WORKMEN'S COMPENSATION

WORKMEN'S COMPENSATION

THE NEW JERSEY EXPERIENCE

MONROE BERKOWITZ

RUTGERS UNIVERSITY PRESS

New Brunswick   *New Jersey*

1960

Copyright © 1960 by Rutgers, The State University

Library of Congress Catalogue Card Number: 59—7510

Printed in the United States of America by Cushing-Malloy, Inc.

FOREWORD

The Institute of Management and Labor Relations has been pleased to lend its research facilities to the preparation of this study by Professor Berkowitz. An objective assessment of the workmen's compensation system in New Jersey has been needed for many years. It is appropriate that such a review be performed by an independent university scholar and equally appropriate that the effort be supported by the Institute. Workmen's compensation, perhaps more than any other social insurance program, evokes issues touching on employer-employee relations. In its financing and administration it relies mainly on private agencies; and formal and informal hearings take the form of adversary proceedings. Involved are employer costs and employee income, accident prevention and man power utilization.

This study is the first in a series of independent appraisals of conceptual and operational problems arising in the several regulatory and social insurance programs which affect the interests of management and workers in New Jersey. In sponsoring such studies the Institute seeks to accomplish its purpose of public enlightenment by giving competent researchers wide scope to collect and examine the facts and to analyze them against a backdrop of our changing conceptions of the role of the social insurance programs in the economy of the state. The findings and conclusions are those of the author and are not necessarily endorsed by the Institute.

> Jack Chernick
> Chairman
> Research Program
> Institute of Management and Labor Relations
> Rutgers, The State University

PREFACE

In 1955 I was asked by the late Carl Holderman, Commissioner of the Department of Labor and Industry of the State of New Jersey, to survey the research, statistical and analysis operations of the Department. This necessarily brought me into contact with the operations of the Division of Workmen's Compensation and some fascinating problems which were outside the scope of the survey. Was it really necessary for workers to be subjected to proceedings which to the uninitiated eye looked like court trials to receive what appeared to be rather modest benefits? How was it possible to tell whether a particular injury arose out of and in the course of employment? Was it necessary to make such distinctions? Was any real emphasis being placed on restoring the injured worker to the labor market? Where could one find information about the costs, effectiveness and satisfactions derived from the workmen's compensation program?

My efforts to find answers to these and other questions led to interviews with participants in the program, and I soon found that both labor and management representatives were unrestrained in voicing complaints. I was told that benefits were niggardly, that insurance adjusters were out to defeat every claim and that workers received benefits to which they were not entitled. Yet, if my respondents were asked for evidence to sustain their complaints, they could only cite particular cases. A search of the literature revealed no recent objective appraisal of the functioning of the program in New Jersey. Representatives of the interest groups had studied the program from their point of view, and the lawyers had been fairly active in probing the legal aspects, but no one had attempted an over-all survey such as this social insurance program seemed to require. I found that there was a modest number of studies on the experiences in the various states and a very few which attempted to deal with the general problems of all jurisdictions. My efforts to bring together the information about workmen's compensation in one state and to correlate it with data about the program in other jurisdictions have resulted in this volume.

The analysis is largely problem centered. After an introductory chapter, there is an account of the trends in the various types of cases which come before the Division of Workmen's Compensation. Chapter 3 is concerned with the adequacy of the various kinds of cash benefits paid under the act. Chapter 4 treats the perplexing problem of permanent partial disabilities — probably the most controversial aspect of the program within the state. The next two chapters deal with administration, which is basic to all problems. Chapter 5 discusses the objectives of administration, the ways compensation acts are administered in the various jurisdictions, and how New Jersey fits into the general patterns. Almost all of the current complaints about the administration of the act have been voiced sometime in the past, and in Chapter 6 something of the findings of the various investigating commissions and the attempts of past Commissioners of Labor to improve the administration of the act are examined.

Unlike any of the other social insurance programs, workmen's compensation in New Jersey is financed without any direct state participation. Chapter 7 examines the role of the private insurance company, the rate-making process and the trends in insurance rates over the years. Employers are concerned with how New Jersey's rates compare with those in other jurisdictions; labor groups maintain that the costs of the program would be less if a state fund were substituted for the private carriers. An interstate comparison of rates and an evaluation of the state fund versus private insurance controversy are included in this chapter.

The next three chapters deal with the specific problems of second injuries, rehabilitation and the challenges posed by the degenerative diseases and radiation hazards. The last chapter is concerned with the future of workmen's compensation: whether it can continue as it has in the past, or whether it is slated to be replaced by alternative methods of dealing with industrial injuries.

I cannot say that my curiosity about the program has been completely satisfied. I would like to know more about the effects of the program on safety measures and the adequacy of medical treatment, for example; but it has proved impossible to secure reliable data in all areas. I have made recommendations for possible changes in most problem areas. I would like to feel that even if the reader disagrees with these recommendations, he will have been presented with sufficient material to draw his own conclusions.

I am indebted to many more persons that I can possibly name here. The list should include the names of many workers, insurance adjusters, lawyers, doctors, labor union officials, industrial relations managers, and employees of the Division of Workmen's Compensation who have been generous with their time and information. William Saley and Ronald Zweig aided me in several tabulations. My acquaintance with Norman Sprague and Lawrence Houstoun, which began with my inquiries into the field, has ripened into personal friendship, and I am grateful for their constant encouragement. Ned J. Parsekian, former director of the Division of Workmen's Compensation, graciously allowed me access to materials in the possession of the division.

The chapter on insurance would not have been possible without the continuing cooperation of Bernard Hamilton and Charles L. Schlier of the Compensation Rating and Inspection Bureau. They were more than patient in explaining the intricacies of rate-making, and they made available all records that were requested. Any student of workmen's compensation is indebted to Anne and Herman Somers for their definitive work in this field. My debt to Herman Somers goes beyond this, since he was good enough to read the entire manuscript and to make a number of valuable suggestions.

The Rutgers Institute of Management and Labor Relations has helped in many ways. Through the Institute I was able to secure the services of two graduate assistants. Joseph N. Seward wrote his Master's essay in the field of second injuries, and Arthur O'Neal wrote his essay in the area of rehabilitation. I have borrowed extensively from their research. In addition, O'Neal has been most helpful in seeing the manuscript through to completion.

For more than three years, I have been guilty of boring Jack Chernick with workmen's compensation problems and taking up an unconscionable amount of his time. In extenuation, I can only plead that if it had not been for him, this book would never have been started in the first place. Needless to say, I, alone, am responsible for any of the errors or ommissions that may remain.

A portion of Chapter 3 dealing with the adequacy of cash benefits appeared as an article in the June, 1958, issue of the *Social Service Review* and is reprinted with permission. Matthew Bender and Co. Inc., publishers of Arthur Larson's two-volume work, *Law of Workmen's Compensation*, have been good enough to allow me to quote from this work.

To Mrs. Louise Chierici fell the thankless burden of typing and retyping the manuscript. She combined unfailing courtesy and an exuberant cheerfulness with an uncanny ability to decipher illegible manuscript; and without all of these qualities, my task would have been much more difficult.

Finally, I must acknowledge my greatest debt, and this is to my wife Shalvo, who has helped immeasurably in more ways than can be detailed.

Monroe Berkowitz

New Brunswick, N. J.
June, 1959

CONTENTS

CONTENTS

WORKMEN'S COMPENSATION

Chapter 1

WORKMEN'S COMPENSATION PROBLEMS AND THEIR SETTING

Income insecurity is part of the price our society pays for continued economic progress. Decisions about starting and discontinuing
businesses are left in the hands of private individuals who are heavily
influenced by market considerations. Firms employ their complement
of labor according to profit expectations and must discard labor if and
when economic conditions darken. The individual worker is expected
to be productive, and if he becomes ill, disabled or too old to work,
his claim to income, his portion of the proceeds of the enterprise, is
sharply reduced if not eliminated. If his life is cut short, his dependents are left to face drastic readjustments. In modern industrial society, most workers are dependent upon wage income. If it is cut off,
they and their families may be left without adequate means of support.

We are a pragmatic people suspicious of any long-range ideological
solutions to social problems. Our industry is diverse and scattered
over a continent; 68 million persons are employed from Maine to California in small one-man service enterprises and in giant manufacturing
corporations, and they represent all shades of political and social
opinion. Our federal system means that we have not one but over fifty
governments concerned with these issues. It is perhaps not surprising
that we have failed to develop a logical, coherent, over-all approach to
the problem of income insecurity.

During the late 1930's, state unemployment insurance programs,
under the administrative supervision of the federal government, were
instituted. The federal government also embarked upon a program of
old-age and survivors insurance designed to provide income for retired workers and to assure a modicum of support to the family in the
event of the death of the breadwinner. These were parts of the Social
Security Act. Included in the act today are various assistance programs operated by the states but supported in part by federal grants-
in-aid, and also a federal program which provides payments to totally
disabled persons.

Following each of our major wars, various types of veterans legislation were passed. These programs now provide eligible veterans
with certain medical services, vocational rehabilitation, survivors insurance, disability compensation and other benefits.

In the 1930's railroad workers were singled out for special federal
treatment. The Railroad Retirement System makes payments to the
retired railroad workers and also provides indemnities for permanent
total or occupational disability. In the event of death, survivors are
entitled to certain claims on the system. The Railroad Unemployment

Insurance System provides benefits for short-term unemployment and temporary disability.

In the 1940's, California, New Jersey, New York and Rhode Island passed laws closely connected with unemployment insurance legislation to provide cash payments to employees out of work because of illness or disability not incurred on the job.

The list of laws and programs could be extended, but the foregoing testifies to our patchwork scheme of social insurances in this country. We have not provided any uniform method of determining payments or eligibility. These vary according to which of the fifty states the employee happens to be working in, the nature of his employment, his veteran status and, above all, the reasons for the interruption of income.[1]

The primary concern of this study is to examine yet another element in this confusing pattern of social insurance—workmen's compensation. This program is designed, in part, to meet the problem of an interruption to workers' income caused by disabilities connected with employment. In New Jersey, as in most other states, a worker becomes entitled to benefits under workmen's compensation legislation if his disabling injury "arises out of and in the course of employment," however that double phrase is interpreted.

The Development of Workmen's Compensation

Workmen's compensation began in New Jersey and other industrialized states before the first world war. A quarter of a century was to pass before the other social insurance programs were initiated. The framers of the modern programs could take advantage of more liberal constitutional doctrines, a more enlightened social conscience and the participation of the federal government to enforce some uniformity among the states.

As early as 1897, New Jersey's Bureau of Statistics and Records began publishing reports on the experience of foreign countries with compensation legislation, on the legal status of the New Jersey employer's responsibility for industrial injuries and on desired remedial legislation.[2] Germany had pioneered with a general workmen's compensation law in 1884; and Great Britain's legislation, which was to

---

[1] The nature and functioning of the American system of social insurance have been analyzed by many writers in the field. See, for example, Eveline M. Burns, *Social Security and Public Policy* (N. Y.: McGraw-Hill and Co., 1956); J. Douglas Brown, "The American Philosophy of Social Insurance," *Social Service Review*, XXX (March, 1956); and J. G. Turnbull, C. A. Williams, and E. F. Cheit, *Economic and Social Security* (N. Y.: The Ronald Press Co., 1957), chapter 2.

[2] A summary description of early New Jersey activity is found in *Summary of Activities of the New Jersey Department of Labor and Industry*, July 1, 1953-June 30, 1954 (Fiftieth Anniversary Report), pp. xii-xiv. See also Philip Charles Newman, *Labor Legislation in New Jersey* (Washington, D. C.: American Council on Public Affairs, 1943), pp. 114-115. A concise history of compensation laws is contained in Stefan A. Riesenfeld and Richard C. Maxwell, *Modern Social Legislation* (Brooklyn: The Foundation Press, 1950), pp. 127-136.

influence strongly the American pattern, started as early as 1897. The United States government passed a rather crude statute covering federal civil employees in 1908. The next year Montana followed with a compensation statute covering the coal mining industry, only to have the courts declare it unconstitutional. A similar fate awaited New York's 1910 law covering employees in specified hazardous occupations.[3] In 1911, however, the dam broke. On April 4, New Jersey's Governor Woodrow Wilson signed a bill establishing a workmen's compensation law that was to become effective on July 4, 1911. That same year, nine other states passed similar legislation, and the compensation movement was well on its way.[4]

Yet the move was a hesitant one. Fears that a compulsory statute might run afoul of prevailing constitutional doctrine were influential in the New Jersey legislature's refusal to make the law binding on all employers. Either party ot the employment contract could decide not to come under its provisions, although, as noted below, the alternatives were not appealing. No broad use of the taxing powers of government were contemplated to transfer the burden of the financial risks from the worker to the community. Instead, the employer was made liable for any payments under the law; and although he could buy commercial insurance, it was not until 1917 that this was made compulsory for most employers. The state's original law did not establish any administrative agency. A worker dissatisfied with the disposition of his case could appeal only to the courts. Administrative tribunals to hear cases and exercise some supervision over awards were not to be established until seven years after the original statute passed the legislature.

If this legislation had come later, the program might have been different. But something more than time is involved here, since it is doubtful that workmen's compensation was conceived of primarily as a

---

[3]*Cunningham* v. *Northwestern Improvement Co.*, 44 Mont. 180 (1911). *Ives* v. *South Buffalo Railway Co.*, 201 N.Y. 271 (1911). The holding in the latter case was that the statute violated the due process clauses of the federal and state constitutions. This is the most famous of the decisions and probably one which aroused the greatest concern. Resentment against this decision did much to stimulate the drive for some sort of workmen's compensation legislation. See Riesenfeld and Maxwell, p. 134, and Herman Miles Somers and Anne Ramsay Somers, *Workmen's Compensation: Prevention, Insurance and Rehabilitation of Occupational Disability* (N. Y.: John Wiley and Sons, 1954), p. 32.

[4] The nine other states were California, Illinois, Kansas, Massachusetts, New Hampshire, Nevada, Ohio, Washington and Wisconsin. The claim is often made that New Jersey's compensation law was the first among the states. The facts of the matter are a bit complicated and do not permit of such a simple statement without qualifications. New Jersey's law was approved on April 4, 1911, to become effective on July 4, 1911. A number of states enacted laws before New Jersey; Kansas and Washington on March 14, 1911, Nevada on March 23, 1911. But of the laws that were enacted before New Jersey's, only Nevada's became effective before New Jersey's, since it went into effect on July 1 of that year. Nevada's act, however, applied only to specific employments, and further it was superseded by another act in 1913. To complicate matters further, Wisconsin, which passed its act after New Jersey (on May 3 rather than April 11), put its statute into effect immediately upon adoption. It is fair to state that New Jersey's law is the oldest statute in point of enactment that has remained in effect. The time difference among the ten states that broke through the barrier in 1911 are rather small. Perhaps it is sufficient to point out that New Jersey was one of the pioneering states in this field of legislation.

program of social legislation designed to meet the problem of income insecurity, and it would be wrong to judge it solely in terms of social insurance criteria. Moreover, the program was conceived of as an extension of the common law of tort liability.

An elaborate jurisprudence based upon the common law of negligence or tort liability has been developed in this country. If you trip on my stairs which I have neglected to keep in good repair, you can recover full damages, including possible payments for inconvenience and suffering, provided you were not contributorily negligent. If I am wholly at fault in an automobile accident, I must be prepared for the financial consequences of my negligence. In general, the law holds me strictly accountable for the results of my activities, and in cases of accidental injuries it is the function of the courts to establish where the fault lies. The injured party must of course bring suit and be able to prove his case according to the legal canons.

Although industrial accidental injuries are but a fraction, possibly one-fifth, of all accidental injuries, it is not difficult to see why they became cause for special concern. The injured workmen found it expensive to bring suit and had difficulty securing competent witnesses from among his fellow workmen since they feared employer reprisal if they testified. The injured employee had the burden of proving his case, and the employer, by the end of the nineteenth century, could fall back on three common law defenses. First was the contributory negligence doctrine, derived from other types of accident cases: The employee could not collect if he was negligent to any degree, quite apart from any possible negligence on the part of the employer. This made recovery difficult enough, but in 1837 there developed the "assumption of risk" doctrine, under which recovery could be denied on the grounds that the worker knew or should have known about the risks inherent in his occupation. Presumably the employee was compensated for the risks in his regular rate of pay; and if he did not wish to assume them, the courts held, he should have declined the job. The third common law defense was the "fellow servant" doctrine, under which the liability of the master was held to be limited to his own actions and not to those of a fellow servant of the injured party. [5] Recovery could be denied under this theory if the employer could show that a fellow worker's negligence contributed to the injury. Also, under the common law, only the injured employee had the right to sue; and if he was killed in an industrial accident, his survivors had no right to pursue the matter in the courts.

This rather harsh legal doctrine was softened only slightly in the early 1900's by the passage of statutes commonly known as employers'

---

[5] A brief account of the leading cases is contained in Domenico Gagliardo, *American Social Insurance* (N. Y.: Harper and Bros., rev. ed., 1955), pp. 368-374. The leading case that established the "assumption of risk" and "fellow servant" doctrines was an English decision, *Priestly* v. *Fowler*, 3 M. Ampers and W., 1, 150 Reprint 1030 (1837). The doctrines were transferred to this country in Justice Lemuel Shaw's decision in *Farwell* v. *Boston and Worcester R.R. Co.*, 4 Metcalf 49 (1842).

liability laws modifying the common law defenses, especially that of the fellow servant doctrine, and in some cases, extending the right to sue to dependents of fatally injured workmen.[6] But, like any other legal doctrine, its effects were influenced by community and social pressures, and by the early twentieth century more liberal interpretations could be discerned. The employee was still required to bring suit against his employer in what was inherently a long-draw-out process, the end result of which remained highly uncertain. If an employee wan his case, however, he was entitled to be made whole; and the amount of money damages received could vary within wide limits, especially when set by a jury of his peers. One employee might fortuitously recover a large sum, whereas another might not receive anything, even though they had suffered comparable injuries and losses in earning power. The uncertainty of the situation did not please employers, many of whom began to insure themselves against their liability for industrial accidental injuries.

The workmen's compensation legislation was designed to solve this problem, and in this sense it was both a social insurance program and an extension of the common law. To the lawyer, the outstanding thing about workmen's compensation is that it does not concern itself with *who* is to blame but establishes instead the liability of the employer for payment in the case of all injuries which arise from the employment relation. Such a drastic change can be rationalized only in terms of social welfare principles.[7] Industrial injuries are conceived of as the inevitable by-product of modern industry. Under the common law of tort liability the economic losses were borne by that portion of the population that could least afford them. To the workers, the losses became a crushing burden they could not anticipate or provide against. Hence, society deemed it wise to transfer these losses, not to the community directly, but to the employer, who in running his enterprise can make provision for them and can also distribute them among the beneficiaries of the enterprise.

But since accidents impose losses on the whole community and since the worker under compensation is theoretically entitled to *certain*

---

[6] In 1909, New Jersey passed an employers' liability law which substantiated the three common law defenses, with the exception of a modification of the fellow servant rule to exclude supervisory employees from classification as fellow servants. (N.J. Laws 1909, ch. 79.)

[7] Many students of compensation have long struggled with attempts to devise a satisfactory theory for the principles involved. Political figures such as Lloyd George and Theodore Roosevelt endorsed the theory of "occupational risk." To Lloyd George is ascribed the oft-quoted slogan, "The cost of the product should bear the blood of the workingman." This theory has been criticized on the grounds that compensation acts only divide the social costs of injuries between labor and industry and that the assumption that all compensation costs can be passed on to consumers is economically naive. Edwin E. Witte has advanced the idea of a "least social costs" principle, which emphasizes that economic losses are reduced to a minimum by compensation legislation. (Edwin E. Witte, "The Theory of Workmen's Compensation," *American Labor Legislation Review*, XX [December, 1930], 411-418.) For a discussion of the compelling reasons why workmen's compensation should be considered as social insurance, see Riesenfeld and Maxwell, pp. 138-140.

benefits, quite apart from assessment of fault, the amount of his benefits was limited to something less than he would have received under the common law proceedings if he could prove the employer wholly negligent. In place of the sometimes larger lump-sum settlements, the compensation statutes substitute a smaller weekly payment computed at some fraction of his weekly wages. This is designed to provide income for the period of temporary disability. In addition, the employee is entitled to some or all of the medical services necessary to heal his injury. In the event the worker is fatally injured, his dependents receive weekly payments for a specified length of time, depending in some cases on the number and age of the survivors. If the worker is permanently and totally incapacitated, his weekly payments extend either for a specified number of weeks or for the balance of his life.

A more thorny problem is raised by permanent partial injuries, and here various statutory schedules relate the number of weeks of payment to the severity of the injury. These schedules take the place of the old jury assessment of damages but leave open many questions. The exact rationale for these payments for permanent partial injury differs in the various jurisdictions. In some they are designed to compensate for loss of potential earning power; in others they are conceived of as an indemnity payment for the injury as such. A problem is posed by the fact that no schedule can possibly anticipate all types of permanent partial injuries, and hence the determination of the extent of disability may have to be left to some tribunal.

Moreover, since the compensation laws extend the common law of tort liability only in the case of work-incurred injuries, it is necessary to devise tribunals to hear cases wherein the origin of the injury is in dispute. This problem has increased in importance as the laws have been interpreted to encompass more and more of the occupational diseases and other ills to which all of us are susceptible. In New Jersey it is possible to receive compensation for heart disease, deafness, tuberculosis, strains, and so on, provided it can be shown that these disabilities arose out of and in the course of employment. Disputes over this question, plus the difficulties of determining the nature and extent of the disability, have perpetuated a litigious atmosphere that many thought would disappear with compensation legislation. These disputes are still resolved by quasi-legal proceedings; and if one listens to these hearings, it sometimes appears that all that has been done is to transfer the forum from the courts to the compensation division. The need to resolve such disputes enormously complicates administrative procedures, but at the same time the transfer of liability to the employers has had the effect of inducing them to devise safety measures and accident prevention programs. One of the clear objectives of the law was to reduce the volume of accidents by making safe working conditions profitable.

Perhaps if workmen's compensation had come in the 1930's instead of in 1911, it would have subordinated liability considerations to the overriding problem of determining an adequate level of benefit payments, regardless of the origin of the disability. Perhaps the taxing powers of government would have been used more freely in the social interest. But we cannot rewrite history even if we should care to. We must recognize workmen's compensation as a program which has inherently graver administrative difficulties than almost any of the other social insurance programs. In none of the others is litigation so common in the determination of benefits; in no other program does such a small proportion of the total cost eventually reach the beneficiaries. All of this may be part of the penalty the program must pay for having arrived first on the social insurance front, but whether these trends must continue is a question that will be examined in later chapters.

New Jersey's Statute

In broad outlines, New Jersey's compensation statute is similar to the laws in the other fifty-three jurisdictions, but no two of the laws are exactly the same.[8] New Jersey's law covers a higher proportion of the labor force than the laws in most jurisdictions. Employers who employ but a single worker are covered under the law (unlike unemployment insurance in the state). Some states exclude agricultural workers, domestic workers, workers in nonhazardous employments or various other groups. New Jersey excludes none of these. All workers who qualify as "employees" are covered, with the exception of casual workers, and the law is quite restrictive in defining these. Casual employment must be unplanned and unforeseen. The courts have held that even if employment was for a single day, the right to compensation, in the event of an injury, could not be denied if the employment was not by chance or pure accident but rather was in accordance with the plans of the employer.[9] Baby sitters and occasional household help qualify as employees under the law. Undoubtedly, many persons, at one time or another, have been employers under the New Jersey statute without being aware of their potential liability in the event of an accidental injury.

Whereas all jurisdictions cover accidental injuries that are industrially connected, not all cover the full range of occupational diseases. New Jersey, together with thirty-three other jurisdictions, provides full coverage for all such diseases, which are considered the same as accidental injuries. Compensation benefits could be denied in New Jersey, however, if the accidental injury was self-inflicted or the

---

[8]The fifty states and Puerto Rico, together with three federal laws, the first covering longshoremen and harbor workers, the second essentially the same legislation but applicable to the District of Columbia, and the third covering federal civil employees, comprise the fifty-four jurisdictions. The best summary description of the provisions of the various laws can be found in *State Workmen's Compensation Laws*, United States Department of Labor, Bureau of Labor Standards, Bulletin 161, rev. August, 1957.

[9]*Malloy* v. *Capital Bakery*, 38 N.J. Super. 516. A discussion of the casual employment relationship can be found in Robert E. Rodes, Jr., "Workmen's Compensation," *Rutgers Law Review*, XI (1956-57), 147.

disease caused by willful self-exposure to a known hazard or if intoxication was the natural and proximate cause of the injury. The burden of establishing these facts is placed upon the employer.[10]

New Jersey's law is not compulsory. As is the case in twenty-four other jurisdictions, employers have the option of accepting or rejecting the compensation provisions of the law. Election to come under the law is presumed, however, unless either party notifies the other, prior to an accident, that the compensation provisions are not to apply. Once covered by the compensation provisions, the parties remain covered unless one or the other "contracts out" by giving written notice sixty days prior to an accident. [11]

If the employer chooses not to be covered by the compensation provisions, he becomes subject to suit in the event of an employee's accidental injury or fatality. Two of the unusual common law defenses are specifically abolished, however. The negligence of a fellow employee or the fact that the worker assumed the risks of the job when employed cannot be considered. The claim might be defeated, however, if it could be demonstrated that the employee was "willfully negligent." The employer must sustain the burden of proof in showing willful negligence, and in the event of a dispute the question is deemed to be a factual one that must be submitted to a jury.[12]

However, even if an employer elects not to be covered by the compensation provisions, the law requires him in most cases to purchase his own liability insurance. So little advantage has been taken of this option that there are no insurance rates existent for these employers. They would have to be created upon demand, but in recent years there has been no necessity for fixing these premiums.

There may, however, be isolated employers throughout the state who have chosen to remain outside the compensation provisions. Although the law's coverage extends to employers of farm labor and domestic help, such employers are not required to insure themselves against their liability under the law. Some of these employers may have "contracted out," but this would not be known unless and until an accident occurred.

Governmental bodies, be they state, county, municipal or fire or school districts, are not given the option of electing or rejecting the compensation provisions. They are required to come under the compensation provisions, but with some exceptions, they are not required to purchase insurance. The only other employers who need not buy insurance belong to a select group of firms which can satisfy the Commissioner of Banking and Insurance as to their financial responsibility.

In eight jurisdictions, employers must purchase insurance coverage from monopolistic state funds. Eleven other jurisdictions, including New York and Pennsylvania, have competitive state funds. New Jersey,

---

[10] N.J. Stat. Ann., 34:15-7, 30 (West, 1958).
[11] N.J. Stat. Ann., 34:15-9, 11.
[12] N.J. Stat. Ann., 34:15-1.

together with thirty-four jurisdictions, falls into another category in that all compensation insurance is written by private carriers.[13] These financing arrangements distinguish workmen's compensation from the other social insurance programs.

The employer or insurance carrier is responsible not only for making the various cash payments but also for providing medical and hospital services. In New Jersey, the worker does not have a free choice of his physician to treat his injuries. He must, in the usual case, use the services of a physician chosen by the employer or insurance carrier. These are but some of the provisions of New Jersey's statute; others will be considered later.

Even though four decades have passed since a compensation law was adopted in New Jersey, time has not erased controversy. As the years pass, the volume of controversy about provisions of the law and its administration appears to increase. Annually, the state legislature has before it bills designed to change one aspect or another of the program as labor and employer groups make known their dissatisfactions. Each of the contending groups points to inequities in the law, to deficiencies in its interpretation and administration, and to areas where New Jersey compares unfavorably with other states. These contentions must be examined in order to evaluate the effectiveness of this social insurance program.

Recent years have witnessed a modest increase in the number of inquiries into workmen's compensation on the national scene, but this program, more than any of the others on the social insurance agenda, is peculiarly a state one.[14] In the aggregate, the amount of disinterested information on this subject within New Jersey is disappointingly small, and much of what is available is couched in terms understandable only to the interested participant in the legal, medical or insurance phases of the problem.

---

[13] The Federal Employees' Compensation Act, covering civil employees, is financed by appropriations of Congress, and hence there is no need for a governmental fund or private insurance.

[14] The outstanding work is the Somerses' *Workmen's Compensation*, a full-dress review of the field. A number of periodical articles have also appeared, including the symposium in the *Industrial and Labor Relations Review*, VII (October 1953), and a penetrating article on benefit levels by Harold A. Katz and Estelle M. Wirpel, "Workmen's Compensation 1910-1952; Are Present Benefits Adequate?" *Labor Law Journal* IV (March 1953), 164-179. Although Arthur Larson's two-volume work, *The Law of Workmen's Compensation* (N. Y.: Matthew Bender and Co., 1952), is essentially a legal tome, the scope of his inquiry is much broader and extends into considerations of general problems of social insurance. Mention must also be made of studies of particular states' experience in recent years. Typical of these is the study by J. Fred Holly and Bevars D. Mabry, *Protective Labor Legislation and Its Administration in Tennessee* (Knoxville: University of Tennessee Press, 1955); and two studies of the Texas law: John P. Owen, *What's Wrong with Workmen's Compensation* (Houston: Bureau of Business and Economic Research, University of Houston, Study No. 4, 1956), and Sam B. Barton, *How Texas Cares for Injured Workers* (Denton: North Texas State College, 1956).

Chapter 2

TRENDS IN WORKMEN'S COMPENSATION ACTIVITY

Immediately before World War II, about 20,000 compensation cases were being closed each year by New Jersey's Division of Workmen's Compensation. In the last few years the annual count has increased to well over 50,000. In dollar terms, the increase has been even greater. Payments incurred in these cases amounted to between $6 and $8 million a year before World War II, whereas the comparable figure in 1957 was over the $36 million mark. The dollar figures are influenced by changes in benefit rates over the years, but this factor has had little effect on the *number* of cases.

An explanation of this increased activity requires an analysis of accident and employment trends, two factors which directly influence the case count. But it is necessary to probe further. The state-wide case totals include awards for all types of disabilities: temporary, permanent partial, permanent total, and fatalities. The cases were closed by agreement between the parties or after an informal or formal hearing. The separate trends for each of these types of disability and methods of settlement must be examined. The state-wide totals must also be broken down to reveal trends in the separate counties. All this may seem unduly complicated, but the analysis will reveal interesting differences in the trends in the several kinds of cases.

National and State Accident Trends

Compensation cases begin with an accidental injury sustained in employment; and if the number of these has been increasing over the years, this will cause a rise in the number of cases. The upper line in Chart 1 shows the estimated number of disabling work injuries in the nation as a whole from 1939 to 1957.[1] The number of such injuries

---

[1] A disabling work injury is essentially a work-connected injury which causes death or permanent impairment, or causes the worker to lose time from his job. Occupational diseases are included, but minor injuries which merely require first-aid attention are not counted. The complete definition as used by the Bureau of Labor Statistics is as follows: "A disabling work injury is any injury occurring in the course of and arising out of employment, which (a) results in death or any degree of permanent physical impairment, or (b) makes the injured worker unable to perform the duties of any regularly scheduled job, which is open and available to him, throughout the hours corresponding to his shift on any one or more days after the day of injury (including Sundays, days off, or plant shutdowns). The term 'injury' includes occupational diseases."

In many of the ensuing statistical comparisons, 1939 is taken as a base year (where the data are available). The choice is arbitrary, but 1939 was a year when the effects of the depression were giving way to the business of defense próduction and in some sense the year can be considered normal. Comparisons are, of course, vitally affected by the choice of a base year; and in most instances the actual data as well as the comparative changes will be shown. Further effects of this choice of the base year are discussed in footnote 4.

10

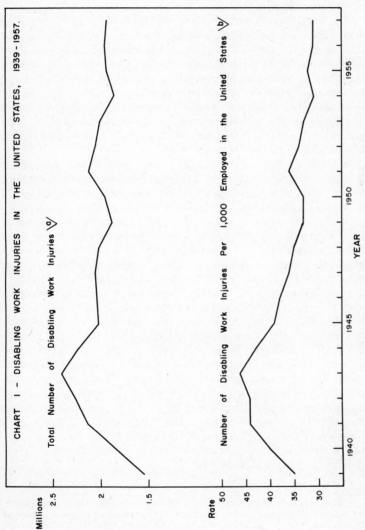

CHART I – DISABLING WORK INJURIES IN THE UNITED STATES, 1939 - 1957.

Total Number of Disabling Work Injuries a/

Number of Disabling Work Injuries Per 1,000 Employed in the United States b/

Source: Industrial Hazards Division, Bureau of Labor Statistics, United States Department of Labor.
a) Includes injuries to self-employed and unpaid family workers, but excludes domestic service. Estimates for Years 1939-1941 have been adjusted to exclude injuries to C.C.C and W.P.A. workers.
b) Total employed labor force excludes domestic service but includes self-employed and unpaid family workers.

moved upward during the period of defense preparation and wartime activity, increasing more than 50 per cent from 1939 to the peak of 1943, when 2.4 million injuries were recorded. From this high, the number of injuries declines, only to rise again in 1950, at the time of the Korean conflict. In 1957 the number of injuries was approximately 25 per cent greater than in 1939.

Since 1939, employment has been expanding, and during the wartime emergencies relatively inexperienced persons were being called into the labor force; they formed a group unused to industrial discipline and particularly subject to accidental injuries. Consequently, when employment is taken into account by computing the disabling work injuries per 1,000 employed persons, as in the lower line of Chart 1, it is not surprising to find that the injury rate increased during the war, but it declined markedly in the postwar years. In 1957, the number of disabling injuries per 1,000 workers was actually lower than in 1939, and of course, considerably lower than the wartime peak.

Much the same accident rate picture emerges if data in narrower categories are examined. The injury frequency rate in the nation's manufacturing industries was 12.0 in 1956, well under the 1939 figure of 14.9 or the wartime rate of approximately 20.0.[2] Nearly 2 million disabling work injuries each year, or an accident frequency rate of 12, is certainly nothing to be complacent about, but accident rates have been declining in the country as a whole.

Unfortunately, comparable data for New Jersey are lacking, but an examination of the record of the "first reports" of accidents filed by employers reveals some broad trends. Employers carrying insurance are required to report all accidents, whereas self-insurers during the period under examination reported only accidents that were expected to develop into compensation cases. Because of the looseness of the definition of the term "accident" in the law, the figures should not be taken as a measure of the actual number of accidental injuries each year. It is of interest, however, that some of the broad national trends can be observed in the New Jersey data in that the wartime and 1951 peaks can be distinguished (upper line, Chart 2). In 1939, 108,759 accidents were reported. Following a wartime peak of 188,739, there was a decline to a low point of 147,204 reports in 1949. If the rise due to the Korean War is disregarded, there has been a steady increase since then to the 1957 high point of over 196,000.[3]

---

[2] The injury frequency rate is the number of disabling work injuries for each million man-hours worked. See *American Standard Method of Recording and Measuring Work Injury Experience*, Z.16.1 (N. Y.: American Standards Association, 1954). The injury frequency rates for all manufacturing industries are compiled by the United States Department of Labor, Bureau of Labor Statistics.

[3] The New Jersey workmen's compensation law does not define just what should be considered as an accident, although the Division of Workmen's Compensation instructs insured employers to report all accidents no matter how small. Some employers undoubtedly reported everything, including the smallest first-aid case, while others may have been more selective. The law and the instructions of the division are clear that the onset of an occu-

These figures can be placed in perspective if the changes in employment are taken into account (lower line, Chart 2). When this is done, the state accident picture looks less foreboding. In 1939, 8.7 accident reports were filed for each 100 workers in nonagricultural employment within the state. In 1942, 11.5 accidents were reported for every 100 employees. Since the war the series has exhibited the familiar irregular decline; in 1953 the rate was the same as in 1939, and in 1957 it was slightly greater than in the base year. The conclusion must be that no spectacular increase in the accident rate can be found within the state.

New Jersey Closed Compensated Cases and Employment Trends

Since the accident rate per 100 employees looks so much different from the raw figures, the question arises as to whether or not the picture would be the same if a compensation case rate, that is, the number of closed cases per 100 employees, were computed. The data on this and related matters are summarized in Table I; but before looking at rates, the actual figures presented in column (1) deserve examination.

Although this is not shown in Table I, the 1939 total of 21,587 cases is fairly representative of the years 1936 to 1939; but at no time since has the annual number been nearly so low. During 1940, the number increased and began its steady climb to 49,515 cases in 1945, 129 per cent higher than in 1939. The number of cases reached its wartime high a few years after the peak in the accident reports. This is not surprising since the figures reflect cases only after they have been processed and finally closed out — an event which may take place a year or more after the accident. The number of closed cases declined after the war, but in 1952 it exceeded the wartime highs and continued to climb upward. In 1954, 57,006 compensated cases were closed, a record high, 164 per cent greater than in 1939. In 1955 the number dropped below 50,000 for the first time after the Korean War, but increased to 58,453 in 1956. The 1955 figure is too low and the 1956 number too high, since a number of cases which should have been statistically processed in time for the 1955 report were held over and show up on the 1956 tabulations. Therefore, not too much significance should be attached to year-to-year changes. The number of cases in 1957 was less than in 1956 but greater than in 1955 and in the immediate postwar period. The average number of closed cases for the years

---

pational disease is to be considered as an accident. The accident reporting rules were changed in 1958. See chapter 5.

All quoted figures of first reports, however, include the reports of the self-insurers on cases in which the accidents resulted in more than seven days lost time or in some permanent impairment. As of the time this is being written, the question of whether self-insurers can be required to report all accidents is a matter in litigation between the Division of Workmen's Compensation and the self-insurers.

Beginning in 1957, the State of New Jersey became a cooperating state in the Bureau of Labor Statistics' program of gathering data on work injury experience. In future years, reliable data on New Jersey industry's experience ought to be forthcoming.

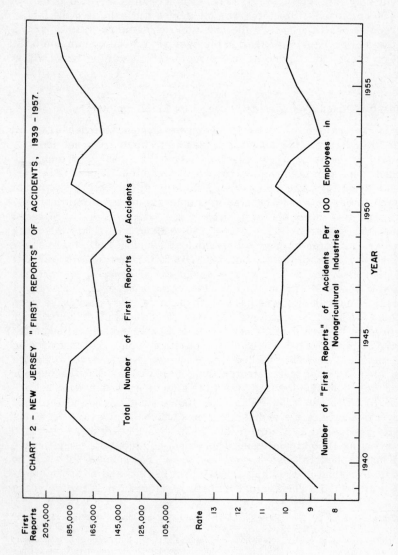

CHART 2 – NEW JERSEY "FIRST REPORTS" OF ACCIDENTS, 1939 - 1957.

Total Number of First Reports of Accidents

Number of "First Reports" of Accidents Per 100 Employees in Nonagricultural Industries

First Reports
205,000
185,000
165,000
145,000
125,000
105,000

Rate
13
12
11
10
9
8

YEAR
1940   1945   1950   1955

Source: New Jersey Division of Workmen's Compensation "Industrial Accident Reports," and New Jersey Department of Labor and Industry, Bureau of Statistics and Records.

Table I. New Jersey Closed Compensated Cases — Employment and Accident Reports, 1939-1957

Year	Total No. of Closed Cases (1)	Total Non agricultural Employment (000) (2)	No. of Closed Cases for Each 100 Employees (actual rate) no. of cases x 100 total nonagricultural employment (3)	No. of Closed Cases for Each 100 Employees (relative number, 1939=100) (4)	No. of First Reports of Accidents (5)	No. of Closed Cases for Each 100 First Reports of Accidents (actual rate) no. of cases x 100 no. of first reports of accidents (6)	No. of Closed Cases for Each 100 First Reports of Accidents (relative number, 1939=100) (7)
1939	21,587	1,244	1.74	100.0	108,759	19.9	100
1940	25,585	1,312	1.95	112.4	127,089	20.1	101.4
1941	31,127	1,499	2.08	119.7	167,923	18.5	93.4
1942	37,094	1,640	2.26	130.4	188,739	19.7	99.0
1943	38,863	1,735	2.24	129.1	187,275	20.7	104.4
1944	47,083	1,693	2.78	160.3	184,315	25.5	128.7
1945	49,515	1,572	3.15	181.6	159,951	31.0	156.0
1946	48,740	1,561	3.12	179.9	161,320	30.2	152.2
1947	44,182	1,622	2.72	157.0	164,796	26.8	135.1
1948	42,682	1,657	2.57	148.5	168,343	25.4	127.7
1949	41,921	1,596	2.63	151.4	147,204	28.5	143.5
1950	40,760	1,658	2.46	141.7	153,175	26.6	134.1
1951	47,145	1,768	2.67	153.7	185,640	25.4	128.0
1952	50,999	1,804	2.83	162.9	179,431	28.4	143.2
1953	54,824	1,850	2.96	170.8	160,257	34.2	172.3
1954	57,006	1,820	3.13	180.5	164,004	34.8	175.1
1955	48,369	1,864	2.60	149.6	181,041	26.7	134.1
1956	58,453	1,930	3.03	174.6	194,021	30.1	151.7
1957	55,041	1,959	2.81	162.0	196,227	28.0	141.3

Source: Data on total number of cases and number of first reports from New Jersey Division of Workmen's Compensation, "Industrial Accident Reports." Data on number of covered jobs from New Jersey Department of Labor and Industry, Bureau of Statistics and Records.

1955 to 1957 was 53,954. This is in contrast to the average number for 1939 to 1941, which was 26,100.

However, some increase in cases is expected because of the rise in employment during this period. In 1939 the division was closing out 1.7 cases per 100 employees (column (3) of Table I). As employment increased after 1939, the number of closed cases increased even faster, reaching a high point of 3.2 closed cases for every 100 employees in 1945. Although the rate subsequently declined from this high point, the number of cases per 100 employees was 2.81 in 1957. In the years 1939 to 1941, the division was closing out cases at the average rate of 1.93 cases per 100 employees. If this rate remained constant over the years, the division would be closing about 36,000 cases a year instead of the approximately 54,000 now being processed each year. The excess of 18,000 cases a year cannot be explained by any changes in employment.

It must constantly be kept in mind that these comparisons are being made with prewar years as the base. The large increases in the number of cases per 100 employees during the war are a perfectly understandable phenomenon. After the war, the tendency was for the rate to decline; but it never again went back to the prewar level. The case rates for the last three years of the table are slightly less than the rates in the immediate postwar years, but greater than in the prewar period.[4]

The reference to the accident picture has already shown that these changes cannot explain the increase in cases. To check this, column 6 of Table I shows the number of closed cases for each 100 accident reports. In 1939 this rate was 19.9; in 1954 it had increased to 34.8; and then it declined to 28.0 in 1957, a rate 41 per cent greater than in 1939.

Since neither accident nor employment trends can account for all of the increase in the number of cases, it is necessary to examine the various categories of cases to determine whether the areas of increase can be isolated.

Trends in Closed Compensated Cases by Type of Disability and Method of Settlement

Since 1941, the yearly count of cases closed by direct settlement or

---

[4] The New Jersey Division of Workmen's Compensation, in its 1956 *Annual Report*, maintains that employment has increased faster than the number of closed cases. It is not possible to quarrel with their arithmetic, but they have chosen 1946 as the base year for their comparisons, a year in which the number of cases was still high, reflecting the war experience, and a year in which the wave of immediate postwar layoffs caused the total number of employed persons to be lower than it was either the year before or the year after. There are other minor differences in the calculations, and it is difficult to agree with their conclusion that employment has increased faster than the number of cases, still it is clear that there has been no significant increase in the case rate in the years 1954 to 1956 as compared with the immediate postwar years. The large increases are those which occur when comparisons are made with the prewar picture. It is perhaps this sort of quibbling that makes people despair of statistical computations, but the inevitable fact remains that comparisons are relative and results depend entirely on the choice of base years.

after an informal hearing has been rather modest in comparison with the increase in the number of formal cases — which has been more than fivefold. Formal cases were but 12 per cent of all cases in 1941, but 36 per cent of the total in the years 1955 to 1957. Direct settlement cases, which accounted for 70 per cent of the total number of cases in 1941, had declined to 48 per cent of the cases in the latter years.[5]

It is possible to classify cases not only by methods of settlement but also by types of disability. All closed cases fall into one of four categories of disability: (1) death, (2) permanent total disability, (3) permanent partial disability and (4) temporary disability only. The first three categories include cases in which payments for temporary disability may or may not have been paid in addition to payments made by reason of a fatality, permanent total disability or permanent partial disability. The last class, however, includes cases in which *only* temporary disability compensation was paid.

Table II shows the annual count of cases since 1941, classified according to method of settlement and type of disability. An analysis of the data in this table shows these trends:

1) The number of death and permanent total cases is a small proportion of cases closed by all methods of settlement.

2) Most of the "temporary only" cases are closed by the direct settlement method. The number of such cases closed at this level is measured in the thousands, and at the other levels, in the hundreds.

3) At each of the stages, the number of temporary cases has actually declined since 1941, with the decline being most marked at the informal stage. The number of death cases has also been declining. The number of permanent total disabilities is so small each year that it is difficult to pick out any trend.

4) For each of the methods of settlement, in recent years, the largest number of cases are the permanent partial disabilities. At the direct settlement stage, the number of permanent partials is comparable to the number of temporary cases, but at the informal and formal stages, the permanent partial disability cases far outnumber any other type.

---

[5]Some of the cases closed by direct settlement were undoubtedly cases in which agreement was reached only after an informal hearing. In one sense, the informal hearing is just another method of reaching an agreement; and up until 1957, the division did not ask the parties to indicate, on the direct settlement or agreement form, whether or not there had been an informal hearing in the case. Consequently, before 1957, the number of cases reported as being closed by informal hearing is too small each year, and the number reported as closed by agreement is too large by this amount. On the other hand, since 1957 the division has been reviewing direct settlements and setting down some cases for informal hearings. This has the effect of increasing the number of informal cases. This change in procedure is discussed in chapter 5. Cases closed out by direct settlement and then later, in the same year, closed out again as, say, a formal case, are classified in the latter category. If, however, a case is closed out as a direct settlement case and then in some later year reopened and closed out as a formal case, the statistics for earlier years are not rectified. Also, the published figures do not reveal just what disposition may have been made of a closed formal case at some prior stage of settlement.

Table II. New Jersey Closed Compensated Cases — By Type of Disability and Method of Settlement, 1941-1957

Year	No. of Cases, All Types of Disability [a]	No. of Death Cases	No. of Permanent Total Disability Cases	No. of Permanent Partial Disability Cases	No. of Temporary Disability Only Cases
Part I. Cases Closed by Direct Settlement					
1941	21,743	90	6	4,894	16,753
1942	24,048	101	1	6,351	17,595
1943	26,069	114	1	7,605	18,349
1944	28,868	115	0	12,084	16,669
1945	31,165	111	1	15,319	15,734
1946	29,153	104	8	10,982	18,059
1947	25,303	97	4	9,628	15,574
1948	24,652	97	3	9,656	14,896
1949	22,623	69	4	8,643	13,907
1950	22,017	63	4	8,540	13,410
1951	24,984	97	6	9,770	15,111
1952	27,421	70	6	12,454	14,891
1953	30,509	92	3	15,010	15,404
1954	31,530	95	10	16,415	15,010
1955	23,597	63	2	12,139	11,393
1956	31,114	78	1	15,705	15,330
1957	23,903	89	0	10,462	13,352
Part II. Cases Closed by Informal Hearings					
1941	5,570	51	2	4,444	1,073
1942	6,655	42	4	5,517	1,092
1943	5,955	38	2	4,795	1,120
1944	6,296	27	5	5,580	684
1945	6,855	24	5	6,227	599
1946	7,413	23	7	6,566	817
1947	7,363	21	4	6,846	492
1948	6,300	23	4	5,824	449
1949	6,787	23	4	6,247	513
1950	6,280	25	8	5,858	389
1951	7,272	24	10	6,816	422
1952	6,635	21	7	6,208	399
1953	6,182	14	4	5,896	268
1954	6,892	17	5	6,604	266
1955	5,803	14	4	5,628	157
1956	8,528	14	4	8,273	237
1957	11,137	21	0	10,855	261
Part III. Cases Closed by Formal Hearings					
1941	3,814	89	12	3,343	370
1942	6,391	131	20	5,655	585
1943	6,839	105	10	6,092	632
1944	11,919	148	23	10,826	922
1945	11,495	81	7	11,106	301
1946	12,174	70	12	11,648	444
1947	11,516	85	18	11,220	193
1948	11,730	55	19	11,387	269
1949	12,511	76	16	12,201	218
1950	12,463	72	17	12,168	206
1951	14,889	92	26	14,607	164
1952	16,943	76	23	16,691	153
1953	18,133	74	26	17,914	119
1954	18,584	83	18	18,373	110
1955	18,969	75	25	18,757	112
1956	18,811	68	19	18,624	100
1957	20,001	68	25	19,822	86

Source: New Jersey Division of Workmen's Compensation, "Industrial Accident Reports."
[a] Does not include reopened cases.

5) The annual number of permanent partial cases has increased over the years according to each method. Since 1941, the number of these cases closed at informal hearings has approximately doubled and the number closed by direct settlement has tripled, whereas there has been a fivefold increase at the formal level.

This analysis leads to a single conclusion. If the increase in the numbers of cases is to be explained, the explanation will have to center around the permanent partial disability cases, particularly at the formal level.

Trends in Permanent Partial Disability Cases

In 1927, when the division closed about 26,000 cases, about one-quarter of these were permanent partial disability cases and about three-quarters were cases in which only temporary disability benefits were paid. In recent years these proportions have been reversed. Three out of four workers in New Jersey who receive a compensation award collect something for a permanent impairment, or, in the words of the law, for "disability, partial in character and permanent in quality...."

An injured worker who loses seven days or less from his job would not be eligible for temporary disability benefits because of the waiting period provision of the law. Yet, if his injury results in a permanent disability, he would still be entitled to a permanent partial award. Consequently, cases classified as permanent partials include cases in which some award has been made for the permanent disability, and possibly temporary disability benefits as well. It is impossible to separate out these payments for all years, but data are available for 1955.

One might suppose that in only a minority of cases would a worker suffer a permanent disability without having lost a week from his job; but the 1955 data show otherwise. Of the 36,524 permanent partial cases closed in that year, nearly half (17,736) were cases in which workers received an award for permanent disability without collecting any temporary disability payments. As a matter of fact, in 1955 more workers received permanent disability awards without temporary disability benefits than the other way around. Less than 12,000 persons received benefits for temporary disability only.[6] It is obvious that workmen's compensation cannot be thought of merely as an income maintenance program.

The very limited evidence at hand indicates that on the average the worker who receives a permanent partial award without also receiving temporary disability benefits suffers from a relatively minor injury. However, care should always be taken not to dismiss even the slightest

---

[6] "Fatal, Permanent Total and Permanent Partial Cases Closed with and without Temporary Disability, 1955" typewritten tables prepared by the Statistical Section of the New Jersey Division of Workmen's Compensation.

disability as inconsequential. In 1955 the average permanent partial disability award received by workers who were not eligible for temporary disability benefits was only $389, or about thirteen weeks of disability at the then maximum rate of $30.[7] This is the number of weeks of benefits that would be awarded if the disability were adjudged at $2\frac{1}{2}$ per cent of total disability or 25 per cent of the first finger. Awards in cases wherein some temporary benefits were collected averaged slightly more than $1,000, but this figure includes an indeterminate number of weeks of temporary disability compensation.

If all permanent partial cases, those with temporary disability benefits and those without, are considered, the most serious cases, as one would expect, are a small portion of the total. Of the nearly 37,000 death, permanent total, and permanent partial cases closed in 1955, only 651 were recorded with "lost time charges" of 1,500 days or more; 1,500 days would be the American Standard Association's time charge for a case adjudged at 25 per cent of total disability or 50 per cent of a hand.[8]

Thus far the discussion has been in terms of cases closed by the Division of Workmen's Compensation. Insurance carriers report on cases as they receive them, and process them in some instances before they are closed by the division. These reports are tabulated by the Compensation Rating and Inspection Bureau according to policy years, each of which embraces two calendar years. Chart 3, based upon these reports, shows the relative trends in several types of cases from policy years 1935 to 1953. The permanent partial cases are divided into so-called "major" and "minor" cases. During this period of time, major permanent partials were defined as cases in which the indemnity award for permanent partial disability alone exceeded seventy-five weeks, or cases in which the total indemnity award exceeded 100 weeks in the aggregate. All other permanent partial cases would fall within the minor category. As can be seen from Chart 3, from policy years 1939 to 1953, the number of major permanent partials about doubled, whereas the number of minor cases increased more than three and one half times.[9] One might conclude from this that the severity of industrial injuries has drastically declined over the years. Unfortunately, little independent data exist on severity rates for New Jersey industry as a whole, but, as will be seen, the available evidence shows no drastic reduction in this measure.

[7]This is based upon the assumption that all workers were earning $45 a week or more in 1955. This assumption is not wholly realistic, but it is not too wide of the mark, as can be seen by reference to the data on wage rates contained in chapter 3.

[8]"Number and Cost of Serious Compensated Accidents, 1955," typewritten tables prepared by the Statistical Section of the New Jersey Division of Workmen's Compensation. The number of days lost does not represent actual time lost from work. It is a combination of the schedule of standard time charges as shown in *American Standard Method of Recording and Measuring Work Injury Experience*, Z-16.1, and the actual number of days lost if temporary disability payments were made.

[9]Later data are not available on a consistent basis because of changes in the definitions of major and minor permanent partial cases. Currently, major permanent partial cases are defined to include all cases in which the worker lost the use of an eye or any limb, cases in-

Trends in the Cost of Closed Compensated Cases

Table III is a record of the yearly incurred costs of cash indemnity payments in closed cases. This is the division's estimate of the eventual cost of all closed cases, but it does not include estimates of the costs of medical or other services. The usual breakdowns for classes of disability are shown, except that from 1939 to 1946 the death and permanent disability cases are combined.

No significant backward step is visible in the upward march of total costs since 1939, or for that matter since 1935, although figures for earlier years are not shown. (The slight dip in 1950 can probably be accounted for by the recession in 1948-49 and the 1955 decline by aberrations in statistical closing dates.) This upward movement is a function of the increasing number of cases, rising wages, and increases in benefit rates because of amendment in the law. The accumulated effects of the changes in the compensation law since 1939 (or 1946, since no changes were made between 1939 and 1946) required an approximate 60 per cent increase in insurance rates.[10] As might be expected from the increase in the number of cases and the rise in wage levels, costs have risen more than this.

In 1939, $6,031,927 were incurred for cash indemnity payments in closed cases. The comparable figure for 1957 was $36,195,336, an increase of 500 per cent. The average award per case in 1939 was $279; the comparable 1956 figure was $600, an increase of 115 per cent. But these comparisons are too gross, since they lump together all sorts of cases.

---

volving impairment to the extent of 80 per cent of an eye or 50 per cent of a limb, and any case which is adjudged at 25 per cent or more of total disability. Minor cases include all other permanent partial cases not serious enough to fit into the major category. Data are available on the basis of the new definitions from policy years 1951 to 1955, too short a period of time to pick out any significant trends. In policy year 1951, 564 major and 25,735 minor cases were recorded. In policy year 1955, 630 majors and 27,091 minors were recorded.

[10]On January 1, 1946, the maximum weekly rate was increased from $20 to $25; fifty weeks were added to the number allowed for permanent total disability, and upward revisions were made in the number of weeks for all schedule awards. Formerly a worker had to remain disabled for seven weeks before being eligible to collect payments for temporary compensation for the waiting period. This seven-week period was reduced to four. Also burial benefits were increased from $150 to $250. The substantial effect of these amendments is attested to by the fact that the Compensation Rating and Inspection Bureau estimated that insurance rates would have to increase by 23.8 per cent to reflect these law amendments.

Effective January 1, 1950, the law was amended to include all occupational diseases, in place of the former specified coverage. The rating bureau evaluated the amendments as requiring a 1.2 per cent increase in insurance rates.

In 1951 the maximum weekly rate for temporary and permanent partial disabilities was increased from $25 to $30, a change which was estimated as requiring an 11.4 per cent increase in insurance rates. The new maximum was made applicable to permanent total cases in the following year. Benefit levels remained stable until the amendments effective January 1, 1957, which increased the weekly maximums and required a 13.2 per cent increase in rates. (Computed from data in New Jersey Compensation Rating and Inspection Bureau, *Annual Reports*. For a more complete examination of changes in insurance rate levels see chapter 7.)

Table III. New Jersey Closed Compensated Cases — Number and Incurred Cash Indemnity Cost, by Type of Disability, 1939-1957

Year	All Cases [a]					Death Cases			Permanent Total Disability Cases		
	Actual No.	Rel. No. (1939 = 100)	Amt. of Compensation Incurred	Rel. Amt. of Compensation Incurred (1939 = 100)	Av. Amt. of Compensation Incurred per Case	Actual No.	Amt. of Compensation Incurred [b]	Av. Amt. of Compensation Incurred per Case [b]	Actual No.	Amt. of Compensation Incurred	Av. Amt. of Compensation Incurred per Case
1939	21,587	100.00	$6,031,927	100.00	$279.42	152	$723,592	$4,439	11	$-	$-
1940	25,585	118.52	7,759,049	128.63	303.27	250	1,285,184	4,673	25	-	-
1941	31,127	144.19	9,167,086	151.98	294.51	230	1,285,579	5,142	20	-	-
1942	37,094	171.83	12,103,899	200.66	326.30	274	1,612,432	5,393	25	-	-
1943	38,863	180.03	12,570,919	208.54	323.47	257	1,451,953	5,378	13	-	-
1944	47,083	218.11	17,653,537	292.67	374.95	290	1,928,023	6,063	28	-	-
1945	49,515	229.37	16,636,388	275.81	335.99	216	1,392,476	6,081	13	-	-
1946	48,740	225.78	18,412,596	305.25	377.77	197	1,536,749	6,860	27	-	-
1947	44,182	204.67	19,393,741	321.52	438.95	203	1,812,424	7,915	26	-	-
1948	42,682	197.72	19,812,046	328.45	464.18	175	1,489,561	8,512	26	199,688	7,680
1949	41,921	194.20	20,499,740	339.85	489.01	168	1,363,764	8,118	24	215,888	8,995
1950	40,760	188.82	19,198,073	318.27	471.00	160	1,320,366	8,252	29	232,598	8,021
1951	47,145	218.40	23,138,233	383.60	490.79	213	1,775,265	8,335	42	356,626	8,491
1952	50,999	236.25	27,709,699	459.38	543.34	167	1,626,042	9,737	36	380,910	10,581
1953	54,824	253.97	30,481,274	505.33	555.98	180	1,796,117	9,978	33	425,080	12,881
1954	57,006	264.08	32,921,717	545.79	577.51	195	2,262,274	11,601	33	454,437	13,771
1955	48,369	224.07	29,894,982	495.61	618.06	152	1,694,467	11,148	31	402,248	12,976
1956	58,453	270.78	33,419,985	554.05	571.74	160	1,831,520	11,447	24	342,150	14,256
1957	55,041	254.97	36,195,336	600.06	657.61	178	2,167,387	12,176	25	248,654	9,946

Source: New Jersey Division of Workmen's Compensation, "Industrial Accident Reports."

[a] Closed cases data do not include reopened cases.

[b] For years prior to 1948, compensations incurred in both death and permanent total disability cases are combined. Separate data became available in 1949.

Table III (Continued)

	Permanent Partial Disability Cases (Includes some Payments for Temporary Disability)					Temporary Disability Only Cases				
Year	Actual No.	Rel. No. (1939 = 100)	Amt. of Compensation Incurred	Rel. Amt. of Compensation Incurred (1939 = 100)	Av. Amt. of Compensation Incurred per Case	Actual No.	Rel. No. (1939 = 100)	Amt. of Compensation Incurred	Rel. Amt. of Compensation Incurred (1939 = 100)	Av. Amt. of Compensation Incurred per Case
1939	7,586	100.0	$4,327,433	100.0	$570.45	13,838	100.0	$980,902	100.0	$70.88
1940	10,149	133.8	5,493,675	126.9	541.30	15,161	109.6	980,190	99.9	65.65
1941	12,681	167.2	6,775,156	156.6	534.28	18,196	131.5	1,106,351	112.8	60.80
1942	17,523	231.0	9,232,446	213.3	526.88	19,272	139.3	1,259,021	128.4	65.33
1943	18,492	243.8	9,508,820	219.7	514.21	20,101	145.3	1,610,146	164.1	80.10
1944	28,490	375.6	14,121,963	326.3	495.68	18,275	132.1	1,603,551	163.5	87.75
1945	32,652	430.4	13,898,123	321.2	425.64	16,634	120.2	1,345,789	137.2	80.91
1946	29,196	384.9	15,061,914	348.1	515.88	19,320	139.6	1,813,933	184.9	93.89
1947	27,694	365.1	16,209,238	374.6	585.30	16,259	117.5	1,372,079	139.9	84.39
1948	26,867	354.2	16,734,200	386.7	622.85	15,614	112.8	1,388,597	141.6	88.93
1949	27,091	357.1	17,610,742	407.0	650.05	14,638	105.8	1,259,346	128.4	86.03
1950	26,566	350.2	16,509,908	381.5	621.46	14,005	101.2	1,135,201	115.7	81.06
1951	31,193	411.2	19,633,912	453.7	629.43	15,697	113.4	1,372,430	139.9	87.43
1952	35,353	466.0	24,145,057	557.9	682.97	15,443	111.6	1,557,660	158.8	100.87
1953	38,820	511.7	26,707,547	617.2	687.98	15,791	114.1	1,552,530	158.3	98.32
1954	41,392	545.6	28,664,697	662.4	692.52	15,386	111.2	1,540,309	157.0	100.11
1955	36,524	481.5	26,616,520	615.1	728.74	11,662	84.3	1,181,747	120.5	101.33
1956	42,602	561.6	29,624,737	684.6	695.38	15,667	113.2	1,621,578	165.3	103.50
1957	41,139	542.3	32,258,553	745.4	784.14	13,699	99.0	1,520,742	155.0	111.01

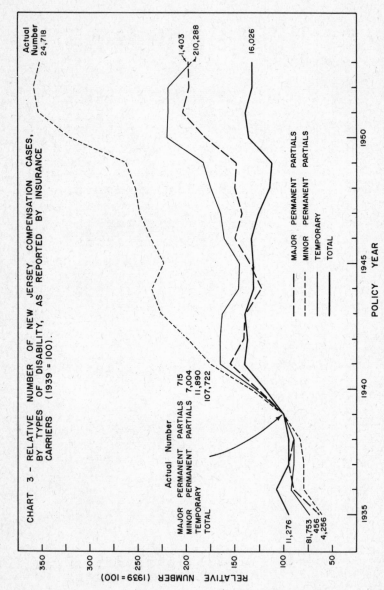

CHART 3 – RELATIVE NUMBER OF NEW JERSEY COMPENSATION CASES, BY TYPES OF DISABILITY, AS REPORTED BY INSURANCE CARRIERS (1939 = 100).

Source: Abstracted from New Jersey Compensation Rating and Inspection Bureau, *Annual Report*, 1956, Exhibit H-1. These data include only losses compensated under the New Jersey Workmen's Compensation Act. Experience accumulated under per capita policies is also excluded.

The total amount incurred in the temporary disability category was $980,902 in 1939 and $1,520,742 in 1957, an increase of 55 per cent. More revealing is the fact that the average award in 1939 was $70.88; in 1956, $103.50; and in 1957, $111.01. If the assumption is made that all workers were eligible to receive the maximum awards in both 1939 and 1956, then in 1939 workers were receiving on the average a temporary disability award for about 3.50 weeks at the $20 maximum then prevailing, and in 1956 for 3.45 weeks at the $30 maximum then in effect. The average number of weeks is about the same for the beginning and end of the period. (Calculations for 1957 would not be meaningful because some high-wage workers injured in 1956 were eligible for the $30 maximum, whereas those injured in 1957 could qualify for the $40 maximum.) If this is any measure of the severity of injuries received, no great change is discernible in the number of weeks of disability.

With the substantial increase in the number of permanent partial disability cases, it is not surprising to find that payments in cases involving this type of disability have increased more than seven times since 1939. But because of the more than proportionate increase in minor permanent partial cases, the average award per employee has increased comparatively little. In 1939 the average payment was $570, whereas in 1957 it was $784.14. This increase of 38 per cent is not sufficient to take care of the rate increases made in the law. Again, using the working assumption that all workers were eligible to receive the maximum rate each year, the average number of weeks compensated was 28.5 in 1939 and only 23.2 in 1956. This decline has been fairly steady through the years. When it is recognized that fewer workers were eligible for the maximum in earlier years, it is safe to conclude that the average award, in terms of weeks of compensation, has actually declined over the years. The increase in dollar totals must be accounted for by the law changes and the increased number of cases.

Insofar as the relative importance of the various types of disability is concerned, the financial information compels the same conclusion as the numerical count. The important category is the permanent partial cases. The fact that these are more than 70 per cent of the cases has been noted; they account for more than this proportion of the compensation dollar. In 1957, eighty-nine cents out of each dollar of incurred costs were spent in awards for permanent partial disability. Both the number count and the dollar count include cases in which temporary payments disability were made in addition to permanent partial awards. At this stage of our inquiry, one can only raise the question of whether these allocation trends represent desirable developments in the use of funds devoted to workmen's compensation.

Compensation Trends by Counties

Thus far the discussion has been in terms of state-wide totals, but it is also useful to look at the breakdown of cases according to New Jersey's twenty-one counties. Table IV shows the total number of cases for each county in 1954, together with information on cases which involve permanent partial disability. As might be expected, the heavily populated and highly industrialized northern counties head the list when it comes to the total number of cases. Hudson County had 12,783 cases in 1954; Essex County, with 11,412, was followed by Union County, with 6,036, and Bergen and Passaic, with totals of about 5,000 each. The experience in these counties contrasts sharply with that in some of the southern, less industrialized counties, in which the annual number of compensation cases is measured in the hundreds. Cape May and Salem Counties, for example, registered totals in the neighborhood of 200.

In light of the population differences, one expects to find substantial variations in the total numbers of cases; less expected, perhaps, are the differences in the proportion of permanent partial cases to all cases in each of the counties. Again, Hudson County led the list with

Table IV. New Jersey Closed Compensated Cases — by Counties, 1954

Counties	No. of Cases		Rank in Order of No. of Permanent Partial Cases	Permanent Partial Cases As a Percentage of All Cases	Av. Award in Permanent Partial Cases[a]	Rank in Order of Amt. of Award
	All Cases	Permanent Partial Cases				
Hudson	12,783	11,106	1	86.8%	$577	21
Essex	11,412	8,997	2	78.8	691	18
Union	6,036	4,770	3	79.0	697	17
Bergen	5,648	4,187	4	74.1	603	20
Passaic	4,383	3,131	5	71.4	641	19
Middlesex	3,672	2,733	6	74.4	747	15
Monmouth	1,760	1,195	7	67.9	936	12
Morris	1,621	1,059	8	65.3	833	14
Mercer	1,733	743	9	42.9	1,055	9
Somerset	955	712	10	74.5	724	16
Camden	1,463	431	11	29.5	1,153	6
Burlington	649	244	12	37.6	1,238	4
Warren	481	239	13	49.7	1,053	10
Ocean	430	224	14	52.1	1,099	8
Atlantic	872	173	15	19.8	1,332	2
Cumberland	642	153	16	23.8	1,295	3
Sussex	315	149	17	47.3	933	13
Hunterdon	253	114	18	45.1	1,030	11
Gloucester	330	110	19	33.3	1,174	5
Salem	194	59	20	30.4	1,563	1
Cape May	209	45	21	21.5	1,152	7
Unclassified	7	6	--	85.7	707	--
Out of State	1,158	812	--	70.1	653	--
	57,006	41,392		72.6%	$693	

Source: Tabulated from information in New Jersey Division of Workmen's Compensation, "Industrial Accident Report," 1954.

[a]Permanent partial cases includes all cases in which some award was made for permanent partial disability. The average dollar award therefore includes payments for temporary disability in those cases in which temporary disability benefits were awarded.

86.8 per cent of its cases in the permanent partial category. Essex and Union Counties had nearly 80 per cent of their cases in this category, while Bergen, Passaic and Middlesex Counties registered proportions between 71.4 and 74.4 per cent. This was in sharp contrast with some of the southern counties, such as Salem, Cape May and Cumberland, in which between 21.5 and 30.4 per cent of the total number of cases were in the permanent partial class.

Although the percentage of permanent partial cases was overwhelmingly higher in the northern counties, the average cash indemnity award for these was lower than in other counties (columns 5 and 6, Table IV). The average award in permanent partial cases in Hudson County in 1954 was $577; in Union County, $697. On the other hand, Salem County had an average award of $1,563. Thus, although fewer in number, the permanent partial cases that were compensated in the southern counties were more serious cases calling for greater dollar amounts of compensation benefits. If the three-year period, 1953 to 1955 is considered, there was a high negative correlation of -.71 between the county's rank in order of number of permanent partials and its rank in order of dollar amount of the compensation awards. In general, counties which had fewest of these cases paid the highest average awards.

The differences among the counties insofar as the percentage of permanent partials is concerned, have been pointed out by many people, including the State Chamber of Commerce and a legislative commission.[11] It has been noted, for example, that Mercer and Camden Counties are industrialized, as are the northern counties; and yet they have a relatively lower percentages of cases in the permanent partial category. Mercer, for example, had 42.9 per cent of its cases in this category, about half that of Hudson County. Camden's percentage ran about 30 per cent.

Data on methods of settlement of the various types of cases by counties are not available for all years, but a detailed examination of the 1954 data for Essex, Mercer, Camden and four southern counties, Cape May, Cumberland, Atlantic and Gloucester, is presented in the appendix to this chapter. Less than one in ten of all cases in the four southern counties was closed out at the formal level, whereas more than three out of ten were settled on this basis in Essex. Camden followed the southern pattern, whereas less than two in ten cases were closed out at this last administrative stage in Mercer County. It is at this formal level that the tendency to grant permanent partial awards is most marked. A good portion of the inter-county differences in proportions of permanent partials may be accounted for by differences in settlement patterns.

---

[11] New Jersey State Chamber of Commerce, "Workmen's Compensation Trends in N. J." (undated, mim., c. 1954). *Report of the Commission to Study Laws Affecting Industrial Development* (Trenton: June, 1957), p. 41.

Further evidence of this is that in the four southern counties and in Camden, three out of four permanent partial cases were settled at informal hearings or by direct settlements, whereas in Essex only slightly more than one-half of the permanent partials were settled at these levels.

Mercer County occupies an intermediate position. In a sense, it has the best or the worst of the two worlds, depending upon the point of view. In 1954, it ranked nearly in the middle (ninth) of all counties in the number of permanent partial cases, and exactly in the same position insofar as the average cash permanent partial award was concerned. The tendency in Mercer was to bring a little less than two out of every ten closed cases to a formal hearing, a proportion smaller than in Essex but greater than in the southern counties or Camden.

In the appendix to this chapter the data for these various counties are standardized to take account of the differences in the number of employees and the different types of employments. When this is done, Essex County's case rate (number of cases per 100 employees) is still approximately 72 per cent higher than that of the four southern counties of Cape May, Cumberland, Atlantic and Gloucester. These comparisons include all closed cases, but the differences would be more extreme if only permanent partial cases or only formal cases were considered, since a greater proportion of Essex County's cases fell into these categories. Apparently there is a higher degree of claims consciousness in Essex County than in the southern counties, with Mercer occupying a middle position. Workers in the southern counties are less willing to file compensation claims, and once they file, are less willing to pursue the case through to the formal stage.

Some Possible Explanations of the Case Trends

The basic purpose of this chapter is to examine and delineate the discernible trends in workmen's compensation activity within New Jersey. The record of the increase over the years in the annual number of all types of cases, and of the permanent partial cases in particular, is there and cannot be erased. All comparisons, however, have been made based upon the prewar period, and it is impossible to conclude, solely on the basis of the record, that the relationships among cases, or the ratio of cases to employment or to accidents, were correct in 1939 and distorted in 1957. The record shows striking differences in case statistics among the various counties, but it fails to tell us whether the northern counties or the southern counties have established the correct relationships.

The state-wide increase in the number of cases in relation to employment or accidents may be the result of an increased inclination on the part of workers to file claims for injuries. Such an attitudinal change may have come about because of the average worker's increased consciousness of social insurance programs generally. Unemployment and old-age and survivors insurance programs have matured significantly only since the war. The federal disability insurance program and the state's temporary disability insurance benefits law are of more recent origin. Social insurance publicists have pointed out that benefits under these programs are a matter of "right" and not "need" and that they should be looked to for income supplements at appropriate times. Possibly, there has been some transfer of this general social insurance consciousness to workmen's compensation. Persons may be more aware of the potentialities of all social insurance programs and more willing to assert their legitimate rights under any one of them.

The increase in the number of litigated cases suggests that workers are more willing to contest claims and are not so satisfied as they once were with settlements offered by employers. Some part of this tendency may have been reinforced by the growth of unions in the state since the late 1930's. "In 14 years, from 1939 to 1953, organized labor in New Jersey more than trebled its membership. It was about 215,000 in 1939 and almost 750,000 in 1953.... The *relative* growth in New Jersey even surpassed that in New York, Pennsylvania, Illinois and Ohio though not that of Michigan or California. Moreover, it markedly exceeded the national growth of approximately 150 per cent."[12] This growing influence of unions may have been felt in a number of ways. The state-wide organizations of labor devote space in their newspapers and other periodicals to the latest developments in the compensation law. Formal educational programs are dedicated to increasing members' knowledge of the various social insurance programs. If the union shop steward is hazy on procedural details, he at least knows the name of a lawyer who has gotten results in other cases. The union also serves as a channel of communication to supplement the usual grapevine methods. If one worker is able to secure a larger settlement only after a formal hearing, then the next injured worker may be less willing to accept a settlement proffered by the insurance adjuster.

In a pre-union era, a worker may have been reluctant to pursue a case for fear of reprisal from his employer. Insofar as the workers' actions are concerned, it makes little difference whether this fear was fancied or real; it still may have prevented him from proceeding with a claim. Although such fears may not be wholly erased with the arrival of the union, the collective bargaining agreement stands as a protection against arbitrary dismissal.

The large number of cases in the highly urbanized northern counties suggests that it may not be the influence of unions alone that makes workers more willing to file and to litigate. Perhaps a whole complex of factors in urban centers produces a knowledgeable, sophisticated worker with a high degree of compensation consciousness and a willingness to test the program to see what can be had. The threads here

---

[12]Leo Troy, "Union Membership in New Jersey," *Review of New Jersey Business*, XIII (July, 1956), 6.

are difficult to disentangle, since the unions are concentrated in these areas and it is here that one finds the concentration of petitioners' lawyers. Lawyers, expert in compensation matters, are an invaluable asset in procuring awards, especially in the doubtful cases wherein the companies' insurance carriers may have denied the existence of any permanent disability.

Before proceeding too far with the thesis that it is the urban environment that is conducive to a claims-conscious state of mind, one is brought up short by the fact that urbanized Camden County shows a relatively low case rate and a percentage of permanent partials less than half that of Hudson and Essex Counties. Whatever effect a change in compensation consciousness may have had, it has made itself felt much more in the northern industrialized counties than in the southern counties, even those which have felt the breath of industrialization and urbanization.

The continued prosperity since 1939 has probably played some part in the general increase in cases in the state as a whole. This may sound strange, since it is usually said that depressed times bring an increased reliance on social insurance programs. In prosperity, a worker is supposed to be reluctant to exchange productive income for a benefit payment. Yet, in the case of permanent partial awards in which no temporary disability benefits are paid, a worker can collect an award without losing a substantial amount of pay. In some instances, the injured worker may be able to continue at his regular task, and in others, the employer may find something for him to do to keep him at work. Perhaps, in former years such a worker would have been grateful that his medical bills were taken care of and that his normal income continued. Today, he may wait a few weeks or months and then, upon advice of his steward, lawyer or fellow employee, file a claim for some residual permanent impairment. The greater security that full employment brings may persuade him that such a course will not bring reprisals, and even if it should, alternative job opportunities may beckon.

Other explanations for the increases in the number of permanent partial cases are suggested by conversations with petitioners' attorneys and labor union officials. As justification for pursuing what might be considered doubtful claims for permanent partial disability, they point to what they consider as low and inadequate rates paid for temporary disability. The feeling seems to be that an injured worker is entitled to more than the pittance allowed and that if it cannot be had in one way, it is legitimate to seek it in another. The whole spirit of the compensation statute favors the injured workman. This is part of the rich history of the law. When the worker exchanged his common law rights for the more certain but more modest compensation awards, administrators were directed to interpret the law in liberal fashion. When statutory rates become low in the eyes of the administrators, if not the legislature, perhaps there is some tendency to compensate for this by being more liberal in the interpretation of the facts or the assessment of the degree of disability. Once the case is brought to the formal level, of course, nothing succeeds like success, and if one doubtful claim is granted, other cases may be resolved similarly.

The differences among counties in the number of cases and proportions of permanent partial cases are striking. When these differences are brought to the attention of the hearing officers, they stoutly maintain that as far as they are concerned, there is no difference in the way South Jersey cases are handled as compared with those in North Jersey. In a sense, they are correct, since in both areas almost all formal cases in which an award is made, carry some award for permanent partial disability. The essential clue to the apparent differences must be found in the fact that there are simply more cases per employee in comparable industries in Essex than in the southern counties, and that more of these cases reach the formal level before they are settled to the parties' mutual satisfaction.

One might speculate that this is because insurance adjusters in South Jersey tend to settle permanent partial disability cases more readily than their counterparts in the north, but the evidence does not bear this out. Although the likelihood of a permanent partial case being settled before the formal stage is greater in the southern counties than in the northern ones, the fact remains that the permanent partial cases are a much smaller percentage of all cases in the southern counties, as compared with the northern counties. The evidence on average dollar amounts of permanent partial awards is relevant here. The higher average awards in the southern counties indicate that the more serious cases are being compensated, perhaps the obvious scheduled disabilities rather than the more controversial nonscheduled back or head injuries or neurological disabilities. Some evidence is presented in chapter 4 to indicate that these latter are the cases that commonly find their way into the formal hearings in Essex County. It may also be that cases of this type tend to be ignored, for one reason or another, by workers in the southern counties. This may be due to the workers' ignorance of the law, the paucity of lawyers skilled in this form of advocacy in the southern counties, or perhaps fear of employer reprisal. Likely, it is in this area of "compensation consciousness" that the explanation of the inter-county differences can be discovered, both as to the filing of original claims and the persistence with which they are pursued through channels. If the Essex County hearing officers and administrative personnel switched places with their colleagues in South Jersey, (a process of rotation which actually was started in 1957), it is likely that each would be surprised at the differences in the compensation climate. But the major inter-county differences would likely persist if these switches were the only changes made. These would not, in and of themselves, alter the fact that the workers in the southern counties may be less willing to file and, when they file, less willing to litigate.

Alternative explanations are that either there are less accidents per job in the southern counties, or the hearing officers are more willing to dismiss cases without compensation. Accident frequency rates are influenced by industrial rather than area considerations, and the industrial differences have been taken into account in the above comparisons. As for the alternative explanation relating to dismissal of cases, the limited evidence on hand indicates no striking differences between Camden County and Essex County.

All signs point to the fact that the differences are due to the higher degree of claims consciousness in Essex, as compared with the southern counties, Mercer being in the middle. Of necessity, it is impossible to isolate these differences in any statistical fashion. These are psychological factors influenced by the differences in the whole socio-economic atmosphere. But, for whatever the reason, there can be no gainsaying the fact that Essex is different from the four southern counties, and these differences cannot be accounted for by any such simple factors as differences in the numbers of jobs or types of employment.

APPENDIX

INTER-COUNTY COMPARISON OF WORKMEN'S
COMPENSATION CASES

In an effort to explore the differences among counties in greater detail, the statistical records of selected counties were examined intensively. The counties chosen for examination were: Essex, representative of the northern portion of the state; Cape May, Cumberland, Atlantic and Gloucester Counties, representing the southern tier; and, because of their particular relevance, Camden and Mercer.

As has been noted, in the state as a whole the number of permanent partial cases at the formal level is greater than at the informal or direct settlement levels. This apparently accounts for some of the differences in the permanent partial picture among the counties. For example, in 1954 in Essex County, of 11,403 cases (on which data were available), 4,080, or 35.78 per cent of the total, were formal cases (Table V). In contrast, in the four southern counties combined, only 6.1 per cent of the cases were decided at the formal level; 93.9 per cent were closed either at the informal level or by direct settlement.

The smallest number of cases occurred in Cape May County — a total of only 209 cases in 1954. Of these, no more than seven reached the formal level; of the seven, two were death cases, so only five cases involving permanent partial disability ever reached the formal level. In Camden County, 7.0 per cent of the cases reached the formal level. In Mercer County, which occupies a somewhat intermediate position between Essex and the southern counties, 18.3 per cent of the cases were decided formally.

With respect to the permanent partial cases alone (Table V), in Essex County 45.0 per cent of these cases received awards at the formal level, whereas in the four southern counties only 24.2 per cent

Table V. New Jersey Closed Compensated Cases — Inter-County Comparison by Type of Disability and Method of Settlement, 1954

County	All Cases					Permanent Partial Cases[a]				
	Total No. of Cases	Formal Cases		Informals and Direct Settlements		Total No. of Permanent Partial Cases	Formal Cases		Informals and Direct Settlements	
		No.	% of Total Cases	No.	% of Total Cases		No.	% of all Permanent Partials	No.	% of all Permanent Partials
Essex	11,403	4,080	35.8%	7,323	64.2%	8,988	4,037	45.0%	4,951	55.0%
Camden	1,462	102	7.0	1,360	93.0	430	100	23.3	330	76.7
Mercer	1,730	316	18.3	1,414	81.7	740	308	41.6	432	58.4
Four Southern Counties										
Cape May	209	7	3.4	202	96.6	45	5	11.1	40	88.9
Cumberland	642	34	5.3	608	94.7	153	32	20.9	121	79.1
Atlantic	872	52	6.0	820	94.0	173	46	26.6	127	73.4
Gloucester	329	33	10.0	296	90.0	109	33	30.3	76	69.7
All Four Southern Counties	2,052	126	6.1	1,926	93.9	480	116	24.2	364	75.8

Source: Tabulated from unpublished data of New Jersey Division of Workmen's Compensation.
[a] Include all cases in which some award was made for permanent partial disability. Since these tabulations were computed independently of the data in Table IV, some slight differences in the counties' case total may be noticed.

of permanent partial cases were decided at this level. In other words, in the four southern counties, 75.8 per cent of the cases that did receive permanent partial awards were closed at the informal or direct settlement levels. Much the same is true of Camden County, but Mercer County presents a slightly different picture in that it more nearly approximates the Essex County pattern; 41.6 per cent of Mercer's permanent partial cases were closed at the formal level, and 58.4 per cent were decided by other methods.

The differences in the total number of cases in the various counties have been noted. But to say that Hudson County has more than 10,000 cases a year, whereas the totals in some of the southern counties are in the hundreds, is only to provoke the natural reaction that this is to be expected in light of population and industrial differences. The differences in the number of employees among the counties can be taken into account, but even this is not enough because the industrial "mix" in each of the counties is so different. One county may have more workers in a relatively hazardous industry like construction; the other may have a higher percentage of its work force in relatively safe service trades or in financial institutions where the accident risks are minimal. Comparisons can be made, however, if the industrial "mix" is standardized for each of the counties.

The results of such a comparison are shown in Table VI. Column 1 shows the distribution of "covered jobs" in Essex County among the various industrial classifications. (The job data are derived from employer reports under the unemployment insurance law and refer to workers who are covered by that law. The term "covered job" rather than "covered worker" is used because of the specialized meaning attached to the latter term in the law.) Broad industrial categories are shown, except in manufacturing, for which it is possible to present finer breakdowns. For the sake of simplicity of presentation, this distribution is shown as parts of 1,000 instead of as traditional percentages. Thus, in 1954, 3 out of 1,000 covered jobs reported in Essex County were in agriculture, forestry and fishing, 1 in mining, 125 in construction, 114 in manufacturing of food products, and so on.

Column 2 shows the number of closed compensated cases per 100 covered jobs in each of these industrial classifications in Essex County. These figures are derived by taking the number of closed compensated cases in each of the categories and comparing it with the number of covered jobs in that classification. Column 3 shows these same calculations for the four southern counties combined. For example, in the southern counties there were 173 closed compensated cases in 1954 in the food manufacturing industries, and there were an average of 4,335 covered jobs reported that year in that classification in these counties. This amounts to 4 cases for each 100 covered jobs in food manufacturing in the four counties. Similar calculations are presented for Mercer and Camden Counties, taking into account their closed cases and the number of covered jobs in each category.

It is not absolutely essential that the statistical comparison be

Table VI. New Jersey Closed Compensated Cases — Inter-County Comparison
of Case Rates, by Industry, 1954

| Industry | Distribution of Essex County Covered Jobs[a] (parts of 1,000) (1) | No. of Closed Compensated Cases per 100 Covered Jobs | | | |
		Essex County (2)	Four Southern Counties[b] (3)	Mercer County (4)	Camden County (5)
Agriculture, Forestry and Fishing	3	17.0	14.4	19.9	14.1
Mining	1	20.7	2.7	--	1.3
Construction	125	12.5	7.3	7.7	6.5
Manufacturing					
Food	114	7.7	4.0	8.0	1.7
Tobacco	2	3.7	--	.5	1.0
Textile Mill	16	4.8	1.7	2.0	3.9
Apparel	14	1.6	.8	1.0	.6
Basic Lumber	7	.9	5.5	6.6	3.9
Furniture	4	4.5	7.9	5.7	.9
Paper	16	4.8	3.9	6.2	2.0
Printing, Publishing	10	2.3	1.4	1.2	6.4
Chemicals	39	3.6	1.2	2.2	1.2
Petroleum Refining	3	8.8	.7	--	5.8
Rubber	3	4.6	1.0	2.0	--
Leather	20	5.9	--	.2	2.3
Stone, Clay and Glass	8	7.6	1.6	2.3	2.2
Primary Metals Industries	54	11.4	5.6	4.0	7.8
Fabricated Metal Products	70	7.5	1.7	.8	2.8
Machinery (except electrical)	67	5.2	4.4	2.6	1.6
Electrical Goods & Machines	60	2.3	1.6	1.7	.7
Transportation Equipment	25	5.9	5.5	9.9	3.2
Instruments & Clocks	6	1.5	1.4	.5	1.0
Misc. Manufacturing	38	2.8	4.0	3.4	1.6
Transportation, Communication and Public Utilities	106	4.2	2.3	2.2	1.4
Wholesale and Retail Trade	104	1.7	1.4	1.3	.9
Finance, Insurance and Real Estate	13	.5	.3	.3	.3
Services	72	3.3	2.4	2.9	1.4
	1,000				

Av. No. of Cases per 100 Covered Jobs
Weighted by Essex County Industrial Distribution

Source: Covered Job Data from New Jersey Department of Labor and Industry, Division of Employment Security. Workmen's compensation case-totals tabulated from unpublished data of Division of Workmen's Compensation. Since the industrial breakdowns for the job and case data are not exactly comparable, it was necessary to make adjustments in the classifications.
[a] For the sake of simplicity of presentation, distribution is shown as parts of 1,000 jobs instead of as traditional percentages.
[b] Cape May, Cumberland, Atlantic and Gloucester.

carried further; for most industrial classifications, the rate in Essex is higher than in the other counties. It is possible, however, to compute an *average* case rate per 100 covered jobs by weighting the case rates in each county by the *distribution of covered jobs in Essex County*. This has the effect of standardizing the industrial composition in each of the counties as it actually exists in Essex County. The average case rate in Essex is 5.86 per 100 covered jobs. This is the average of all the case rates in each of the industrial classifications, weighted by the number of jobs in these classifications in the county. The average number of cases per 100 covered jobs in the four southern counties is substantially less, 3.41.

If Essex County had the same number of cases per 100 covered jobs in each of the industrial classifications as did the southern counties, then Essex's average would have been 3.41 cases per 100 covered jobs. As it is, Essex's rate of 5.86 is approximately 72 per cent higher. This difference cannot be accounted for by differences in employment or the fact that the counties have different industrial makeups, because the southern counties' average has been weighted by the distribution of jobs within Essex County. When the averages are computed in the same manner for Mercer and Camden Counties, similar results are noted. Mercer's average is 3.80 cases per 100 covered jobs, whereas Camden's is lowest of all, with 2.65 cases for each 100 covered jobs.

These comparisons are on the basis of *all* closed compensated cases and not just permanent partial disability cases or cases closed at the formal level. But it has already been shown that Essex has a higher percentage of its cases in these categories than do the southern counties. To examine either or both of these categories separately would only expose more extreme differences than have already been noted.

Chapter 3

THE ADEQUACY OF WORKMEN'S COMPENSATION PAYMENTS

Workmen's compensation is the only social insurance program in which the worker gave up pre-existing rights for promised benefits. In none of the other programs did the worker have a prior right, under the common law, to recover amounts from his employer in the event of unemployment, retirement or off-the-job disability. When society deemed it wise to stop the injured employee from proceeding against his employer for recovery of damages, the employee had to rely on the implicit promise that the cash benefits and medical services provided would somehow be an adequate substitute. No one would claim that the average injured employee should receive, under the compensation laws, the highest award that he might fortuitously recover under the common law; the presumed certainty of the benefit is supposed to compensate for the fact that it is lower in amount.

The framers of the early laws had some idea about the amount of these awards and their relationship to what the worker earned on the job. What toll have the passing years taken of these concepts? How do the various states compare in the matter of benefit levels? Let us concentrate first on the temporary disability benefit, since the relationship between income loss and benefit level is clearer here than in any of the other types of disability. Permanent total disability benefits and death benefits will be examined later. Also pertinent to this discussion is the information on benefits available to workmen's compensation receivers from other public social insurance programs and from private group supplemental plans.

Income and Benefit Levels in Temporary Disability Cases

All social insurance programs have common problems in setting benefit levels. In general, three methods can be used: (1) Benefits can be fixed at some percentage of productive income. (2) They can be fixed in accordance with some criteria of assumed average or individual "need." (3) A flat-rate system can be used under which all eligible recipients receive the same dollar amounts, with perhaps some adjustments for dependents. Of course, variations and combinations of these basic methods may be adopted.

From the start, workmen's compensation jurisdictions, with two exceptions, have adopted the first method, and the other social insurance systems in this country have followed suit. The second method is used in public assistance programs and other aid programs which

37

require clients to pass some "needs test" of eligibility. Vocational rehabilitation programs, for example, supplement indigent clients' incomes while they are undergoing training or physical rehabilitation, but only after the rehabilitation counselor is satisfied that family income is insufficient to meet the extra burden. The flat-rate method is used in the workmen's compensation programs in Washington and Wyoming but has otherwise been uniformly rejected in this country; however, it is used in other countries, notably Great Britain.[1]

The rejection of the flat-rate system must be explored. Although this pattern presumably is not used in workmen's compensation, circumstances threaten to, or already have, converted our wage-related benefit system into a flat-rate one. Reasons for preferring a system that related benefits to wages have been admirably stated by Eveline Burns: "...a wage related system is especially well devised for large and economically heterogeneous communities, for it enables them to apply a uniform principle to all citizens wherever they reside and at the same time maintain any desired differential between benefit and normal earnings, as well as occupational differentials."[2] Burns was referring to the national scene, but her remarks apply with equal effect to the industrially heterogenous State of New Jersey.

The hallmark of a free enterprise economy is a system of differential rewards based upon incentive, and these differentials should be preserved when a worker receives social insurance benefits. The differences in wages received result in different levels of living, and these must be continued when disability strikes. Automobile installment payments must be met, mortgage payments fall due, and the amounts of these continuing obligations vary with income levels. A survey conducted among persons receiving unemployment compensation in the Pittsburgh area shows, quite clearly, that families find it difficult to readjust spending patterns when they meet income reverses.[3] The whole American climate argues for a wage-related benefit system rather than one which pays a flat rate to all.

In none of the social insurance programs, however, are benefits related exactly to wages. The principal compromises made are in: (1) the formula used to relate wages and benefits, (2) the payment of

---

[1] In Great Britain, the flat benefits payable vary with age, marital status and number of dependents in the unemployment and pension programs. Under the workmen's compensation program, flat rates are paid for periods of what we would term temporary disability, but specific disablement benefits and additional benefits in cases of continued unemployability, special hardship, etc., are also made. See Douglas Potter and D. H. Stansfeld, *National Insurance (Industrial Injuries)* (London: Butterworth, 1950).

In 1958, the government in Great Britain proposed a new national old-age pension plan with graduated contributions and pensions linked to the level of earnings. See "Britain Proposes Higher Pensions," *The New York Times*, October 15, 1958, p. 9.

[2] Eveline M. Burns, *Social Security and Public Policy* (N. Y.: McGraw-Hill Book Co., 1956), p. 38.

[3] *Survey of Unemployment Compensation Beneficiaries in the Pittsburgh, Pennsylvania, District*, September 1, 1953-August 31, 1954 (Pittsburgh: Duquesne University, March 15, 1955).

dependent's allowances, (3) the imposition of minimum benefit levels, and (4) the fixing of maximum levels.

The benefit formula used in the federal Old-Age, Survivors, and Disability Insurance program (OASDI), for example, is weighted in favor of workers in the low income groups; they receive a higher percentage of their average wages than other workers. New Jersey is the only jurisdiction which alters its workmen's compensation *formula* according to income levels. All other jurisdictions which relate benefits to wages pay a specified percentage of wages to workers with the same number of dependents, but there is a stated maximum. The percentage is usually 66 2/3, the figure used in New Jersey from 1919 until the amendments of 1957 replaced this constant percentage figure with a schedule relating wages and benefits. Under this schedule, the benefits for workers with wages up to $45 a week are roughly two-thirds of their wages, but for those with higher weekly wages the proportion is smaller.

The concept of need also enters the determination of benefits wherever dependents' allowances are made. Fifteen states pay dependents' benefits under workmen's compensation; under unemployment insurance programs about one-quarter of the states pay these allowances, as does the federal government under the OASDI program. New Jersey does not take the number of dependents into account in fixing either temporary disability workmen's compensation, unemployment insurance or temporary disability benefits for nonoccupational disabilities.

The laws in all states except Arizona specify minimum weekly benefits in cases of temporary disability, but in at least nineteen jurisdictions a worker cannot collect more than his actual wage as a benefit.[4] If his wage is less than the minimum specified benefit, he is entitled only to his actual wage.

New Jersey's original law specified a minimum of $5 per week for temporary disability. This was increased to $6 in 1919, to $8 in 1923 and finally to $10 in 1929. The original law's minimum was a provisional one in that workers who earned less than $5 received their actual wages as a compensation benefit.[5] The present law specifies an actual minimum of $10 per week, which applies even if greater than

---

[4]Information about the workmen's compensation laws in the various jurisdictions here and in succeeding references is taken from several different sources. The basic source is *State Workmen's Compensation Laws*, United States Department of Labor, Bureau of Labor Standards, Bulletin 161, August, 1957. The data have been supplemented by unpublished information furnished by the bureau. Mrs. Clara Beyer and Mrs. Beatrice McConnell of the bureau have been most kind in making information available in this rapidly changing field. The United States Chamber of Commerce publishes a useful comparison of state laws called *Analysis of Workmen's Compensation Laws*, but the latest edition available at the time of this writing was that of January, 1957. The various studies that have been made of the experience in individual states have also supplied useful comparative information.

[5]For a discussion of the differences between the provisional and flat minimums, see Arthur H. Reede, *Adequacy of Workmen's Compensation* (Cambridge: Harvard University Press, 1947), p. 145.

the worker's actual wage. The minimum benefit figure is not of great importance in the state because of the method used to calculate wages.[6] A worker may be a part-time employee, but as long as he is working in an employment where the customary hours of work are eight a day, he would have to be earning less than $37\frac{1}{2}$ cents per hour before the minimum would have any relevance.[7]

The provisions for alteration of formulas and for dependents' allowances and the fixing of minimum benefits interfere with the idea of relating benefits to wage levels; but the existence of fixed weekly maximums threatens to destroy entirely the concept of relating benefits to wages. In all wage-related social insurance programs, the problem exists as to where benefit levels should be set in relation to wages. The guiding principle is that benefits should not be set so high that workers will prefer benefit status to employment, nor so low as to defeat the purposes of supplying maintenance income. In New Jersey's original law the level chosen was 50 per cent of wages. In 1919 the law was amended to make the level conform more nearly to that in other jurisdictions; it was set at 66 2/3 per cent, the level retained until 1957.

The percentage itself, whatever it may be, means that there is a maximum weekly benefit for the individual worker, and it might be

---

[6] A wide variety of methods is used to calculate the wage in the various jurisdictions. Unlike the situation in unemployment insurance, the purpose of the wage calculation in workmen's compensation is not to test past attachment to the labor force but to estimate the claimant's future earning capacity. The problem is stated by Arthur Larson as follows:

> The computation of average weekly wage is frequently based upon actual wages during the preceeding year, if claimant's employment has been substantially continuous, and upon the wages of employees in similar work if it has not. Since the entire objective is to arrive at as fair an estimate as possible of claimant's future earning capacity, a claimant who has made only part-time earnings should have his wage basis figured on part-time wages only if the employment itself or his relation to it is inherently a part-time one and likely to remain so; otherwise his earnings should be converted to a full-time basis. When an employee, who regularly holds two concurrent jobs, is injured in one of them, his wage will usually be based upon his earnings in both if they are in a similar line of work, but on the earnings in only the one producing the injury if they are unrelated in character. (*The Law of Workmen's Compensation* [Albany: Matthew Bender and Co., 1952], II, 69.)

The laws of some states are quite specific as to the method that should be used to calculate the average wage. The Vermont statutes, for example in Chapter 353, Sect. 8104, state: "Average weekly wages shall be computed in such manner as is best calculated to give the average weekly earnings of the workman during the twelve weeks preceeding his injury." They then go on to say how this shall be done in cases of casual employment, etc. Essentially the New Jersey law defines wages as the money rate at which services were being performed at the time of the accident. Provision is made for converting part-time wages to a full-time basis, since the law states that the hourly wage is to be multiplied by the "customary number of working hours constituting an ordinary day in the character of the work involved" in order to determine the daily wage. Under any circumstances, the weekly wage upon which benefits are based is found by multiplying the daily wage by a minimum of five days.

[7] Eight hours times $0.375 per hour equal $3 as a daily wage. Five times $3 would be $15 per week. As long as the employee's weekly wage is at least $15, he is eligible for the minimum weekly benefit.

thought that no other limitation should be included in the law. This was the thinking of a committee which prepared a Uniform Draft of an Employee's Compensation Code in 1910 and 1911, following a conference of all state commissions. The committee observed: "...we have inserted no maximum for the weekly benefit receivable. It involves an inequality of treatment if the percentage of wages is to form the basis of compensation...."[8] The weekly maximum is in effect a maximum imposed upon a maximum, and there is yet another maximum limitation in that, in New Jersey, a worker cannot receive temporary disability compensation payments for more than 300 weeks. One might well echo Burns's comment: "The purposes of these limits are not always easy to determine."[9]

It is possible to find some rationalizations for the weekly maximum benefits. In part, these were imposed as a concession to the social character of the programs. Workers at the upper end of the wage scale were to receive a smaller percentage of their wages so that low income workers might receive more adequate benefits without increasing the program's over-all costs. Also, employer groups could probably defeat a law which provided only a single limitation of a stated percentage of wages. Under the two-thirds rule, a man earning, say, $150 a week would be eligible for a compensation benefit of $100 a week, a sum which might simply be considered as being too high. Social insurance programs still carry a faint stigma which all the writings in the world cannot erase. Accusations of abuse and malingering which are prevalent now would probably be increased greatly if there were no weekly maximum benefit. But it is one thing to impose a maximum and another to fix it at such a low level that the worker earning the average wage can qualify to receive the maximum benefits.

Chart 4 shows, for the years 1911 to 1957, the average weekly wage in New Jersey and the minimum wage that an employee would have to receive in order to qualify for the maximum benefits.

In the first years of the law, average wages were about $11 per week; the statutory compensation rate was 50 per cent of wages, and the weekly maximum benefit was $10. Thus the average worker earned less than $20 and could actually receive 50 per cent of wages as a benefit. In 1919 the 50 per cent was increased to 66 2/3 per cent, but the maximum was raised only to $12, thus lowering the minimum weekly wage necessary to qualify for maximum benefits to $18. This was probably less than the average weekly wage, although accurate wage data for New Jersey for these years are not obtainable. The situation was not helped greatly when the weekly maximum was

---

[8]Conference of Commissioners on Compensation for Industrial Accidents, *Proceedings* (1910), p. 351. Quoted in Harold A. Katz and Estelle M. Wirpel, "Workmen's Compensation 1910-1952: Are Present Benefits Adequate?" *Labor Law Journal*, IV (March 1953), 164-179. We are indebted to this article by Katz and Wirpel and have made for New Jersey some of the same comparisons they have made for Illinois.

[9]*Social Security and Public Policy*, p. 51. The rationalizations for maximums mentioned in ensuing paragraphs are discussed by Burns.

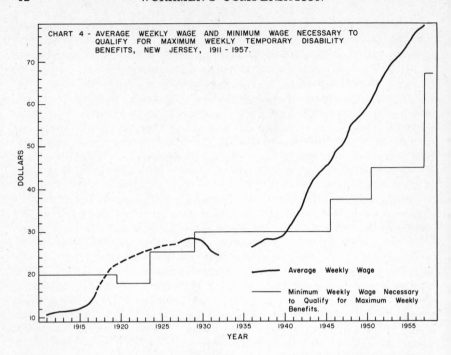

CHART 4 - AVERAGE WEEKLY WAGE AND MINIMUM WAGE NECESSARY TO QUALIFY FOR MAXIMUM WEEKLY TEMPORARY DISABILITY BENEFITS, NEW JERSEY, 1911 - 1957.

Sources: Average weekly wage data for the various years are not entirely comparable. Data from 1913 to 1916 inclusive are abstracted from the annual reports of the New Jersey Bureau of Statistics of Labor and Industries. The 1917 figure is from the *Industrial Directory of New Jersey*. The figures for 1919 and 1923 are not New Jersey wages. They are from the United States Bureau of Labor Statistics series on production workers in manufacturing industries and pertain to the entire country.

Data from 1927 to 1932 inclusive are computed from the monthly figures in the *Industrial Bulletins* published in those years by the New Jersey State Department of Labor. The figures are not twelve-month averages in all cases. In 1927, a nine-month average was used, in 1928, an eleven-month average, in 1931, a ten-month average and in 1932, a five-month average. It was not possible to secure reliable data for the years 1920-1922, 1924-1926 and 1933-1935.

From 1936 to 1957, figures are the indicated average wage rates from unit statistical individual accident reports as reported to the New Jersey Compensation Rating and Inspection Bureau. (See the *Forty-First Annual Report*, 1958, p. 27.) It should be noted that these data are invariably lower than the reported figures on average wages for workers in manufacturing industries in New Jersey since they encompass only workers involved in accident cases. Also, they pertain to policy years, each of which covers two calendar years. The data for the last five years are subject to revision. Data for 1956 and 1957 are estimated by correlation with national wage statistics.

The minimum weekly wage for maximum benefits is the maximum weekly benefit paid in temporary disability cases divided by the statutory percentage for each year except 1957. In that year the minimum weekly wage necessary to qualify for maximum benefits was stated in the law.

increased to $17 in 1923, but in 1929 the maximum was upped to $20, raising the minimum wage necessary to qualify for the maximum benefit to $30, a sum above the average wage then prevailing. As the depression set in and wages dropped, the average worker could once again be assured that he would receive two-thirds of his wages as a compensation benefit. It is ironic that the statutory percentages become truly meaningful only when the economy has sickened with depression.

Wages rose during the period of defense preparations for the second world war and have continued upwards since then. In 1940, the average wage was approximately equal to the minimum wage necessary to qualify for maximum benefits; but in each year since then, the average weekly wage has been greater than this minimum. Although weekly maximums were increased three times after the close of the war, since 1940 the average worker has received less than two-thirds of his wages as a benefit. In 1957, the average worker and, as a matter of fact, the worker who receives $10 less than the average would be eligible to receive the maximum weekly benefit. This means that we are approaching, if we have not already reached, what amounts to a flat-rate system, with all its attendant disadvantages.

Table VII shows for the years 1936 to 1957 the estimated average weekly compensation rate for temporary disability benefits in New Jersey. This is an estimate of the average percentage of wage loss which is actually covered by the temporary disability benefit payments. Insurance rate-makers must make these calculations when they evaluate the cost of changes in the maximum weekly benefits. In computing this average rate, account is taken of the fact that some low-wage workers will receive more than the statutory percentage of wages as a compensation benefit since they will be eligible to receive the minimum specified in the law. Others will receive exactly the statutory percentage, whereas still others will receive less than the statutory percentage since they will receive the maximum weekly benefit.[10]

In 1936, the estimated average rate was 60.46 per cent; and as wages increased, this declined to 42.65 per cent in 1945. The next year, the weekly maximum was increased to $25; but the average percentage of wage loss compensated rose only to 48.11 per cent and then promptly declined in ensuing years. In 1950, the year before the weekly maximum was increased to $30, the average rate had declined to less than 40 per cent; and the new maximum raised it to only 45.41 per cent. The 1957 statutory increase in the maximum brought the average rate up to but 47.37 per cent.

---

[10] The concept of the average or what is called the "effective rate" of compensation is from Reede, chapter X. Since Reede's work was published, newer wage distribution tables have become available, and these have been used. These tables and an explanation of their use can be found in Barney Fratello, "Workmen's Compensation Injury Table and Standard Wage Distribution Table," *Proceedings of the Casualty Actuarial Society*, XLII (1955), 165-166.

Table VII. Average Weekly Wage and Temporary Disability Benefit
Comparisons, New Jersey, 1936-1957

Year	Av. Weekly Wage[a]	Max. Weekly Compensation Payments for Temporary Disability	Min. Weekly Wage Necessary to Qualify for Max. Weekly Benefit[b]	Est. Av. Compensation Rate[c]
1936	$26.68	$20	$30	60.46%
1937	27.88	20	30	59.23
1938	28.48	20	30	58.59
1939	28.47	20	30	58.60
1940	29.60	20	30	57.44
1941	32.22	20	30	54.73
1942	35.83	20	30	51.11
1943	40.40	20	30	46.74
1944	43.44	20	30	44.01
1945	45.37	20	30	42.65
1946	48.46	25	37.50	48.11
1947	51.49	25	37.50	45.91
1948	54.75	25	37.50	43.65
1949	56.47	25	37.50	42.53
1950	58.73	25	37.50	39.31
1951	62.56	30	45	45.41
1952	66.72	30	45	43.08
1953	69.64	30	45	41.51
1954	71.78	30	45	40.47
1955	73.62	30	45	39.53
1956	77.00	30	45	37.94
1957	77.55	40	67.51	47.37

[a] These are the indicated average wage rates from the unit statistical individual accident reports received by the New Jersey Compensation Rating and Inspection Bureau. See *Forty-First Annual Report*, 1958, p. 27.
[b] For all years up to 1957, this is the maximum weekly benefit rate divided by the statutory percentage. Beginning in 1957, this weekly wage was stated in the law.
[c] See explanation in footnote 10. In essence, this is the estimated average percentage of wage loss covered by the compensation benefits paid for temporary disabilities.

The 66 2/3 level was a fiction for the majority of workers long before it was abandoned in the 1957 amendments, which substituted a "wage and compensation schedule." Under this schedule the traditional percentages were adhered to fairly closely for workers earning wages of $45 a week or less. For workers who earn more, the statutes specify benefits which are less than 66 2/3 per cent of their wages. A $60-a-week worker is entitled to a compensation benefit of $36, or 60 per cent; a worker earning $67.51 or more is entitled to the maximum weekly benefit of $40. For the worker earning exactly $67.51, the percentage would be 59.3 per cent. This undoubtedly was the product of a practical political compromise wherein the higher weekly maximum was exchanged for the lower percentage figures in the wage brackets above $45 a week. Cash in hand is probably a good exchange for obsolete percentage figures, but whether the statutory percentage is 66 2/3 or 60 is probably meaningless when the average wage is approaching

$80 a week. The weekly maximum has nullified the statutory percent-
ages, whatever they may be, for the majority of workers.

Maximum Weekly Compensation Benefits and the Price Level

Competitive prices are volatile, and monopoly prices tend to be
sticky, but "legislative prices" are the most sluggish of all. Although
benefits are not prices, in most social insurance programs the amount
of money involved can be changed only with legislative consensus; and
changes are not made quickly in response to economic changes either
in depression or inflation.

Chart 5 shows the average weekly wage and maximum weekly compensation rate in *real* terms from 1913 to 1957 in New Jersey. These
are the actual figures adjusted by prices measured in terms of the
dollar values prevailing in the period 1947 to 1949. The $10 maximum
weekly benefit in 1913 was actually worth more than twice this amount
in terms of constant dollars, but as prices rose in the period before
the first world war the real value of the benefit declined. In the middle
and late twenties the price level remained fairly constant, but the
plunge of prices during the depression increased the real value of the
weekly benefits. In terms of the 1947 to 1949 dollars, the $20 maximum
in 1933 was worth $36.17. In real terms, the benefit level has never
again been so high, although the maximums have been increased three
times. The increase to $40 on January 1, 1957, placed the benefit level
in real terms just about where it was back in 1939. The actual maximum then was only half of what it was in 1957, but prices had increased
just about 100 per cent.

Even if benefits had kept pace with the increasing price levels, this
would have been sufficient merely to keep benefits at a constant level
of purchasing power. In a dynamic economy, however, there is no
reason to be satisfied with social insurance benefit levels that just
match rises and falls in price levels. This would ignore the fact that
our economy is becoming increasingly productive with the passing
years. Chart 5 graphically portrays the upward march of the real
average weekly wage in New Jersey. These wage figures have been
adjusted by exactly the same index of prices that was used for the
benefit levels. The gap between the real wage and the real maximum
has been widening since the depression, and it was greater in 1957 than
in the years when the maximums were $10 and $12 a week. The more
fluid wage rates have managed to keep pace with or outstrip the rises
in prices, but the stickier benefit levels have increasingly fallen behind.
Perhaps, because of the method by which they are set, benefit levels
are doomed to lose the race with prices and wages in an inflationary
economy, but the question remains as to whether they have to finish
such a poor third.

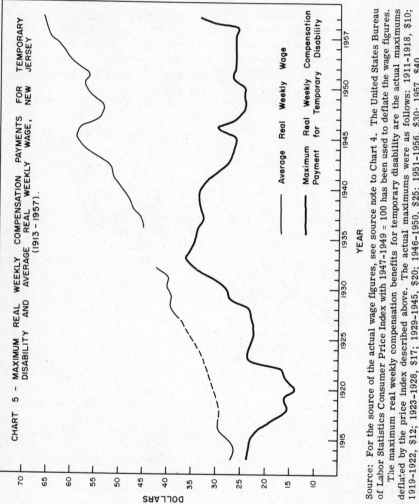

CHART 5 – MAXIMUM REAL WEEKLY COMPENSATION PAYMENTS FOR TEMPORARY DISABILITY AND AVERAGE REAL WEEKLY WAGE, NEW JERSEY (1913 – 1957).

Average Real Weekly Wage

Maximum Real Weekly Compensation Payment for Temporary Disability

Source: For the source of the actual wage figures, see source note to Chart 4. The United States Bureau of Labor Statistics Consumer Price Index with 1947–1949 = 100 has been used to deflate the wage figures. The maximum real weekly compensation benefits for temporary disability are the actual maximums deflated by the price index described above. The actual maximums were as follows: 1911–1918, $10; 1919–1922, $12; 1923–1928, $17; 1929–1945, $20; 1946–1950, $25; 1951–1956, $30; 1957, $40.

Interstate Comparison of Benefits for Temporary Disability

Thus far we have been discussing the adequacy or inadequacy of the New Jersey program's benefits in relation to changes in wages levels, percentage of wage loss restored, and the movements of the price levels; the conclusions are not very encouraging. Let us turn now to the experience of other states. Of course, the New Jersey worker must live on benefits paid in his state, and it may be small comfort to him to learn that others are worse off.

Comparisons among the fifty-four jurisdictions are complicated. The laws may vary in at least the following six ways with reference to the calculation of the weekly rate for temporary total disability:[11]

1) Length of waiting period: All jurisdictions, with the exception of Oregon, specify some waiting period between the date of accident and the date compensation payments may begin. The period ranges from two days in Hawaii to the most common provision of seven days.

2) Length of retroactive periods: In all but seven jurisdictions, if a worker remains totally disabled for more than a specified number of days, he can collect benefits for the waiting period. These retroactive or "reversion" periods range from five days in the case of Oklahoma, North Dakota and Nevada to seven weeks in California. Oregon, of course, needs no such provision.

3) Percentage of wage compensated: Wyoming and Washington pay a flat rate to injured workers regardless of wages, but all other jurisdictions pay a stated percentage of wages, ranging, in the case of a single worker, from 50 per cent in Montana and Oregon to 80 per cent in North Dakota.

4) Maximum weekly benefits: All jurisdictions impose a weekly maximum, ranging from $25 in Mississippi and Puerto Rico to Arizona's $150 in the case of a single worker. Thirteen of the jurisdictions have a maximum of $40 a week or more for workers with no dependents, thirty-five have a maximum rate ranging from $30 to $39, while in six the maximum is less than $30.

5) Number of dependents: Twelve jurisdictions out of the fifty-four allow some additional amounts to a worker with dependents. This may be accomplished by allowing a higher weekly maximum or by providing a higher stated percentage of wages. An injured worker in Illinois with the maximum number of dependents may receive up to $97\frac{1}{2}$ per cent of wages, with, however, a weekly maximum of $45. The law covering federal employees allows up to 75 per cent of wages when the worker has the maximum number of dependents, a realistic percentage when it is considered that the weekly maximum is $121.15.

6) Minimum weekly benefits: All jurisdictions with the exception of Arizona specify some weekly minimum benefit. In nineteen

---

[11] For sources of information on comparative provisions of the laws in the several jurisdictions, see footnote 4.

jurisdictions the so-called "provisional" minimums exist so that a worker cannot collect more than his actual wage if it is less than the stated minimums.

Within each of the categories above, there may be variations. In some states, a wife is a dependent, whereas in others the only dependents are children under eighteen. Wages are defined in various fashions. Also, in addition to the limitations imposed by the statutory percentages and the weekly maximums, there are limitations on the total amount a worker may collect or the maximum period during which he is eligible for payments. This limitation is less important in temporary disability cases than it is in death and permanent disability cases.

The moral of all this is simply that one law cannot be adjudged more liberal or less liberal than another on the basis of any one of its provisions. These must be read together to determine how they apply to a worker who becomes injured. Although it is impossible to devise a comparison which will reveal, at a glance, how the various jurisdictions rank insofar as liberality of benefits is concerned, such a ranking may be approximated by making certain uniform assumptions about the worker's wage, number of dependents and length of time out of work because of the effects of his injury.

Such comparisons have been made in Table VIII. It has been assumed that the worker is earning $80 per week, or at least that these are his "wages," however that term is defined in each of the jurisdictions. Also it is assumed that he is out of work for four weeks, thus eliminating many of the differences which arise solely because of differing waiting periods. Also it assumed that the worker has a wife and one child. Under these assumptions the worker could collect at least two-thirds of his wage loss only in Arizona, Hawaii and the three federal jurisdictions; an additional ten jurisdictions would allow him one-half or more of his lost earnings, and of these ten, four, including New Jersey, would pay exactly 50 per cent. But in over 70 per cent of the states, he would receive less than this proportion of his wage loss. In sixteen jurisdictions he would receive less than 40 per cent of his lost income when he is out for four weeks, a length of time that covers most temporary disability cases.[12]   In these comparisons, New Jersey shares the twelfth rank with Illinois, Maryland and Michigan. In eleven jurisdictions, the worker with a wife and one child would be treated more generously than in New Jersey, whereas in thirty-nine states he would receive less.[13]

---

[12]It is estimated that roughly three-quarters of all temporary disability cases would not last more than twenty-one days. See Fratello, Exhibit E, p. 136.

[13]Dependent's allowances are relevant in these comparisons. Three other states would pay this hypothetical worker the same total amount as New Jersey. In both Maryland and New Jersey, the $160 total is derived simply by multiplying four weeks by the maximum weekly rate of $40, which would be paid whether the worker was single or with dependents. In Michigan the $40 rate is applicable because the worker has a wife and one child, each of

Table VIII. Inter-Jurisdictional Comparison of Compensation Paid for First Four
Weeks of Temporary Disability to an $80-per-Week Worker
with Wife and One Child, September, 1957[a]

Jurisdiction	Total Compensation Received for First Four Weeks of Disability (to nearest dollar)	Percentage of $320 Wage Loss Compensated
U. S. Federal Employees	$240	75.0%
Arizona	217	67.8
District of Columbia	213	66.6
Hawaii	213	66.6
U. S. Longshoremen	213	66.6
Nevada	200[b]	62.5
Wisconsin	196	61.3
Alaska	186	58.1
Oregon	185[b]	57.8
Connecticut	180	56.3
Minnesota	180	56.3
Illinois	160[b]	50.0
Maryland	160	50.0
Michigan	160[b]	50.0
New Jersey	160	50.0
Wyoming	154[b]	48.1
Washington	154[b]	48.1
Massachusetts	152[b]	47.5
Missouri	150	46.9
California	148	46.3
Idaho	148[b]	46.3
New Hampshire	148	46.3
Indiana	144	45.0
Arkansas	140	43.8
Delaware	140	43.8
Maine	140	43.8
North Carolina	140	43.8
Oklahoma	140	43.8
South Carolina	140	43.8
Texas	140	43.8
North Dakota	137[b]	42.8
New York	135	42.2
Utah	134[b]	41.9
West Virginia	132	41.3
Kentucky	128	40.0
Rhode Island	128	40.0
Tennessee	128	40.0
Vermont	128[b]	40.0
Florida	126[c]	39.4
Alabama	124	38.8
Montana	124[b]	38.8
Ohio	121	37.8
New Mexico	120	37.5
Pennsylvania	113	35.3
Colorado	110	34.4
Iowa	107	33.4
Louisiana	105	32.8
Kansas	102	31.9
Nebraska	102	31.9
Mississippi	100	31.3
Puerto Rico	100	31.3
Georgia	90	28.1
South Dakota	90	28.1
Virginia	90	28.1

Source: Replies to questionnaire sent to all jurisdictions, July 9, 1957. Since that date, New
York has increased its maximum weekly benefit to $45.
[a]Sixteen laws specify that benefits for the waiting period will be paid when a worker is out for
four weeks. It is not always clear whether this is interpreted as just four weeks or more than
four weeks. To avoid such difficulties, it has been assumed that the worker is out for four
weeks plus one day; but for simplicity of presentation, the compensation payments for just the
first four weeks are shown. The time period of four weeks and one day would be sufficiently
long for a worker to collect waiting period benefits in all jurisdictions which have such retroactive provisions, except California (49 days), Colorado (six weeks), Louisiana (six weeks),
Nebraska (six weeks), New York (35 days), Ohio (five weeks), and Pennsylvania, South Dakota,
and Virginia (six weeks).
[b]In these jurisdictions, a higher level of benefits will be paid if a worker has a greater number
of dependents.
[c]Based on a five-day work week.

Whatever else might be said about the adequacy of New Jersey's rates for temporary disability, it cannot be said that she ranks anywhere near the bottom on the basis of comparisons with other jurisdictions. However, the differences between New Jersey's payment and that of the top-ranking jurisdiction is considerable. Under the act covering the United States federal employees the worker can collect $240, or 50 per cent more than New Jersey's $160. It also must be noted that the wage chosen for the hypothetical worker approximates the average wage in New Jersey and other industrialized states. The comparisons have not been made in terms of the average worker's wage in each of the states. If this had been done, New Jersey would appear in a less favorable light insofar as the rankings are concerned.[14]

Permanent Total Disability Benefits and Budgetary Standards

Another test of adequacy of any benefit payment is to relate it to some budgetary standard. At the outset we confess to some bias against this sort of traditional comparison. Budgetary standards are delicate instruments that are useful in the hands of the trained social worker who has the task of evaluating a particular client's needs. They lose much of their meaning when some arbitrary standard is used to judge the needs of a whole group of workers, who, individually, may find themselves in radically different economic and social positions. A worker who is temporarily disabled cannot quickly readjust his whole living pattern to some artificial norm. His family needs are geared to his wage level, and the best test of adequacy is to determine how closely the benefits come to matching his wage loss. We have already seen that workmen's compensation benefits do not score high on this count.

Budgetary standards may assume more relevance, however, in the case of the workers who are adjudged to be permanently and totally disabled. In these cases, the worker may be in for a long siege. His initial period of benefits in New Jersey is 450 weeks, and during this period he may find himself without any wage income. If he does not respond to rehabilitation, he may be disabled for life and left with a pension, which, at the most, will be set at the weekly maximum. These maximums have by and large been the same as for temporary

---

whom is classified as a dependent; if the employee had only a wife, or only a dependent child, the weekly rate would be $36, and the total amount received would be $144. In Illinois, the $40 rate is paid because the worker has a wife and one child, but only the child is classified as a dependent. A worker with a dependent child but no wife would still be entitled to this rate in Illinois; however, a married man with no children could collect a rate of only $39 a week. If another child is added to the family, the benefit amounts in Illinois increase to $168 (4 times $42) and in Michigan to $180 (4 times $45).

[14]See Alfred M. Skolnik, "Trends in Workmen's Compensation: Coverage, Benefits and Costs," *Social Security Bulletin,* XXV (August, 1958), 7.

disability, except that the increase from $25 to $30 was made in 1952 instead of in 1951, as for the temporary disability recipients.

The erosion of the real value of the weekly maximums due to increases in prices is particularly relevant in the cases of permanent and total disability because the legislature has never made any retroactive adjustments. The worker who was permanently and totally disabled back in 1950 still receives weekly benefits today of no more than $25 a week, the maximum prevailing in New Jersey in 1950. As of July, 1956, there were 500 permanently and totally disabled workers receiving benefits of less than $30 per week, and in some instances their weekly rate was as low as $17.[15]

It is true that the permanent total disability cases, by reason of the length of time cash payments are made and the heavy medical expenses entailed, are the most costly of all types of cases.[16] From policy year 1950 through 1954 there were twenty-one permanent total cases wherein estimated incurred costs exceeded $50,000. These are huge sums, although it should be recognized that they are estimates and might be cut radically if the recipients should die before the actuarially expected age. Yet, in spite of the magnitude of these incurred costs, we are left with the cold fact that compensation payments are made on a weekly or semimonthly basis and families must live on current payments. Logic compels the conclusion that we are throwing these persons back on their friends, family or the community for support, quite contrary to the fundamental purposes of the law.

Let us ignore for the moment those persons who have become disabled in the past and concentrate on the worker who currently becomes permanently and totally disabled and is eligible for the maximum of $40 a week. Such a worker would receive a cash indemnity award of $173.33 a month. How does this meet available budgetary standards?

The relief agencies in New Jersey also use budgetary standards that are rather strict and cover only basic requirements. A client who comes to the Bureau of Assistance of the State Department of Institutions and Agencies must demonstrate need before he can be eligible for old-age assistance payments or any other assistance program payments. His needs are determined on the basis of a maintenance budget that uses food allowances from the low-cost diet plan of the American Home Economics Association. It is assumed that the client has an adequate wardrobe, and therefore the budget is intended to provide only for normal replacements and recognized expenses of cleaning and maintenance. The personal incidental allowance is nominal and comes to only $5.20 a month for an adult. Table IX shows the budgetary allowances for various types of families.

---

[15]This information is from a staff report prepared by the New Jersey Division of Workmen's Compensation. See also Joseph N. Seward, "New Jersey's One Per Cent Fund," unpublished M. A. thesis (Rutgers University, 1957).

[16]Information on incurred costs is from New Jersey Compensation Rating and Inspection Bureau, *Fortieth Annual Report*, 1957, p. 32.

Table IX. New Jersey Minimum Assistance Budgets for Basic
Requirements, July, 1957, by Type of Family

Type of Family	Monthly Budget Allotment
Man and Wife Each engaged in minimal activity	$136.80
Man and Wife with One Male Child Between 13 and 18 Years of Age Man — minimal activity Wife — moderate activity	209.00
Man and Wife with One Male Child and One Female Child Each Between 13 and 18 Man — minimal activity Wife — moderate activity	232.20

Source: New Jersey Department of Institutions and Agencies, Division of Welfare, "Minimum Standards and Allowances for Basic Requirements" (mim., rev., November, 1956). This source includes the allowances for food, clothing, personal incidentals, fuel for heating and utilities. No specific allowances are set for cost of shelter since actual cost will be allowed if reasonable. In the case of a man and wife living alone, a $40-a-month shelter cost was allowed; in the other two cases, a $50 shelter allowance was made. In each case, it has been assumed that the man is not gainfully employed.

Only in the case of a man and wife engaged in minimal activity and no gainful employment (thus saving on incidental occupational expenses) would the current $40 maximum payment meet this low-standard budget. And even for this small-sized family at this subsistence level, the budget calls for more than would be forthcoming if the man received an award at the $30 maximum prevailing before 1957.

For larger families, even the $40 maximum falls below the required amounts. A man and his wife with one male child between thirteen and eighteen years of age could receive approximately $209 a month if they had no other sources of income. Of course this man would have to disclose his complete financial situation. If legally responsible relatives are located, they are called upon to contribute to his support if they are able. Granted that the processes of investigation of these matters have become much more humane under the professional canons of the social worker, nonetheless the family must certainly demonstrate need before becoming eligible for any payments; and when this is done, they qualify only for what will keep body and soul together. On the other hand, a man who becomes permanently and totally disabled as a result of an industrial injury supposedly has some equity in the matter. To the extent that he is forced to turn to relatives or to the community, the law is not fulfilling its primary obligation.

Again, however, it must be pointed out that whatever the defects in the adequacy of New Jersey's treatment of the permanently and totally disabled, these defects are present in other jurisdictions as well. In some respects, New Jersey's law is more liberal. In New Jersey and in thirty other jurisdictions, benefits continue for the term of eligibility or as long as the man lives. Twenty-one jurisdictions, however, still specify a maximum number of weeks in permanent total cases, ranging from 330 in Vermont to 550 in New Mexico and Tennessee. Comparisons among jurisdictions as to weekly maximum rates in these cases yield approximately the same results as the comparisons in the case of temporary disability. In no jurisdiction is the weekly total for permanent disability higher than that for temporary, and in some it is less.[17]

Permanent Partial Disability Benefits

A disabled worker collects temporary compensation payments for the time he is out of work or during the healing period of his injury; these are designed as income maintenance payments. If he is found to have some permanent impairment, further benefits will be paid irrespective of actual wage loss and in addition to whatever allowances for temporary disability may have been made. Permanent partial awards are not meant as income substitutes, and hence it is meaningless to portray them against a backdrop of earnings, prices or budgets. Problems posed by these permanent partial disability payments are discussed in Chapter 4.

Death Benefits

Compensation for death is computed differently from awards for the other types of disability in New Jersey, since dependents' allowances are made but are based on a lower percentage of wages. Since the inception of the law in the state, death benefits have been fixed at 35 per cent of wages in the case of one dependent survivor, and this percentage increases by 5 per cent intervals until a maximum of 60 per cent is paid in the case of six or more dependent survivors. As with awards for permanent total and temporary disability, a maximum of $40 is imposed. Also, as with the permanent total disability cases, the legislature has never seen fit to raise the weekly maximum for widows and children of workers who were fatally injured sometime in the past to the newly adopted maximum. Paradoxically enough, if the increased maximums were retroactively applied to survivors in death cases, the increases in benefits would not be so great as they would be if these maximums were applied to permanent total disability cases.

---

[17]Alaska, which pays a maximum of $100 a week for temporary total disability, fixes a lump-sum payment in the case of permanent total disability according to the number of dependents. In both temporary and permanent total disability cases, Massachusetts allows a maximum of $35 for the first thirteen weeks of disability and $40 a week thereafter. Oklahoma has a $35-a-week maximum in the temporary cases but reduces this to $30 in the permanent total cases. California's permanent total disability maximum of $50 is $10 less than its allowance in temporary cases. Wyoming and Oregon also have lower rates for permanent total disability. The figures quoted pertain to the case of a worker with no dependents.

In death cases, the benefits were fixed at such a low percentage of wages that some survivors could not qualify for even the previous maximums. The minimum payment of $10 a week obtains in death cases as in other types of cases.

Payments to survivors are also subject to a duration maximum. The original law limited payments to the widow to 300 weeks. In 1923, the law was amended to provide benefits to the widow for 300 weeks and to surviving children until they reached sixteen years of age. This was changed to eighteen years in 1946, and in 1957 the duration of payments to a widow was increased from 300 to 350 weeks.

Table X compares various weekly death benefits with the minimum budget allotments provided by the agencies which administer the assistance programs. This is the same budget that was used in the permanent total disability comparisons, adjusted for the fact that one adult male is missing. Only in the case of the widow without minor children does the compensation benefit meet the relief budget. If there are more dependents, the situation gets progressively worse. It is true that if there are more than four dependents, the statutory percentages increase from 50 to 55 and 60; but the weekly maximum is $40, which happens to be exactly 50 per cent of the $80 wage assumed for the fatally injured worker.

How does New Jersey compare with other states in these compensation payments to survivors? In all but two jurisdictions (which pay lump-sum benefits) the survivors are alloted a weekly amount based, in most states, on a percentage of the worker's wage, just as in the case of temporary total disability.[18] However, many more

Table X. New Jersey Minimum Assistance Budgets for Basic Requirements
July, 1957, and Compensation Death Benefits to
Survivors of an $80-per-Week Worker

Type of Family[a]	Budget Allotment	Amt. of Monthly Compensation Death Benefits
1) Widow Alone	$104.70	$121.24
2) Widow and One Child	164.90	138.56
3) Widow and Two Children	204.00	155.88
4) Widow and Three Children	232.00	173.33
5) Widow and Four Children	272.50	173.33
6) Widow and Five Children	298.90	173.33

Source: See footnote to Table IX.
[a] In all cases the budgetary allowances for the widow engaged in moderate activity was chosen. In case 2 a boy between ages 13 and 18 is assumed; in case 3 one boy and one girl, each between ages 13 and 18; in case 4 the same as case 3 plus an additional child between ages 10 and 12; in case 5 the same as case 4 plus an additional child between ages 4 and 9: and in case 5 an additional baby age 3 or less is assumed. Cost of shelter is estimated at $40 a month for a widow alone; at $50 a month if there are one, two or three children; and at $60 a month if there are four or five children.

---

[18] In addition to these periodic payments, most jurisdictions, including New Jersey, will make a lump-sum allowance for funeral expenses.

jurisdictions will, like New Jersey, pay a sliding percentage scale of the worker's wage according to the number of surviving dependents.

Thirteen jurisdictions pay these benefits for the period of widowhood and/or until the children reach eighteen. One might say that since college education is becoming increasingly common, the age limit should be increased; but thus far no jurisdiction has increased it. New Jersey and five other states pay benefits to the widow for only a specified number of weeks, although thereafter some payments are made until the children are eighteen, whereas the remaining jurisdictions specify either a maximum number of weeks, a maximum lump-sum, and/or an aggregate dollar maximum that effectively limits the number of weeks.

Again, comparisons in the case of death benefits cannot be made on the basis of the legal provisions, but it is possible to compare the effect of the application of the various laws. Assume that the worker who had earned $80 a week leaves a widow who dies twenty-five years after the fatal accident without having remarried.[19] The widow is left with three dependent children who are exactly, one, three and ten years of age on the day of fatality. (Birthday coincidences simplify calculations.) It is now possible to calculate the total aggregate family benefits in what is a more meaningful fashion, always recognizing that a change in the weekly wage, number, and/or age of the dependents will change the rankings.

The weekly benefit (Table XI) would be greatest in California (50 per cent greater than in New Jersey), but the total benefits, because of a statutory limit, would be half that of New Jersey's. On the other hand, although the weekly rate payable under the United States federal employees' law is slightly lower than in California, the total benefits in this jurisdiction, which allows payments during the period of widowhood and to children until eighteen, amount to nearly $65,000, more than twice New Jersey's total. This is the most generous jurisdiction, although Hawaii's aggregate benefits closely approximate those paid under the federal employees' law.

The weekly benefits are probably of greater immediate importance to the family, although it is obvious that in most jurisdictions painful readjustments have to be made in the family's level of living if compensation benefits are the sole source of income. Family income would be cut at least in half in thirty-six states, including New Jersey and Massachusetts, where the weekly rate is $40, and Pennsylvania, where the benefit is $37.50. New Jersey shares the seventeenth rank insofar as these weekly benefits are concerned.

In the long run, duration of benefits must be considered. The family would receive a total of more than $55,000 in six jurisdictions, and between $35,000 and $55,000 in five states. In twelve jurisdictions, the family would receive more than in New Jersey, and in forty-one, less.

---

[19] In most jurisdictions benefits are cut off if the widow remarries. In New Jersey, she is entitled to some dower rights: either the balance of her award or $1,000, whichever is less.

Table XI. Weekly Amounts and Total Benefits Payable to Widow and Three Children of an
$80-per-Week Worker Who Dies as a Result of Compensable Accident in New Jersey, 1957

Jurisdiction	Weekly Benefit	Total Aggregate Benefits[a]
California	$61.75	$15,000
U. S. Federal Employees	60.00	64,986
Delaware	56.25	29,745
Arizona	53.33	55,599
District of Columbia	53.33	56,922
Hawaii	53.33	63,790
U. S. Longshoremen	53.33	56,922
Wisconsin	48.65	21,933
South Dakota	46.93	9,000
Connecticut	45.00	58,500
Michigan	45.00	20,250
Minnesota	45.00	17,500
Washington[b]	44.31	49,622
Illinois	44.00	13,000
Utah	42.35	11,638
Ohio	40.25	12,000
Massachusetts	40.00	42,750
New Jersey	40.00	30,936
New York	40.00	44,304
Wyoming[b]	37.62	13,350
Missouri	37.50	12,000
Pennsylvania	37.50	21,091
Oregon[b]	37.33	38,520
New Hampshire	37.00	12,617
Nevada	36.95	41,520
Colorado	36.75	11,466
Montana	36.50	18,250
Indiana	36.00	14,400
Arkansas	35.00	12,500
Florida	35.00	12,250
Louisiana	35.00	14,000
Maine	35.00	10,000
North Carolina	35.00	9,600
South Carolina	35.00	10,000
Texas	35.00	12,600
Kansas	34.00	12,480
Nebraska	34.00	11,050
Iowa	32.00	9,600
Tennessee	32.00	11,000
Alabama	31.00	9,300
Idaho	30.00	12,000
Kentucky	30.00	12,000
New Mexico	30.00	16,500
North Dakota	30.00	32,320
Vermont	30.00	9,900
Virginia	30.00	9,000
West Virginia	27.12	27,903
Georgia	25.50	10,000
Maryland	25.00	10,000
Mississippi	25.00	8,600
Rhode Island	24.00	14,032
Puerto Rico	17.31	9,000
Alaska[c]	----	14,400
Oklahoma [c]	----	13,500

Source: Replies to questionnaire sent to all jurisdictions, July 9, 1957. Since this date, New
York's rate was increased to $45.

[a] Based on the assumption that widow remains unmarried until her death twenty-five years
after husband's fatal accident and that the three dependent children were exactly ages 1, 3 and
10 years on day of fatality. Does not include burial or funeral expenses.

[b] In Washington, benefits are payable on a monthly basis: $125 monthly for widow alone plus
$30, $25, and $12 for dependent children, or a total of $192 monthly for a widow and three
surviving dependent children. In Wyoming and Oregon, also, the monthly rate by 4.333 in order
to make the data roughly comparable with those for the other jurisdictions.

[c] Benefits paid in one lump sum. In Alaska: $9,000 for widow plus $1,800 for each dependent
child. In Oklahoma: $13,500 regardless of the number of dependents.

In seventeen jurisdictions the aggregate family benefit ranges from $12,000 to $15,000. In twelve other states, the totals would amount to $10,000 or less.

The family of a worker who is killed in Connecticut would be entitled to more than six times as much as the family of the worker whose accident occurred in Mississippi or Virginia. The worker's family in Pennsylvania would receive about two-thirds the amount awarded to the New Jersey family, who, in turn, would receive only a little more than half the amount that would be forthcoming if the worker were killed in Connecticut.

Under these comparisons, New Jersey's rank among the states in survivor benefits is not significantly different from its rank in temporary disability benefits. The picture changes, however, if only the widow of the $80-a-week worker survives. In that event, California would head the list with its weekly payment of $49.40. In four other jurisdictions, the widow would receive at least $40 a week, or 50 per cent of her husband's earnings. But these are the high-paying states, and New Jersey is not among them. Thirty jurisdictions would pay a weekly benefit higher than New Jersey's $28 (35 per cent of $80) if the widow alone survived. Also, in New Jersey, these benefits would cease at the end of 350 weeks, whereas in thirteen jurisdictions, they would continue during the entire period of widowhood.

There appears to be no rational explanation for these benefit variations. Exact and complete uniformity among the states would probably be undesirable, but the amount of variation that exists is the result of allowing the individual states to set their own benefit levels.

Workmen's Compensation Benefits and the Federal Social Security Program

Thus far the discussion of adequacy of benefits has been in terms of the amounts that an industrially injured worker could actually receive from the workmen's compensation program itself. However, under our nonintegrated system of social insurances, it is possible that a worker or his family might also qualify for benefits from some other program. The chief possibilities relate to the federal Old-Age, Survivors, and Disability Insurance program (OASDI), the temporary disability insurance laws of four states, and the private programs established by a company or a union, or jointly through the collective bargaining process.

Difficult problems are involved in coordinating the state workmen's compensation programs with the federal social security system since the programs are administered by different levels of government. Also, most compensation systems are financed exclusively by employers, whereas employees contribute to OASDI. Although a worker's contribution is matched by his employer, nonetheless the worker builds some equity in the program; and benefit payments, once he meets eligibility requirements, are his as a matter of right. A retired worker receiving an old-age insurance payment may still work at productive employment as long as his earnings do not exceed the statutory limitations. If he becomes injured on the job, he is eligible to receive the normal compensation payments in addition to his old-age insurance stipend. The payments are made at the same time, but for different reasons.

The worker who is receiving lifetime permanent and total disability benefits under workmen's compensation can also collect old-age insurance benefits when he reaches sixty-five if he has accumulated sufficient credits. The social security payment is due because of accumulated contributions made during the worker's productive life by himself and his employer. He becomes entitled to it upon attaining a certain age and effectively retiring from the labor market. And the award for permanent and total disability? This is paid either because of a specific physiological incapacity, or because of loss of earning power, or both. To the extent that the disability benefit is an income maintenance payment, it is illogical to pay it to a retired worker who has no income loss. However, logic is one of the first virtues sacrificed in a nonintegrated social insurance program. Of course, the fact that the permanent and total disability removed the worker from the labor market before his normal retirement age would possibly reduce his monthly retirement payments under the federal program. However, none of the state laws attempts to supplement the old-age insurance payments to bring them up to the level that the worker would have received had he been able to continue at work until he reached retirement age. This would require a degree of coordination between the two programs that has not yet been achieved. Minnesota, however, has provided an offset to its workmen's compensation permanent total disability benefits for social security payments.

The 1956 amendments to the Social Security Act established a program of benefits for the permanent and totally disabled. To be eligible, a person fifty years of age or over must be permanently and totally disabled. The tests for determining this are both economic and medical. The claimant must have been unable to engage in any substantial gainful activity because of a physical or mental impairment for at least six full consecutive months; and this impairment must be permanent, in that it is expected to result in death, or continue for a long, indefinite time. Monthly payments under this program cease when the worker becomes entitled to normal retirement benefits, at age sixty-five for men and sixty-two for women.

Although the federal tests of disability are not the same as under New Jersey's workmen's compensation law, a worker could qualify for and receive both the federal benefit and the state compensation payment.[20] In the State of New Jersey, a permanently and totally disabled

---

[20] The OASDI program originally provided that the federal disability insurance payment was to be reduced by the amount of the workmen's compensation benefit. The 1958 amendments to the Social Security Act eliminated this offset provision.

worker receiving the maximum weekly compensation payment of $40 a week could also collect as much as $127 per month under the federal program.

Since 1939, the Social Security Act has provided survivor benefits. If the worker dies while fully insured, the widow is entitled to three-fourths of his primary benefit when she reaches the age of sixty-two, and dependent children under eighteen are also entitled to benefits. In addition, the law allows a nominal lump-sum death benefit. If we revert to our previously cited example of an $80-a-week worker who is fatally injured and who leaves a wife and three children aged, one, three, and ten, and assume that the worker is entitled to the maximum primary benefit, the family benefit under the federal law would be $254 a month until the first child reached eighteen. Computed benefits are higher but are subject to an overriding maximum of $254 a month. They would then be reduced to $232 and finally to $174 until the last child attained eighteen. If the worker died while fully insured, the widow when she reached age sixty-two would be entitled to $87 a month if she had not remarried by that time.

Table XII shows the compensation payments and the social security benefits this family would receive under the assumed circumstances. In each of the periods of time, the benefits under the federal act would be higher than the benefits under the New Jersey workmen's compensation statute. The family, if eligible for each of these types of payments, could collect both simultaneously.

No real question of adequacy can arise about the total benefits from both programs. While two of the children are under eighteen years of age, the payments from both programs exceed the income the family received when the breadwinner was alive. Of course, not all families would be eligible for the social security benefits. The widow would not receive the federal survivorship benefits if she had no children under eighteen in her care; the worker may not be covered under the federal act or may die while in an uninsured status. Even though the family may receive both sets of benefits, both occasioned by the death of the

Table XII. New Jersey Compensation Benefits and Social Security Benefits
Payable to Widow and Three Children, Ages, 1, 3 and 10.
Based on Wages of an $80-per-Week Worker Entitled to
Maximum Primary Benefit of $116

Time Period	Monthly Workmen's Compensation Benefit	Monthly Social Security Benefit	Total Monthly Benefit
First 350 Weeks	$173.33	$254	$427.33
Next 66 Weeks	155.88	254	409.88
Next 364 Weeks	138.56	232	370.56
Next 104 Weeks	121.24	174	295.24
Total Amt. over the 884 Weeks (17 years)	$30,936	$48,048	$78,984

principal wage earner, one ought not lose sight of the fact that two different sets of "rights" are involved. It is a sad commentary on the adequacy of workmen's compensation benefits that the family's plight will be alleviated only if it can qualify for simultaneous benefits under some other social insurance program.

Workmen's Compensation, Temporary Disability Insurance and Private Group Supplements

How does workmen's compensation fit into collectively bargained insurance and welfare plans? Workmen's compensation payments may be supplemented under pension plans, group life and accidental death and dismemberment insurance provisions, cash indemnity plans for wage loss from accidents or illnesses, and paid sick leave plans.[21] In addition, some collective bargaining agreements specifically provide for separate supplementation of temporary disability workmen's compensation payments.

Pension plans may provide payments to employees who retire early because of disability as well as to employees who retire at age sixty-five. It is common in these retirement plans to deduct the amounts of workmen's compensation payments from the pensions received by the employee, although some contracts specifically exempt permanent disability compensation payments payable before the retirement age of sixty-five. Other agreements provide that there shall be no deduction whatsoever by reason of any workmen's compensation payment; however, pensions are available to employees only after they have retired, and only employees who are receiving some permanent type of workmen's compensation benefit would collect both pension and benefit.

Group life insurance normally provides payments in the case of death, whether from occupational or nonoccupational causes, and hence it provides an important supplement to survivor benefits under workmen's compensation. If the life insurance plan includes accidental death and dismemberment coverage, this can be written to cover only nonoccupational injuries or extended to a so-called "twenty-four hour" basis so as to include both occupational and nonoccupational hazards. Schedules, analogous to those set forth in the workmen's compensation statutes, list the amount of payments for specific physiological losses. Provisions may also be included for payments in the case of permanent and total disability.

Many variations in these plans are found in collective bargaining

---

[21] For an excellent discussion of these private supplements, see Duncan McIntyre, "Workmen's Compensation and Private Benefit Programs," *Industrial and Labor Relations Review*, VII (October, 1955). Illustrative contractual provisions are found in Bureau of National Affairs, *Collective Bargaining: Negotiations and Contracts*, 44:901-903 (July 15, 1955.) Liberal use has also been made of the file of New Jersey collective bargaining agreements in the library of the Institute of Management and Labor Relations of Rutgers, The State University.

agreements in New Jersey; however, the extent of each type of plan is not known. Thus the workers in one company are covered by a noncontributory plan which provides for group life insurance including accidental death and dismemberment features, but this latter policy is written on a nonoccupational basis.[22] Another firm's collective bargaining agreement provides group life insurance including permanent and total disability benefits before age sixty, plus the accidental death and dismemberment clauses, which are written on a twenty-four hour basis.[23]

An important supplement to temporary disability workmen's compensation payments is contained in those plans which provide for cash indemnity payments when the employee is sick or disabled. The temporary disability insurance laws of four states, California, New York, Rhode Island and New Jersey, provide benefits to workers during periods of nonoccupational illness or disability. Railroad workers are also covered under such a law.[24] Rhode Island permits concurrent payments under workmen's compensation and temporary disability insurance, subject to a maximum limitation. In California and in the railroad industry, if the temporary disability insurance payment during a given week is higher than the workmen's compensation payment, the worker may receive the difference. Otherwise, the California, New York and New Jersey and the railroad laws do not permit a worker to collect both types of benefits for the same week and the same disability. Of course, defining a non-work-connected injury may be as difficult as defining an injury which arose "out of and in the course of" employment. In an effort to free the disability insurance agencies from having to make these causal determinations, the programs generally relate eligibility to nonreceipt of workmen's compensation benefits rather than to the cause of disability. If there is some doubt about whether the worker is entitled to the workmen's compensation benefits, he may collect the temporary disability insurance benefit, but he must repay it if he should later receive workmen's compensation benefits.

The temporary disability programs and the workmen's compensation programs are both state-controlled, and problems of coordination are thereby eased. The New York law is administered by the same agency that supervises the compensation statutes. On the other hand, New Jersey's law is administered by the state's unemployment insurance agency; and coverage, eligibility and benefits, for the most part, are uniform in the two programs. In 1958, New Jersey's maximum weekly benefit was $35 under both the temporary disability insurance law and the unemployment insurance law, in contrast to the permissible

---

[22] Contract between American Smelting and Refining Company and Perth Amboy Smelter and Refinery Workers Union, Local 365 (IUMM & SW), July 3, 1956.

[23] Contract between Bendix Aviation Corporation — Eclipse-Pioneer Division and United Automobile Aircraft and Agricultural Implement Workers (AFL-CIO), Local 153, October 20, 1955.

[24] Alfred M. Skolnik, "Temporary Disability Insurance Laws in the United States," *Social Security Bulletin*, XV (October, 1952). Also, United States Department of Labor, Bureau of Employment Security, *Comparison of Temporary Disability Insurance Laws* (January, 1954).

$40 weekly maximum under workmen's compensation. However, in New Jersey and California, employers are allowed the option of providing coverage through a commercial carrier or self-insurance. In New Jersey, as of 1957, about 37 per cent of all covered workers were under the state plan, while the balance were insured under one of the alternative arrangements. As far back as 1944, some of these temporary insurance plans covered by private insurance provided for a maximum weekly payment of $40 a week and more.[25]

The existence of these nonoccupational disability payment plans creates certain anomolies in that a worker injured outside the plant may conceivably collect more than the employee who sustains an occupational injury, at least insofar as weekly benefits for the period of incapacity are concerned. This, quite naturally, has spurred the move to increase private group supplements of workmen's compensation. In some cases, the supplements are directly tied in with the wage indemnity or sick leave plans, and in other cases they are treated separately. As a matter of fact, all combinations and permutations can be found.

Whether separately or in combination with some other plan, the company may guarantee a supplement which is completely independent of the workmen's compensation benefit; or it may specify a total amount the employee is to receive in case of a compensable injury. In the latter case, the company supplements the state's compensation benefit by whatever dollar amount is necessary to bring the worker's total benefit to a predetermined total.[26] As an example, one collective bargaining agreement provides separate plans for occupational and nonoccupational disabilities. The nonoccupational plan provides higher benefits than the state's temporary disability insurance benefits, and the occupational plan supplements the workmen's compensation payments. Under the latter plan, benefits start the fourth day of disability and extend for a maximum of thirteen weeks for any one period of disability. The workmen's compensation supplements, which are in addition to the state-determined payments, range from $4.20 per week for the lowest wage employee to a maximum supplement of $16 per week.[27] In similar fashion, agreement in another company provides for supplementation of workmen's compensation payments up to a maximum combined payment of $60 per week.[28]

Some collective bargaining agreements specifically provide that the company's sickness or accident payment plan shall not apply to injuries covered by workmen's compensation; in contrast, other provide that occupationally injured workers are to receive full pay for a limited

---

[25]For a discussion of New Jersey's law, see Jack Chernick, "Social Legislation," in S. J. Flink, ed., *The Economy of New Jersey* (New Brunswick: Rutgers University Press, 1958).

[26]Harland Fox, "Company Supplements to Workmen's Compensation," National Industrial Conference Board, *Management Record*, XVII (January, 1955), 20.

[27]Bakelite Co., Bound Brook Plant, and Chemical and Crafts Union, Inc. (Ind.), April 5, 1956.

[28]American Can Company (Newark plants) and United Steelworkers of America, October 1, 1955.

period of time. One company pays an employee injured in the shop the difference between his normal wages and the amount of compensation provided in the law. As is common in these plans, there is a waiting period (in this case, payments commence on the third day of disability), and the payments are limited to a maximum period of thirteen weeks.[29]

In some instances, the company attaches conditions to the receipt of this supplemental compensation which are different from those associated with eligibility for workmen's compensation. For example, one agreement obliges the company to pay the difference between the compensation benefit and employee's wages for a period of ten weeks but qualifies this by saying the payments will be made "provided that his injury was not the result of a violation of rules, or misconduct on his part, and provided further that a competent physician selected by the company, if it desires, finds that the employee concerned is unable to work because of such injury."[30]   The last condition also attaches to receipt of workmen's compensation, although, in the event of a dispute, it is a matter of determination by the compensation officials rather than the physician selected by the company. However, an employee is entitled to the state's workmen's compensation benefits even if his injury was the result of a violation of rules. Only if it is found that the occupational injury was self-inflicted, or caused by intoxication, would compensation be denied under the state statutes.

Where supplementation is provided for, not in the collective bargaining agreement, but as a matter of company policy, the company may reserve the right to use its discretion in adding to compensation payments. For example, one plan states that the company *may* assume reasonable expenses in connection with corrective operations on non-compensated, nontraumatic hernias in addition to providing full pay for the subsequent period of temporary disability. Also, the company may assume reasonable expenses for special training, treatment and other measures in cases where rehabilitation procedures seem necessary. Under this plan, company payments over and above the statutory requirements may be made if it is deemed necessary, and statutory requirements covering funeral expenses may be exceeded.[31]

---

[29]Agreement between Hercules Powder Company (Burlington plant) and Oil, Chemical and Atomic Workers International Union, AFL-CIO Local 12-669, June 19, 1956.

Supplementation up to an employee's normal wages is, of course, the maximum supplementation. In some instances, the first days of the disability may be supplemented at lower rates. For example, an agreement provides for 80 per cent of pay for the first five days of disability and up to full pay thereafter for a maximum of 120 days, including the workmen's compensation benefit. Another provides supplemental benefits of three-fourths of a day's pay for the fourth and fifth consecutive working days lost and one-half of a day's pay for the next thirty-five consecutive working days lost; but the total of this and the workmen's compensation benefits may not exceed the employee's normal pay for any one day. (Bureau of National Affairs, *Collective Bargaining Negotiations and Contracts*, 44:901-903 [July 15, 1955]).

[30]Agreement between New Jersey Power and Light Co. and International Brotherhood of Electrical Workers (AFL-CIO), Locals 327 and 749, May 1, 1955.

[31]E. I. Du Pont de Nemours and Co., "Industrial Relations Plans and Practices" (rev. September 1, 1955).

Since these extra payments are discretionary with the company, they may operate to discourage the worker from filing a formal petition. The difference between the compensation benefits provided in the law and the employee's full wages plus extra payments can be considerable. The fact that income is not reduced must remove some part of the injured worker's incentive to contest the employer's offer of a direct settlement, in the hope of getting something, or something more, in the way of a permanent partial disability award.

Private supplementation of any public social insurance program inevitably results in two opposing sets of pressures insofar as liberalization of benefits is concerned. On the one hand, employers called upon to supplement existing benefits may endorse moves to raise public benefits. Even under a noncontributory program, such as workmen's compensation, this may shift some costs from the individual firms to the group. On the other hand, employees assured of full wages or some supplementation may lose some of their enthusiasm for general increases in benefit levels.

One final point must be noted in connection with these private group supplements. Additions to temporary disability compensation benefits are far more numerous than supplements to payments made in the event of permanent partial disability. Also, pension plans which deduct temporary compensation benefits usually do not deduct fixed statutory scheduled benefits, for example, for the loss of a limb. This may be one more reason why claims for temporary disability compensation have decreased relatively over the years, while claims for permanent partial awards have increased.

Adequacy, Equity and Abuse: Summary and Conclusions

Difficulties are involved in attempting to define "adequate" benefit payments, but by whatever method they are measured, the current compensation benefit levels fall short. The indictment against them may be summarized in the following manner:

1) The system purports to relate benefits to wages, but the existence of a maximum weekly benefit below the average weekly wage threatens to create a flat-rate system that ignores occupational and income differentials. The statutory rate of 66 2/3 per cent of wages had lost much of its meaning, even before it was formally abandoned in 1957.

2) Although the basic theory of workmen's compensation contemplated that the worker would bear some portion of the wage loss due to accidental injuries, at present he bears more than half of the loss in cases of temporary disability, an amount in excess of the portion envisaged when the law was amended back in 1919.

3) The rising price level has eroded the real value of benefits. In terms of dollars of constant purchasing power, the $40 maximum is

worth about the same as the $20 dollar maximum was worth in 1939. During the same period of time the real value of the average wage has about doubled.

4) If the breadwinner becomes permanently and totally disabled, or is fatally injured, the family will be left with an income which, in most cases, is less than that set by the minimum budget for basic requirements used in the assistance programs under which families must pass a needs test.

This indictment of inadequacy applies to other states besides New Jersey. In no case is New Jersey the most generous of the jurisdictions. In the case of temporary disability benefits, she ranks twelfth among the fifty-four jurisdictions, using comparisons based upon a hypothetical worker making $80 a week who is out of work for four weeks. In the case of weekly death benefits, New Jersey ranks thirty-first if only the widow survives and seventeenth if the widow and three dependent children are left. In terms of total aggregate benefits, New Jersey ranks thirteenth in the case of our assumed hypothetical family.

It is significant that we have been able to say little, one way or the other, about the adequacy of permanent partial disability benefits because of their vague relationships to wage loss, and because these awards may be paid in addition to temporary disability benefits. It is in the category of permanent partial disability claims that cries of abuse are most often heard. This is mentioned here because the problem of abuse and malingering is intimately related to the problem of adequacy. Awards for permanent partial disability are sometimes justified on the grounds that the benefit levels for temporary disability are inadequate. The feeling among petitioner's attorneys, and perhaps among some compensation officials, is that the worker is entitled to something more than the low weekly award for temporary disability. On the other hand, opponents of higher rates justify their position on the grounds that some workers receive unwarranted awards for permanent partial disabilities. As one employer spokesman put it, "A worker may not be able to live on what he gets from the temporary disability benefit, but in the majority of cases, this is supplemented by an award for a permanent injury, even though the permanent impairment cannot be discovered by any objective evidence.

In a sense this is a vicious circle. Easy awards are encouraged because rates are low, and the low rates are justified because of the allegations of abuse. Yet the evidence gathered condemns the temporary disability benefit levels as inadequate, and this fact must be faced. To the extent that loose administration permits malingering, to that extent the problem must be solved, but as a separate problem. The sheer equity of the situation requires that the problem of adequacy and the problem of abuse be viewed separately. Even the most vocal of critics would not contend that all the awards are unjustified.

Discussion of adequacy of *present* rates and payments in cases of death and permanent total disability does not take into account the plight of those who must live in the present, but on rates set sometime in the past. The issue of increasing benefit payments to those already on the rolls has been complicated by the thorny problem of how to finance such increases. Insurance carriers must set up reserves at the time of the accident and understandably object to becoming liable for some unforeseen sums in the future. Also, insurance companies and private employers come and go; and although their assets may be sufficient to meet their known obligations, they are not sufficiently elastic to take care of indefinite obligations of the future. The proposal has been made that the second injury or One Per Cent Fund be tapped for this purpose. Objections have been raised by employer groups who claim that the amounts in this dedicated fund have been accumulated for a specific purpose and should not be used for purposes foreign to their original intent.

Even if the legislature should consent to use the money in this fund, this would not be the final solution. We are living in an inflationary climate, and it is likely that increases in prices will continue. If the fund is tapped once, it may have to be tapped again when benefit levels are again increased. It would seem preferable to set up a separate fund specifically designed for this purpose. The fund could be financed by a charge against premiums of carriers and benefits paid by self-insurers. The original payments for the accidental injury or fatality would be assessed against the particular employer and affect the insurance rates in his classification; the subsequent increases would be a burden in which all employers would share. If such a move is made, it would seem wise to program it in orderly fashion, since the 1957 increase in compensation benefits is certainly not the last. Such a fund could have maximum limitations so that companies would not be required to contribute continually.

If we can see the problem of adequacy separately from the problem of abuse, there remains the question of the adequacy of the current benefit levels. The devil in the piece is the maximum weekly rate, the purposes of which have already been explored. If, in spite of the fact that the statutory percentages or the compensation schedule already set one maximum, the program requires an additional maximum stated in terms of dollars per week, ways and means must be found to make this maximum more flexible. The legislative process of fixing maximum weekly benefits cannot keep up with the rapid changes that are occurring in the wage and price levels in our present economy. The legislature, however, does have the power to fix, not a specific maximum, but a method of determing this maximum.

The choices are multiple. The maximum could be adjusted according to some measure of prices or according to some budgetary standard. The second method would be subject to all sorts of value judgments, and the first would involve many difficulties, including that of choosing some base period. A more feasible method would be to tie the maximum to some percentage of average wages. The legislature could direct that the maximum be adjusted either up or down, say once each year. Such a change may be too drastic to accomplish at once, but it could be approached in stages. Also, if it were feared that adjustments might be too rapid from year to year, certain limitations on the extent of the movement, either up or down, could be written into the law.

We have noted the trend toward supplementation of workmen's compensation benefits of all types, especially temporary disability payments. Once the pattern of private supplementation of social insurance benefits became popular, it was inevitable that workmen's compensation would be included in the fold, although since this is such a different kind of program, supplementation is not nearly so usual as in the case of pensions and unemployment insurance programs. For the worker who is fortunate enough to be covered under a particular collective bargaining agreement, the problem of adequacy of benefits for him and his family is closer to solution. Although the extent of such supplemental programs is not known, it is certain that they do not cover the entire labor force and cannot, in themselves, be relied upon to solve the problem of inadequate benefit levels.

Chapter 4

PERMANENT PARTIAL DISABILITIES

Before the amount of benefits in any type of compensation case can be fixed, it must be determined whether the accidental injury arose "out of and in the course of" employment. Once such a determination has been made, the least serious cases, those involving only temporary disabilities, and the most serious, those involving fatalities pose relatively few difficulties. In permanent disability cases, however, the problem of measuring the extent of the disability is also present. There are relatively few permanent total disability cases in comparison with the number of permanent partial disability cases which occur each year.

If the temporarily disabled worker cannot qualify for workmen's compensation, he may still receive temporary disability insurance benefits in four states. The family of the fatally injured employee may receive survivor benefits under the Social Security Act. The totally disabled person may qualify for benefits under the federal statute. However, unless the worker is covered by some private group plan, it is likely that only under workmen's compensation will he receive benefit payments for a permanent partial disability.

The trend in the number and cost of these permanent partial cases in New Jersey has already been discussed in Chapter 2. Only one set of statistics will be cited here to recall their importance. During calendar year 1956, 72 per cent of all closed compensated cases involved a permanent partial disability issue, and these cases accounted for 89 per cent of the compensation benefits awarded. At the formal hearing level, 99 per cent of all cases were in this category, and ninety-five cents of the benefit dollar awarded at this level went to these claimants.[1] These data testify to the importance of these cases, although it should be remembered, that cost figures include the weekly payments for temporary disability compensation as well as permanent partial disability awards.

Employer groups in New Jersey complain about the ever increasing number of permanent partial cases "where there is no apparent disability and little or no loss of time or wages."[2] In 1957, the report of the Commission to Study Laws Affecting Industrial Development stated, "The major problem in workmen's compensation is the payment of

---

[1] New Jersey Division of Workmen's Compensation, *Annual Report*, 1956, p. 3.

[2] *Summary of Employer Proposals to Improve the New Jersey Workmen's Compensation Program* (undated printed material submitted by New Jersey State Chamber of Commerce, New Jersey Manufacturers Association and New Jersey Self-Insurers at time of legislative consideration of amendments effective January 1, 1957).

many claims for permanent partial disability in amounts up to $800 where there is no apparent disability, little or no loss of time or wages, and where the claim often rests on subjective complaints."[3] Following the recommendations of employer groups, the commission proposed changes in the statutory definitions of disability and the tests used in evaluation. Such changes have been vigorously opposed by labor groups on the grounds that present procedures are adequate; they proposed that statutory definitions be liberalized and not restricted.[4] Needless to say, the area of permanent partial disabilities is not the only one in which the interested parties do not see eye to eye, but this is the area in which the controversies are most basic and feelings most intense.

The Importance of Permanent Partial Cases in Various States

The Somerses used 1951 data to show that in New Jersey the proportion of compensation cases in the permanent partial category was higher than in the industrially important states of Illinois, New York, Pennsylvania and Wisconsin. Moreover, New Jersey was the state with the lowest average award per case.[5]

The hazardous nature of over-all comparisons among states is well recognized. Each state has a different industrial composition, a different law, and a different method of keeping statistical records. An attempt to meet some, but not all, of these difficulties was made by Joseph S. Keiper in a study sponsored by the Commerce and Industry Association of New York. Keiper examined the number and cost of all types of compensation cases reported by employers within comparable insurance classifications in several states.[6] The nature of these classifications is discussed in Chapter 7. Essentially they are categories into which companies doing similar work, or making similar products, are grouped for insurance rate purposes. Examples of such classifications are: "breweries," "painting and decorating," "airplane manufacturing," and so on.

Keiper used these data, covering a five-year period ending December 31, 1951, to compare New York's experience with the combined experience in ten industrial states: New York, California, Connecticut, Illinois, Maryland, Massachusetts, Michigan, Missouri, New Jersey and Wisconsin. The same basic data can be used to compare New Jersey with the combined states.

---

³*Report of the Commission to Study Laws Affecting Industrial Development* (Trenton: June, 1957), p. 40.

⁴"Memorandum of New Jersey State CIO Council Regarding Employers' Proposals for Modification of the Workmen's Compensation Act" (undated, mim.), pp. 2-12.

⁵Herman M. Somers and Anne R. Somers, *Workmen's Compensation: Prevention, Insurance and Rehabilitation of Occupational Disability* (N. Y.: John Wiley and Sons, 1954), pp. 74-79.

⁶Joseph S. Keiper, "The Imbalance Between Costs and Benefits" in Joseph S. Keiper, M. William Zucker, James J. Regan, and Mahlon Z. Eubank, *Studies in Workmen's Compensation* (N. Y.: Commerce and Industry Association of New York, 1954). A full list of the classifications used and a comprehensive description of the method are contained in this study.

Table XIII. A Comparison of Compensable Disabilities per $1 Million of Payroll in 65 Selected Classifications in New Jersey and 10 Industrial States Combined, 1946-1951

% by Which N.J.'s Disability Rates Exceed Rate for 10 States Combined	All Compensable Disabilities		Deaths		Perm. Total		Major Perm. Partial		Minor Perm. Partial		Temporary Only	
	No. of Class.	% of All Class.	No. of Class.	% of All Class.	No. of Class.	% of All Class.	No. of Class.	% of All Class.	No. of Class.	% of All Class.	No. of Class.	% of All Class.
More than -70.0	—	—%	3	4.6%	—	—%	—	—%	—	—	—	—%
-69.9 to -60.0	—	—	3	4.6	—	—	—	—	—	—	1	1.5
-59.9 to -50.0	—	—	3	4.6	1	1.5	1	1.5	—	—	8	12.3
-49.9 to -40.0	1	1.5	6	9.2	1	1.5	—	—	—	—	10	15.4
-39.9 to -30.0	1	1.5	7	10.8	—	—	—	—	—	—	17	26.1
-29.9 to -20.0	1	1.5	6	9.2	2	3.1	1	1.5	1	1.5	17	26.1
-19.9 to -10.0	4	6.1	1	1.5	1	1.5	1	1.5	—	—	7	10.8
-9.9 to -0.1	10	15.4	5	7.7	1	1.5	3	4.6	—	—	2	3.1
0 to +9.9	15	23.1	14[a]	21.5	50[b]	76.9	3	4.6	—	—	2	3.1
+10.0 to +19.9	14	21.5	8	12.3	1	1.5	6	9.2	—	—	—	—
+20.0 to +29.9	7	10.8	2	3.1	—	—	4	6.1	1	1.5	—	—
+30.0 to +39.9	3	4.6	1	1.5	—	—	5	7.7	2	3.1	1	1.5
+40.0 to +49.9	4	6.1	1	1.5	—	—	3	4.6	1	1.5	—	—
+50.0 to +59.9	3	4.6	—	—	—	—	5	7.7	2	3.1	—	—
+60.0 to +69.9	1	1.5	1	1.5	—	—	8	12.3	—	—	—	—
+70.0 to +79.9	—	—	—	—	1	1.5	1	1.5	1	1.5	—	—
+80.0 to +89.9	—	—	—	—	—	—	3	4.6	—	—	—	—
+90.0 to +99.9	—	—	—	—	1	1.5	3	4.6	4	6.1	—	—

(Table rotated 90° on the page. Column headings for the individual classification groups are not printed on this page; each group is identified below only by its median‑percentage figure. The range categories shown here (+100.0 and above) are the upper tail of a distribution that begins on preceding pages, so the sparse columns carry most of their data — and full totals of 65, 100, etc. — on earlier pages.)

Range	Grp A N	Grp A %	Grp B N	Grp B %	Grp C N	Grp C %	Grp D N	Grp D %	Grp E N	Grp E %	Grp F N	Grp F %
+100.0 to +109.9	—	—	—	—	2	3.1	3	4.6	2	3.1	—	—
+110.0 to +119.9	—	—	2	3.1	—	—	2	3.1	—	—	—	—
+120 0 to +129.9	—	—	—	—	—	—	4	6.1	6	9.2	—	—
+130.0 to +139.9	1	1.5	—	—	—	—	3	4.6	3	4.6	—	—
+140.0 to +149.9	—	—	—	—	1	1.5	2	3.1	1	1.5	—	—
+150.0 to +159.9	—	—	—	—	—	—	—	—	3	4.6	—	—
+160.0 to +169.9	—	—	—	—	—	—	1	1.5	5	7.7	—	—
+170.0 to +179.9	—	—	—	—	—	—	1	1.5	3	4.6	—	—
+180.0 to +189.9	—	—	—	—	—	—	2	3.1	5	7.7	—	—
+190.0 to +199.9	—	—	—	—	—	—	1	1.5	5	7.7	—	—
+200.0 to +209.9	—	—	—	—	—	—	1	1.5	4	6.1	—	—
+210.0 to +219.9	—	—	—	—	—	—	1	1.5	3	4.6	—	—
+220.0 to +229.9	—	—	—	—	—	—	—	—	5	7.7	—	—
+230.0 to +239.9	—	—	—	—	—	—	—	—	—	—	—	—
+240.0 to +249.9	—	—	—	—	—	—	1	1.5	1	1.5	—	—
+250.0 to +259.9	—	—	—	—	—	—	2	3.1	2	3.1	—	—
+260.0 to +269.9	—	—	—	—	—	—	3	4.6	3	4.6	—	—
+270.0 to +279.9	—	—	—	—	—	—	—	—	—	—	—	—
+280.0 to +289.9	—	—	—	—	—	—	1	1.5	1	1.5	—	—
+290.0 and over	—	—	2	3.1	3	4.6	2	3.1	1	1.5	1	1.5
Total	65	100	65	100	3	100	65	100	65	100	65	100
Median Percentage		+10.3%		−3.0%		+5.3%		+60.6%		+171.6%		−32.0%

Source: Based on Joseph S. Keiper, "The Imbalance Between Costs and Benefits," in *Studies in Workmen's Compensation* (N. Y.: Commerce and Industry Association of New York, 1954). The 10 industrial states combined were N. Y., Calif., Conn., Ill., Md., Mass., Mich., Mo., N. J., and Wisc.
a Includes twelve classifications in which no deaths occurred in New Jersey, although some occurred in other states.
b Includes five classifications in which no disabilities occurred either in New Jersey or in the 10 states combined, and forty-four classifications in which no disabilities occurred in New Jersey, although some occurred in other states.

In New Jersey, a so-called "compensable disability rate" is computed by calculating the number of compensable disability cases per $1 million of payroll in each of sixty-five different insurance classifications. In order to expose differences among the various types of disability cases, compensable disability rates were calculated separately for cases involving deaths, permanent total disabilities, major permanent partial disabilities, minor permanent partial disabilities and temporary only cases. The same calculations were made based upon the combined experience of the ten states. Table XIII shows the classifications in which New Jersey's disability rate is higher or lower than in other states, and also the percentage by which New Jersey's rate exceeds that of the ten states combined. (A minus percentage figure shows that New Jersey's rate was less than in the combined states).

When all compensable cases, regardless of type of disability, are considered together, or when the death cases or permanent total cases are considered separately, the average disability rate in New Jersey is not significantly different from the rate in the combined ten states. With reference to all compensable disabilities, on the average, New Jersey's rate is 10.3 per cent greater than in the combined states; its rate for death cases is 3 per cent less, whereas its rate for permanent total cases 5.3 per cent greater. These are the median percentages by which New Jersey's disability rates exceed that for the ten states combined. In light of the difficulties involved in comparing the experience among states, these must be considered as small differences.

Striking differences can be observed, however, in the remaining three categories. On the average, New Jersey's rate for cases which involve only temporary disability is 32 per cent less than in the ten states combined. This difference is more than made up for in the permanent partial disability cases. In the major permanent partial cases, only six of the sixty-five classifications in New Jersey have disability rates which are less than in the other states. In eighteen classifications, New Jersey's rate exceeds that in the other states by more than 100 per cent. The median percentage by which New Jersey's rate is in excess is 60.6.

In only one classification, "electric light and power," is the number of minor permanent partial disabilities per $1 million of payroll less in New Jersey than in the other states. In each of the remaining sixty-four classifications, New Jersey's rate is in excess by amounts ranging from 20 per cent upwards. Fifty-three out of the sixty-five classifications show disability rates which exceed the rates for the combined states by more than 100 per cent. In twenty of New Jersey's classifications, minor permanent partial disability rates are more than 200 per cent greater than those in the combined states. The median percentage rate by which New Jersey's disability rate exceeds the ten states combined is 171.6.

When New York's experience is compared with these same ten states, on the average, its rates are also greater than in the other states.[7] Its rate of excess is greater than New Jersey's for all types of cases except those involving permanent partial disabilities. On the average, in the major permanent partial cases, New York's rate is only 1 per cent higher than the combined states, whereas New Jersey's rate is 60.6 per cent higher. In the minor permanent partial cases, New York's rate is, on the average, 60.6 per cent greater, in contrast with New Jersey's rate, which on the average is 171.6 per cent greater.

Undoubtedly there are many deficiencies in these comparisons since one can never be sure that the firms are classified in exactly the same way in the various jurisdictions. Moreover, there are differences in wage levels, statutory provisions and reporting patterns among the states. On the other hand, the method of comparison does *understate* the percentages by which New Jersey's rate exceeds that in the other states. For one thing, when reporting payroll to the insurance carrier for the purpose of fixing insurance premiums, New Jersey employers with minor exceptions report *all* wages and salaries in all classifications. In other states, employers report payroll only up to a certain limit, such as $100 per week for each individual. This limits the amount of wages of an individual employee that is subject to insurance premiums to a maximum amount. This has the effect of inflating the payroll base and understating the disability rate, which is computed on the basis of the number of cases per $1 million of payroll. For another, it must be noted that New Jersey, itself, is one of the ten states making up the combination of states with which New Jersey is being compared. If New Jersey were removed from the ten states, the percentages by which New Jersey's rates exceed those of the combined states would increase substantially.

In discussing adequacy of compensation benefits, the shortcomings in New Jersey's benefits were pointed out, but it was also noted that the benefits in other states are inadequate. However, these interjurisdictional comparisons of disability rates do not lead to the conclusion that whatever the situation in New Jersey, it is about the same as in other industrial states. In the permanent partial categories, New Jersey's disability rate exceeds that in the other states by substantial amounts in nearly every classification.

Methods of Assessing the Number of Weeks of Compensation in Permanent Partial Disability Cases

An important reason for the wide variation among the states in the proportion of permanent partial disability cases is that they use different methods to determine the nature and extent of permanent partial disability.

Larson claims that "the distinctive feature of the compensation system, by contrast with tort liability is that its awards (apart from medical benefits) are made, not for physical injury as such, but for 'disability' produced by such injury." In his view the central problem

[7] Keiper, Zucker, Regan, and Eubank, Table 6, p. 21.

becomes one of analyzing the rather complex legal concept which has been built up around the term "compensable disability."

The key to the understanding of this problem is the recognition, at the outset, that the disability concept is a blend of two ingredients, whose recurrence in different proportions gives rise to most controversial disability questions; the first ingredient is disability in the medical or physical sense, as evidenced by obvious loss of members or by medical testimony that the claimant cannot make the necessary muscular movements and exertions; the second ingredient is *de facto* inability to earn wages, as evidenced by proof that claimant has not in fact earned anything.[8]

It is recognized that the two ingredients may be found together but that one may be present without the other. Thus a man could be a physical wreck yet by sheer perseverance or ingenuity contrive to earn a living, whereas another man might be quite capable of working but be denied a job because of his employer's prejudice against hiring anyone with his "disability."[9]

The basic problem is how the two ingredients, wage loss and physical impairment, are to be combined in assessing the degree of disability. There are many solutions to the problem, and the differences among them are a matter of the relative emphasis which is placed on the importance of one or the other ingredient. Employers tend to favor methods which emphasize the worker's loss of wages, whereas labor groups prefer to de-emphasize this criterion and to stress instead the physical impairment of the worker.

James L. Hill of the Ford Motor Company makes a strong representative case for a strict wage-loss theory. He claims that allowing a compensation benefit for an injury which entails no actual loss of wages is in the nature of payment for damages, a principle which was intended to be discarded when the compensation system was adopted. It is his claim that no objective procedures exist to determine the effect of a worker's injury on his future earning capacity. Consequently, compensation officials resort to some arbitrary standards. When officials attempt to rate certain disabilities without reference to wage loss, the inevitable result is to emphasize a worker's disability rather than his residual capacities. This has the effect of discouraging efforts to rehabilitate the injured workman.

It is admitted that, in theory, an injured employee who returns to work at his pre-injury rate of earnings may have suffered a loss in his wage-earning capacity. However, in Hill's view, employment at pre-injury earnings should create a presumption against the idea that the worker experienced any loss in earning capacity. He argues against

---

[8] Arthur Larson, *The Law of Workmen's Compensation* (Albany, N. Y.: Matthew Bender and Co., 1952), II, 2.

[9] In addition to Larson's discussion, see Henry Kessler, "Whole Man Theory," in *Workmen's Compensation Problems*, IAIABC *Proceedings*, 1956 (United States Department of Labor, Bureau of Labor Standards, Bulletin 192), pp. 76-79.

trying to estimate a worker's possible future loss of earnings on the grounds that it is not possible to do this accurately, and that it is unrealistic to attempt it since the award would have to be based on considerations which go beyond the facts in the case.[10]

Those opposed to the wage-loss theory attack it on several grounds. They point to the fact that a company may re-employ the injured employee and then keep him on the payroll only during the period for which he would be eligible to receive compensation benefits. When his services are terminated, he may find it difficult to secure another position. It is claimed that an injury to a worker is in the nature of a capital impairment; if there has been a physiological disturbance, this is bound to affect his earning power sooner or later. It is also claimed that certain administrative problems are present if a strict wage-loss theory is adopted since cases may have to be kept open for a number of years. If, however, administrators are concerned only with rating the extent of the worker's physical disability, the case can be closed after the hearing.

It is pointed out that in a dynamic labor market rates are constantly changing, making it difficult to calculate a worker's wage loss. A man may be removed from the labor market because of his injury, and upon his return may earn the same wages as before. If, however, he had continued to work, his wage might have been higher because of rate increases, and more important, he might have had opportunities for advancement. Objections are also raised that under a strict wage-loss theory two persons with identical injuries may receive awards which differ in amount. The difficulties involved in explaining these differences to workers loom large in labor's objections to the wage-loss theory.

There is ample evidence of these two points of view within the state. In 1956, employer groups in New Jersey proposed an amendment that was written into the law to the effect that no determination of permanent partial disability, except in actual amputations and enucleations, should be made before the expiration of a twenty-six-week period after date of injury, date of return to work or date of last active medical treatment, whichever is later.[11] They also proposed, but without success, that a legal presumption should be established that no permanent disability existed if the employee continued at work during the twenty-six-week period and lost no more than seven days' wages.[12] Needless to say, such amendments were vigorously opposed by labor groups, who pointed out that "the partial permanent award is given for damage or injury to a human being, which injury is as permanent as the human being himself." They pointed to the examples of employees who continued at work only on sufferance of their employers and maintained that these arrangements were not necessarily permanent. Also

---

[10] James L. Hill, "Actual Wage Loss Theory," in *Workmen's Compensation Problems*, IAIABC *Proceedings*, 1956, pp. 72-76.

[11] N.J. Stat. Ann. (West, 1958), 34:15-16.

[12] "Joint Employer Proposals to Amend the New Jersey Workmen's Compensation Law" (undated, mim.), pp. 12-13. A summary of these proposals has been cited in footnote 2.

it was argued that it is contrary to the entire theory of social or remedial legislation to erect, as barriers, further artificial presumptions against an employee's claim, especially since he now has the legal burden of proving his case.[13]

The choice between these two relative positions is complicated by the fact that the laws in all jurisdictions contain some sort of a schedule which sets forth the number of weeks of compensation to be paid to a worker with a specific impairment. The New Jersey schedule allows 15 weeks of compensation benefits for the loss of a toe other than the great toe, 60 weeks for the loss of hearing in one ear, 75 weeks for the loss of a thumb, and 300 weeks for the loss of an arm, to cite but some of the listings. The schedules in the various jurisdictions differ, not only in the number of weeks allowed for various disabilities, but also in the extensiveness of their listings.

These price lists for the parts of the body were designed originally to inject an element of certainty into compensation proceedings and to simplify the task of the administrators. Jury awards in the pre-compensation days were notoriously chaotic and highly uncertain; the schedules, which presumably could be understood by anyone, were supposed to provide guidance for the worker and insurance adjuster, thus saving the time of litigation and the annoyances of prolonged controversy.

Presumably, the original purpose of these schedules was to provide a list of the number of weeks of benefits which would compensate the average worker for his actual or presumptive wage loss.[14] A rough attempt was made, following the schedules developed in the compensation laws of European countries, to evaluate the loss of earning power which may result from the loss of one part of the body as compared with another. The schedules were meant to be internally consistent, but they apply to workers of different ages in different occupations. Obviously the loss of a finger would not have the same effect on the future earning powers of a violinist and a truck driver. If a man starting out on his career and a worker about to retire suffered the same anatomical loss, their eventual wage losses would be very different.

Of course, since most schedules list benefits in terms of weeks rather than dollars, and since workers receive a certain percentage of their wages as compensation benefits, the difference in wages earned by injured workers has some effect on the weekly dollar benefits. Only one state, California, has instituted a multifactor schedule which takes into account such factors as occupation and age in assessing the number of weeks of benefits due for a particular disabling injury. The difficulties of applying the California schedule, which encompasses

---

[13] "Memorandum of N. J. State CIO Council," p. 11.

[14] For some interesting early comment on the development of these schedules and comparison with experience in foreign countries, see Carl Hookstadt, *Comparison of Workmen's Compensation Laws of the United States and Canada up to January 1, 1920* (United States Department of Labor, Bureau of Labor Statistics, Bulletin 275), pp. 74-90.

literally thousands of separate combinations of factors, argue against its adoption in the other states which adhere to the flat-rate schedules.[15] The gross averaging process, implicit in a schedule such as New Jersey's, is justified on the grounds that a social insurance program with an annual case load of over 50,000 cases requires treatment in terms of the probabilities of the average worker's wage loss, rather than an evaluation of an individual worker's loss of earning power in terms of his age, occupation and ability to compete in the open labor market.

But if these schedules were based originally on presumed average wage loss, time has tended to blur this relationship. Schedules are amended according to political pressures, or as a result of particularly dramatic cases which one side or the other feels have been wrongly dealt with under the schedules Little unformity exists among the jurisdictions, and it is commonplace to note that a New Jersey hand is worth more than the loss of an entire arm in Alabama and twenty-four other states, and that wide variations can be found in the schedules in adjoining states.[16]

The achedules apply not only in cases of actual loss of limb but also in cases in which the worker has experienced a "loss of use" of a particular limb. These cases range from the rather obvious situations in which the man's limb is completely paralyzed to the cases in which the main evidence of loss of use of the limb is the employee's subjective complaints of constant pain. In such cases, the schedules do not provide the same degree of certainty as is present when the worker loses a limb. Someone, be it insurance adjuster or compensation administrator, must estimate the degree of disability in terms of the number of weeks. Thus if the disability is estimated at 50 per cent of the loss of use of an arm, the worker would be entitled to 50 per cent of the 300 weeks allowed for total loss of the arm in New Jersey's schedule. Further uncertainties are introduced when it is recognized that the worker, unfortunate enough to have suffered a clean-cut amputation of the arm, may receive an award not only for the loss of the arm but in addition for a resulting neurosis. The schedule provides little guidance in assessing the number of weeks of benefits for neurological disabilities, and it is necessary to move to a consideration of the so-called nonscheduled cases.

The area of nonscheduled awards will be great or small depending upon the extensiveness of the schedules used in the various jurisdictions. It is in this area that the sharpest conflicts between emphasis

[15]An early analysis of California's disability schedule can be found in Edison L. Bowers, *Is It Safe to Work?* (N. Y.: Houghton Mifflin Co., 1930), chapter 4. Somers has made a thorough analysis of the implications of this schedule, and in general, he sees little to recommend it. See "Disability Rating: Veteran's Administration Contrasted with Workmen's Compensation Experience," in *Compensation for Service-Connected Disabilities* (84th Congress, 2d Session, House of Representative Committee Print, No. 281, 1956), pp. 226-234.

[16]Max D. Kossoris, "An Appraisal," in *Workmen's Compensation in the United States* (United States Department of Labor, Bureau of Labor Statistics, Bulletin 1149, 1954), p. 5.

on wage loss or physical impairment are most apparent. The number of cases in which the anatomical schedules offer little guidance in assessing the number of weeks of benefits are increasing, and probably constitute the bulk of the permanent partial cases in New Jersey.

In general, there are two main methods by which a jurisdiction might decide these cases. One method, which supposedly emphasizes the wage-loss aspects of disability, attempts to evaluate the loss in the worker's wage-earning capacity without reference to any schedule. Actual earnings before the injury are contrasted with earning capacity after disablement. This necessarily involves something more than a mechanical comparison of the worker's earnings at two points of time. Discounts may have to be made for such factors as changes in the general wage level, the claimant's age, training, hours of work, and also post-injury earnings which may be accounted for only by the employer's sympathy. Consideration must also be given to whether or not post-injury earnings will necessarily be permanent.[17] Jurisdictions which attempt to evaluate the employee's loss in earning capacity in determining benefits may also allow specific awards for disfigurements. These awards may be rationalized on the grounds that a disfigurement may interfere with the employee's ability to get and hold a job; but the tendency has been to enlarge this concept, and to compensate for loss of teeth and scars on the body which normally would not be visible if the employee worked in the usual occupations.

There has been a tendency, in jurisdictions which attempt to measure changes in wage-earning capacity, to place increasing reliance on the criterion of physical impairment *per se*, in large part because of the administrative difficulties of measuring loss of earning capacity. Another factor involved is the sense of injustice which arises when some serious injury is compensated meagerly because there is no loss of earning capacity, and a less grave injury receives a greater award because of the loss in earning capacity due to the employment situation. It has been stated: "...a combination of practical and ethical considerations has caused the *de facto* shift. But while we now have in practice a mixture of both physical impairment and loss of earning capacity criteria, with considerable emphasis on the former, the theoretical rationale, stated in the laws, remains almost exclusively in terms of earning capacity. Doctrine generally lags behind fact and action."[18]

The other major method, used in New Jersey and several other jurisdictions but in no two in exactly the same way, is to rate the non-scheduled disability in percentage terms. The 100 per cent figure may be derived from the schedule itself. In New Jersey's schedule (Table XIV), the loss of a leg is scheduled at 275 weeks, an arm at 300 weeks, and the loss of the whole body, as it were, is listed at 550 weeks. If the disability is rated at 5 per cent of the leg, 13 3/4 weeks will be

[17]For a discussion of the difficulties involved in applying these tests, see Larson, *Workmen's Compensation Law*, II, 10-25.

[18]"Disability Rating: Veteran's Administration Contrasted with Workmen's Compensation Experience," in *Compensation for Service-Connected Disabilities*, p. 244.

awarded; if at 5 per cent of the arm, 15 weeks will be paid; and if the worker suffers some orthopedic injury to the back, for example, this may be rated at 5 per cent of what has been termed "partial total," or 27 1/2 weeks (5 per cent of "total" or the 550 weeks allocated for the whole body).[19]

Table XIV. New Jersey Schedule of Disabilities, Effective January 1, 1957

Per Cent	Thumb, 1st & 2d Finger or Hand 230 Wks.	Arm 300 Weeks	Thumb 75 Weeks	Fingers				Leg 275 Weeks	Foot 200 Weeks	Toes		Eye 200 Weeks	Hearing		Partial Total Based on 550 Weeks
				1st 50 Weeks	2d 40 Weeks	3rd 30 Weeks	4th 20 Weeks			Great 40 Weeks	Other 15 Weeks		1 Ear 60 Weeks	2 Ears 200 Weeks	
1	2.3	3.	¾	½	.4	.3	.2	2¾	2	.4	.15	2	.6	2	5½
2½	5¾	7½	1⅞	1¼	1	¾	½	6⅞	5	1	⅜	5	1½	5	13¾
5	11½	15	3¾	2½	2	1½	1	13¾	10	2	¾	10	3	10	27½
7½	17¼	22½	5⅝	3¾	3	2¼	1½	20⅝	15	3	1⅛	15	4½	15	41¼
10	23	30	7½	5	4	3	2	27½	20	4	1½	20	6	20	55
12½	28¾	37½	9⅜	6¼	5	3¾	2½	34⅜	25	5	1⅞	25	7½	25	68¾
15	34½	45	11¼	7½	6	4½	3	41¼	30	6	2¼	30	9	30	82½
20	46	60	15	10	8	6	4	55	40	8	3	40	12	40	110
25	57½	75	18¾	12½	10	7½	5	68¾	50	10	3¾	50	15	50	137½
30	69	90	22½	15	12	9	6	82½	60	12	4½	60	18	60	165
33⅓	76⅔	100	25	16⅔	13⅓	10	6⅔	91⅔	66⅔	13⅓	5	66⅔	20	66⅔	183⅓
35	80½	105	26¼	17½	14	10½	7	96¼	70	14	5¼	70	21	70	192½
40	92	120	30	20	16	12	8	110	80	16	6	80	24	80	220
45	103½	135	33¾	22½	18	13½	9	123¾	90	18	6¾	90	27	90	247½
50	115	150	37½	25	20	15	10	137½	100	20	7½	100	30	100	275
55	126½	165	41¼	27½	22	16½	11	151¼	110	22	8¼	110	33	110	302½
60	138	180	45	30	24	18	12	165	120	24	9	120	36	120	330
65	149½	195	48¾	32½	26	19½	13	178¾	130	26	9¾	130	39	130	357½
66⅔	153⅓	200	50	33⅓	26⅔	20	13⅓	183⅓	133⅓	26⅔	10	133⅓	40	133⅓	366⅔
70	161	210	52½	35	28	21	14	192½	140	28	10½	140	42	140	385
75	172½	225	56¼	37½	30	22½	15	206¼	150	30	11¼	150	45	150	412½
80	184	240	60	40	32	24	16	220	160	32	12	160	48	160	440
85	195½	255	63¾	42½	34	25½	17	233¾	170	34	12¾	170	51	170	467½
90	207	270	67½	45	36	27	18	247½	180	36	13½	180	54	180	495
95	218½	285	71¼	47½	38	28½	19	261¼	190	38	14¼	190	57	190	522½
100	230	300	75	50	40	30	20	275	200	40	15	200	60	200	

For each natural tooth lost — 4 weeks.

Source: State of New Jersey, Department of Labor and Industry, *Workmen's Compensation Law*, 1957, p. 89. This is the schedule in the form used by the parties and the administrators.

[19]The use of the confusing term "partial total" is justified, since if the worker is actually permanently and totally disabled, his initial award would run not for 550 weeks but for 450 weeks. After this 450-week period, the status of his case is re-examined; and if he is still eligible, benefits can continue for the rest of his life.

Under this system, wage-loss concepts are present only if one makes the assumption that the 550 weeks are based upon the presumed wage-loss for total incapacity. But this is a far departure from a factual inquiry into the question of whether or not there is, or will be, any actual loss of earning capacity. It may be argued that wage loss need not be proved since it was presumed when the schedule was drawn up, but all of the energies and talents of the hearing officer in disputed cases will be devoted to determining the extent of the physical disability and translating this into percentage terms without concern whether the worker lost a day of work, or whether he might eventually be handicapped in an employment sense.

Larson argues that once you cut loose from the earning capacity concept, it is practically impossible to contrive a substitute principle which will give a rational guide to determine which injuries are covered and how much compensation they merit.[20] On the other hand, Somers makes a persuasive case for dropping this test and frankly recognizing that awards are based upon physical disability *per se*, but he does not underestimate the difficulties surrounding a physical impairment test.[21]

It is of a paramount importance to recognize that in New Jersey the claimant seeking a permanent partial award need not experience any actual wage loss or prove that he has suffered from a disability that will interfere with his future wage-earning capacity. This was established early in the history of the compensation program. One of the early writers on the state's compensation law points out that the fact that a man has resumed his calling with no reduction in his wages is no bar to his receiving compensation payments for permanent disability. The term disability "embraces any loss of physical function which detracts from the former efficiency of the body or its members in the *ordinary pursuits of life.*"[22] To the extent that wage-loss concepts operate in the state, they do so only because the schedules may be interpreted as being based upon the presumed average wage loss for the disability.

If tests involving loss of wage-earning capacity are abandoned, it is possible to distinguish three general methods of "rating" the disability to determine the number of weeks of benefits. The distinctions among them are not always clear, and is perfectly feasible for administrators in various states to use a combination of these methods. One method would be to extend the schedule to all or nearly all disabilities; another would be to depend upon the time-tested virtues of adversary

---

[20] Larson, *Workmen's Compensation Law*, II, 51.

[21] "Disability Rating: Veteran's Administration Contrasted with Workmen's Compensation Experience," in *Compensation for Service-Connected Disabilities*, p. 244.

[22] R. Robinson Chance, *The Workmen's Compensation Law of New Jersey*, 2d ed. (Newark: Soney and Sage, 1918), pp. 60-61. Cases cited in affirmation of this point of view are, *Burbage* v. *Lee*, 87 N.J.L. 36; *Pressy* v. *De Zeng Standard Co.*, 86 N.J.L. 469, *affirmed* 88 N.J.L. 382; *Burd* v. *Richardson and Boyonton*, 40 N.J.L. 84.

proceedings in which the interested parties each present their point of view to a hearing officer who must decide the case. The third method allows the case to be decided, in whole or in part, by a panel of impartial physicians.

No matter which method is used, great reliance must be placed upon medical testimony; but it is doubtful if medical testimony alone can decide the case. It is one thing for a physician to state that, in his expert opinion, the worker has suffered a linear fracture, that there is poor alignment with consequent restriction of movement, and so on. It is another thing to translate these medical findings into the appropriate percentage of the number of weeks allowed for loss of an arm. It is one thing for the doctor to state that, in his opinion, the X-rays show some damage to the lumbar region; it is another and possibly more difficult task to translate this into the correct percentage of 550 weeks which should be allowed. Two physicians may honestly disagree about the extent of the injury, and they may be far apart on the percentages.

More than a quarter of a century ago, the difficulties involved in evaluating disabilities were recognized by Dr. Henry Kessler. Addressing a meeting of the American Association of Industrial Physicians and Surgeons, Kessler stated: "... in industrial accidents several basic methods have been employed, for example, in a stiff elbow following fracture four doctors will give as many different opinions as to the estimate of disability ranging from nothing to 100 per cent. It may be said that doctors are prejudiced and have personal interests at stake. It has been my experience, however, that more often the differences of opinion are honest and sincere; the trouble is we are not all talking the same language. One man is thinking in terms of reduction of earning capacity, the second of vocational handicap, the third of the structural condition as in fractures, while the fourth of the functional condition. All cannot be right but someone is." [23]

Kessler believes that it is possible to devise an acceptable method of measuring loss of function. [24] If this were done and extended to other types of disabilities, the result would be a schedule to cover these disabilities, just as the schedule now covers the loss of limbs. If this method were carried to its logical extreme, the problem of non-scheduled disabilities would be solved by their elimination. The idea of scheduling disabilities that are not now scheduled is opposed on the grounds that it would require the employee to be subject to long-drawn-out examinations and that this would be too expensive for insurance carriers.

New Jersey makes full and frank use of the second method, adversary proceedings. If one spends a few days visiting one of the large, active hearing centers in Newark or Jersey City, one is impressed with

---

[23] Reported in *The Newark News,* May 27, 1925.
[24] Henry Kessler, *Accidental Injuries* (Philadelphia: Lee and Febiger, 1941). Kessler has written extensively on this subject. See, for example, his article "Whole Man Theory," in *Workmen's Compensation Problems,* IAIABC *Proceedings,* 1956; also his *Low Back Pain in Industry* (N. Y.: Commerce and Industry Association of N. Y., 1955).

the resemblance that formal compensation hearings bear to ordinary court trials. Doctors, known frankly and openly as petitioner's physicians, circulate rapidly from courtroom to courtroom testifying about the results of their examinations of injured employees. They are opposed by other doctors, retained by the insurance carriers or large self-insurers, who give opposing testimony about the nature and extent of the worker's disability. These are the professional testifiers, who testify by day and examine by night.

The unschooled layman may recoil at these procedures, but it is easier to criticize what has been called "court-house medicine" than it is to find acceptable substitutes. Given the basic theory of deciding cases by the adversary method and given the large volume of cases the deputies hear each day, the professional testifiers serve a purpose. As one deputy director remarked to the writer, "I couldn't get along without these fellows, they know their business and I know their biases."

In a typical case, in which the only issue involved is the nature and extent of the worker's disability, the petitioner's doctor will give his opinion about the nature of the disability, and then in response to a question from the petitioner's attorney, will estimate the extent of disability at so many per cent of the limb, or of "partial total." If the case involves both an orthopedic and a neurological issue, two physicians may testify on behalf of the worker. In similar fashion, the insurance company's doctor will go through the same process and make his estimates. As in any other adversary proceeding, it is expected that the estimates of the extent of disability will not agree: that the petitioner's doctor will maximize the extent and that the insurance company's doctor will minimize it. Neither the deputies nor the parties are surprised about this, and although the doctors may be subject to cross-examination, if they are truly professionals at this sort of thing, they take this in stride. They may be able to anticipate most of the routine questions and are quite proficient in giving the "correct" answers from the point of view of "their" side.

The deputy hearing the case has the responsibility for making the decision, but now he has some guideposts delineating the outside limits. Using his expert knowledge, gained perhaps from years of experience, he will make his decision somewhere between the estimates of the two sides. The deputies become disturbed, not when there is some difference of opinion between the doctors representing the two sides, but when there is a "wide" divergence between their estimates. It is impossible to define the exact dividing line between normal and wide divergences, but what is fascinating about this is that the deputies have very definite ideas about what constitutes a reasonable or unreasonable divergence.

If the divergences are wide, the deputy is left with a difficult problem. Can he then call upon the services of a disinterested physician to examine the man and to testify as to his findings? There is little doubt that if both parties consent to this procedure, the deputy may call upon a third physician; and a recent case decided on appeal seems to establish that he has the right to call upon an impartial doctor without the consent of the parties.[25]

This procedure of calling in an impartial physician comes close to, but is not exactly the same as, using an impartial panel of physicians to estimate the extent of disability. Under present New Jersey procedures, the impartial physician would not be called upon unless the deputy felt that the testimony of the opposing physicians did not afford him sufficient guidance. Under the panel system, the testimony of impartial physicians would displace that of the physicians retained by the parties.

In discussing the respective merits of the two systems, one deputy pointed out that the impartial examiner is apt to proceed on the theory that medicine is a strict science. According to the deputy, however, the opinion of the physician depends upon the recording and interpretation of symptoms, and this can lead to a multiplicity of diagnoses, differential in character. A majority of a committee of deputy directors which considered this problem felt that the common-sense method of having the deputy decide the case according to the testimony of opposing physicians was the better approach.[26]

A member of the division's medical department stated that the lawyers and most of the doctors to whom he spoke felt that the adversary system is the best system that has yet been devised; that every injured man is entitled to his day in court; that every injured man is entitled to have someone testify in his behalf; and that, in the final analysis, doctors do have their individual points of view. His conclusion, after much study, was that it is possible to rely on the wisdom of the individual deputy director to assess properly the testimony given by individual doctors. The deputy realizes that a particular doctor is representing a definite point of view; and in arriving at his ultimate decision the deputy attaches to the testimony the weight he feels it deserves under the circumstances.

A system of adversary proceedings on medical issues requires doctors who are familiar with the nature of the legal process and the methods used to evaluate a disability in compensation terms. A

---

[25] *Roman Polulich* v. *J. C. Schmidt Tool Dye and Stamping Co.*, Essex County Court, Law Division, Docket No. A-116. This case was heard by a deputy director who subsequently became the director of the division. The respondent's doctor had testified that the petitioner's disability due to neurosis was $2\frac{1}{2}$ per cent, while the petitioner's doctor estimated it at 50 per cent. The deputy in his opinion stated: "Because of the marked divergence between the findings and estimates of opposing medical experts, ... I felt that the evidence presented did not provide a basis upon which I could render a reasonable decision." He thereupon had the petitioner examined by a neuropsychiatrist recommended by the medical director of the division. Counsel for the respondent objected to the impartial expert's testimony but was overruled by the deputy, who was sustained in this respect by the court.

[26] This and subsequent opinions of personnel of the division are from the minutes of the Workmen's Compensation Board meeting of April 21, 1956. Discussions of these topics were prompted by the series of articles which Max Weiner had published in the *The Newark News*. Because of the closed nature of the board meetings, and since the deputies were not speaking for publication, the identity of various board personnel has not been revealed.

recurrent theme among the discussions of the deputy directors is that more doctors should participate in these proceedings, but, inevitably, grave obstacles must be surmounted before this becomes common practice. One difficulty is that the average physician is a busy man who hesitates to come into the compensation courts and perhaps lose a half of a day or more testifying, or waiting to testify. The proposal has been made that physicians who testify only occasionally be given priorities in the scheduling of cases, but it is not easy to do this. If it could be done, one set of rules would exist for scheduling cases in which the professional testifier gives evidence and another set for cases in which the doctor who comes in only occasionally is called to the stand. The professionals, who would probably resent the outsiders anyway, would likely object to these practices and would hardly be comforted by being told that they would be around all day anyway.

The doctor unfamiliar with the compensation proceedings may have a rather hard time on the witness stand. According to one of the deputies, when these doctors are called in, they are subjected to veiled sarcasm and innuendo on cross-examination and then leave the hearing feeling humiliated and exasperated. According to this deputy, it is the responsibility of the hearing officer to protect the witnesses from the onslaught of the lawyer who is trying only to display his cleverness; but it is probable that there is only so much the deputy can do in this regard. The division has made constant efforts to increase the number of doctors who testify, but this is an uphill fight since the system, as devised, so obviously favors the professional testifier. He is familiar with the lawyers, the other doctors, the hearing officers and the general procedures. He knows exactly what is expected of him, and he is an expert in calling the numbers, that is, in estimating the percentages of disability.

Whatever the virtues of the adversary proceedings, it should not be surprising to find that under this system an increasing number of the permanent disability cases are being litigated. What does seem surprising is that any except the obvious schedule cases and the more minor nonscheduled ones are ever settled by direct agreement between the parties. As a matter of fact, only a few of the more serious cases are closed without coming to the formal disputes level; however once these cases arrive there, the parties are often able to settle them through the good offices of a referee or deputy director.

A Comparison of Permanent Partial Awards in Essex and Camden Counties

Since, under the system, the evaluation of disability varies from jurisdiction to jurisdiction and county to county, it should not be surprising to find that the settlement of awards likewise varies from place to place. Here also, decisions depend a great deal upon the opinions of the parties and administrators.

The differences within New Jersey may be further illustrated by a sample of cases that have come up in two counties, Essex and Camden. The proportion of permanent partial to all compensation cases varies in the several New Jersey counties and the number of minor permanent partial cases has increased (see Chapter 2).

Table XV shows the number of weeks of compensation benefits awarded at the formal hearing in 262 Essex County cases and 50 Camden County cases, classified according to scheduled and non-scheduled awards.[27] One thing is noticeable in this tabulation. The nonscheduled award is relatively more frequent in Essex than in Camden; 180 out of the 262 Essex cases, or approximately 69 per cent, fall into the nonscheduled category, in contrast with 27 out of 50, or 54 per cent, of the Camden cases.

A given disability, however, may fall into both categories. A man may receive a scheduled award for loss of limb or loss of use of a limb and, in addition, some award based upon a percentage of 550 weeks because some part of his body not listed on the schedule was also involved in the injury. Such combination cases have been included under the nonscheduled category in Table XV. Although such combination awards occur in only a minority of the sample cases, they are more frequent in Essex than in Camden. Ten of the 180 nonscheduled awards in Essex also include some award for a scheduled disability, whereas only 1 of the 27 Camden cases was of the combination variety. In both counties workers in most cases received relatively small awards, although this is more apparent in Essex than in Camden.[28] Twenty per

---

[27] In order not to interfere with the work of the Division of Workmen's Compensation, the cases were examined as they were processed by the statistical section of the division, that is, after they were closed. An attempt was made to secure all Camden County formal cases involving any permanent partial issue which were processed by the statistical section during the month of July, 1957. Since it was thought necessary to have at least 50 Camden closed compensated cases, some cases processed in June were included. The Essex County cases were chosen at random from among the cases statistically processed in July. The thought was that at least five times as many Essex as Camden cases should be included. Because of the time lag involved in the processing of cases, it was possible to include only cases in which the accident occurred prior to January, 1957; as of that date, the twenty-six-week rule went into effect requiring the division, in the usual case, to postpone making any determination until after the expiration of the six-month period. Had determination made before both and after this rule went into effect been included, the sample would not have been homogeneous.

Because of the relatively small number of cases included and the method of choosing the sample, small differences should not be given undue importance; yet it is believed that the sample is relatively representative of the experience in each county.

A total of 291 Essex cases and 59 Camden cases were examined. Of the 291 Essex cases, 9 were discontinued, 7 with the payment of some compensation and 2 without; 13 cases were dismissed, 7 before trial and 6 after trial because of such factors as failure of the petitioner to prove the occurrence of a compensable accident, failure to file in time or, in one case, failure to establish a casual relationship; one case was not moved; another involved only medical payments; 5 cases were reopened cases in which there had been previous activity at the formal level. This left 262 closed compensated cases in Essex for which it was possible to secure data on the type and amount of permanent partial awards.

Of the 59 Camden cases, 4 were discontinued, 2 with compensation and 2 without. Four cases were dismissed, 3 before trial and 1 after; and 1 case was not moved. Thus a total of 50 Camden cases were used.

[28] In tabulating the number of weeks of compensation benefits received in the permanent

Table XV. Number of Weeks of Compensation Incurred in Sample of Formal Closed Permanent Partial Cases in Essex and Camden Counties, New Jersey, 1954

		Essex County						Camden County					
		Nonschedule Awards		Schedule Awards		Total		Nonschedule Awards		Schedule Awards		Total	
No. of Weeks of Compensation	% of 550 Weeks	No. of Cases	% of Cases	No. of Cases	% of Cases	No. of Cases	% of Cases	No. of Cases	% of Cases	No. of Cases	% of Cases	No. of Cases	% of Cases
0 - $13\frac{3}{4}$	0 - 2.5%	36	20%	35 [a]	43%	71	27%	3	11%	6	2%	9	18%
14 - $27\frac{1}{2}$	2.6 - 5	84	47	24	29	108	41	8	30	7	30	15	30
$27\frac{3}{4}$ - $41\frac{1}{4}$	5.1 - 7.5	26	14	15 [b]	18	41	16	1	4	3	13	4	8
$41\frac{1}{2}$ - 55	7.6 - 10	11	6	5	6	16	6	6	22	2	9	8	16
$55\frac{1}{4}$ - $82\frac{1}{2}$	10.1 - 15	8	4	1	1	9	3	3	11	2	9	5	10
$82\frac{3}{4}$ - 110	15.1 - 20	3	2	2	2	5	2	0	—	1	4	1	2
$110\frac{1}{4}$ - $137\frac{1}{2}$	20.1 - 25	5	3	0	—	5	2	4	15	0	—	4	8
$137\frac{3}{4}$ - 165	25.1 - 30	2	1	0	—	2	1	1	4	0	—	1	2
$165\frac{1}{4}$ - 220	30.1 - 40	3	2	0	—	3	1	0	—	2	9	2	4
$220\frac{1}{4}$ - 275	40.1 - 50	1	1	0	—	1	0.4	1	4	0	0	1	2
$275\frac{1}{4}$ - 330	50.1 - 60	1	1	0	—	1	0.4	0	—	0	—	0	—
Totals		180	100%	82	100%	262	100%	27	100%	23	100%	50	100%

Source: Abstracted from records of closed cases in files of New Jersey Division of Workmen's Compensation.

[a] Includes one case for which there had been a previous award, the amount of which is unknown.

[b] Includes one case in which an additional $34\frac{1}{2}$ weeks were awarded for double indemnity.

cent of the nonscheduled cases in Essex were given awards based upon 2.5 per cent of permanent partial total or less, in contrast with 11 per cent of the cases in Camden. Forty-three per cent of the Essex scheduled cases received payments for 13 3/4 weeks or less, in contrast with 26 per cent of the Camden cases (2.5 per cent of 550 weeks is equal to 13 3/4 weeks). Sixty-eight per cent of the Essex cases and 48 per cent of Camden cases received awards of 27 1/2 weeks or less.

Each of these Camden cases was closed only after a full trial, which culminated in a formal determination by a deputy director. In Essex, the cases are first brought before a formal referee or deputy director who attempts to settle the issues involved in conference with the parties. In some few cases a so-called "formal settlement" will result, and the case will be closed without further procedures. However, of the total of 18,811 cases closed at the formal level in 1956, only 79 cases were disposed of this fashion. A more usual result of the pre-trial conference is that the parties agree on the amount of the award, perhaps after hearing the preliminary and unofficial opinion of the deputy; but in order to protect themselves and sometimes in order to assure an adequate attorney's fee, the parties insist on a consent judgment. This follows a so-called "streamlined trial" after which the judgment, which has already been agreed upon, is entered. In the state as a whole, half of the 1956 cases disposed of at the formal level fell into this category. If no agreement can be reached at the pre-trial conference, the hearing officer attempts to narrow the issues in dispute, and the case is set down for a full trial at a later date at which a formal determination will be made. Only 48 out of the 262 Essex cases were disposed of by a formal determination and award; the balance were closed by stipulation and consent judgments. Thirty-five of these were nonscheduled cases, and 13 were awards based upon the schedule.

Some information about the nature of the injury in the scheduled and nonscheduled cases in both counties is presented in Table XVI. The sample is too small to show all possible injuries, but the prominent role that back injuries play in both counties is obvious. One-third of the nonscheduled Camden cases and slightly more than one-third of the Essex cases involved the back exclusively. More than half of the nonscheduled cases in both counties involve the back plus some other injury, usually a neurological involvement.

The charge has been made that many of awards in the back cases

---

partial disability case that finds its way to the formal level, a dilemma must be resolved. In many of these cases workers have already received some benefits either as a result of a direct settlement or an informal hearing. (The reopened cases, those in which workers received awards at a prior formal hearing, have been excluded.) If one wants to get some idea of the nature of the work at the formal level, the previous actions should be excluded, and only the awards made by the deputy directors should be included. On the other hand, if the object is to determine the total compensation received for permanent partial disability, then the prior weeks of compensation, either received or incurred, should be included. In Table XV, the latter course has been chosen. Included in the number of weeks of compensation are the settlements previously made in 30 of the 262 cases in Essex and in 13 of the 50 Camden cases.

Table XVI. Nature of Injury in Sample of Formal Closed Permanent Partial Cases
in Essex and Camden Counties, New Jersey, 1954

Type of Case	Essex County		Camden County	
	No. of Cases	% of Cases	No. of Cases	% of Cases
I. Nonscheduled Cases				
Back cases exclusively	66	37%	9	33%
Back injuries plus other injuries.	29	16	5	19
Total back cases	95	53	14	52
Neurological exclusively	15	8	0	—
Neurological plus other injuries.	40	22	6	22
Total neurological cases	55	31	6	22
All other nonscheduled cases	45	25	12	44
Total Nonscheduled Cases[a]	180	100%	27	100%
II. Scheduled Cases				
Thumb, 1st and 2d finger or hand	27	33%	6	26%
Arm	6	7	4	17
Thumb[b]	5	6	0	—
Fingers or toes	5	6	3	13
Leg	16	20	4	17
Foot	14	17	5	22
Eye	9	11	0	—
Hearing	0	—	1	4
Total Scheduled Cases	82	100%	23	100%

Source: Abstracted from records of closed cases in files of New Jersey Division of Workmen's Compensation.
[a]Columns add up to over 100 per cent because there is some overlapping of back and neurological cases.
[b]Includes one case in which there was additional compensation for the left second finger (11 1/4 weeks were granted for the thumb; 4 weeks for the finger).

are based upon subjective complaints and that the awards are therefore unwarranted. Such a charge cannot be proved by the statistical record; but for whatever it is worth, it can be noted that of the 66 back cases in Essex, 15, or 23 per cent, of them resulted in compensation awards amounting to 2 1/2 per cent of partial total or less, while 55 cases, or 83 per cent of the 66, resulted in awards of 5 per cent or less.[29] It is impossible to give any meaningful breakdown for the Camden cases since only 9 were involved.

Fifteen of the awards in Essex nonscheduled cases were based exclusively on some neurological involvement, whereas no such cases

---

[29]The statistical record cannot prove this charge not only because of the inherently sterile nature of the statistics but also because of the difficulties associated with the concept of "unwarranted." As Kessler has pointed out, the emotional factor is significant in all illnesses and especially those associated with the lower back. A specific award may not be "unwarranted" even if no objective findings of injury to the back are discovered. There are still the neurotic symptoms to be considered and controlled. See his *Low Back Pain in Industry*, esp. p. 192.

were found in Camden. However, in both counties awards were made for neuroses in addition to some other injury or disability. Fifty-five of the Essex cases were in this category, as were 6 of the 27 non-scheduled Camden cases. There is some overlapping of cases in these counts since a back injury which also involved a neurological award was counted under both categories.

New Jersey's lack of emphasis on the wage-loss aspects of disability is illustrated in Table XVII, in which the sample cases are classified according to the number of weeks of temporary compensation allowed.[30] Fifteen, or 30 per cent, of the 50 Camden cases received no allowance for temporary disability whatsoever, either because the claimant lost no time from work or because he lost less than one week's time. In Essex, 123 out of 262 cases, or 47 per cent of the cases, received no temporary disability benefits.

This is not to say that workers who receive permanent partial awards without payments for temporary disability are necessarily receiving unjustified benefits. In the judgment of the deputies, these

Table XVII. Number of Weeks of Temporary Disability Compensation Paid or Awarded in Sample of Formal Closed Permanent Partial Cases in Essex and Camden Counties, New Jersey, 1954

No. of Weeks of Temporary Compensation Already Paid or Awarded	Camden County No. of Cases	Essex County No. of Cases
0	15	123
1/7-1	2	19
1 1/7-2	2	16
2 1/7-3	2	14
3 1/7-4	0	3
4 1/7-5	3	13
5 1/7-6	0	14
6 1/7-7	2	6
7 1/7-8	0	7
8 1/7-9	2	6
9 1/7-10	2	3
10 1/7-15	5	18
15 1/7-20	4	7
20 1/7-25	5	7
25 1/7-30	2	2
30 1/7-35	1	
35 1/7-40	1	1
Over 40	2	2
Unspecified		1
	50	262

Source: Abstracted from records of closed cases in files of New Jersey Division of Workmen's Compensation.

[30]Included in the number of weeks of temporary disability compensation are both the number of weeks awarded at the formal hearing and the number of weeks which had already been paid or which the company or insurance carrier had already agreed should be paid. In most formal cases, the number of weeks of compensation for temporary disability is usually not at issue, since this matter is usually settled before the case reaches the formal level.

people were permanently disabled. Even if wage-loss concepts loomed more importantly than they do in the state, it would still be possible for workers to receive awards for permanent disability without any actual loss of time from work, if their disability lessened their future earning power.

As noted above, amendments to the law effective January 1, 1957, forbade the division to make determinations in certain permanent partial cases before the expiration of twenty-six weeks. Employers advocated this amendment on the theory that it would help to eliminate cases in which the employee received an award without actually suffering any permanent disability. The amendment provides that the twenty-six-week period shall run from the date of the employee's final active medical treatment or his return to work, whichever is earlier. If no time is lost, or no treatment is rendered, then the disability is not to be determined until twenty-six weeks after the date of accident. Even before this ruling, relatively few cases were determined in less than six months. Table XVIII shows the time lags for the sample cases (processed under the old rules) from date of accident until date of formal disposition. It is not possible to discover the exact date of final medical treatment or return to work. In Camden, only 4 of the 50 cases were determined in less than six months. The average time lag in Camden was 16.1 months and the median time lag, 11 months and 14 days.

In Essex, it is useful to compare the time lags in the cases that

Table XVIII. Time Lag From Date of Accident to Date of Disposition in Sample of
Formal Closed Permanent Partial Cases in Essex and
Camden Counties, New Jersey, 1954

No. of Months	Essex County		Camden County
	No. of Stipulations and Consent Judgments	No. of Determinations and Judgments (Awards)	No. of Determinations and Judgments (Awards)
Less than 4	0	0	0
4 but less than 5	9	2	2
5 - 6	42	3	2
6 - 7	42	5	2
7 - 8	21	2	4
8 - 9	21	6	5
9 - 10	18	4	7
10 - 11	9	3	2
11 - 12	4	3	2
12 - 18	30	7	9
18 - 24	11	5	5
24 - 30	3	2	5
30 - 36	2	1	2
Over 36	1	6	3
Total Cases	213	49	50
Average Time lag	9.5 mos.	16.2 mos.	16.1 mos.
Median Time lag	7 mos. 13 d.	10 mos. 24 d.	11 mos. 14 d.

Source: Abstracted from records of closed cases in files of New Jersey Division of Workmen's Compensation. Sample does not include reopened, discontinued or dismissed cases.

went to full trial (determinations and judgments), and those that were disposed of by consent judgment. In the cases that were tried the time lags were about the same in the Essex and Camden cases, that is, sixteen months on the average. The quick dispositions, however, were made in the consent cases; but even in these, the average time lag was 9.5 months, and the median time lag was 7 months and 13 days. Only 9 of the 213 cases in this category were determined in less than 5 months, but in an additional 42 cases, the time lag was more than 5 months but less than 6 months.

Under the 1957 amendments, determination of disability can be made in less than six months with the consent of the employer or insurance carrier. Consent judgment cases are not in the same category as direct settlements, but such cases are closed with the consent of the parties. If the carrier's representative feels that the time for determination is not yet at hand, he can delay matters further by insisting on a full trial. Of course, the nature of the settlement available at the time may argue against further delay.

Future Directions

In the State of New Jersey the evaluation of permanent partial disabilities presents problems of many different kinds. There is vocal opposition to present methods of evaluating disability; and granted that complete consensus among the parties-at-interest is not possible, there must be some fundamental agreement, lest the program be constantly subject to controversies and fail to meet community approval. Also the differences among counties of the state must be considered. Although people may not be able to agree on who should be given a permanent partial award, it is certain that no one would contend that the accident of geographical location should be a relevant factor.

A system of evaluating the extent of disability according to an employee's wage loss has much to commend it. There is no need under such a system to evaluate the extent of physical disability or to distinguish among permanent total, permanent partial, and temporary disabilities. A disabled person would receive a percentage of his wages during the period in which he was unable to work because of his disability. Once he returned to work at his pre-injury earnings or at a greater figure, he would no longer receive any benefits. If he could find employment but only at a lesser wage, he would receive a benefit equivalent to a percentage of the difference between his pre-injury and post-injury earnings.

Such a system would have the advantage of providing a seemingly definite basis for the making of awards, since it would not be necessary to make fine rating distinctions based upon the employee's physical condition. The always difficult problem of determining whether the employee's injury arose out of his employment would be a bit easier to solve if the employee were not eligible for benefits if he lost no wages.

But there are also difficulties under such a system. How long should a case remain open? Some would say that a case should stay open and the worker remain eligible for potential benefit payments during the entire compensable period. Thus if the maximum number of weeks were, say 550, a man would be eligible for 550 weeks of full or partial payments if he could show some wage loss during that number of weeks. These would not necessarily be consecutive weeks; a man may be employed and then lose his job because of his disability. Conceivably, his case could remain open for as long as he lived. (Under the act covering federal employees, wage-loss concepts are emphasized, and there is no limitation on the number of weeks or total amount of benefits that a person may draw for total disability.) Whether or not a maximum number of weeks were set, such a system would pose all the administrative problems involved when cases remain potentially active for long periods of time. This would bring pressures for lump-sum settlements to close out cases just to be rid of future liabilities. The basic theory of a compensation system that is supposed to pay benefits in the same manner as wages would be defeated if such a practice became widespread.[31]

The most enthusiastic advocates of one form or another of the wage-loss theory would not eliminate the schedule awards for loss of a specific part of the body.[32] A person who lost an arm in an industrial accident would receive the appropriate schedule award, regardless of wage loss, whereas the person who suffered a comparably grave disability not listed on the schedule would not receive any permanent disability award if he returned to his job at his pre-injury rate of earnings. This leads to anamolous results which are difficult to explain to workers on the grounds that the schedule award is based upon presumed wage loss, whereas the other award is based upon actual wage-loss. As a result, some tests of loss of wage-earning capacity inevitably creep into the wage-loss concepts. The administrators attempt to compare the claimant's actual post-injury earnings with what he would have earned had his injury not occurred, taking into account the appropriate discount factors. Or, as advocated by employers in New Jersey, if the employee experiences no actual loss of wages, this creates a presumption against payment of benefits, but this presumption can be overcome by the worker. The former test of comparing earnings sacrifices some of the element of certainty, whereas the latter test may create inequities.

The other side of the coin is that the person with the nonscheduled injury may receive much more than the person with a scheduled injury who may actually have experienced a greater wage loss. However, this

---

[31]S. Bruce Black, "The Anomolies of Workmen's Compensation," *Industrial and Labor Relations Review*, VII (October, 1953), 45.

[32]James L. Hill, whose viewpoints on the wage-loss theory have been set forth above, reluctantly admits that although in his opinion the schedules do fit into the workmen's compensation system as he sees it, he would leave the schedules in the law but reduce them to a minimal basis. See *Workmen's Compensation Problems*, IAIABC *Proceedings*, 1956, pp. 85-86.

can be resolved by regarding the schedule awards as minimal; further payments could be made if a continuing wage loss can be demonstrated.

The wage-loss tests also require the administrators to determine, even after the employment connection of the original accident is admitted, whether continuing unemployment is due to the disability or to a host of other causes. This cannot be a self-administering system, especially in times of less than full employment. Experience with the administration of the unemployment compensation system testifies to the difficulty of determining an employee's genuine attachment to the labor force.

If these are some of the strong and weak points of a system that would stress wage loss, what are the advantages and disadvantages of the New Jersey system which concentrates on evaluating the physical disability as such? The advantages of one system are the disadvantages of the other. Once a case is closed in New Jersey, it remains closed, unless and until there is some change in the disability, and even this must be brought to notice before the statute of limitations has tolled. It is possible to estimate incurred liability with a great degree of accuracy, to the advantage of insurance carriers and employers. The pressures for granting lump-sum payments are lessened.[33] Also, there is at least a superficial consistency between the scheduled and nonscheduled awards. The nonscheduled awards are based upon some percentage of 550 weeks, and this is related to the lesser numbers of weeks specified for the various parts of the body listed.

Under New Jersey's system there is no necessity to test attachment to the labor market or to measure loss of wages or changes in wage-earning capacity, and these are advantages; but there are also disadvantages. One of these is the almost inevitable tendency to broaden the types of disability which become compensable. It is exceedingly difficult to determine the cause of an injury under any system; but in the absence of an automatic eliminating factor which would bar awards if the claimant could not show wage loss or loss of wage-earning capacity, hosts of minor cases based upon subjective complaints come to the fore. Some of these, and probably the majority, will be genuine disabilities which arose out of and in the course of employment. Some few will be brought by outright malingerers who would probably learn to beat almost any system devised; but there is also another category. These are cases of claimants who may, for example, be experiencing genuine pain from a low-back injury, the origin of which is totally obscure. A physician, in response to a hypothetical question from the worker's counsel, will concede that such an injury could result from the man's employment. Such proof of causal relationship may be sufficient and may be all that is obtainable. The physician testifying

---

[33]In contrast with states which operate on a theory which emphasizes wage-earning capacity tests, New Jersey has been able to keep these payments within bounds. During calendar year 1956, only 203 petitions for commutation were received by the division; and of these, 30 were approved and 173 disapproved. See New Jersey Division of Workmen's Compensation, *Annual Report*, 1956, p. 7.

for the carrier may dispute this, and then it is up to the deputy to make the determination and resolve the issue. Since this is a matter of conflicting opinions, the courts will regard it ordinarily as being in the factual field and will not disturb the deputy's finding if it is supported by the necessary amount of evidence. The whole compensation tradition argues for a liberal interpretation of the law in favor of the claimant; and since no wage-loss tests are necessary, the feeling seems to be that if the man suffered an injury, he is entitled to something.

The lack of objective standards in the evaluation of disabilities results in more and more cases being litigated. Either because the standards are so flexible or because the insurance carriers are so niggardly in their settlements, some petitioners' attorneys boast that they can take any case in which there has been a direct settlement, either before or after an informal hearing, reopen it, and get an increased permanent partial award for the petitioner. There is nothing in the statistical picture to indicate that they are exaggerating very much. Whatever the reasons for this, it is indicative of how much the element of certainty of benefits has been eliminated from these determinations.

Because of this lack of certainty, moreover, some persons who are aware of the possibilities take advantage of them and collect awards. Others, who may be in much the same physical condition may never be aware of the possibilities. They may not be convinced that they are "disabled," and, consequently, they may never file for benefits; or if they file, they may fail to litigate. The difference in levels of sophistication about these matters in various parts of the state may account for the differences in the county patterns.

Continuation of present trends carries with it the danger that employer discontent with the program may result in drastic legislative remedies of the buckshot variety. Mere postponement of the determination of permanent partial disability for six months is no grand solution, although it is indicative of legislative distrust of the administrators' judgment. It may not be equitable to move to a strict wage-loss theory, and attempting to evaluate loss in wage-earning capacity seems to be as difficult as evaluating physical disability under the present system. Yet some reforms are necessary if the compensation system is to be preserved in its present form.

The prime objective of any reforms should be to restore a modicum of certainty to the determination of permanent partial awards to prevent excessive litigation. Also, a way must be found to prevent persons with obviously minor disabilities from collecting such a large proportion of the compensation dollar. The system of adversary proceedings may be much better suited to disputes over the causal relationships between employment and the disability than it is to the technical evaluation of the nature and extent of the disability itself.

It is encouraging that deputies may use impartial physicians to aid them in making these disability determinations. Perhaps the idea of a panel of physicians ought not to be summarily dismissed, but such changes do not go to the heart of the problem. There is a method used by the deputies to evaluate the percentage of disability, and if it were more widely publicized, evaluations could be made by the parties without resort to litigation. Call this scheduling of disabilities not now listed or call it what you will. Unfortunately, too many people react to labels rather than ideas. A number of prominent physicians have expressed the opinion that it is feasible to draw up schedules on impairment of physical and mental function, that would encompass many of the present disabilities not presently scheduled. Such schedules should not be drawn up by the legislature, for they should be changed as medical science progresses and as understanding of the disability produced by various injuries changes. But the schedules could be drawn up in accordance with legislative mandates and limitations, and the results could be subject to review.

As will be discussed in the next chapter, any system that encouraged direct settlements would have to be closely supervised by the compensation division. It is not enough to have only physicians participate in this process of drawing the schedules. Disability, as the term is used in workmen's compensation, is inevitably a blend of medical incapacity and inability to function in the labor market. The talents of employment and labor market technicians should be utilized to help determine the amounts of indemnity payments in particular cases.

Some of the important problems involved in evaluating permanent partial disabilities will be looked at again when the heart cases and radiation hazards are examined in Chapter 10. It is obvious, however, that some reforms are necessary. Unless something is done to improve the handling of permanent partial disabilities, it is likely that it will be impossible to achieve the consensus necessary to solve other problems, such as the inadequate level of benefit rates.

Chapter 5

ADMINISTRATION OF WORKMEN'S COMPENSATION CLAIMS

It is obvious that a law is only as good as its administration, and it is just as obvious that good administrators can be hobbled by a poor law. It is exceedingly difficult to compare laws among the several jurisdictions, but it is even more difficult to compare the quality of administrations or even to evaluate the administration of one law. One is forced to look at the dry administrative provisions, the rules and regulations, the methods followed in processing cases, and to slight the rich human element that influences all of these. Strong-spirited personalities can do much in the administration of a law encumbered with obsolete provisions, whereas flaccid administrators can do little with the best of statutes. The student of social insurance does not have the license of a novelist to describe his offhand impressions, although these cannot always be avoided; he must attempt to analyze and describe, always recognizing that some important variables are missing.

An attempt to formulate the objectives of administration leads promptly and surely to questions of the basic purposes of a compensation act. Kossoris claims that the primary purposes are to assure the injured workmen prompt benefit payments, adequate and competent medical services and prompt and adequate rehabilitation and to work for accident prevention. Consequently he believes that "the primary objective of administration is to make sure that the law is observed and that an injured worker gets everything to which the law entitles him."[1] Given this objective, the conclusion must be that the administrative agency has the positive duty to follow through on claims and to supervise them. The administrators cannot operate on the assumption that it is the responsibility of the injured person to look after his own rights, thus leaving the primary administrative function as one of adjudicating contested claims.

The Somerses agree that the primary objective should be to see that the law is enforced, but they go on to say that it is the administrators' function to see that the parties know their rights and obtain them. In other words, the administrators have positive duties not only to adjudicate contested claims or administratively recognize resolved claims but also to ascertain that rights and obligations are actually met. In the Somerses' view, this implies disseminating information about the law, enforcing coverage and insurance requirements, supervising claims settlements, hearing contested claims, supervising

---

[1]Max D. Kossoris, "An Appraisal," in *Workmen's Compensation in the United States* (United States Department of Labor, Bureau of Labor Statistics, Bulletin No. 1149, 1954), p. 3.

96

medical and rehabilitation provisions, promoting safety and industrial hygiene and collecting and analyzing data on accidents, claims, settlements and benefit payments.[2]

Social and economic conditions have, of course, changed since compensation laws were first introduced, and the administrator may no longer have to act in paternalistic fashion to protect the interests of workers; still he has the active obligation to see that the law's provisions are known, to check on their observance even in noncontested situations and to gather and analyze the information so that both he and the community can evaluate the performance of the program. The parties are entitled to prompt disposition of claims, and the public must be assured of the efficient workings of administrative procedures at the minimum costs consistent with performance objectives.

The Administrative Structure

Administrative structures among the jurisdictions vary. Some states still retain court administration; in others, administration is in the hands of a single director or of a commission located in one of the state departments or set up as an independent agency. In New Jersey, primary administrative responsibilities are centered in the Division of Workmen's Compensation of the State Department of Labor and Industry. The chairman of the division is the Commissioner of the Department of Labor and Industry, but the actual administration of the division is in the hands of a director, who acts subject to the supervision and direction of the Commissioner.[3]

New Jersey's single director supervises the work of the administrative and clerical personnel and has the responsibility of assigning cases to hearing officers. The director may be able, by reason of his personality and position, to influence the hearing officers, but he has no authority to reverse any of their rulings. The hearing officers enjoy the protections of civil service status. The director may also have such protection if he has tenure as a deputy director; but as director, he is appointed by the Governor with the advice and consent of the Senate and serves during the term of office of the Governor appointing him, and until his successor is appointed and qualified.[4]

The central office of the division is located in Trenton. Here the

---

[2] Herman M. Somers and Anne R. Somers, *Workmen's Compensation: Prevention, Insurance and Rehabilitation of Occupational Disability* (N. Y.: John Wiley and Sons, 1954), p. 143.

[3] The director may also serve as a deputy director of compensation and hear cases. The law requires him to be an attorney-at-law of the State of New Jersey, a requirement which also pertains to each of the deputies and the formal referees with the exception of those referees who had occupied that position for five years prior to the introduction of this rule in 1952. (N.J. Stat. Ann. [West, 1958], 34:1A-12.1, 12.2.)

[4] N.J. Stat. Ann., 34:1A-12. This section of the statutes also spells out the duties of the director, including the fact that he is also to serve as secretary of the division. The secretary has various legal responsibilities, including the docketing of cases and certification of transcripts.

employers' and insurance carriers' reports are processed, and the paperwork connected with the direct settlement or agreement cases is handled by clerical personnel. All petitions for formal compensation hearings are filed initially in the Trenton office, where they are docketed, and sent eventually to the appropriate regional hearing center.

The administrative work involved in the handling of informal hearings is done largely at the hearing centers by clerical personnel. The cases are heard by referees, who are assisted by the staff of the medical department. This department is headed by a medical director, a full-time employee of the Department of Labor and Industry, who has the duty of providing general guidance on medical matters and also assists in the work of the Rehabilitation Commission. On his staff are the state medical examiners who do the examining work in informal cases.

The Commissioner, the director, the deputies and certain key personnel meet monthly as the Workmen's Compensation Board. At these meetings common problems are discussed and reports are received from committees on outstanding issues.[5] Some time during these meetings is usually devoted to educational symposiums concerned

---

[5]The scope of the administrative activities of the New Jersey Division of Workmen's Compensation is suggested by a listing of the committees in existence as of September, 1956. Not all of these committees reported to the Workmen's Compensation Board.

Committee	Duties
1) Administrative	To consider whatever matter is referred to them by the Commissioner.
2) Appeals	To consider changes in appeals procedures.
3) Apportionment of fees	To consider matters related to apportionment of counsel fees between the parties.
4) Adjournments	A special committee to consider problems arising out of rules for adjournment of cases.
5) Max Weiner articles	To consider issues raised by this series of articles in The Newark News.
6) Conflicts of Interests	To study and report on outside employment of state employees. This was a department-wide committee.
7) Disputed medical bills	To study and report on data concerning disputed medical bills and complaints concerning doctors' charges.
8) Informal hearings	To study generally the problem of adequate reports at the informal level and to study questions of state doctors' estimates.
9) Legislative	To study and make recommendations on proposed legislation.
10) Medical	To confer with medical societies on matters of common interest.
11) Medical fees	To report on a schedule of fees for medical testimony and reports.
12) One Per Cent Fund	To suggest forms and procedures in these cases.
13) Chemical and radiation poisonings	To study problems arising from occupational diseases from these sources.
14) Rehabilitation	To study problems in area of coordination of rehabilitation referrals and services.
15) Rules	To make recommendations on rules.
16) Statistical and research	To make recommendations in this area.

with developments in the field of medicine or compensation generally. The board promulgates the rules and regulations governing administrative procedures.[6]

The Division of Workmen's Compensation does not have sole responsibility for all matters within the scope of the objectives of workmen's compensation administration as outlined above. Responsibility for accident prevention and safety work lies primarily with another section of the Department of Labor and Industry, the Bureau of Engineering and Safety. Rehabilitation of injured workers is a responsibility the division shares with the Rehabilitation Commission. Problems of liaison, difficult as they are, are eased somewhat, since the Rehabilitation Commission is also a division of the Department of Labor and Industry. Although the Division of Workmen's Compensation has a statistical section which compiles reports, it has no independent research facilities and must depend upon its operating personnel or persons from the Bureau of Statistics and Records of the Department of Labor and Industry for analytical help. Lastly, it might be noted that although the division has many lawyers on its staff, it does not have its own counsel. Prosecution of employers for failure to carry insurance, or any other such legal work, is a responsibility of the Attorney General's Office. This is in accordance with the administrative patterns established in the state government in 1948, when all such legal work was centralized in one agency.[7]

Administering Noncontested Cases

In New Jersey, which has no state insurance fund, compensation benefits are paid either by the employer or by the insurance carrier. Consequently, the division neither processes nor pays claims; its task is to supervise these payments, to see to it that adequate payments are made promptly and in accordance with the rights of the parties.

Not all jurisdictions use the same method of administering payments in noncontested cases. At least three different methods can be distinguished, although combinations of these methods are possible.[8] One is the so-called "direct payment" method identified with the State

---

[6] N.J. Stat. Ann., 34:15-64, authorizes the Commissioner, director and deputy directors to make rules and regulations for the conduct of hearings not inconsistent with the provisions of the statute. N.J. Stat. Ann., 34:15-102, authorizes the division to make rules and regulations, as are necessary for the purpose of carrying out that section of the statutes which requires reports from employers and insurance carriers.

[7] Under this same reorganization plan, Chapter 446 of the New Jersey Laws of 1948 established the Department of Labor and Industry as a principal department in the executive branch. The then existing Bureau of Workmen's Compensation was made a division of the department. These changes were effective as of January 1, 1949.

[8] The Somerses distinguish four methods of administration of noncontested cases. In addition to the three listed above, they include the "triple-form" method used in Ohio under which the injured worker fills out a long, detailed form, and then gets his doctor and employer to fill out similar forms. In their view, this system has worked poorly. (See Somers and Somers, *Workmen's Compensation*, pp. 153-154.)

of Wisconsin. The injured worker is not required to initiate action for payment; nor is he required to sign agreement forms or any other papers, except, perhaps, receipts for payments. Payments are supposed to be automatic and to begin promptly after the date of injury. The insurance carriers are required to file reports with the administrators showing the date and amount of benefit payments, or reasons why payments are not being made. Wisconsin's workmen's compensation commission operates on the theory that it has an obligation to inform the injured employee of his rights, and to see to it that he receives all compensation benefits that are due him with a minimum of legalistic procedures. If a dispute should arise about these benefits, the administrators make an attempt to resolve it up by a careful scrutiny of reports and the perusal of other information garnered either by correspondence or by informal conference. If it cannot be so settled, the case may then go over to the contested realm; a hearing will be held and a formal decision made.[9]

Another method of administering noncontested cases is the "hearing method" identified with New York State. Under this method, which would seem to afford maximum protection to the rights of injured workers, compensation payments may begin without the filing of a claim by the worker, but the case ordinarily will not be closed until after a hearing has been held or the parties have had the opportunity of refusing such a hearing. This requirement imposes a heavy administrative burden on the New York administrators, and various devices have been adopted to lighten the load. A "motion calendar unit" in the claims division disposes of a large number of cases in which the injury is minor and in which there is no controversy. Cases are listed on the motion calendar together with a notice advising the parties of the proposed disability findings and compensation award. The parties are advised that they need not appear on the date set for a hearing; and since the proposed award usually confirms the payments the carriers have already made, it is usually accepted by the carriers' representatives. If either party objects, in writing, or at the hearing, the case is placed upon the trial calendar. If there are no objections, the case is closed on the day set for the hearing, and a copy of the decision is sent to the claimant, advising him that what had been proposed has now been done. The referee, on his own motion, may decide that the matter is important enough to be placed upon the trial calendar; but since he handles over three hundred cases each day, he usually cannot give any one of them detailed consideration.[10]

---

[9] Marshall Dawson, *The Development of Workmen's Compensation Administration in the United States and Canada* (Washington, D. C.: International Association of Industrial Accident Boards and Commissions, 1951). Dawson's excellent report to the IAIABC contains a good description of the workings of the various types of administrative systems.

[10] For a description of New York's procedures and some recommendations for change, see the report of the Moreland Act Commissioner, Joseph M. Callahan, *Costs, Operations, and Procedures under the Workmen's Compensation Law of the State of New York* (N. Y.: January 28, 1957), pp. 35-36.

This is a rather cumbersome procedure and proposals have been made to streamline it further. It probably made more sense in an earlier day when protection of the interests of workers was of paramount concern. Also, as Dawson has pointed out, such a complex system could not work at all without administrative energy and ability of the highest order.[11]

The third system is the "agreement method," used in one form or another in the majority of states. Under this system, the employer offers the injured worker a settlement, which the worker either accepts or rejects. If accepted, an agreement form embodying the terms of the settlement is normally signed by the employee and then filed with the administrators. Payments may begin immediately or after what is usually a rather routine approval by the administrative body. If the proposed settlement is not accepted, then either party has the right to contest the case and seek a hearing, in accordance with the procedure in the particular jurisdiction. Dawson has this to say about the workings of the agreement system: "In theory, it has the advantage of giving the injured worker a chance to look over the proposed settlement and correct possible errors or injustice in computing the payment. In practice, the worker may not know his rights under the compensation law; neither is he in any position to bargain with the employer or insurance carrier; and consequently, it is open to question whether he should be required to sign an agreement before receiving the benefits specified in the statute. Investigations have shown that in the absence of vigilant supervision by the State agency, the agreement system affords little protection to the injured worker."[12]

In the eyes of some authorities in the field, the direct payment method used in Wisconsin is thought to be preferable to the other two, but it is difficult to determine whether the object of praise is the method per se or the sound and tight administration characteristic of Wisconsin. New York's hearing method is unique; but the substantive differences between the direct payment and the agreement methods seem to lie, not in whether the employee is asked to sign an agreement, but rather in the degree to which the state agency involves itself in supervising the promptness and the adequacy of the benefit payments.

Under the direct payment method, Wisconsin is concerned with publicizing the standards for awards, in checking on the over-all performance of insurance carriers, and in seeing to it that adequate payments are made in a particular case. The philosophy in some of the states that follow the agreement method, or if not the philosophy at least the practice, seems to be that if the parties have agreed upon a settlement, then it must be all right, unless, of course, it is obvious that some errors have been made.

---

[11] Dawson, *The Development of Workmen's Compensation Administration*, p. 17. For a more critical view of New York's administration, see Joseph S. Keiper, *Forces That Spiral Compensation Costs* (N. Y.: Commerce and Industry Association of New York, 1953).

[12] Marshall Dawson, *Problems of Workmen's Compensation Administration* (United States Department of Labor, Bureau of Labor Statistics, Bulletin 672, 1940), p. 120.

New Jersey's procedures can fairly be described as being within the "agreement" category, although an attempt has been made to eliminate purely routine checks of the agreements. Since 1956, the division has conducted, at least a spot-check review of the adequacy of settlement proffered by insurance carriers; and beginning in 1958, it introduced new accident reporting rules designed to give the division more information about a worker's injuries. Both changes were accomplished by administrative regulation, and without benefit of amendments to the statutes. Actually, the statutes do not spell out any agreement procedure, although repeated references are made to the "agreement to pay compensation" and to the reports required of employers and insurance carriers.[13]

Under the new rules, the employer is required to file a report (Form WC-1) for each accidental injury which causes the worker to lose time from his regular duties after the working day or shift on which the accident occurred, or which requires more than routine first-aid treatment. The report calls for comprehensive information about the accident and is designed to allow the state eventually to publish statistics which will be useful for safety programs.[14] Once it is known that the accidental injury has caused some permanent injury or a disability which requires the worker to be out of work for more than the seven-day waiting period, the insurance carrier or self-insured employer files a so-called "Initial Report of Accident" (Form WC-2). Within twenty-one days after the accident, another report is due: the "Statement of Wages and Agreement to Care for Case" (Form WC-2A). Both of these reports are fairly simple, calling for information about the employee, the date of accident and a history of developments subsequent to the filing of the original report.

Payments of at least the temporary disability benefits can begin, once the employee is out of work for more than seven days. At the close of the temporary disability period, or when the extent of any permanent injury is determined, whichever point in time is later, the "Final Report of Accident" (Form WC-3) is due. This embodies the "agreement to pay compensation," or, as the division refers to it, the "direct settlement." The first sections of this form are carbon copies of information on the two preceding forms, whereas the later sections call for medical information about the disability and a statement of the type and amounts of compensation benefits paid, or to be paid, the

---

[13] N.J. Stat. Ann., 34:15-22, 27, 39, 50, 51, 96-102.

[14] See "Notice" filed in office of the Secretary of State on July 25, 1958, by the Commissioner of the Department of Labor and Industry as a supplement to the rules and regulations of the department and the Division of Workmen's Compensation. The new reporting rules were effective as of October 1, 1958. The onset of an occupational disease also requires the filing of the report regardless of whether or not any working time is lost.

Information from these new forms should serve to fill out the accident information picture in the state. The old reporting forms were deficient in many respects. They failed to distinguish between the accident, that is, the circumstances which caused the injury, and the injury itself. They failed to define the term "accident," and hence employers were never sure just when the reports should be filed.

employee. A copy of the direct settlement form is given to the employee, although his copy omits detailed information about the physician's diagnosis and X-ray findings.

Under the old procedures, the employee was supposed to sign these forms. If he refused to sign, they were to be filed anyway with a notation to that effect; and the lack of signature did not stop the payment of benefits. The new forms do not call for the employee's signature.

Also, under the former method of processing these forms, the division would check the direct settlements only for the arithmetical correctness of the computations, proper signatures, and so on. If nothing untoward was found, the division "approved" the settlement and so notified the employee. At the same time, he was told that the settlement was not final, that he had the right to reopen his claim, and to proceed to an informal hearing or file a formal petition.

The employee's copy of the new direct settlement form does not indicate quite so clearly as before that the terms of the settlement have been approved by the division. He is advised that this form shows the history of his case as reported by the insurance carrier and the terms upon which the carrier has settled the matter. Addresses of offices of the division at which he may receive further information are listed on the reverse side of the form, and he is told that he may reopen the claim if his condition worsens or if payments are not made as shown on the form.

The detailed medical information called for on the new forms allows the division to review each case to determine if the settlement is adequate. But even when the old forms, which called for less medical information, were in use, the division began to replace its formerly cursory review with a more detailed examination. From January to June, 1958, referees reviewed 2,778 reports of direct settlements. Since approximately 30,000 of these direct settlements are filed each year, this constitutes only a fraction of all such cases.

Only 37 per cent of the direct settlements reviewed were found to be adequate on their face; 63 per cent, or 1,767 cases, were selected for further examination. The procedure adopted was to set these suspect cases down for an informal hearing. In 664 cases, additional cash payments were made to the petitioner after the hearing; and in 85 of the cases, the hearing produced evidence to indicate that the payments were adequate. Four hundred and fifty-four cases were still pending as of the time of the report. In 315 cases, the employee did not appear for the hearing or advised the division that he did not wish a hearing. In the remaining cases, the employee had already taken his case to a higher level, or he was advised by the division to file a formal petition.[15]

The division claims that the total additional cash obtained for the injured workers was seven times the amount originally paid on direct

---

[15] New Jersey Division of Workmen's Compensation, "Report of Review and Survey of Direct Settlements," consolidated semiannual report, January to June 30, 1958.

settlements. It is not known how many of these direct settlements would eventually have found their way to the contested stages, but the sheer number of cases and the amounts of additional payments made after an informal hearing are indicative of the shortcomings of the direct settlement or agreement procedures. In part, these stem from the lack of certainty surrounding the evaluation of permanent partial disabilities. (There is usually little quarrel over the number of weeks of temporary disability benefits in these cases.) In part also, they are the result of years of neglect of and in attention to what should probably be the most important stage of the whole compensation proceedings.

Informal Hearings

The compensation statutes do not specifically authorize informal hearings; and nowhere in the law are the provisions for any informal hearings spelled out.[16] However, the division, since 1914, has had one system or another of informal hearings. As a matter of fact, the practice of having referees informally settle compensation claims antedates the system of formal hearings, which was not authorized until 1918.

Whatever their defects, and many have been alleged from time to time, the informal hearings have always had the virtue of being truly informal and accompanied by a minimum of technical procedures. The division itself may send a case to a referee for an informal hearing, but more usually the injured employee or the insurance carrier requests such a hearing, either before or after an agreement has been reached in a case. The informal hearing must take place within the time period set forth in the statute of limitations, and before a formal claim petition is filed.

Informal referees sit in various locations throughout the state and are served by assignment bureaus located in Camden, Trenton, Newark, Jersey City, Paterson and Hackensack. A claimant may appear in person at one of these bureaus or apply in writing for a hearing. In either event he is asked to complete a rather simple form which asks for the minimum of pertinent information about the date of accident, the name of the insurance carrier and employer, and so on. Possibly 2,000 such applications are received each month in the state as a whole. Each of the major insurance carriers usually has a particular day set aside for hearing its cases, and ordinarily an applicant can secure a hearing within two to four weeks of the date of his application.

A number of applicants usually appear for their hearings at the same time. The referee interviews them individually in the hearing room and then refers them to the state medical examiner, who sees them in the examining rooms which adjoin the hearing room. The

---

[16] However, N.J. Stat. Ann., 34:15-50, obligates the division to do what it can to bring about a settlement of a pending claim.

medical examiner, after diagnosis of the case and perusal of the medical records, records his findings and his estimate of the percentage of permanent disability for use by the referee. According to the rules, the claimant or the employer is to present to the doctor, on demand of the referee, the reports of the attending physician or physicians, including X-rays, reports of X-rays and laboratory tests.[17]

If no specialist's examination is required, the claimant, after examination, returns to the hearing room to wait for his case to be called. When his turn comes, he appears before the referee together with a representative of his employer or the insurance carrier. The claimant may or may not be represented by an attorney. Based upon the evidence and discussion with the parties, the referee will recommend a particular settlement. In most cases, the discussion and recommendation will be concerned with the percentage of permanent partial disability.

The referee's recommendation need not be accepted by either side. According to the rules, if this decision cannot be made on the day of the hearing, the employer is supposed to notify the referee, within two weeks, of his acceptance or rejection of the recommendation. It is difficult, however, to check up on whether this is followed, since if the employer accepts, he would then simply file the necessary agreement or direct settlement forms.

If the employer either denies liability or refuses to accept the recommendation, the referee is obliged to inform the claimant of his right "to consult an attorney at once for the protection of his rights and further to state that said attorney is not permitted to demand a fee in advance."[18]

As noted above, the claimant may have the advice and services of an attorney at the informal hearing, and he may also submit reports of private medical and X-ray examinations in order to strengthen the presentation of his side of the case to the referee. The referee may allow counsel fees and fees for these examinations and X-rays. The rules speak of these fees as being based upon standard considerations of reasonableness, and also state that in allowing these fees, the hearing officer is supposed to keep in mind "the purpose and function of informal hearings and the policy of the Division of Workmen's Compensation to provide a prompt remedy to claimants without undue expense and hardship."[19] In practice, the maximum fees allowed counsel, in the usual case, do not exceed 10 per cent of the compensation benefits. In contrast, a statutory maximum of 20 per cent is allowable in formal proceedings. Moreover, at the formal level, the fees are apportioned between the parties, whereas at the informal level, they are assessed only against the claimant.

---

[17]New Jersey Division of Workmen's Compensation, "Rules Adopted in Pursuance and by Virtue of Revised Statutes of New Jersey; Title 34, Chapter 15, Section 64" (filed in Office of Secretary of State on October 11, 1954), Section I, rule 3.

[18]New Jersey Division of Workmen's Compensation, "Rules," Section I, rule 6 (1954).

[19]New Jersey Division of Workmen's Compensation, "Rules," Section I, rule 8 (1954).

Complaints by one side or the other about some aspect of the informal hearing procedure have been made since at least 1928. Complaints made during the earlier years will be discussed in the next chapter, and discussion here will be confined to recent proposals for statutory changes.

The employers, in 1956, protested against what they termed an "unsatisfactory, overly legalistic system for processing and determining claims resulting in time-consuming and costly procedures of paying compensation and final award."[20]   The suggested remedy was for a system of informal hearings in the nature of arbitration proceedings to reduce the number of formal petitions. The referee would be obligated, under these proposals, to prepare a memorandum of the proceedings of the informal hearing, including a history of the accident or disease as related by the claimant. (This would put the employee's case on the record.) Attached to this memorandum would be the findings of the state medical examiner. A copy of the memorandum would be supplied to either party upon request, and could be offered in any subsequent formal proceedings with agreement of the parties. If such agreement was not forthcoming, then either party could subpoena the referee, or the state doctor, or both, to testify at a formal hearing.

Although the referee's recommendation would not be absolutely binding, it would be given a degree of finality if accepted by both sides. In that event, the referee's recommendation would be binding at any subsequent proceedings only with respect to the degree or amount of permanent disability, unless it were established that the disability of the employee had subsequently increased or decreased.

If the employee retained counsel at the informal hearing, the referee could award a counsel fee not to exceed 10 per cent of the difference between the amount of benefits recommended and the amount already paid or offered by the employer. In certain "minor" cases wherein the claimant does not avail himself of the informal hearing procedures, it was proposed that the counsel fees at the formal level be limited to 5 per cent of the difference between the amount awarded at the formal level and the amount offered or already paid.[21]

Labor groups objected vehemently to these suggestions, both to the principles involved and to the methods suggested to implement these principles. "Apparently what the employers abhor is observation or supervision by third or independent parties in their dealings with employees who have been maimed or disabled by industrial accident."[22]

---

[20]*Summary of Employer Proposals to Improve the New Jersey Workmen's Compensation Program* (undated printed material submitted by the New Jersey State Chamber of Commerce, New Jersey Manufacturers Association and New Jersey Self-Insurers at time of legislative consideration of amendments effective January 1, 1957). This was accompanied by a draft bill incorporating suggested revisions in the compensation statutes.

[21] Somewhat these same recommendations were made in the New Jersey Legislature, *Report of the Commission to Study Laws Affecting Industrial Development* (Trenton: June, 1957), p. 42.

[22] "Memorandum of New Jersey State CIO Council Regarding Employer Proposals for Modification of the Workmen's Compensation Act" (undated, mim.), pp. 14-15.

After quoting the statistics showing the number of cases closed by direct settlement or after informal hearings, the CIO Council stated, "We think there are too many and not too few direct settlements, and that the legislative purpose and policy as expressed in the existing act would be better served by broader supervision."

The proposal for giving the referee's recommendation a degree of finality was objected to by the council on the grounds that this would tend to convert the informal proceedings in to formal proceedings but without the benefit of the protection a worker has in a formal case. "Above all, the employers don't want lawyers around when they discuss workmen's compensation with their employees. The lawyer is the petitioner's technical expert." It was pointed out that the employer or insurance carrier has expert adjusters or other representatives present at each stage of the proceedings, whereas the employee may appear alone. "The employer comments would create the impression that these 'voluntary' settlements are arrived at in a simple informal discussion between two laymen representing divergent interests, but nevertheless equally inexpert. It just isn't so."

The referees went on record as being opposed to the employers' proposals on the grounds that the informal hearings are settlement discussions and that it would be undesirable to handicap these discussions by using what is said or done as an admission against interest at a later formal hearing. The thought was that this would interfere with the chances of settlement and would result in fewer cases being closed out at the informal level. Objections were raised to the idea of having referees testify at formal hearings on the grounds that this would not be practical in light of the heavy hearing schedules of these officials. Also, there was opposition to the idea of giving the recommendations the degree of finality envisaged by the employers, on the grounds that the carriers have the benefit of representation at these hearings, whereas the claimant often comes alone. The fear was expressed that this might lead to the evil of having recommendations accepted only when the recommended award was on the conservative side.

The referees, however were in favor of the idea of giving the informal hearings statutory recognition. They also agreed that minor cases involving hands, feet, fingers and toes should go through the informal hearing procedure before any formal hearing, with the proviso that the referee be given authority to apportion the claimant's counsel fee between the parties.[23]

The respective positions of the parties at the time the 1957 amendments were being considered represent as good an example as any of the conflict over the theory and practice of the informal hearings. Both sides see the informal hearings as a type of a mediation process. The employers are anxious that it be continued as such, but at the same

---

[23] New Jersey Division of Workmen's Compensation, "Minutes of Regular Meeting of the Referees," June 16, 1957.

time, they want to pin down the position of the claimant for possible later examination at the formal level. As the referees correctly point out, there is something inconsistent in seeking the advantages of the informal settlement and yet, at the same time, wanting to use the parties' negotiating positions as admissions against interest in later proceedings.

On the other hand, the representatives of the employees argue that although this is a mediation process, it is not between equal parties since the claimant may not be represented by his expert, the claimant's lawyer. In their view, this can be tolerated only because the mediator is without power to make binding decisions. They oppose any efforts in the direction of giving him such powers unless the claimant is put on equal footing with the employer, and the argument is that this cannot be done until provision is made for adequate counsel fees apportioned between the parties.

Formal Hearings

An employee, at any time between the date of his accident and the expiration of the statute of limitations, can petition for a formal hearing. This can be done before the insurance carrier offers a direct settlement, or after the direct settlement has been approved by the division and the employee is already receiving benefits.[24] The law does not require that an informal hearing be held before formal proceedings are instituted.

It may seem illogical for a worker to seek out a lawyer and file a formal petition before any attempt has been made to settle his case on a voluntary basis, but this does happen. The worker may feel that he will not be treated fairly by the insurance adjuster, or he may simply not be aware of the procedures for direct settlement. If a lawyer refuses the worker's case and advises him that he should first attempt to settle, the lawyer runs the risk that the worker will merely seek counsel elsewhere. The lawyer can receive no fee in advance, for he is compensated only on the basis of a percentage of the amounts that the worker receives at the formal hearing, over and above that which is "offered, tendered in good faith or paid" to the worker at a reasonable time prior to the hearing.[25]

At any rate, there is nothing in the law which prevents the filing of the formal petition at any time within the statute of limitations, and once this is done, the character of the efforts to settle the case changes. Now the insurance adjuster is bound to work through a lawyer rather than deal with the client directly; and, more important, whatever

---

[24] N.J. Stat. Ann., 34:15-34. An approval of an agreement for workmen's compensation is not a determination on the merits. It does not have the force of a judgment binding parties. An agreement that is not approved by a deputy in open court does not operate as a bar to formal determination of any controversy. *Ferraro* v. *Zucker*, 12 N.J. Super. 231.

[25] N.J. Stat. Ann., 34:15-64.

efforts the division may be making to bring about a settlement will be stopped.

The formal petition form is a rather simple one on which the employee states that he sustained an injury which is alleged to be compensable under the act. The petition calls for basic data about the parties, the accidental injury and the employee's contentions. Once it is docketed and clerically processed in the Trenton office, a copy of the petition is served upon the employer or insurance carrier. The respondent has ten days in which to send in his answer, which, according to the law, should admit or deny the substantial averments of the petition and state his contentions with reference to the matters in dispute as disclosed by the petition. A copy of the answer is sent to the petitioner's attorney, and the case is then assigned to the appropriate regional hearing center. In some centers, the parties will be called in for a pre-trial conference before a formal hearing is scheduled. Pretrials may be assigned to deputies but are usually handled by formal referees. Each major insurance carrier has a specified day in which its pre-trial list is heard.

The rules provide that there shall be full exchange of all medical reports, including X-rays and medical findings, and that if such information is not exchanged, it may be excluded at the formal hearing at the discretion of the deputy. To assure the elimination of the element of surprise, the attorney for each side is required within ten days of service of written demand to furnish his adversary "the complete medical findings and diagnosis, including X-ray and other laboratory data, but not including the history and estimate of disability or recommendation for reserve." [26]

The fact that such information may not be available until the pre-trial conference gives some clue as to why cases can be settled at this level, but not earlier. It also raises some questions about why all of this information is not forthcoming earlier; why it is not in the possession of the division and used to bring about a prompt settlement of the case. The questions are rhetorical and are asked merely to emphasize that the formal petition produces more information than may have been available to the division before, although provision for exchange of information is also made at the informal level.

If, after the pre-trial conference, the parties are able to agree upon the essential issues, including the quantum of disability, the case may be closed by a formal settlement, which is approved by the formal referee or deputy director; or evidence may be heard, a record taken and a consent judgment entered. As noted in the discussion of permanent partial disabilities, some cases which go through all the forms of a contested adversary proceeding are actually cases in which both parties have agreed on the extent of disability and the amount to be awarded, but one side or the other wants to complete a formal record.

---

[26] New Jersey Division of Workmen's Compensation, "Rules," Section II, rule 7-A (1956).

Only a small fraction of the cases at the formal level actually involve genuine adversary proceedings.

Reasons for preferring the formal record may be multiple, including the desire to protect counsel and witness fees and also the finality of the award. Agreements to pay compensation may be reopened at any time within the statute of limitations, whereas final awards can be reopened only if there is some showing that the extent of the disability has increased or decreased.

Clogged calendars are a perennial problem in the compensation courts; and if the parties seek adjournments or appear at the pre-trial proceedings unprepared, this aggravates matters. One method of control is through the assessment of counsel fees. If a case has been set down for pre-trial on two successive listings and has not been moved for failure of the respondent to have medical examinations or reports available, according to the rules, the case is placed upon the trial list. If a formal award is made, the deputy is instructed to assess the entire counsel fee against the respondent. The rule is not to apply if failure to have the medical examination is due to the petitioner's neglect or refusal, in which event the case is to be marked "not moved."[27]

If the case is not closed in one fashion or another after pre-trial conference, the results of the conference are noted in the file, together with an estimate of the time needed for trial, number of witnesses, and so on; and the case is set down on the trial list of a deputy director. The nature of these trials has been discussed in the chapter dealing with permanent partial disabilities, and the details will not be repeated here. Suffice it to say that they have all of the outward aspects of a trial in a court of law. A stenographic record is taken, although this is not necessarily transcribed unless ordered by either party. Witnesses are heard. In the usual case the main witnesses are the doctors for each side, who describe the nature of the disability, answer a hypothetical question as to causation and estimate the percentage of disability. In more complicated cases, other witnesses may testify. If an occupational disease issue is involved, the testimony of industrial hygienists and toxicologists may be heard. The decision of the deputy is made at the close of the hearing or, if reserved, is due within one month after the completion of the hearings or from date of filing of briefs, which are due within twenty days.

Over the years many complaints and investigations about the unethical conduct of lawyers and doctors in compensation proceedings have been made. Yet in a series of articles written in 1955, Max Weiner notes that allegations of ambulance chasing were still being

---

[27] New Jersey Division of Workmen's Compensation, "Rules," Section II, rule 7-C (1956). Rule 6 (1954), which sets forth the pre-trial procedure, provides: "For failure to appear at a pre-trial conference or to participate therein or to prepare therefor, the Deputy ... may make such order with respect to the imposition of costs and counsel fees and with respect to continued prosecution of the case as is just and proper."

made.[28] The Commissioner, under present rules, is authorized to investigate cases of misconduct or unlawful charges and, on notice to the attorney involved, conduct a hearing. If the Commissioner finds the complaint justified, the matter is referred to the Supreme Court or the Bar Association's Ethics Committee, or he may take such action as he deems necessary. The solicitation of cases or payments of referral fees to anyone not an attorney is forbidden; and there have been instances of suspension of attorneys from practice before the division for violation of these rules. [29]

The law limits the amounts of attorney's fees and prohibits lawyers from receiving a greater portion of the award than actually allowed by the hearing officer.[30] In the past, checks for accrued compensation benefits were sent directly to the petitioner's lawyer, who would distribute the sums involved. This is no longer done. Accrued compensation is paid directly to the petitioner, less any deductions allowed for medical and hospital expenses, attorney's fees and other items. The respondent employer or insurance carrier forwards checks for these allowances directly, as instructed by the deputy or referee.

State doctors and other employees of the division are forbidden to testify in any formal proceedings except in special circumstances. In the past, the conduct of the parties at the hearings has been subject to criticism, as has the general decorum in the hallways and anterooms surrounding the court rooms. Doctors at one time made a practice of examining clients in odd, out-of-the-way places adjacent to the hearing rooms. Doctors who are not state employees are forbidden to make examinations on premises where cases are heard except with special permission. Such rules might seem to be unnecessary and unworthy of the dignity of the professional persons involved. Sad to say, the rules have a solid basis in a past history of these complained-of activities.[31]

The administrators must work within the framework of the statute, and this constitutes a limiting factor in eliminating many of the road blocks in the way of a more prompt disposition of cases. To the credit of the administrators themselves must be listed two procedures designed to eliminate unnecessary testimony and hearings in formal cases.[32] The first of these has to do with medical testimony in cases

---

[28] Published in *The Newark News*, November 14 to 23, 1955. Reprinted as a pamphlet, *Workmen's Compensation in New Jersey*; see chapter 7, "The Ambulance Chasers." This should be read together with the series by the same writer published in January, 1957, and reprinted as a pamphlet entitled *Workmen's Compensation in New Jersey — A Postscript* (The Newark Evening News, February, 1957).

[29] New Jersey Division of Workmen's Compensation, "Rules," Section II, rules 21, 26 (1954).

[30] N.J. Stat. Ann., 34:15-64.

[31] New Jersey Division of Workmen's Compensation, "Rules," Section II, rules 22, 23, 24 (1954).

[32] Other rules of the New Jersey Division of Workmen's Compensation not mentioned in the text are designed to assure speedy disposition of formal cases. Carriers are admonished to have sufficient personnel on hand to dispose of the volume of scheduled cases (Section II, rule 10 [1954]). Once a trial is started, it is to proceed without interruption to its conclusion (Section II, rule 9 [1954]). Any case listed pre-emptorily, or within the first ten for hearing on a trial calendar, or set down for a hearing for the second time, in which the

at the formal level in which the amount of the award is agreed upon, but the settlement is affirmed in open hearing and is required to be supported by medical findings. In such cases, if the allowance for permanent disability does not exceed 2 per cent of "partial total," or its equivalent at the maximum rate, a declaration of administrative policy, effective February 15, 1956, states that the personal appearance of medical witnesses for either party is deemed unnecessary. Medical reports or stipulations are to be submitted in lieu of personal testimony by doctors. This not only speeds dispositions but also results in lower costs; smaller fees are allowed for reports without testimony than would be allowed if the physician made a personal appearance. The justification for personal appearances by doctors in any settlement case is not crystal clear, but again it must be remembered that these hearings have the form if not the actual content of adversary proceedings. If medical testimony were not allowed in any of these cases, fees would be reduced, and petitioners could argue that they would not be able to attract physicians with the necessary skills. This policy was adopted with the concurrence of the Workmen's Compensation Association, a group composed of representatives of all the interest groups concerned with workmen's compensation in the state.

The second procedure concerns minor cases which, it is felt, should be settled at some level below the formal hearing stage. The purist might argue that many of these cases ought to be settled at the noncontested agreement level, but the division has, at least, adopted a declaration of administrative policy to encourage their settlement at the informal hearing level. The method of control, if there has been no informal hearing, is through lowering counsel fees to a maximum of 5 per cent of the award in all formal cases involving fingers and toes, regardless of the amount of recovery, and in all cases involving the foot or hand in which the award is less than $425. This policy is supported by petitioners' attorneys and is undoubtedly of great help in eliminating these minor cases from the formal calendars. Nothing in the policy compels settlement, but it does assure that some attempts at settlement will have been made by the time the cases reach the formal level.[33]

Each of these rules and policies is illustrative of the attempt to lessen the work load at the formal level and to facilitate settlement between the parties at an earlier stage of the game. Whether they go to the heart of the administrative difficulties is another matter, but they are steps in the right direction.

---

petitioner does not appear, or which is not adjourned for good cause, is to be marked "not moved" and is not to be restored to the calendar except on motion. Another rule provides: "The counsel fee normally allowed shall be reduced 20 per cent for each time a case has been marked NOT MOVED." (Section II, rule 11 [1954]).

[33] New Jersey Division of Workmen's Compensation, Administrative Policy No. 3 (April, 1957).

Appeals

There is no appeals tribunal within the Division of Workmen's Compensation. If not satisfied with the judgment of the deputy director, either party may take his case to the county court by filing notice of appeal within forty-five days after the judgment has been rendered.[34] The party taking the appeal must file with the county court a certified copy of the transcript. Each side files briefs, which may be typewritten. The appeals are argued orally and are based exclusively on the transcript and testimony.[35] These trials are for the purpose of "providing a new mind for the consideration of the testimony adduced."[36] The appeal is concerned with the facts as well as the law, although the courts have held that the ambit of the hearing on appeal cannot be broadened to include issues not comprehended by the moving papers or the conduct of the trial.[37] Also, the county court must give due consideration to the deputy director's opportunity to judge the credibility of witnesses in a compensation proceedings, but it still has the duty to consider the appeal as a trial *de novo* on the transcript of the record and testimony and to make its own findings of fact and conclusions of law.[38]

Appeals from the decision of the county courts are made, in the usual case, to the Appellate Division of the Superior Court and from there, in accordance with New Jersey's procedure, to the Supreme Court. Thus there are three possible appeal stages after judgment has been rendered by the deputy.

Ever since deputies were given original jurisdiction in 1918, proposals have been made to amend the three-stage appeals procedure. Objections have been raised that the present appeals procedures are expensive and time-consuming. It should be recognized, however, that the number of appeals taken is not great. During 1956, only 214 cases were appealed to the county courts, a larger number than in any previous year. Thirty-two appeals were taken to the second stage, but this number has run as high as 56 cases (1949). Only seven cases reached the Supreme Court in 1956, whereas the number was twice this in 1953. These numbers are small in comparison with the total number of judgments rendered by the deputies. Still the time taken to reach a decision at the highest level averaged eighteen and one half months for

---

[34] N.J. Stat. Ann., 34:15-66.

[35] Rules Governing the County Courts as Promulgated by the New Jersey Supreme Court, rule 5:2-5 (d). The rules governing workmen's compensation appeals are reproduced in Division of Workmen's Compensation, *Workmen's Compensation Law* (Trenton: 1957), Appendix B.

[36] *Huber* v. *New England Tree Expert Co.*, 137 N.J.L. 549, *affirmed*, 2 N.J. 15. *DeMonaco* v. *Renton*, 32 N.J. Super. 450, *reversed on other grounds*, 18 N.J. 352.

[37] *Kraemer* v. *Nitroform Co.*, 33 N.J. Super. 220, *reversed on other grounds*, 36 N.J. Super. 178, *reversed on other grounds*, 20 N.J. 497.

[38] *Augustin* v. *Bank Building and Equipment Corp.*, 41 N.J. Super. 187, *affirmed* 44 N.J. Super. 242.

the cases appealed during 1954-1956.[39] Also it is probably true that most of the cases that were appealed to the Supreme Court involved serious injury or death, and as a result persons often in great need of compensation are compelled to wait for a long time.[40]

There is probably greater sentiment for some change in the appeals procedure than there is for any particular proposal. One idea, advanced by the division and supported by the State CIO and AFL, and also some representatives of insurance companies, would not eliminate any appeals stage but would substitute for the county court a review board of three deputies within the division.[41] This would probably assure closer control of the deputies' decisions and administrative practices. As matters stand now, each of the deputies is an individualist with the prerogatives of a law judge. The director may conceive of new directions for this social insurance program, but he is limited to "educating" the deputies or to promulgating rules or formal administrative policies. Having a review body of expert deputies within the division would conceivably assure quicker response to some ideas of the director and other administrators on such matters as rehabilitation and supervision of medical practices. Also, if standards for evaluation of disabilities are devised, a review board within the division could compel the individual deputies to adhere closely to these standards.

At any rate, it is argued that a review board would bring to its task a specialized technical knowledge, which judges, concerned with other matters, generally lack. Such review boards are common in compensation agencies of other states and in other administrative agencies.

On the other hand, the review board proposal has been opposed by the New Jersey Manufacturers Casualty Insurance Company and some petitioner's attorneys. (This is one issue on which the interest groups do not line up neatly on opposing sides.) The objections are raised that the review board would be too close to the deputies, that it would not eliminate any appeal stage, and that the deputies on the review board would not have sufficient duties to occupy them full time.

An alternative proposal is to eliminate the county courts and have appeals taken directly from the deputies' judgments to a special panel of the Appellate Division of the Superior Court composed of three judges. Only if their work load became light, would these judges be assigned to other duties. To eliminate the costs of printed briefs, it is proposed that appeals be made on the transcript with typewritten briefs, as is now the practice in the county courts.[42]

This does not exhaust the proposals for change which have been

---

[39] New Jersey Division of Workmen's Compensation *Annual Report*, 1956, p. 9.

[40] Statement of Ned J. Parsekian, Director, Division of Workmen's Compensation, at hearings before Governor's Committee on Judicial Review of Workmen's Compensation Cases, *Trenton Evening Times*, July 25, 1957.

[41] *The Newark News*, July 25, 1957.

[42] New Jersey Manufacturers Casualty Insurance Company, "Memorandum Concerning Appeals Procedure Submitted to Governor's Committee on Judicial Review of Workmen's Compensation Cases," July 29, 1957. Also, *The Newark News*, July 25, 1957.

made, but these are the two most popular proposals advanced recently. Both would have the advantage of having "experts" handling appeals. The second would eliminate one appeals step, although a proposal has also been made that the appeals end with the Appellate Division, which would eliminate the Supreme Court stage at the opposite end of the procedures. The first could have the advantage of eliminating some of the legalistic procedures that have characterized workmen's compensation deputies but it is not obvious that this would be the result.

In light of the relatively small number of cases appealed, and in light of the other administrative problems that cry for solution, this matter of appeals probably cannot be classed as a major item of highest priority. Our legal traditions require review of compensation decisions, but this does not mean that the present procedure must be endorsed. One might agree with the editorial conclusion of *The Newark News*, "...the principle that workmen's compensation appeals should be made shorter, quicker and cheaper is beyond dispute."[43]

---

[43] July 29, 1957. Proposals for administrative reforms will be found at the end of the next chapter.

Chapter 6

THE ADMINISTRATIVE HISTORY OF NEW JERSEY'S ACT

The Establishment of Basic Procedures, 1911-1921

The administrative character of New Jersey's compensation program with its reliance on quasi-judicial procedures has been shaped by the original 1911 law. This statute created no administrative machinery. The rates and schedules of compensation benefits were set forth, but in the event of controversy the only place of appeal was to the Court of Common Pleas (now known as the County Court). A petition could be brought for a hearing if the parties could not agree, or if, after agreement, payments were not forthcoming, or if the worker sought to have his weekly payments commuted to a lump sum.

The legislature did provide for an Employers' Liability Commission, not to administer the act, but to observe its operations and to report yearly to the legislature on recommendations for changes and improvements.[1] In its first report, issued in 1912, the commission traced the limited experience under the act and in general found much to praise in the way it was working in its beginning year. It was pointed out that before the law was passed the worker received no compensation in nine out of ten cases of permanent disability, but that the reverse was the case under the law.[2] The commission also praised the fact that practically all the outlay of the employer now was collected by the injured worker, instead of 75 per cent being wasted in litigation, as under the former system of combat between employer and employee.[3] The fact that the law did not require employers to insure their liability was a bit disturbing, since the worker could receive no benefits if the employer was insolvent, but the commission deferred making concrete recommendations, pending the accumulation of more experience.

---

[1]N.J. Laws 1911, ch. 24, 520. The membership of the commission was identical with that of the Commission on Employers' Liability, whose recommendations had been responsible for the passage of the act itself. The commission was appointed by the Governor and was tripartite; two of its members represented the employers' interest, two were members of the legislature and two represented organized labor. The members served without remuneration and had a secretary but no other staff. They were, however, authorized to call upon the state Department of Labor for clerical and statistical assistance.

[2]The commission went on to say: "Moreover, the average amount paid under our present law to permanent disability cases according to the best figures available, appears to be fifteen times greater than the average received under the old laws. At the same time, the actual cost to the employer, while necessarily higher pending the natural adjustment of insurance rates and the installation of preventative appliances, has not increased in anything like this proportion." (New Jersey Employers' Liability Commission, *Annual Report*, 1912, p. 10.)

[3] *Ibid.*, p. 11.

By the next year, observers of the law were beginning to recognize the administrative deficiencies of the new system.[4] Commissioner of Labor, Lewis T. Bryant was less than satisfied with the way the law was operating. According to the Commissioner: "It has become apparent that the ordinary laboring man is woefully ignorant of the Liability Law. The merest percentage of them have ever seen a copy of the Act. They do not know its provisions nor where a copy of the law can be obtained. The Department has an abundant supply of pamphlets of the Act for free distribution but it is difficult to place them in the hands of interested persons." Bryant complained that many employees did not receive correct compensation payments. He recognized that some of the errors were unintentional but felt that others were deliberate, and in either case the Department had no authority "even to call the attention of the injured to the error much less require the employer to live up to the agreement entered into by him when he accepted the protection against law suits which the compensation section affords him."[5]

Bryant asked for authority to take up these irregular settlements with the parties. Anticipating the agreement procedure that was to be adopted some years later, he suggested that it would be advisable to require the filing with the department of an agreed-upon statement of fact in each case. This would be signed by each party and would set forth the exact character of the injury received, the conditions under which it occurred and the compensation to be paid. "The Department could then notify the injured workman of any apparent discrepancy in the settlement, offer its good services to both sides in adjusting the situation and direct attention to the fact that the matter could be further adjudicated in the Court of Common Pleas."[6] In spite of these recommendations, nothing was done. The administrative procedures of the act were not changed during the first five years of its operation.

One significant influence which helped pave the way for changes was a report of the Social Insurance Committee of the American Association for Labor Legislation. Under the direction of its secretary, John Andrews, the association had made a hasty survey of the compensation laws in Washington, Ohio and Massachusetts, and then in 1914 he succeeded in raising money for a thorough study of the New Jersey law. "New Jersey was selected as being the first American state

---

[4] The National Civic Federation had appointed a joint labor-management commission which was inquiring into the operations of the compensation laws in various states (United States Senate, *A Study of the Report of the Commission of the American Federation of Labor and the National Civic Federation* [Document 419, 63d Congress, 2d session, January 15, 1914], incorporates the findings of this survey). This commission met with William E. Stubbs, the secretary of the New Jersey commission to discuss aspects of New Jersey's law. Stubbs estimated that workers in the state were getting only about 80 per cent of what they were entitled to under the law. In his opinion, no workmen's compensation law could be devised which would work with perfect satisfaction automatically. It was his position that some central board or authority should be established to exercise general supervisory powers over the operation of the law (*The Newark News*, October 2, 1913).

[5] New Jersey Department of Labor, *Annual Report*, 1913, p. 21.

[6] *Ibid.*, p. 22.

permanently to put into effect a compensation system.... The law frequently has been recommended as a model in noncompensation states by groups of insurance men and employers. Certain enthusiasts of their numbers even hailed it the 'one compensation law in America which is satisfactory to all concerned.' Under the circumstances, a careful investigation of the New Jersey plan appeared to be most desirable."[7]

The actual investigation was done by S. Bruce Black, who was later to become president of the Liberty Mutual Insurance Company, and Solon De Leon. Their report was far from complimentary. They condemned the general lack of administrative supervision of compensation benefits on a number of grounds, pointing out that accident statistics were not being compiled and that without these insurance rates could not be computed or accident prevention measures undertaken.[8] In cases where settlements were made, the committee found many situations where benefits were not paid in accordance with the law. It estimated that not over 60 per cent of the amounts due under the statute were actually being paid to injured workers.

In addition to these alleged underpayments, or nonpayments, the committee complained of the delays involved in court procedures, the costs of the appeals to the courts, and the inexpertness of the judges who heard compensation cases. On the general matter of court administration the committee concluded: "In short, administration of a workmen's compensation law through the courts, a number of separate and scattered tribunals already overburdened by their ordinary business and more or less likely to be unfamiliar with the law, results harmfully in that: (1) serious delays occur, defeating one main purpose of a compensation law, namely to care for the injured or his dependents financially during a period of no earnings; (2) fees necessarily paid to attorneys eat up large portions of the awards; (3) settlements in violation of the law are frequently sanctioned by the courts or even ordered by them on their own initiative; (4) conflicting opinions are handed down, confusing and complicating the whole system and making justice a matter of location, not of law; and finally (5) many meritorious claims are not pressed for fear that court action will result in dismissal from employment. A more unsatisfactory system, from the injured worker's

---

[7] American Association for Labor Legislation, "Three Years Under the New Jersey Workmen's Compensation Law" (Report of an investigation under the direction of the Social Insurance Committee), reprinted with introductory material in *American Labor Legislation Review*, V (March, 1915), 31-102. The quotation cited appears on p. 34.

[8] Although an accident reporting law had been passed in 1912 (N.J. Laws 1912, ch. 156, p. 225), requiring all death cases and accidents involving two weeks of disability or more be reported to the Department of Labor, the committee, after investigation, concluded that only about half of the accidents were being reported. According to the committee, "... thousands of accidents must be occurring each year which are subject to compensation but in which there is no record whatever of any settlement that may have been made. For all administrative purposes these cases are irretrievably lost. The injured worker and his dependents may have received only a part of their legal benefits, or more probably were deprived of them altogether. In the absence of a central administrative body, there is no way of determining which." ("Three Years Under the New Jersey Workmen's Compensation Law," p. 39).

point of view, would be hard to devise."[9] This was not the full extent of the committee's complaint; it also criticized to the law scale of compensation and the lack of compulsory insurance requirements.[10]

The interrelationship of the various problems became apparent in 1915, when the New Jersey Senate held hearings on amendments recommended by the Employers' Liability Commission to increase compensation rates, establish compulsory insurance requirements and set up a Workmen's Compensation Bureau to administer the act. Attorneys for employer groups criticized the proposed amendments on the grounds that if the rates were increased, workmen would maim themselves deliberately. It was also claimed that to allow employees to appeal to the proposed bureau would only cause constant trouble, since no employee was ever known to be satisfied with the amount of compensation he received. This provoked bitter comment from labor representatives, who claimed that the men who were praising the laws, as they stood, were the very same men who opposed the compensation legislation when it was first introduced.[11]

The next year, however, amendments establishing a Workmen's Compensation Aid Bureau did pass the legislature.[12] The aid bureau, headed by the Commissioner of Labor, was to report on the operations of the law in much the same manner as the Employers' Liability Commission, which had been abolished. The aid bureau also had the responsibility for record-keeping formerly entrusted to the Department of Labor, but, most important, the bureau was to "approve" settlements arrived at between the parties. This latter provision probably served to eliminate the more obvious kinds of under payments.

In addition to approval of agreements, the aid bureau was authorized, by language which is still in the law, to endeavor to bring about settlement of pending claims if agreements were not filed within twenty-one days. Acting under this authority, two referees, both attorneys, were hired to adjust claims. Working in somewhat the same manner as the present-day informal referees, these men traveled throughout the state hearing and settling disputed claims. They had no power to make final decisions; but if after consultation with the parties they were unable to bring about a settlement, they could certify the case to the county courts. In some cases, the threat to certify the case was sufficient to bring about an amicable settlement. The law provided that if the court found that the employer had no reasonable excuse for

---

[9] American Association for Labor Legislation, "Three Years Under the New Jersey Workmen's Compensation Law," pp. 57-58.

[10] The chairman of the New Jersey Employers' Liability Commission, speaking at the same meeting at which the report was presented, made what he called a plea in extenuation. He pointed out that New Jersey was a pioneering state and that the people had not been generally aware of the complex problems involved. He emphasized that the commission itself had been critical of the operations of the act but that progress had to be made slowly since the various problems were interrelated. (*American Labor Legislation Review*, V [March, 1915], 130-132.)

[11] *The Newark News*, March 3, 1915.

[12] N.J. Laws 1916, ch. 54, p. 97.

failure to pay adequate compensation, then all reasonable expenses of the workmen, including "medical and legal services and loss of working time in prosecuting his claim," could be assessed against the employer or insurance carrier.[13] Attempts were made the following year to amend the act to give the aid bureau original jurisdiction in disputed cases; and finally, in February, 1918, a bill was passed creating a Workmen's Compensation Bureau in the Department of Labor, with the Commissioner of Labor as chairman.[14]

The practice of holding informal hearings was to continue under the new law; but now, in the event of disagreement, a petition could be filed with the bureau and the case would be set down for hearing before a deputy, in much the same manner as today. Appeals from decisions of the deputies were to the county courts, where a trial *de novo* would be held. It was not until three years later that the act was amended to provide that trial of the appeals was to be based upon the transcript of the record and testimony as certified by the bureau.[15]

The freeing of the administration of the act from court control was thus a gradual process. In summary, no administrative machinery whatsoever was created in the beginning, but the legislature did create a watch-dog committee, the Employers' Liability Commission, to observe and make reports. Five years after the act was passed, the aid bureau took over the commission's responsibilities and also the task of adjusting disputes, but it was without power to make decisions. Two years later, the Workmen's Compensation Bureau was established and its employees given power to hear and decide cases, but still appeal could be made to the court, where the trial would begin again. Not until more than a decade had elapsed were the courts confined to hearing the appeals based upon the record made and certified by the bureau, but still today these are trials at which the court has power to review findings of fact as well as law. Although the law has been amended countless times since 1921, no really basic changes have been made by the legislature in administrative procedures since that date. The original act had the impress of court procedures, and this has remained.

Early Amendments — Legislation by Collective Bargaining

There have been seven Commissioners of Labor since the original 1911 act.[16] Lewis T. Bryant, Commissioner at the time of the original

---

[13] A sympathetic account of the workings of the aid bureau is found in a feature story in *The Newark News*, August 5, 1916, entitled "State's Umpire Assures Justice in Workmen's Compensation Cases."

[14] N.J. Laws 1918, ch. 149, p. 429. Walter Edge, who was an Assembly member of the original Commission on Employers' Liability and a Senate member of the Employers' Liability Commission, was Governor at the time this fundamental change was made in the law.

[15] N.J. Laws 1921, ch. 229, p. 734.

[16] Some information about each of these men and their tenure is found in *Summary of Activities of the New Jersey Department of Labor and Industry*, July 1, 1953- June 30, 1954 (Fiftieth Anniversary Report), pp. lvi-lvii.

passage of the act, served until his death in 1923; and to him and his aides must be given a good share of the credit for freeing the act from court administration. Bryant evidently had the happy facility of being able to bring the interest groups together to agree upon amendments for submission to the legislature.

In the early part of 1922, a committee had been formed under the auspices of the New Jersey Chamber of Commerce. The committee was widely representative of the various interest groups, since it had on it not only members of the Chamber but also representatives of the State American Federation of Labor and the New Jersey Medical Association, together with Colonel Bryant and a member of the New Jersey Rehabilitation Commission.[17]   The group conducted a joint investigation and submitted amendments for consideration by the legislature.[18]   Although most of its recommendations were turned down, they were reintroduced in 1923 after further conferences with the manufacturing and labor groups, under the auspices of the New Jersey Department of Labor. After many meetings between the two groups, and in keeping with the traditions of collective bargaining, the parties finally agreed on a compromise settlement. Agreement was reached to increase the maximum benefit rate from $12 to $17, representing a concession of a $2 increase on the part of the employers and a $1 decrease on labor's part, as contrasted with their earlier positions.[19]

The employers, however, won their point that the matter of coverage of occupational diseases should be deferred, pending a study of the problem by a joint commission. The ten-day waiting period was left unchanged, but a retroactive or reversion period of "more than seven weeks" was written into the law. The employers conceded that the maximum number of weeks for the assessment of nonscheduled permanent partial disabilities should be increased from 400 to 500. This was a concession obtained by Bryant, who hailed it as "a new step in social administration," and one which would add 20 per cent to the compensation payments for this class of disabilities. The 300-week period of death benefits was also extended to provide payments to each child

[17]The New Jersey Manufacturers Association, which had declined an invitation, was the only organized body representing a significant interest group which was not represented (*The Newark News*, February 19, 1922).

[18]By this date the maximum weekly rate had increased from the original $10 to $12, and the group recommended a further increase to $18. Also it was proposed that penalties for noncompliance with the compulsory insurance provisions, which had been written into the law earlier, be strengthened; that occupational disease provisions be included; and that the allowances for medical provisions be liberalized. Due in part to the depressed economic conditions prevailing in the state at the time, most of the amendments failed of passage, but the provisions liberalizing medical allowances were passed. The maximum allowance of $50 for medical and hospital treatment was eliminated; and in its stead the medical and hospital allowances were separated, and a maximum of $50 was placed on each. The time limits during which these services had to be provided were eliminated, and provision was made that payments in excess of $50 for medical and $50 for hospital treatment could be made upon application to the bureau. (N.J. Laws 1922, ch. 245, p. 500.)

[19]It should be noted, however, that the New Jersey Chamber of Commerce backed labor's point of view that the maximum should have increased to $18.

until the age of sixteen. Provisions were also made for a lump-sum payment for burial expenses of $150. This also was a compromise; the labor groups wanted this sum to be $200, whereas the employer groups argued that $100 was sufficient.[20]

This whole experience was probably a salutary one. With all due respect to the abilities of the legislators, it is difficult for a body which has so much other business to transact, and so little time to do it in, to become fully cognizant of all of the issues in such an inherently complicated field. One way for the legislature to proceed is by relying on agreements reached among the parties-at-interest.[21] This requires that the interest groups be in agreement on basic principles, such as the validity of the operating theory, the essential worthwhileness of the program and the integrity of its administrators. It also implies that each group has some room in which to maneuver and some willingness to be flexible in its position. This was probably easier in 1923, when the law was still in its developmental stages, than it is today. Such a procedure is also aided by a strong Commissioner able to use his good offices to persuade the interest groups to come to some agreement. For one reason or another, this procedure of having the parties publicly agree on amendments to be submitted to the legislature has not been frequent in the history of the program. Whatever private agreements may be made prior to passage of amendments cannot be known; but publicly, in the usual case, the parties have appeared as combatants before the legislative body.

Administrative Problems and Investigations

The atmosphere of cordiality was not to last long after Bryant's death. He was succeeded in office by Dr. Andrew F. McBride, who was to serve until the depression year of 1929. The early years of McBride's tenure were comparatively calm, but by 1928, some strikingly modern problems rose to plague the administrators. Representatives of the AFL were evidently dissatisfied with the treatment workers were receiving at the informal hearings when they were examined by state doctors who, then as now, estimated the extent of permanent partial disability.

Doctors retained by the state were allowed to carry on a private practice, and some were examining compensation clients for insurance carriers. The president of the State Federation of Labor protested that an employee who was examined by a state doctor retained by insurance carrier could later come before this same doctor for an impartial estimate of his disability at the informal hearing. McBride answered this protest by claiming that none of the state doctors was actually on the payroll of an insurance company, and he also pointed to the

---

[20] *The Newark News*, February 6, 1923.

[21] For a recent critical examination of this type of procedure, see Gilbert Steiner, *Legislation by Collective Barbaining* (Urbana: University of Illinois, Institute of Labor and Industrial Relations, 1951).

difficulty of getting competent physicians to examine for the state unless they were allowed some outside practice.[22]

To find a solution to this problem, McBride appointed an unofficial commission to look into the whole matter. The commission was composed of representatives of labor, employer groups, physicians, the New Jersey Bar Association and social welfare organizations. As could be expected, the inquiry sometimes went beyond the narrow question of dual employment of physicians. The labor groups protested the low estimates of disability given by state physicians in particular cases, and the doctors complained that referees sometimes disregarded their findings. Some of the state doctors, who admitted to the dual practice, claimed that they did not estimate disability of patients whom they had seen privately unless the extent of the disability was obvious. The head of the medical department of the bureau admitted that he did some work for the insurance carriers, but agreed with the suggestion that he might give this up.

In its final report, the majority of the members of the commission stated that they did not believe that the practical results of dual practice were inimicable to the purposes of the compensation law or harmful to the interests of injured persons, but they recommended that dual practice be discontinued since it might have these tendencies. The minority report, submitted by the AFL representative, was much more vigorous in its condemnation of the administration of the compensation bureau. It pointed out that all but two of the state doctors had been employed by carriers or employers, and inferred that this was the reason for the low estimates of disability at informal hearings. The natural consequence, according to the AFL representative, was the increase in the number of formal cases.[23]

McBride went out of office in 1929 and was succeeded by Colonel Charles R. Blunt, who promptly became involved in much the same administrative problems. Under his aegis, the first comprehensive drafting of rules and regulations (which had been authorized when the statute was amended in 1918) was accomplished. One of the main purposes of these rules and regulations was to control certain alleged practices among lawyers practicing in the compensation courts. According to Blunt, lawyers or their agents would come into the rooms where informal hearings were being conducted and "slip the man

---

[22] *The Newark News* conducted an informal poll among physicians to learn how seriously the conditions complained of were in conflict with sound theory and practice but could find no doctor who would justify this dual employment. The chief medical examiner of the New York State Department of Labor said that the practice was absolutely wrong, that at one time it had been tolerated in New York, but that it had been stopped. One doctor stated that a man in such dual employment would have to be possessed of the morals of the Angel Gabriel and the wisdom of an Abraham Lincoln to avoid favoring the side from which he derived the larger financial return. A representative of an insurance company defended the practice, claiming that unless the state used doctors with extensive industrial experience, it was not giving the injured worker the attention he deserved. Also, in his opinion, competent physicians could not be bought or sold, whether employed solely by a carrier or in a dual capacity. (*The Newark News*, April 3, May 7, 17, 1928.)

[23] *The Newark News*, May 17, July 13, November 23, 1928.

seeking compensation his business card and advise him to make an application for a formal hearing."[24] Blunt complained about the fact that checks for compensation awards, which were made out in the name of the petitioner, were sent to the office of the latter's attorney, who would deduct his fees. In some cases, according to Blunt, the lawyers received more than the fee authorized by the hearing officer. This was to be curbed by the new rules. If abuses continued, the checks were to be handed out in the presence of the lawyer and his client. Violations would result in suspension of the lawyer from practice before the compensation courts for one year. Other rules covered such matters as adjournments, fees, medical examinations, settlements and commutations.

In a news release, dated March 7, 1930, Blunt amplified his charges of ambulance-chasing doctors and lawyers, stating that they constituted a ring and that their actions had reached the point where the bureau might be shaken to its foundations. He complained that although the rules had been in operation for more than four months, no lawyer had been cited for an infraction of these regulations. Yet, in his view, it was a matter of common knowledge among persons in contact with the bureau that solicitation and subsequent irregular handling of cases had continued. Blunt's concern was further stimulated by a series of articles in *The Newark News* which cited cases of lawyers tacking on additional fees after they had their clients out of court. The articles alleged that some lawyers maintained a system of runners and contact men, with whom they split fees, and that the lawyers were allied with doctors who practiced fraud and forgery.[25]

Blunt moved on a number of fronts. He shifted the deputy directors around, appointed a supervising referee for informal hearings, and put into effect a system of preliminary formal hearings, the forerunner of present-day pre-trial procedures. Also, he forbade deputies to attend manufacturers' conventions as guests, with their expenses paid by employer groups, and he promised a full-scale investigation by a commission whose members were to be appointed by the various interest groups. The leaders of the medical and legal societies promised swift disciplinary action against any of their members cited for unethical practices by the investigating commission.[26]

The investigating commission, called the Workmen's Compensation Advisory Commission, issued a unanimous report in March, 1931. Their major recommendation was that the entire compensation law be

---

[24] *The Newark News*, November 3, 1929.

[25] *The Newark News*, March 10, 11, 15, 1930.

[26] At about this same time, Blunt suspended the deputy commissioner in charge of the Newark office. Personality differences may have played some part in this action; the deputy had been with the New Jersey Department of Labor for eighteen years, and evidently was a candidate for the Commissioner's job at the time that Blunt was selected. A hearing was eventually held before the New Jersey Civil Service Commission, and the dismissal was upheld. In its opinion, the deputy had violated instructions from his superior in that he had represented clients in accident cases and had used the services of some employees in the compensation bureau to assist him in work incidental to such cases. (*The Newark News*, March 22, 24, April 29, June 4, 1930.)

revised, not because it was unsound, but rather because it was in a state of confusion due to the various amendments which had been passed over the years. Also, it recommended that the appeals procedure be changed to allow an appeal directly to the Supreme Court, thus bypassing the county court. (Proposals to accomplish this were still being made in 1958.) Several recommendations were made to step up the processing of cases and to improve the efficiency and speed with which cases were being processed. The matter of outside employment of state physicians was still a live issue. The practice at the time was for the Rehabilitation Commission to conduct clinics which were closely associated with the compensation courts. Rehabilitation clinic doctors evidently still were retained from time to time by insurance carriers or petitioners in compensation matters, and the investigators believed that this practice should be prohibited.

The always confusing matter of the nature of the informal hearings was a matter for comment. The commission hoped for a procedure under which all cases would have to go through the informal hearing stage as a condition precedent to a formal hearing. In their view, many cases could be informally adjusted by a referee without delay, but owing to the intervention of certain lawyers and doctors, "whose chief interest seems to be in obtaining the allowance of fees, these cases are not permitted to be informally adjudicated but are set down for a formal trial."

On the matter of evaluation of permanent partial disabilities, the now familiar complaint was made that some petitioners received awards, although apparently complete recovery had been made. One solution suggested was the employment of a panel of disinterested physicians to advise the referees and deputies. As to the complaint of ambulance-chasing, the commission stated: "...we have considerable evidence indicating the practice before the bureau on the part of certain attorneys and physicians is becoming commercialized, that there is a certain amount of ambulance chasing on the part of doctors and lawyers and this practice is being carried on in the quarters of the Department of Labor." According to the commission, the activity of these professionals was, in part, responsible for cases being thrown into formal hearings rather than being settled at the informal level.[27]

Blunt claimed that he made some reforms, but no basic legislative changes were made as a result of the commission's recommendations. None of the amendments passed in 1931 substantially affected administrative procedures.

The depression necessarily brought strains to the compensation program and was also responsible for shifting political currents within the state. The legislature authorized a new investigating commission with representation from the legislature and the various interest groups. The chairman of the commission was Dr. Andrew McBride,

---

[27]New Jersey Workmen's Compensation Advisory Commission, *Report to the Commissioner of Labor* (Trenton: March 11, 1931).

the former Commissioner, who now represented the medical society.[28] Hearings before the commission were held during the latter part of 1933.[29] The chairman of the Essex Bar Association's compensation committee complained of physicians lounging around the Newark hearing rooms waiting for lawyers to bring them cases. When the lawyers did show up, it was his claim that the doctors made prefunctory examinations, either in the halls or the anterooms, and then offered lengthy testimony when the cases came to trial. He also alleged that hearing officers had a list of preferred lawyers and that they offered this list to claimants seeking counsel.[30]

A representative of the New Jersey Manufacturers Association complained of loose administrative practices and maintained that the compensation hearings were a disgrace to the state. He argued for more dignity, promptness and better scheduling of formal hearings.

Representatives of the State Federation of Labor submitted a number of recommendations, but these concerned deficiencies in the law, as they saw them, rather than mere administrative deficiencies. They complained of the low estimates of disability and claimed that the referees should be instructed to resolve doubts in favor of the injured worker. They maintained that the worker ought to have free choice of a physician, that a state insurance fund should be established, and that the formal hearings should be entirely separated from any record made at the informal ones. The employer representatives had expressed the opinion that the informal hearings should be a condition requisite to the formal ones, whereas the labor representatives argued against maximizing the importance of the informal stage. They felt that the interests of the injured worker were better protected at the formal level.

Accusations and opinions were plentiful at the hearings of the commission; but possibly because of lack of funds, very little in the way of concrete data as to the operations of the bureau were forthcoming. An exception was the testimony of James Gribbin of the Bureau of Statistics and Records of the Department of Labor. Gribbin presented an analysis of the contested cases heard in Newark in the early months of 1932, together with an account of the lawyers' fees and the names of the lawyers handling these cases. This substantiated the opinion, previously expressed, that the compensation legal work was

---

[28]N. J. Laws 1933, Joint Resolution 16. The authority to continue the work of the commission was given in N. J. Laws 1934, Joint Resolution 5. The commission was formally known as the Workmen's Compensation Investigating Commission but published its report as the *Report of the Joint Commission on Study of the Workmen's Compensation Act and Practices* (Trenton: April 12, 1935).

[29]In the meantime, as if the bureau did not have troubles enough, a special investigator of the Newark office in charge of trust funds set up in certain death cases, was arrested on charges of embezzling $15,000. This opened up a whole new area of investigation, since evidently the records of these funds were sparse and the general financial housekeeping procedures lax. This incident was to be grist for the mills of the legislative commission. The investigator eventually was found guilty of embezzling compensation funds and was sentenced to serve a term of two to three years (*The Newark News*, December 6, 1933).

[30]These hearings were reported in *The Newark News*, October 23, 30, 31, November 6, 20, 27, 1933.

rather highly concentrated among attorneys who specialized in this field. Also, the data showed that these lawyers tended to rely heavily on a limited number of physicians for testimony. [31]

The managing editor of the *Union Labor Messenger* discounted previous testimony of a lawyer-doctor racket in the compensation courts. He blamed the insurance companies for building up that impression and stated that the worst racket of all arose from the inadequate supervision of settlements made by the insurance carriers. He pointed out that only a small proportion of informal cases went on to the formal stage, and that comparatively few formal cases were ever appealed to the courts. This was cited as evidence that the system was working well. He was opposed to anything that would cut down the fees of lawyers, pointing out that strong representation was the only protection the injured worker had against the practices of insurance carriers. His solution to the problems was to eliminate the private insurance carriers and substitute a state fund and to increase the number of hearing officers.

Members of the commission were critical of his testimony, and the AFL representative questioned his right to speak for organized labor. The chairman drew from him the admission that he saw nothing wrong in lawyers soliciting work, or in doctors examining claimants in the hallways. Outside of such views, however, his opinions, with their emphasis on the deficiencies of private insurance and the necessity for strong legal representation for the injured worker, reflect modern present-day labor opinion fairly well.

The commission's final report was made public on March 22, 1935, nearly two years after it had begun its work. [32] Although few of its important proposals for administrative changes were adopted, some contain ideas which are applicable to the current picture. One of these had to do with the creation of a general supervisory and appeal board within the bureau, consisting of a physician, a representative of labor, the employers and the general public and a lawyer. The board was to lay down general rules, fix fees and act as an appellate body to hear appeals from the deputies' decisions.

Their treatment of the problem of informal hearings was also interesting. They recommended abolishing informal hearings and substituting informal conferences at which the parties would state their positions, and at which the referee would attempt to settle the case or, if necessary, make a decision. If this was not acceptable, he would

---

[31] Gribbin further testified that although the law limited legal fees to 20 per cent of the award, he had found 108 cases wherein the fees exceeded this limit. In many of these cases, according to his testimony, the fees, portions of which were assessed against the insurance carrier, amounted to more than 100 per cent of the award. One of the deputies explained that in some cases the higher fees were a matter of agreement between counsel of both sides.

[32] New Jersey Legislature, *Report of the Joing Commission on Study of the Workmen's Compensation Act and Practices* (Trenton: April 12, 1935). Space does not permit the detailing of all of the commission's recommendations or of the two minority reports that were filed.

certify the information and the facts as he found them; and the disputed case would be set down for a formal hearing.

The commission also recommended that fees for lawyers and doctors be allowed on the basis of the amount of work done, rather than the amount of the awards. Also, it was recommended that no physician engaged by the state for compensation and rehabilitation work should be permitted to have an outside practice. In their view, these men should be appointed from a list certified by the medical society.[33]

John Toohey succeeded Blunt at the beginning of 1934; and like all previous Commissioners, he had a program to eliminate difficulties in workmen's compensation.[34] Disturbed by the lack of dignity at the compensation hearings, Toohey's remedy was to formalize the hearing atmosphere; the deputies were ordered to wear black judicial robes when they sat in compensation courts. As far as is known, New Jersey is the only state with this practice. This is not important in and of itself, but it is one indication that the administrators look upon formal hearings as essentially legal proceedings.

The Commissioner was also concerned with the perennial problem of speeding up the disposition of cases so as to eliminate backlogs. New rules were drafted, under which adjournments of cases would have to be granted by the hearing officers, rather than taken as a matter of right, as had been the practice before. Plans were also made for pretrial conferences, at which the issues could be narrowed in the hopes of eliminating unnecessary testimony. The Workmen's Compensation Board was established with power to suspend an attorney guilty of receiving more than the allowed fees.[35] The rules on informal hearings were tightened, and once again it was reiterated that representatives of either the petitioner and/or respondent would not be allowed to attend the physical examination of the claimant by the state doctor.

In 1944, Walter Edge, the same man who had been so prominent in

---

[33] The majority of the commission also recommended that workers be given their free choice of physician provided that the employer had the right of consultation. This recommendation was opposed by two minority members, who proposed that the workers' choice be made from a panel of doctors selected by the employer and approved by the medical society.

[34] Indications that the rackets in the field were not entirely ended were present when four men were picked up for questioning by the Union County prosecutor's office. In an effort to end ambulance-chasing activities, the bureau had been doing some investigating on its own. Investigators who had bandaged themselves to look like injured workers were approached by the four men, who suggested that they have their cases handled by a Newark law firm. The case charges against the law firm were referred to the Newark Bar Association.

Commissioner Toohey was active in trying to stamp out these practices and was able to secure affidavits from other men who worked as runners for attorneys in Newark. These men lounged around factories and bar rooms to seek out injured workmen. The lawyer was supposed to give the runner $10 for each client, although in some cases failure to deliver the promised fees evidently contributed to the willingness of the runners to testify. (The Newark News, June 19, 1935.)

[35] The power of the board to suspend an attorney for unethical practices was used when a Jersey City lawyer was suspended for appropriating compensation checks meant for the claimant and the physician in the case. Another lawyer was suspended for violating the rules against obtaining a written retainer for 50 per cent of the award and keeping this portion after the case was decided. (The Newark News, September 19, 1940.)

the passage of the original law, was elected Governor, and in his inaugural message he stressed the need for improvements and liberalization of the compensation law. The state established a postwar economic commission, and its recommendations were responsible for increases in the maximum weekly rates and the partial disability schedules, and also an expansion of the second injury fund.[36] With the new Governor came a new Commissioner, Harry C. Harper, who soon was embroiled in the same sorts of problems that had plagued his predecessors.

The postwar period saw an acceleration of the trend toward formal cases, with a consequent backlog of pending cases. In an attempt to speed their disposition, the system of having formal referees hear cases, in which the parties agreed on a settlement at the formal level, was established. Also, supervising deputy commissioners were appointed in the larger hearing centers. These were noncontroversial matters, but Harper soon found himself involved with the lawyers and doctors. The old problems of decorum, ethical practices and fees came up for consideration, if not solution. Harper objected to doctors examining claimants, and to lawyers conferring with their clients, on the stairs and in the halls near the compensation court rooms. His solution was a bit more constructive than merely issuing orders prohibiting such practices; he provided conference rooms for professional consultations. He also instituted the practice of having compensation checks sent directly to the beneficiaries rather than to the lawyers for distribution. Lawyers' and doctors' fees were to be sent out by separate check.

Harper had also complained about the high legal fees and the fact that compensation practice was concentrated in a relatively few firms.[37] Petitioners' lawyers responded, that as compensation benefits increase (new rates were to go into effect on January 1, 1946), lawyers' fees should increase correspondingly. It was pointed out that the fees were small, as compared to fees allowed in damage suits, in which the lawyer could receive one-third of the award. Also, it was claimed, that only those lawyers who handle a great many compensation cases, could afford to represent compensation clients, and that statistics on average

---

[36] New Jersey Commission on Post-War Economic Welfare, *Labor Security in the Post-War Period*, Second Report (Trenton: 1945).

[37] Harper encountered difficulties when he allegedly acted to reduce the fee schedule for lawyers and doctors. The rumor was that he had ordered that lawyers' fees be cut to 10 per cent of the awards and that doctors be given no more than $25 per case. The Commissioner later denied this, but at the same time, expressed the opinion that something would have to be done to encourage more parties to settle their cases informally so as not to burden the formal level with unnecessary petitions. When word of the alleged reduction reached the lawyers, some of them staged what might be termed a short-lived strike, in that they walked out of the courts before their cases were called. The next day, after conferring with about forty doctors and lawyers, it was agreed to maintain the *status quo* while an investigating committee looked into the whole fee matter. The committee met with Harper a number of times, but in the end, the agreement was that fees should be fixed on practically the same basis as before. The amount of the fees was to be left to the discretion of the deputies, within the maximum allowances fixed by the statute but with no fixed bureau schedule. (*The Newark News*, April 13, 14, November 30, 1945.)

fees did not take into account the fact that the lawyer received no fee, if no award was forthcoming. It was maintained that lawyers are an essential part of the compensation system, and should be encouraged to represent their clients; that they are now being shut out of work by the informal hearings, and that if the lawyers are discouraged from representing clients, the insurance carriers would benefit at the expense of the injured workers.[38]

On the other side of the picture, lawyers representing insurance carriers credited Harper with trying to straighten things out. It was admitted that many conscientious lawyers worked hard on their cases and deserved their fees, but it was claimed that many others created work for the sake of the fees; that the bulk of these cases could be settled by informal hearings, but that some lawyers insisted on formal hearings because of the bigger fees involved. And so the controversy ran, but to no definite conclusion. By this time, the pattern of formal hearings with legal representation had been firmly established. So long as the injured worker was convinced, or could be convinced, that he could collect more by pursuing his case right through to the deputy's level, the trend was going to continue.

The Nelson Report

On July 1, 1950, Percy A. Miller, Jr., took office as Commissioner. Under the reorganization act, effective January 1, 1949, the Workmen's Compensation Bureau had become the Workmen's Compensation Division of the New Jersey Department of Labor and Industry, and the deputy commissioners were now known as deputy directors. Like each of his predecessors, Miller found it necessary to spend time studying the processing of workmen's compensation cases. According to Miller, bottlenecks were developing in the handling of the 16,000 to 18,000 cases that went before the nine deputies for formal hearings. The tack Miller chose in seeking a solution was not to turn to yet another investigating committee composed of representatives of the interest groups but rather to hire a consultant to survey the situation and to make recommendations to help speed up the disposition of cases. He chose a man who was probably the foremost authority in the country on such matters, Harry A. Nelson, the director of Wisconsin's Workmen's Compensation Department and the president of the International Association of Industrial Accident Boards and Commissions. Nelson's report was submitted in May, 1951. Unfortunately, space does not permit a detailed analysis of its contents, but some summary of the main points is essential since time has not dulled most of the recommendations or the analysis upon which they rest.[39]

In discussing the efficacy and value of administrative procedures, Nelson called to mind the aims of the original compensation laws.

---

[38] *The Newark News*, July 24, 1945.

[39] Harry Nelson, "Report of Study of New Jersey's Workmen's Compensation Act" (typewritten), May, 1951.

Most states, he pointed out, set up boards or commissions to carry out the provisions of the act, on an administrative rather than a purely traditional basis. They wished to get away from legalism and to substitute a system with rules easily, speedily and inexpensively carried out by an agency which, above all, must be expert in its field. The purpose was to avoid technical and complex rules. Some states which clung to court procedures in the beginning later supplanted them, but they still tended to preserve the features of legalism with its concomitant objectionable features. In Nelson's view, to the degree that a compensation act combines the factors of speed, simplicity, certainty and low expense with the greatest economy to labor, industry and the consumer of goods, it will have attained its original objective. To the degree that the remedy fails to attain these objectives, it will have fallen short of the avowed goal.

In many respects, this was a fresh breath of air. For years, the investigations of the compensation program had dealt with the picayune bickerings of the interest groups and with surface difficulties, without anyone calling to mind the fact that there were discernible objectives of the program as a whole that should not be dropped from sight. It was recognized that the problem of a backlog of formal cases could not be dealt with by manipulations of procedure at that level alone, but that the whole procedure had to be examined.

Nelson cited the advantages of having the system work automatically. His recommendations for change embraced many features that had worked well in Wisconsin, some of which have already been discussed. These included the supplying of information to employees immediately after an accident was reported and the substitution of the direct payment system for the agreement system. Final reports of cases that had not been contested should be accompanied by meaningful physician's reports, which would allow the administrators to determine if payments complied with the law. It was recognized that if workers could be persuaded that they would receive fair treatment at this stage of the proceedings, there would be less resort to formal procedures. Also recommended were procedures for checking on promptness and continuity of payment and for appraising the performance of insurance carriers.

A series of recommendations were made to improve the informal hearing procedures, some of which had been recommended by other investigators who had gone before him. For one thing, it was proposed that much could be done by way of correspondence, following careful scrutiny of reports by the division to eliminate the necessity of personal appearances by the parties. This is in line with the general philosophy of the direct payment system, whereby administrators take it upon themselves to see that correct amounts of compensation benefits are paid as due. Beyond this, however, Nelson suggested, that informal hearings be given legislative sanction and that they be made a condition precedent to any further proceedings.[40]

---

[40]To insure that this would not simply be a *pro forma* step, it was suggested that some financial penalties be assessed. If an employer rejected an informal award, and if such an

Nelson recognized the many problems connected with the evaluation of permanent disabilities and recommended that standards for estimating permanent disability be devised and that training courses be instituted for state medical examiners to acquaint them with the standards.

An interesting forecast is made in this 1951 report of the six-months' rule on permanent partial disabilities, which was made part of the law in 1956. According to Nelson, proceedings should be stayed until a clear showing has been made that the time for the determination of the extent of permanent disability has arrived. It was his suggestion that a period might be fixed of, say, six months after the end of the healing period, providing that compensation was being paid during the period of the stay. In amplifying his reasons for this suggested delay, Nelson stated that he was impressed with the fact that many cases of permanent disability were decided before the ultimate condition had been attained; that there was much lost motion and failure to arrive at the true facts in attempting to decide these cases too early; and that the longer, within reasonable limits, the decision as to permanent disability could be postponed without prejudice to the parties, the more likelihood an accurate decision would be reached.

In passing on to problems of formal hearings, Nelson commented that lawyers will contend that unless they are retained to assist clients, a fair hearing and determination cannot be had. Doctors, who profit financially, will protest that unless their expert services are utilized, the results will be detrimental to the employee. Compensation administrators are sometimes reluctant to admit that the proceedings could be made more simple, rather than more complicated and legalistic. The consumer, however, who must ultimately foot the bill, has little knowledge of the processes involved or how to relieve himself of any charges that are imperceptibly added to the cost of the product he purchases. Nelson concluded that in the light of these facts it was not surprising that a greater demand for simplicity, speed and low expense was not made.

Along with these factors, according to Nelson, comes an increasing demand on the part of labor to have cases decided on a generous basis, to the point where some rather ridiculous decisions, based neither on actual disability nor on wage loss, may be made. This may not be in accord with the principles adopted in 1911; but since it meets with the approval and wishes of so many groups involved, it is difficult to overcome resistance to change and convert to a system that would render to the worker speedily, inexpensively and adequately the compensation to which the law entitles him.

Nelson had several recommendations to make to improve the formal hearings, some of which he had already made in his discussion

---

award were later sustained at a formal hearing, then all costs would be assessed against the employer. If an employee rejected the informal award, and if later the formal hearing produced no greater award, then the employee would have to bear the brunt of whatever nominal fees would be allowed.

of informal and noncontested cases. These had to do with the payment of compensation when due, even in advance of determinations, the undesirability of premature evaluation of disabilities and the exercise of general supervision of the over-all performance of the carriers and employers. He also argued for simplification of the pleadings in formal cases and for a full exchange of relevant medical information between the parties. He further recommended allowing the deputy the opportunity to call in independent medical examiners in cases of doubt about the determination of extent of disability.

Nelson would have the deputy regarded as an officer with full investigating power, whose function would be to bring out all pertinent facts at the hearing rather than to act as a judge who listens to testimony and makes a decision based upon this testimony. The deputies, in his view, should in no way be circumvented from obtaining factual and scientific information from any source whatsoever and should not have to be confined themselves to the information presented by the parties.

Perusal of the record of compensated cases necessarily brought Nelson in touch with what he termed "consolation awards," awards not based on actual wage loss or disability, but made in order to close out a case and to satisfy the claimant. A fully healed fractured rib is generally considered to be as strong and functionable as before the injury, according to Nelson; and yet he found that, at times, a small percentage of disability would be allowed. Frequently, in such cases, a small percentage of disability would also be added for a supposed element of neurosis. In Nelson's view, as a matter of sound economy and wise apportionment of funds available for compensation purposes, payment should be made only for actual or reasonable prospective wage loss, or in cases of scheduled injuries, for actual loss of function to a part. The use of compensation funds where disability does not exist deprives those who have suffered a wage loss or disability of amounts which could or should be awarded them. Nelson believed that, either by law or administrative procedures, a uniform practice should be set up to avoid such objectionable practices. Labor, in his opinion, is shortsighted in demanding that compensation be paid in cases in which, according to common sense and good medical opinion, no real physical disability or wage loss exists.

On the controversial matter of attorneys' fees, Nelson recommended a system that would allow fees based not only on the amount of the award but also on the service afforded, the amount of work involved and the necessity of the service, both as to time and quality. In cases of simple issues, the attorneys' fees should not necessarily be fixed at the same percentage of the compensation award as in cases of involving complex issues, in which a smaller award and greater services are involved. Nelson saw that in many cases the statutory maximum of a fee of 20 per cent would be justified and that in others a greater percentage should be allowed, but also that many cases do not call for the 20 per cent fee.

It is difficult to judge the effects of Nelson's report on the administration of New Jersey's law. His recommendations for pre-trial procedures (recommendations that had been made by earlier investigators) were probably responsible for establishing this practice on a firm basis in the large hearing centers. His condemnation of frequent adjournments probably led to the institution of continuous trials. Other recommendations for streamlining formal procedures were absorbed into the system, but his recommendations for fundamental changes were largely ignored. Little has been done to strengthen the informal procedures, to promulgate standards of disability, to eliminate legalistic procedures or to institute a direct payment system.

Administrative Reforms

There are many approaches to administrative reforms. At one extreme, it is possible to talk of a complete law revision, a change in administrative philosophy and financing arrangements. At the other, one can seek ways and means to eliminate obvious shortcomings within the present framework. In this regard it must be noted that the latter-day administrators have made progress in reviewing direct settlements, in attempting to keep minor cases out of the formal channels, in attempting to eliminate unnecessary medical testimony, and in seeking ways and means to assure ethical practices and to speed up the disposition of cases. But there are limits to what can be done, given the present statute, which carries with it the heavy freight of its historical development; and it is not easy to achieve the consensus among the interest groups necessary for amendments.

One looks in vain for any strong disinterested group pressing for sound administrative reforms. Both labor and employer groups press for particular proposals, but always with a strong measure of self-interest. A speedy, simple disposition of cases at minimum cost, and in line with the original objectives of the law, sometimes seems almost incidental to their other purposes. The employer groups press hardest for certain reforms, but one wonders whether their representatives in compensation matters, the insurance carriers, are doing their utmost to achieve these objectives within the present framework. Undoubtedly, consideration of what should be an extraneous matter, the size of petitioners' attorneys' fees, influences the number of cases brought to the formal level. However, the law is specific in stating that these fees are based only on the difference between the amounts awarded at the formal level and the amounts paid or offered at previous stages. It is obvious that the closer the correspondence between these amounts, the less the incentive to bring cases to the final level. Granted that there are many reasons to explain the carriers' actions — it is said that cases are sometimes not brought to their attention soon enough, that the standards for evaluating disability are vague, and so on — still the question can be raised as to whether the insurance companies are doing all they can to achieve desirable administrative practices. Labor too may be shortsighted in insisting on awards in dubious cases, instead of pursuing the goal of more adequate treatment of those who suffer, or who will suffer, extended interruptions to their normal productive incomes.

The history of the administration of the act leads one to the conclusion that piecemeal reforms have their definite limitations. Although progress has been made, many of the practices and attitudes complained of as much as a quarter of a century ago, or more, are still with us. Without underestimating the difficulties involved in making any changes, it may be said that what is needed is a new administrative orientation. The fact that the program developed out of the common law of tort liability, and the fact that financing arrangements are private in character, must not be allowed to prevent workmen's compensation from taking its place as one of a group of social insurance programs. If this is to be accomplished, the one group available to press for administrative and legislative reforms are the administrators of the act. Their primary function is not to adjudicate differences among the interest groups, but to administer the program in light of the objectives outlined at the beginning of chapter 5; and this requires a host of changes.

On the noncontested level, progress has already been made with new reporting forms and the division's review of direct settlements. These, however, still retain the vestiges of the agreement system which has developed over the years. References to agreements and agreement procedures should be deleted from the law. In their place could be substituted a simple statement to the effect that the carrier and self-insurer are obligated to pay compensation as it becomes due and to report the full facts of the case to the division. It is also necessary that standards for the evaluation of permanent disability be devised and publicized. For administrative purposes, the basis on which this is done is less important than the fact that it be accomplished. If these changes were made, the administrators, operating under a direct payment philosophy, could concentrate on seeing to it that adequate compensation payments are made promptly and with a minimum of legalistic procedures.

There is no good reason to wait until the formal hearing before all relevant medical information is produced. This should be forthcoming at the time the carrier files its final report of accident, as is contemplated with the use of the reporting forms introduced in 1958. Each of these reports should be screened and reviewed by competent personnel with authority, under the law, to require the insurance carrier to produce additional relevant records, and to have the employee examined by a state physician if necessary.

Much can be accomplished by correspondence at this stage. Unless there is some unusual dispute, the overwhelming majority of cases which involve only questions of the quantum of disability ought to be disposed of at the noncontested level. This assumes that the standards of disability evaluation can be made definite and clear and that carriers would feel no obligation to make payments in cases in which the employee's disability was nonexistent.

Carriers should be judged on the basis of their over-all performance in making adequate payments speedily. If a carrier is continually deficient in meeting its obligations, the law should provide for a hearing procedure at which these matters could be heard and decided. Appropriate penalties could be provided for recalcitrant carriers, including the suspension of their privilege of writing compensation insurance within the state.

Only if it is impossible to adjust the case at the noncontested level should it be allowed to move into the informal hearing stage. The informal hearings need not be thought of as negotiating sessions at which an attempt is made to settle a dispute between equal parties. As long as this remains the thinking, labor groups are perfectly correct in arguing that if the employer has expert advice, then the employee has need of the same. These should be fact-finding sessions, which would not be scheduled unless the division felt that it was necessary to secure further information by direct contact with the parties. With the direct payment philosophy in force, the referee (a title that should be changed) would not seek agreement, but would merely point out to the carrier the appropriate payments to be made in the case, if these could be determined. Even with these changes, the disposition at the informal level need not be binding on the parties. If dissatisfied, then they should be given the opportunity to proceed to a formal hearing. But the law should require all unsettled cases to go through the informal stage before proceeding further. Some chance should be given to those whose duty it is to administer the law to see if a genuine dispute exists, before a case is brought to the forum which adjusts disputes.

The formal stage would then be reserved for cases which involve complicated disputes over the relationship between the employment and the accident, cases which involve complex diseases, or those which present some novel problem. To burden the formal stage with cases concerned with nothing more than the routine assessment of the quantum of disability is to admit to administrative deficiencies at the lower levels. It is a sheer waste of resources to utilize scarce medical and legal talent to process cases that could just as easily have been settled directly by the insurance carriers.

At present, the division exercises control over cases coming into the formal hearings by paring counsel and witness fees in certain small cases that it feels could best be settled at the informal stages. Such practices might well be continued and extended, but in the final analysis the most effective deterrent to the flow of unnecessary cases to the formal level can only be the assurance that both parties can receive full justice at the lower stages.

Throughout the history of the act, the matter of counsel fees and the concentration of legal work in a few hands have caused concern to administrators and investigators. Given the existing limitation on counsel fees, the only lawyers who find it profitable to operate in this field are those who spend most of their time in the compensation courts. If the changes outlined above were made, the number of cases at the formal level should decline drastically, but those that do reach that level may require extensive legal and medical research. The law should allow the deputy director wide discretion in fixing legal fees, in accordance with the amount of work necessary to prepare and present the case rather than the amount of the resulting award. This same reasoning would apply to fees for medical and other witnesses. Such a change would require the parties to have a high degree of confidence in the judgment of the deputies, but none of the proposed changes would have any chance of working without administrative personnel of the highest caliber.

To attract such personnel to hear cases and to review final reports of employers will probably require greater funds to administer the law than have been forthcoming in the past. The administrative costs of the division, which range around $700,000 a year, are met largely by appropriations from state revenues.[41] But other social insurance schemes are financed out of contributions, and there is no logical reason why this program should not be underwritten by a portion of premium costs. (At present, the funds allocated for administration of the division amount to about 0.8 per cent of annual earned premiums of insurance carriers.) In the end, a sound administration should lead to greater over-all economies. Weak administration is one of the most expensive of luxuries.

It might be much easier to find ways to change and improve the administration of the program than to bring about the fundamental reorientation in attitude and philosophy necessary to make these changes meaningful. Yet much is at stake here. No statutory change, no matter how well intended, can accomplish much unless accompanied by an active alert administration sympathetic with the goals and purposes of the program.

---

[41] The Legislature may authorize the transfer of up to $50,000 a year from the One Per Cent Fund for general administrative purposes of the division when the balance in the fund exceeds $1,250,000. (N.J. Stat. Ann., 34:15-94.)

Chapter 7

FINANCING THE PROGRAM – PRIVATE INSURANCE

The Employer Obligation

Most employers subject to New Jersey's compensation law are required to make provision for their financial liability under that statute. The exceptions are employers of farm or domestic labor, and the various levels of government.[1] Experience under the Social Security Act has demonstrated the practicality of having employers of farm and domestic labor pay the payroll taxes under this federal program, and it is likely that no great administrative obstacles stand in the way of requiring such employers to carry compensation insurance. As a matter of fact, many farmers and employers of domestic labor do insure, as do some governmental bodies, even for occupations for which the law does not require insurance coverage.[2]

Not all employers who are required to make provision for their financial liability under the law need purchase commercial insurance. If they can satisfy the Commissioner of Banking and Insurance that they are financially responsible, they may qualify as self-insurers.

---

[1]It should be noted that if any private employer did not elect coverage under the compensation act but remained under the employer liability provisions, the law (N.J. Stat. Ann. [West, 1958], 34:15-72) still requires him to insure or make sufficient provisions for the payment of his obligations. As of December, 1958, the Compensation Rating and Inspection Bureau had no knowledge of any employer who came under the employer liability provisions.

According to N.J. Stat. Ann., 34:15-43, all employees of governing bodies, state, county, municipal, or any board or commission, and all officers, appointed or elected, must come under the compensation provisions of the law. This specifically includes active volunteer firemen doing public fire duty, and every active first-aid or rescue squad worker doing public first-aid or rescue squad work. In general, the governing bodies are not required to insure, or qualify as self-insurers, with one exception. N.J. Stat. Ann., 34:15-74, requires that they provide compensation insurance for volunteer firemen, volunteer first-aid and emergency squad workers and fire marshals. These employees ordinarily do not receive wages, but the law (N.J. Stat. Ann., 34:15-75) provides that in the event of an accident, their compensation should be based upon a weekly wage that would entitle them to the maximum compensation payment.

[2]Residences employing domestic labor pay for their insurance coverage based upon the number of servants hired rather than the wages paid them. In New Jersey, for policy year 1955, nearly 43,000 policies were issued on a per capita basis, which gives some rough idea of the number of employers who insure their liability for injuries to domestic labor, even in the absence of legal requirements. On the basis of the number of policies issued in what appear to be agricultural classifications, it is estimated that about half of the employers of farm labor carry insurance coverage. This leaves the other half of the approximately 9,000 employers of farm labor in the state carrying rather heavy liabilities without such coverage.

Less than one-quarter of the state's municipalities carry insurance for street and maintenance employees. The State of New Jersey does not carry insurance for its employees, although presumably it meets all of the requirements of a self-insurer in that it is financially responsible, and it employs a large number of people in a variety of jobs.

Actually the term "self-insurer" may be misleading, since the firms are not required to set up reserves for anticipated losses on an actuarial basis. In reality, they are non-insurers who have convinced the Commissioner of their financial capabilities and business stability.

During 1957, 180 employers qualified as self-insurers in New Jersey, but as might be expected, these were large employers, many of whose names could be found on any honor roll of American industry. Self-insured employers constitute approximately 0.1 per cent of all employers, but they pay about 15 per cent of all compensation benefits.[3] The self-insurers must meet not only the indemnity and medical costs of compensation cases but also the burden of processing claims and defending them in the compensation courts — expenses that would fall to the insurance carriers if these companies insured.

The economic motive may not be paramount in the decision of a company to self-insure; it may value the idea of controlling the administration of its compensation claims. On the other hand, some self-insurers hire adjusting agencies to process claims and undoubtedly feel that their total costs are less than if they were to buy insurance. There is some evidence of a trand away from self-insurance. Since 1946, the relative amount of compensation benefits paid by self-insurers has declined.[4]

Insurance Companies

With the exception of the employers exempt by statute, and the self-insurers, all other New Jersey employers are compelled to insure their liability under the law with one or another of the 162 insurance companies authorized to do business within the state.[5] Only 149 of these insurance companies actually wrote liability premiums, of this type

---

[3] A list of the self-insured employers can be found in New Jersey Compensation Rating and Inspection Bureau, *Forty-First Annual Report*, 1958, Exhibit J. The amount of compensation benefits paid is based upon contributions of self-insured employers to the One Per Cent Fund.

[4] New Jersey Division of Workmen's Compensation, *Annual Report*, 1956, pp. 21-22.

[5] Any such employer who fails to insure may be guilty of a misdemeanor. N.J. Stat. Ann., 34:15-79, provides that upon conviction of a misdemeanor, the employer shall be punished by a fine of not more than $1,000, or by imprisonment for not more than sixty days, or both. In cases wherein the compensation award is not paid at the time of sentencing, the court may suspend sentence and place the defendant on probation with an order to make payments to the worker through the probation office. A contractor placing work through a subcontractor is liable for any compensation awarded to an employee of the subcontractor if the subcontractor fails to carry the required insurance. All fines collected under these provisions are to be credited to the account of the Rehabilitation Commission.

A check of the records of the Attorney General's office reveals that during calendar year 1956, 177 cases were referred to that office by deputy directors of Division of the Workmen's Compensation because of some doubt as to whether the employer was properly insured. In 44 of these cases, at the end of the year, the Attorney General's office was either still investigating the cases and checking on the insurance coverage or still awaiting final determinations in the cases by the compensation division. In another 21 cases, no compensation award was granted, either because the case was discontinued or dismissed or because the petition was not moved. In 28 other cases, investigation by the Attorney General's office revealed that the employer actually did carry insurance at the time of the acci-

during 1957; and, as can be seen from Table XIX, a relatively few companies succeeded in capturing the lion's share of the business. One company alone, the New Jersey Manufacturers Casualty Insurance Company, had for approximately one-quarter of the business. Four-fifths of the premiums written during 1957 were written by 25 companies.[6]

Table XIX. Written Compensation Premiums of Five Leading
New Jersey Insurance Companies, Calendar Year 1957

Company	Written Premiums	Percentage of Total Written Premiums
N. J. Manufacturers Casualty Insurance Co.	$20,716,065	23.1%
Liberty Mutual Insurance Company	8,825,318	9.8
Travelers Insurance Company	5,655,637	6.3
Aetna Casualty and Surety Company	3,623,100	4.0
Hartford Accident and Indemnity Company	3,076,140	3.4
Total for Five Leading Companies	$41,896,260	46.74%

Source: New Jersey Compensation Rating and Inspection Bureau, *Forty-First Annual Report*, Exhibit B.

---

dent. This leaves 84 cases, of which 40 were closed at the end of the year and 44 were still pending. The disposition or status of these cases was as follows:

	No. of Cases	
Compensation award paid by employer	34	
Employer not required to insure (employee a domestic)	5	
Employer prosecuted	1	
Total closed cases		40
Employer given opportunity to make payment	24	
Partial payment made by employer	7	
Referred to county prosecutor	13	
Total pending cases		44
Total cases		84

It is apparent from the above tabulation that the Attorney General's office has been concerned, principally, with seeing to it that the petitioner receives his award. In 65 of the 84 cases, the employer either paid the award, was currently paying it, or was being given an opportunity to make some arrangements to pay it. Presumably, if the employer shows some evidence of good faith and can arrange to pay the petitioner, no prosecution will be undertaken. In 13 of the cases, however, the matter was referred to the appropriate county prosecutor. In only one case had the employer been indicted for a misdemeanor. In that one case, the court placed the defendant on probation for a period of five years, during which time he was to pay the compensation award of $5,514.14. Of course, the employer could have been fined or imprisoned in any of the cases that were referred to the county prosecutors.

N.J. Stat. Ann., 34:15-80, requires employers to post notices of the fact that they are insured or qualified for self-insurance in a conspicuous place about their premises. Inspectors of the Department of Labor and Industry check for these notices when they make routine safety or wage and hour inspections. Cases in which employers presumably have failed to comply with the insurance requirements are referred to the compensation division and, from there, to the Attorney General's office. This procedure has the advantage of allowing a check to be made on insurance status, prior to an accident and subsequent compensation claim.

[6] New Jersey Compensation Rating and Inspection Bureau, *Forty-First Annual Report*, Exhibit B. Any statistics of concentration are influenced by the dominant position of the

The important carriers within the state are organized either as stock companies or as mutual associations. The mutuals are incorporated groups which elect officers and transact business in the corporate name. Policyholders are members of the association or company; they are entitled to vote at meetings and have rights of participation in the profits of the company. Stock companies carry on business, not as an associate matter, but rather as one of commercial speculation with the insurer making a hedged bet against the contingencies. They accept insurance at a premium designed to cover the hazards of loss and the expenses, and they hope to receive a profit from the underwriting.[7]

Mutuals gain their greatest percentage of business through direct writings, or contact by salaried representatives, and hence they tend to seek out the large risks. Stock companies, on the other hand, operate through brokers and commission agents, a factor which naturally increases their acquisition costs. In general, mutuals have lower administrative costs and are able to return dividends to their policyholders. On the other hand, stock companies claim to offer superior services to counterbalance their higher net charges.

The formerly clear distinctions between these two types of carriers have blurred in recent years. At one time, the mutual's policyholders paid a moderate policy fee and were assessed for losses as they occurred. Today, they operate in much the same manner as stock companies and do business on an advance premium basis, with no assessments. The introduction of prospective experience rating, retrospective rating and advance premium discount plans has tended to better the competitive position of stock companies; and the mutuals, in an effort to expand business, have invaded the field of the smaller risks. Also, and probably most important, some, but not all, stock companies write policies which carry rights of participation in the profits of the company.

In the 1920's, participating companies in New Jersey wrote about 30 per cent of all premiums, but this percentage has gradually increased. Since 1947, the participating companies have accounted for

---

New Jersey Manufacturers Casualty Insurance Company. It must also be realized that this is a highly specialized line of insurance; many companies that are authorized to write compensation business write policies only to accommodate customers who have placed other insurance with them.

This has become increasingly possible with the popularization of the multiple-line concept, under which a single insurance company is allowed to write a variety of casualty and surety lines. See G. F. Michelbacher, ed., *Multiple-Line Insurance* (N. Y.: McGraw-Hill Book Co., 1957), esp. chapter 1, "The Multiple-Line Idea."

Kulp points out that for insurance companies, compensation business has always been a favorite opening line or business-getter for other lines. "No other underwriter has as many legitimate occasions to keep in touch with the insured — through auditor, safety engineer, and claims representative. It is worthwhile then to carry compensation as an accommodation." Kulp goes on to say that this is possible only when the other lines are showing underwriting profits. (C. A. Kulp, *Casualty Insurance*, 3d ed. [N. Y.: The Ronald Press Co., 1956], p. 151.)

[7]Clarence W. Hobbs, *Workmen's Compensation Insurance* (N. Y.: McGraw-Hill Book Co., 1939), p. 329.

one-half or more of the total earned premiums each year, with the major portion falling to the two leading carriers within the state, both of whom operate on a participating basis.[8]

The Compensation Rating and Inspection Bureau

All insurance is affected by a public interest, but probably none so much as compensation insurance which is compulsory and which secures payment, not to business firms which suffer casualty losses, but to industrial workers whose incomes are interrupted. Testimony to its unusual nature is the fact that for many years insurance carriers felt that this was a line on which underwriting profits should not be made.[9] Also, almost from its inception, workmen's compensation insurance has been subject to a high degree of state regulation. State laws require not only that rates charged by compensation insurance carriers be filed with some supervisory authority but also that the entire rate structure be subject to approval by the insurance commissioner. The object of such regulation is to see to it that the rates charged are neither excessive nor discriminatory, but that they are at the same time adequate to produce the necessary revenues to cover losses. It goes without saying that a free market for insurance does not exist; employers similarly situated will pay the same initial insurance rates. The existence of the various rating plans, together with the fact that some companies return dividends to policyholders, guarantees a degree of price competition, but always within the framework of the over-all rate regulation.

Although state control over the rate-making process, itself, began in 1912 in New York when a statute was adopted regulating and supervising rate-making associations for all branches of insurance,[10]

---

[8]New Jersey Compensation Rating and Inspection Bureau, *Forty-First Annual Report*, Exhibit C-1. The rating bureau does not issue breakdowns showing the relative business of stock and mutuals in New Jersey, largely because the largest carrier in the state is formally organized as a stock company but operates on a participating basis.

If the nation-wide business of mutual and stock companies which operate in the State of New York is considered during the years 1948 to 1956, the stock companies accounted for about 60 per cent of the earned premiums of both classes of companies, while the mutual companies accounted for the remaining 40 per cent. (Alfred M. Skolnik, "Trends in Workmen's Compensation: Coverage, Benefits and Costs," *Social Security Bulletin*, XXV [August 1958], Table 10.) The earned premium figures disregard dividends to policyholders. The distribution of business is influenced by the fact that there are more stock companies than mutual carriers. In 1954, in the casualty insurance field as a whole, there were 321 stock companies and 240 mutuals. (Kulp, pp. 417-420.)

In addition to these classes of carriers, a fraction of private compensation insurance, less than 2 per cent, is underwritten by reciprocal or interinsurance exchanges and Lloyds' associations. The subscribers to a reciprocal exchange arrangement do business through an attorney-in-fact who exchanges contracts among the members. As Kulp states, "Each member covers every other member at the same time he is covered." The liability is that of the individual subscribers and not the group. (Kulp, pp. 423-427.)

As will be discussed below, various state funds may write all or a portion of the compensation insurance in their respective jurisdictions.

[9]Kulp, p. 151.

[10]Stefan A. Riesenfeld and Richard C. Maxwell, *Modern Social Legislation* (Brooklyn: The Foundation Press, 1950), p. 372.

New Jersey, in 1917, was the first state to establish a Compensation Rating and Inspection Bureau by legislative act.[11] In most states today, the necessary statistical and actuarial information for rate-making purposes is gathered and analyzed by the National Council on Compensation Insurance, which makes the rates, subject to approval by state authorities. The council, composed of representatives of both stock and mutual carriers, was established in 1921. New Jersey's bureau, like the bureaus in the seven other states which followed New Jersey's lead in establishing independent rating bureaus, cooperates with the National Council but is independent of it.

New Jersey's Compensation Rating and Inspection Bureau occupies a unique place in the structure of state government. Technically it is not part of the state government, but rather an instrumentality of the state under the supervision of the State Commissioner of Banking and Insurance. Each insurance company authorized to write compensation insurance within the state must, by law, be a member of the bureau and is entitled to one vote in its affairs. The duality of its structure is illustrated by the fact that the Commissioner appoints a deputy to act as ex officio chairman of the bureau; and, as a matter of practice, this same man has been selected by members of the bureau as its manager or chief executive officer.

During calendar year 1957, the bureau employed an average 94.1 employees, but only the deputy commissioner, the actuary and his four assistants are under the state civil service program. In recent years, the normal expenditures of the bureau have amounted to slightly more than $400,000 a year, or a bit more than one-half of 1 per cent of the insurance companies' written premiums.[12]

The principal job of the bureau is to establish the compensation rates. The insurance company members elect a governing committee composed of representatives of six carriers, and it meets with the manager of the bureau and other top officials about four times a year. The governing committee has the task of approving the rates and regulations for submission to the Commissioner. In practice, the rates evolved by the bureau staff are usually accepted by the governing committee and, when so accepted, are normally approved by the Commissioner.

Rate-Making — The Determination of Pure Premiums

A detailed examination of rate-making procedures is contained in

---

[11] N.J. Laws 1917, ch. 178, p. 522.

[12] N.J. Stat. Ann., 34:15-93, provides that each insurance company shall pay one-quarter of 1 per cent of net premiums to the state tax commissioner for the purposes of defraying the costs of the Commissioner of Banking and Insurance in carrying out his rate-making functions. In addition, the insurance carriers pay all the expenses of the bureau except for the civil service salaries and the costs of certain machine equipment used in determining rates. During calendar year 1957, the total expenditures of the bureau amounted to $473,227.21, or 0.53 per cent of written premiums. This total included, however $21,666.78 for alterations and improvements in bureau premises. (New Jersey Compensation Rating and Inspection Bureau, Forty-First Annual Report, p. 14.)

the appendix to this chapter, and only a brief summary description will be given here.

An *insurance rate* is the price of insurance and is quoted in terms of a unit of exposure, which is usually $100 of covered payroll. In the case of domestic servants' classifications, however, the unit of exposure is on a per capita basis.

Compensation rate-making rests, in good part, on the theory of probability, which is, essentially, that the number of times an event occurs in an exposure, sufficiently great in time and extent, determines the number of times an event will occur in a like exposure in the future.[13] Since the usual unit of exposure is $100 of payroll, rate-makers attempt to place experience under categories that give some indication of being similar from one year to the next. Such categories, called *classifications*, are well-defined industries, processes or occupations. About 683 such classifications, each given a code number, and described in a classification manual, are in use in New Jersey. Since most insurance carriers operate in several states, it is to their advantage to have some uniformity in manual classifications, and in New Jersey the bulk of the classifications are those of the National Council on Compensation Insurance. Some, however, are special to the state, and New Jersey does not use some of the national classifications.

A fairly detailed set of rules is available to enable carriers to classify employers properly. Usually, an employer receives one classification, the one which most accurately describes his operations; however, in some cases standard exceptions are provided, and employers are allowed to divide their payrolls and apply rates separately for each of the classifications involved.[14]

Manual rates, that is, the rates shown in the manual for each classification, are made up of the *pure premiums*, which are the amounts of expected losses per unit of exposure, and the *expense and other loadings*. Determination of the pure premium for each classification adjusts the *rate relativity* among the classifications; it indicates the hazard of one classification as opposed to another.

The bureau must have certain basic information for each classification before it can decide whether existing pure premiums should be changed. It must know the actual experience of employers over some past period; how many compensation cases occurred, what types of cases they were, how much they cost, and so on.

Under the so-called "unit statistical plan," each insurance carrier must report payrolls, earned premiums and losses segregated by type

---

[13] Hobbs, p. 513.

[14] As of July, 1958, there was no experience recorded in about 60 of the 683 classifications. In addition to the usual payroll-rated classification, there are four per capita classifications covering domestic servants and some special classifications covering vessels and the chemical and dyestuffs rating plan. Certain classifications, such as clerical office employees, salesmen, drivers, and so on, are usually separately classified, and their payrolls are separately listed and rated. When an employer has more than one classification, the most important one is listed as the governing classification, and this is used when companies are divided into categories for statistical purposes.

of injury, under each policy it issues. The bureau assembles these data by classification and by policy year. A policy year is the period during which all policies issued in a specific calendar year are in effect. Since a policy runs for a term of one calendar year, but may be issued at any time during the year, one policy year runs over two calendar years. The policy year 1957 began on January 1, 1957, but did not end until December 31, 1958.

The older these data, the more likely the estimates of incurred losses will reflect reality; but unfortunately the more aged the experience, the less likely it is to reflect current conditions. The bureau takes the most recent policy-year data available and adjusts it to reflect current conditions. Because of the inevitable time lags involved in having the insurance carriers evaluate the experience, the most recent data available in the middle of any one year pertain to the policy year dated three years earlier. Even this is only the first of five eventual reportings the carriers will make on the experience of this policy year. But one policy year's experience is not enough; hence the bureau uses a total composed of data for the most recent year available and the four preceding policy years, adjusting each year's information to reflect current conditions.

Payrolls and medical losses are used as reported; but indemnity loss estimates are adjusted to the level they would have been if the current law had been in effect during each of the policy years, and premiums are changed to reflect the latest manual rates. Medical losses are not adjusted, in part because of the difficulty of securing an adequate index of changes in these costs.

Past experience is used in order to adjust the rate relativity for the future, and this requires some delving into the types of losses. Indemnity losses are classified into serious and nonserious categories, and losses in individual cases are limited to a maximum amount. The basic rationale here is that the frequency of occurrence is more significant, as an indication of what to expect in the future, than the severity, which is more influenced by chance factors. The losses eliminated must be taken into account later when the final rates are set. In effect, this procedure spreads the cost of a few fortuitous cases over the entire rate structure, so that they do not influence the rates for any one classification.

Once these various adjustments have been made, the bureau has before it the payrolls for five policy years and the so-called modified losses. Dividing losses into the payrolls allows the computation of pure premium rates based upon the "five-year indications" for each of the classifications. At the time of the rate revision, each classification has a current or "present" pure premium, and this is adjusted so as to permit comparison with the five-year indications. Which of these pure premiums should be chosen to underlie the new level of rates in the classification? This depends upon the credence or statistical reliability that should be attached to the five-year indications. A table of credibility values, related to claim frequency, is used to test the five-year indications. If, for example, in the serious category, multi-plying the present pure premium rate by the payroll shows, on an expected loss basis, the equivalent of fifty average losses, then the indicated pure premiums will be given full credence. If it falls below this, then the indications are held to be deficient; and they must be supplemented by giving weight to the present pure premiums.

Similar credibility factors are applied to the nonserious losses and to the medical losses. In effect, whenever the indications are not given 100 per cent credibility, the pure premiums are determined by a formula under which the indications are averaged together with the present pure premiums. If the indications are given, say 30 per cent weight in this average, the present pure premiums are given the com-plement of this, or 70 per cent, as their weight. In most instances, the total formula pure premiums are used as the pure premiums to under-lie the new rates.

The fact that the experience of five policy years is used lends stability to the classification pure premiums. If losses, over the years, are moving either up or down, the use of only the experience of the last year would mean that rates would fluctuate widely. The five-year moving average tends to dampen these fluctuations, a tendency rein-forced by a rule of the bureau that classification pure premiums should not change by more than 20 per cent at any one rate revision.

Once pure premiums are adopted for each classification, the rate-maker has a measure of relative hazard. The pure premiums must still be translated into manual rates, but before this can be done, the important decision as to whether the *general rate level* should be changed must be made.

Adjusting the General Level of Rates

In adjusting the general level of rates, the bureau makes use of the calendar-year information filed by carriers on so-called schedule W. This is, in effect, a running inventory from the individual carrier's accounting records. It shows earned premiums and losses during each of the last six calendar years for all policies which became effective in each of the last twenty-two years. Once these data are aggregated for all carriers, the over-all premiums and incurred losses for the latest calendar year can be abstracted by deducting the premiums and losses at the end of the previous year from the comparable totals at the end of the last year shown. At the time of the July, 1958, rate revision, for example, it was possible to secure the schedule W premiums and losses for calendar year 1957. This would not show the experience under policies written during 1957 alone. Some 1957 experience would be included, but the figures would reflect premiums of several of the past years and loss experience under some policies written perhaps decades ago.

One advantage of schedule W is that it provides some check on the insurance companies' reporting of outstanding losses. If these losses are estimated too generously at the time the accident occurs, this has the effect of increasing the loss ratios — the percentage that losses are of earned premiums. Eventually, however, the estimated losses become paid losses; and if the amounts actually paid are less than those estimated, the difference is eventually reflected in the schedule W reports, and loss ratios are correspondingly deflated.

The important thing about the schedule W information is that it gives the bureau some idea of the over-all loss experience of the insurance carriers. For calendar 1957, the earned premiums amounted to approximately $86.5 million, and incurred losses were estimated at about $52.5 million, giving a loss ratio of 60.66 per cent. When premiums are placed at the latest collectible level and losses are adjusted to reflect the current law level, the loss ratio is reduced to 59.97 per cent.

This loss ratio must now be tested to determine whether it is too high, too low or just right. This is done by contrasting the latest modified loss ratio with the *permissible loss ratio,* the percentage of earned premiums which had been expected to be paid in losses. It so happened that at the time the permissible loss ratio was 58.08 per cent, or about 3 per cent less than the modified loss ratio. This was a signal to the bureau that the general rate level should be increased, as was done at the time of the July, 1958, rate revision. If the 1957 schedule W modified experience had shown a loss ratio less than the permissible one, the general rate level would have been decreased.

Obviously the permissible loss ratio is the crucial factor. It is determined entirely by the standard expense loadings, which remain fairly constant from year to year except for changes in the tax factors. These expense loadings range around 42 per cent of the earned premiums, leaving about 58 per cent for losses. In other words, if things worked out each year as expected, about two-fifths of the premiums would be allocated for the various costs of the insurance companies, and the balance would be allocated for indemnity and medical losses.

Table XX shows these expense loadings as a percentage of the

Table XX. New Jersey Compensation Insurance — Expense Ratios, All Industry Groups, July 1, 1958

Expense Items	Standard Loadings	Excluding Loss and Expense Constant	Tax Items	
Acquisition	17.50%	17.50%	Gen. State Premium	2.00%
Taxes	3.70	3.70	2d Injury Fund	0.45
Claim	8.20	8.32	Rate Supervision	0.25
Inspection	2.47	2.50	Misc. Federal Fees	0.50
Home Office	6.11	5.52	Security Fund	0.50
Payroll Audit	1.86	1.48	*Total*	3.70%
Profit	2.50	2.50		
Total	42.34%	41.52%		
Permissible Loss Ratio	57.66%	58.48%		

Source: New Jersey Compensation Rating and Inspection Bureau, "July 1, 1958, Rate Revision," Exhibit IX.

premium level. The largest single item is the 17.5 per cent acquisition expense, fixed to take into account the stock companies' commissions to agents and brokers. Since all companies, however, charge the same manual rates, all would benefit by rate fixed with a 17.5 per cent acquisition expense, regardless of whether business is secured through brokers, salaried representatives or direct writing.

Other expense items cover the costs of adjusting claims, the inspection of the employer's premises, the expenses involved in auditing payrolls and the costs of the home office. The two remaining items are taxes and profits. The tax items (shown separately in Table XX) involve certain fixed statutory obligations, and also the contributions to the second injury fund and the security fund.[15] Since the law provides limitations on contributions to these funds once they reach predetermined levels, the tax loadings fluctuate from year to year.

The profit item is a source of controversy. At one time, the loadings did not include any profit item, but beginning in 1952, in New Jersey, a 1.5 per cent profit loading was introduced, and in 1957 this was changed to 2.5 per cent as other expense loadings were reduced.[16] This revaluation of the expense items was based upon surveys made by the National Council on Compensation Insurance and reflected countrywide rather than New Jersey experience, particularly.

Some critics of private insurance tend to lump all the expense items together and to regard them as profits for the insurance companies. Although this is wide of the mark, the fact remains that some portion of the premiums allocated for other expense items may wind up as profits if casualty losses are less than expected. On the other hand, if losses exceed the expected level, companies will sustain underwriting losses, despite the profit loadings.

All policyholders pay a so-called *loss and expense constant*. Table XX shows the expense loadings, both with and without the constants. Actually, in New Jersey, as of July 1, 1958, the loss constant was zero, and, in effect, the loss and expense constant is an expense constant alone. This amounts to $10 for all payroll-rated policies and $5 for per capita-rated ones. As its name implies, the expense constant is a flat charge added to the premium of the risk, designed to offset the fact that the expense loading on the smaller risk does not yield enough money to cover the minimum cost of issuing and servicing a policy.[17]

The expense constant was advocated by the stock carriers, who

---

[15] N. J. Stat. Ann., 34:15-103-120, provides for the creation of separate security funds for the mutual and stock carriers. Each carrier pays a sum equal to 1 per cent of its net premiums each year. Contributions cease, however, when the sums in the funds equal 5 per cent of the loss reserves of the carriers. The funds are used for compensation claims that remain unpaid by reason of default of an insolvent insurance carrier. The current status of each of the funds is reported each year in the annual report of the Compensation Rating and Inspection Bureau. As of December 31, 1957, the stock security fund stood at $2,442,812.02, and only $504.89 was paid in claims during the year. The mutual security fund stood at $787,321.55, and no claims were paid.

[16] Inspection, home office and payroll audit expense loadings were reduced. The over-all change in the total expense loadings were insignificant.

[17] Hobbs, p. 416.

claimed that one of the causes of their underwriting losses was the disproportionately large expense connected with the small risk. Since the dollar amounts available for expenses are determined as a percentage of premiums, in the higher premium ranges the amounts may be excessive, whereas in the lower ranges they may be insufficient. The introduction of the expense constant increases the amounts available for expenses. More recently, the introduction of premium discounts, either directly or through retrospective rating plans, has had the effect of reducing the flat percentage expense loadings for the large risks.

The high proportion of the premiums allocated for the expense loadings lends ammunition to those who advocate state insurance funds in place of private insurance. Of course, regardless of how the program is financed, it must receive in premiums an amount larger than that which is to be paid in indemnity and medical losses. The costs of audit, inspection, overhead, and so on, are there, and they must be met, in one fashion or another. In the final analysis, the question is not whether there should be an amount allocated for expenses, but whether some other sort of a system could do the job less expensively.

Setting the Manual Rates

Since pure premiums have already been determined for each classification, each of these rates must now be translated into manual rates. To simplify matters, the expense loadings are taken into account by multiplying the pure premiums by an appropriate factor. This multiplier reflects not only the expense loadings but also the losses previously eliminated in converting the individual classification experience and any necessary changes in the general rate level.

As an example, one classification, "wire insulating or covering," had an adopted pure premium for the July 1, 1958, rate revision of $1.06, which, when multiplied to reflect the increase in the rate level and the expense loadings, becomes $1.766; $0.02 is added to this rate as a catastrophe loading,[18] making the annual premium $1.786, which, under the interval system used, rounds off to $1.80. This becomes the rate per $100 of payroll, unless it is adjusted by experience rating, retrospective rating or the premium discount plan. Regardless of the size of the risk, $10 would be added to its total premium as the expense constant. The minimum premium charged would be $19 per year, computed on the basis of five times the rate plus the expense constant.

Experience Rating

In setting insurance rates, an individual company's experience is considered together with that of other companies in the same classification. The manual rate may be an accurate measure of the insurance

---

[18] Catastrophes are accidents that involve two or more claims.

cost for the classification as a whole, but it may be highly inappropriate as a measure of the hazard in any one company. An individual firm's safety efforts might be stimulated if it were convinced that its insurance rate would be responsive to changes in its accident rates. Prospective experience rating is one method of modifying an employer's rate to take into account the individual firm's experience. It is common to refer to prospective experience rating, in which the risk's current experience is used to modify its future rate, merely as experience rating, without the qualifying adjective. In retrospective rating, the risk's current experience is allowed to influence its rate for the current period.

Only the relatively large employers who can qualify for experience rating. If a risk has developed premiums of at least $1,600 during the last year, or the last two years, of its experience period, it automatically qualifies for rating.[19] If an employer is eligible, he has no choice in the matter. His experience will be scrutinized without application on his part, and he will receive a rate that may be greater or less than the manual rate for his classification.

One major problem is to determine how much weight any individual firm's experience should be given. Its experience must be compared with that of the classification as a whole in such a way as to give the maximum responsiveness of the rate to *significant* changes in the risk's experience.[20] Once an accident occurs, the severity of the resulting injury is greatly influenced by chance. Consequently, it is the frequency of accidents that is given major weight. This is accomplished by reviewing the actual losses of the insured as reported under the unit statistical plan. Losses are brought up to the present law level, individual losses are limited to a maximum value, and, if large enough, are split into two components. One is the so-called "normal" loss, which is limited to $2,000, whereas the balance of the incurred loss, up to a maximum value, is included as the "excess" loss. Since the normal portion of the loss more nearly reflects frequency, it is given greater weight in the comparisons.

The manual premiums for the classification are also brought up to current levels, segregated into normal and excess portions, and multiplied by the expected loss factors to determine the expected losses for the classification as a whole. It now becomes a matter of averaging together the risk's adjusted losses and the expected losses for the classification. Just as when the pure premiums for the classification are determined, it is necessary to assign credibility factors to weight each of these amounts. The credibility factors, which have a range from 0 to 1, give greater weight to the actual adjusted losses as the risk increases in size.

The complement of the credibility factor used to weight actual

---

[19] The basic data on New Jersey's experience rating plan can be found in a publication of the Compensation Rating and Inspection Bureau entitled *New Jersey Experience Rating Plan* (Newark, 1923, with periodic supplements).

[20] Kulp, p. 504.

experience is used to weight the expected losses. Take the extreme case as an example: If a risk developed sufficient experience, its actual experience would be given a credibility factor of 1, and the expected losses would be given a weight of 0, or for all practical purposes disregarded. Such large risks are, in effect, self-rated. On the other hand, a small risk which just meets minimum eligibility requirements cannot expect that its experience will be given much credence. Primary weight would be attached to the expected losses of the classification as a whole.

In computing the averages, the normal and excess components are averaged separately and then added together. The resulting total adjusted losses are then divided by the expected losses for the classification to arrive at a percentage experience modification factor.

If this percentage figure is less than 100 per cent, the risk would pay less than the manual rate; if greater, it would pay more. On balance, the amounts of credits tend to be greater than the amounts of charges. Of the 12,331 risks rated in calendar year 1957, 7,998 received a credit or a decrease in their manual rates, 11 remained normal, whereas 4,322 risks received an increase. The increases or decreases can be considerable; the percentage experience modification factor ranges from 20 per cent to a high of 200 per cent. On the average, however, risks which received decreases paid 77 per cent of manual rates, whereas those whose rates went up paid 123.6 per cent of the manual rates. Risks that are experience rated are usually about 10 per cent of the total number, but their importance is indicated by the fact that they may develop about 80 per cent of the total premiums.[21]

The essential justification for experience rating is that the system is supposed to reward or penalize an employer for his relative success in controlling the frequency and severity of industrial accidents. Yet the very theory of experience rating does not make it applicable in the plants that probably need it most. Large departmentalized plants, with thousands of employees, usually have a high degree of safety consciousness, stimulated, perhaps, by an organized safety program under the guidance of a trained safety engineer. In part, the motivation may be to reduce insurance rates, but it is doubtful whether this is the sole, or even important, motivation. If experience rating were to disappear tomorrow, these safety programs would probably continue in force. To account for these safety developments by financial considerations, such as rate concessions, would be to ignore the development of public relations and the increased community consciousness of many of the units of big industry. In a tight labor market, it pays a plant to have a reputation as a safe place to work, quite apart from any credits on the insurance premium. A spectacular industrial accident can interfere with morale and hiring, and cost a great deal more money in indirect

---

[21] These data are from: Compensation Rating and Inspection Bureau, *Forty-First Annual Report*, Exhibit E.

losses than any possible increases in rate premiums. Also, many
companies are unionized, and union officials tend to interest them
selves in safety matters and are quick to file grievances relating to
unsafe conditions.

The smaller plant, which is not so much in the community's eye
and which may not have any organized safety program, may well be
tempted by rate concessions to busy itself with reducing injuries. In
too many cases, however, such a plant would not generate sufficient
premiums to qualify for rating. Most plants are not large enough to be
experience rated.

Premium Discounts and Retrospective Rating

Premium discounts and retrospective rating were introduced in
New Jersey only at the end of 1956, although retrospective rating was
first used in Massachusetts twenty years earlier. Prospective ex
perience rating cannot be immediately responsive to changes in the
risk's experience, since modifications of the present insurance rate
are always being made on the basis of the experience of the past
period. Retrospective rating is essentially a method of determining an
employer's insurance rate by basing it upon losses of the current
insurance period. Something of this sort is available to risks who
insure with participating companies; the dividends they receive are
based, in part, upon the insurance carrier's loss experience for the
current period. With retrospective rating, which ties rates to a risk's
current experience, the nonparticipating companies have a competitive
weapon to induce large risks to insure with them rather than the par
ticipating companies, or rather than self-insure.

Both premium discount plans and retrospective rating, which, as
will be seen, are alternatives, allow the large risk a discount on the
expense portions of its premiums. When manual rates are deter
mined, acquisition expense and other expense loadings are set as a
percentage of the premiums paid by an employer. This means that an
employer who pays a $20,000 premium would be paying twice as much
commission to the insurance agent as an employer who paid a $10,000
premium. Both the retrospective plans and the discount plans allow
for a graded acquisition expense; a feature about which the commission
agents are less than enthusiastic. [22] Of course, to the extent that these
plans allow stock companies to capture risks that were previously
self-insured, or insured with a participating carrier, no real sacrifice
is being made by the agent.

Unlike experience rating, which is compulsory for eligible risks
the retrospective rating plans are optional with employers. In spite of
the fact that they were introduced on the urging of stock carriers, in
the interests of equity they are available for both participating and
nonparticipating carriers, although the plan for each class of carrier

---

[22] Kulp, pp. 531-532.

is different. Neither retrospective rating nor premium discount plans supersede the experience rating plan. Every insured employer who qualifies for experience rating continues to be rated just as if a retrospective rating plan had not been chosen. If, however, a large employer does not choose retrospective rating, he will automatically receive a premium discount if his premiums are large enough.

There are two plans of retrospective rating, designated as plan A and plan B. The choice between these two plans would seem to depend largely upon the employer's temperament. Under plan A, the standard premium is the maximum premium that the risk can be called upon to pay. The minimum premium is a percentage of the standard premium, and this percentage decreases as the standard premium increases.[23]

Under plan B the employer gambles a little bit. The minimum premium and basic premium[24] are lower than under plan A, but the maximum premium is greater than the standard premium. The percentage that the maximum premium is of the standard premium decreases as the standard premium increases.

To qualify for retrospective rating, a risk must develop at least $5,000 of premiums at standard rates. Assume, for example, that an employer has a standard premium of $7,500 and that he insures with a nonparticipating stock carrier under plan A. Assume that his incurred losses amounted to $3,750, or exactly one half of the standard premium. His retrospective premium will depend upon his actual losses, as converted, the basic premium and an amount for taxes. The basic premium will vary with the size of the standard premium. The minimum-size eligible risk (standard premium of $5,000) would pay a basic premium of 28 per cent. This declines slowly and gradually as standard premium increases, until employers with standard premiums of $500,000, and over, pay a basic premium of 18.9 per cent.[25] The basic premium declines principally because of the graded expense features. These graded expense values are identical with those used in the discount plans.

Adding together the basic premium, the converted losses, and the taxes gives an indicated retrospective premium of $6,585,38. Since this less than the standard premium (the maximum he would pay under

---

[23] New Jersey Compensation Rating and Inspection Bureau, "Circular Letter #791," October 31, 1956.

[24] The basic premium charge is made up principally of that portion of the administrative expense common to all eligible risks and classifications, and also a net insurance charge based upon the differences between the maximum and minimum premiums. Any losses above the maximum premium are the responsibility of the insurer and not the insured. No employer can be called upon to pay more than the maximum premium, regardless of the extent of his incurred losses. On the other hand, he is called upon to pay the minimum premium even if he has no losses or if his losses plus his basic premiums and taxes are less than the minimum premium. As Kulp points out, "The effect of adding these pooling or insurance provisions is to set an upper and a lower limit to the self-rating feature of retrospective rating." (Kulp, p. 523.)

[25] The values cited are as of May, 1957. New Jersey Compensation Rating and Inspection Bureau, "Manual Amendment Bulletin, #214," May 10, 1957.

plan A) and more than the minimum (85 per cent of the standard premium or $6,375), it would be the premium he actually would pay.[26]

If he had chosen plan B, his indicated retrospective premium would have been slightly less ($6,422.68), but he would have been taking more of a chance. His maximum premium could have been as high as $12,750 (170 per cent of his standard premium of $7,500). On the other hand, if his losses were low enough, he could have paid only the minimum premium of $4,350 (58 per cent of $7,500).[27]

As an alternative to retrospective rating, any employer with a total standard premium of over $1,000 can qualify for a premium discount according to the schedule below.[28]

Total New Jersey Standard Premium	Applicable Discount (per cent)	
	Schedule Y Nonparticipating Companies	Schedule X Participating Companies
First $1,000	----	---
Next $4,000	9.0	3.0
Next $95,000	14.0	6.0
Over $100,000	16.5	8.5

The basic rationale for premium discounts is the same as for retrospective rating in that it allows a graded expense feature for large insurers. The employer with a standard premium of $7,500 would pay a net premium of $6,975 if insured with a nonparticipating company, more than under retrospective rating plan A or B. Of course, with the discount plan, he takes no chances; his net premiums do not depend upon his loss experience.

Retrospective rating is relatively new in New Jersey, and it is still too early to determine its effect. However, the minimum-size requirements prevent it from being applied to any but a small minority of employers. During policy year 1955, for example, when there were more than 122,000 risks on an annual basis, only about 2,300 of them developed premiums of $5,000 and over. During 1957, only 228

---

[26] Since his standard premium is $7,500, his basic premium is $2,100 (.28 x $7,500). When losses are adjusted to include claims expenses, they become $4,275 (1.14 x $3,750). The basic premium plus the adjusted losses amount to $6,375. When the tax factor is added (1.033 x $6,375), the indicated retrospective premium becomes $6,585.38. (Values as of May, 1957.)

[27] Any employer with a standard premium of $25,000 or over can purchase a loss-limitation feature according to the rules of the plan. Loss limitation can be bought for 5 per cent of standard premium multiplied by the loss conversion factor. In determining the retrospective premium, any loss that exceeds the purchased limit is reduced to that limit before it is added to total losses. (New Jersey Compensation Rating and Inspection Bureau "Circular Letter #791," October 31, 1956.)

[28] New Jersey Compensation Rating and Inspection Bureau, "Manual Amendment Bulletin # 214," p. 5.

employers chose retrospective rating: 94 under plan A and 134 under plan B.[29]

Premium discount plans are applied to approximately 11,000 employers. Nothing in the discount plans purports to offer any additional incentives to safety programs. Because of the graded expense features, they do allow the large employer the opportunity to buy his insurance at less than manual rates.

Assigned Risks

Although the law requires all employers, with stated exceptions, to carry compensation insurance, some employers are unable to place their business with one or the other of the private companies. Carriers may be reluctant to underwrite an individual risk because of some extra-hazardous conditions, because of the unwillingness of the firm to comply with suggestions about safety and accident prevention procedures, because of some unfavorable loss experience in the past, or perhaps because of the firm's unwillingness or inability to meet premium payments promptly. Each insurance carrier sets its own standards for the risks it chooses to underwrite; and given the press of competition among carriers, most employers are able to place their business with some insurance company. Some employers, however, are unable to find any insurance company willing to take their business on a voluntary basis, and yet the law compels them to insure.

Assigned risk plans have been developed to meet this problem.[30] New Jersey's plan dates from 1932. Under it, employers who are unable to place their business apply to the Compensation Rating and Inspection Bureau for assignment to an insurance carrier who must underwrite their risks and at no increase in manual rates. The risks are assigned to the carriers roughly in accordance with the percentage of business done by the carriers within the state.

Prior to 1951, the number of assigned risks in New Jersey was small, but in that year the generally unfavorable loss ratios experienced by carriers resulted in a re-examination of their underwriting policies. The number of assigned risks in 1951 was more than double the number in 1950. The numbers and premium volume continued to increase until 1954, when 5,364 risks with earned premiums of over $3.5 million were under the assigned risk plan. Since then, the premium volume and number of policies have declined, although the beginning months of 1958 again showed an increasing number of employers seeking insurance under the assigned risk plan.

---

[29] New Jersey Compensation Rating and Inspection Bureau, *Forty-First Annual Report*, p. 2.

[30] In 1956, in the nation as a whole, there were twenty assigned risk plans in nineteen states and in the District of Columbia that were administered by the National Council on Compensation Insurance. In nine additional states, including New Jersey, the assigned risk plans were under the jurisdiction of state administrative bureaus, while seventeen states had state funds which either by statute or administrative ruling were required to take any risk offered for insurance. (*The Insurance Almanac*, 1956 [N. Y.: The Underwriting Printing and Publishing Co.].)

The overwhelming number of assigned risks are firms with relatively few employees, although in 1957, 60 assigned risks had premiums of $5,000 or more. As might be expected, the loss ratios for the assigned risks tend to be greater than for the average risk. In spite of the rather significant increase in the number of risks over the years, the assigned risks in policy year 1955 were only 3.2 per cent of the total number of policies, and they accounted for 4.8 per cent of the total earned premiums.[31]

From the point of view of the Compensation Rating and Inspection Bureau, the assigned risks constitute something of a problem. They must be allocated among the insurance carriers, and the bureau must see to it that all employers are assigned, in one fashion or another. Also, they constitute a barometer of conditions in the market for insurance. When the number of assigned risks is on the increase, this is a sign that market conditions are beginning to tighten. Although these factors are highly important to the insurance industry, from a broader point of view the most important aspect of the assigned risk plan is simply that it exists. It constitutes one solution to the problem of providing insurance to every employer who can afford to meet normal premium costs. Undoubtedly there are a number of employers each year who do not accept assignment once it is offered to them, because they cannot, or think they cannot, meet the premium payments.[32] These employers must either go out of business or take their chances on running afoul of the law by operating without insurance protection.

Trends in Insurance Rates and Costs

It is possible to depict the trends in insurance rates and premium costs in a variety of ways, including the following:

1) Earned premiums according to policy year experience (column 1 of Table XXI). This measures the premiums earned during the effective period of all policies written during a single calendar year. In 1939, the total amounted to $17,979,341. By policy year 1943 it had more than doubled; it decreased in 1944, but in the following year more than made up for this decline. The next two years showed substantial increases, and then the volume declined in 1948 and 1949. Earned premiums increased in 1950 and in each year since then up to policy year 1955, when they amounted to $77,220,621, an increase of approximately 330 per cent over the 1939 volume.

2) Earned premiums according to calendar year experience (column 2 of Table XXIV). These data are from schedule W, which, as explained above, is a running inventory from the insurance companies'

---

[31]Data on assigned risks are from the New Jersey Compensation Rating and Inspection Bureau, various *Annual Reports*.

[32]This is cited as one of the reasons why over a sixth of the employers assigned under the National Council on Compensation Insurance plans failed to accept the insurance provided. (Kulp, p. 155.)

accounting records.[33] Insofar as trends in earned premiums are concerned, the calendar-year data show the same over-all direction as exhibited in the policy-year experience. During calendar year 1939, earned premiums amounted to $16,088,072. They have increased each year since then with the exception of a slight dip in 1945 and more substantial declines in 1949 and 1950. The calendar-year data are in the nature of a running average and iron out some of the changes shown in the policy-year experience. In calendar year 1957, earned premiums amounted to $86,495,504, an increase of approximately 437 per cent over the 1939 volume.

Table XXI. New Jersey Workmen's Compensation Insurance — Policy Year Experience, 1939-1956

Policy Year	Earned Premiums (1)	Incurred Losses (2)	Loss Ratio (3)
1939	$17,979,341	$10,316,278	57.38%
1940	23,103,755	13,143,882	56.89
1941	30,160,846	15,666,180	51.94
1942	35,443,061	16,453,032	46.42
1943	37,561,520	18,254,715	48.60
1944	35,983,919	17,655,713	49.07
1945	39,492,010	19,061,827	48.27
1946	51,151,558	22,168,780	43.34
1947	53,278,791	23,719,808	44.52
1948	48,859,913	24,158,068	49.44
1949	40,330,181	24,608,450	61.02
1950	44,827,087	31,547,153	70.38
1951	51,985,876	36,644,071	70.49
1952	62,295,550	36,091,971	57.94
1953	71,653,392	37,363,729	52.15
1954	73,106,664	38,378,887	52.50
1955	77,220,621	40,714,311	52.72
First Six Months 1956	43,588,154	24,379,972	55.93

Source: New Jersey Compensation Rating and Inspection Bureau, *Forty-First Annual Report*, Exhibit C.

---

[33] When policy year data are examined, we have the advantage of looking at the experience for a definite period. Policy year 1955 data, for example, show the experience during the effective life of all policies written during calendar year 1955. One disadvantage is that we will not know the complete experience for policy year 1955 until more than five years after, when the last reportings are made. Calendar-year data allow a more current look. The earned premiums for calendar 1958 are calculated by adding together all premiums earned on policies written during the last twenty-two years to the end of 1958, and subtracting from that figure the premiums earned up to the end of the preceding calendar year.

Each policy year shows premiums earned and losses incurred over two calendar years. On the other hand, each calendar year shows the losses incurred over a number of past years and the premiums earned, for the most part in portions of two policy years. Strictly speaking, policy-year experience and calendar-year experience are simply not comparable.

3) The average compensation insurance rate or cost per $100 of payroll (column 3 of Table XXII). Earned premium volume changes because of two factors. One is the change in insurance rates, best measured by changes in the general level of rates, and the other is the change in payrolls (column 1 of Table XXII) against which the rates are applied. One is the multiplier and the other the multiplicand. If the general level of rates remains the same but payrolls increase, then the earned premium volume will increase, and the reverse is true.

Table XXII. New Jersey Workmen's Compensation Insurance —
Payrolls, Earned Premiums and Average Rates,
"Payroll Rated" Business

Policy Year	Payroll (in hundreds of dollars) (1)	Earned Premiums (2)	Av. Rate (Col. 2 - Col. 1) (3)	Index of Av. Wage Rates (1939=100)[a] (4)
1939	$1,126,834,3	$17,197,753	$1.53	100.0
1940	1,356,776,2	22,270,969	1.64	104.0
1941	1,735,544,2	30,011,497	1.73	113.2
1942	2,032,524,5	36,089,356	1.78	125.9
1943	2,296,780,1	37,216,182	1.62	141.9
1944	2,328,546,3	35,727,736	1.53	152.6
1945	2,361,738,6	38,873,948	1.65	159.4
1946	2,701,352,3	50,108,049	1.85	170.2
1947	3,003,633,8	51,978,066	1.73	180.9
1948	3,235,386,2	47,484,212	1.47	192.3
1949	3,326,790,4	39,162,224	1.18	198.3
1950	3,845,581,3	43,882,448	1.14	206.3
1951	4,316,458,1	51,002,776	1.18	219.7
1952	4,668,353,0	61,294,697	1.31	234.4
1953	4,987,974,6	70,569,861	1.41	244.6
1954	5,119,543,1	71,971,580	1.41	252.1
1955	5,527,942,8	76,044,013	1.38	260.0
1956	———	———	1.32	266.9
1957	———	———	1.53	275.6

Source: New Jersey Compensation Rating and Inspection Bureau, various *Annual Reports*, average rates for 1956-1957 estimated by rating bureau.
[a] Data derived from statistics of indicated average wage rates from individual accident reports. (New Jersey Compensation Rating and Inspection Bureau, *Forty-First Annual Report*, p. 27.)

If earned premiums are divided by payrolls in hundreds of dollars, we get the so-called average rate per $100 of payroll. For policy year 1939, this average rate was $1.53. Although the exact data are not available, the average rate for policy year 1957 is estimated at exactly the same figure of $1.53. The rate increased from 1940 to 1942, decreased the next two years, and then increased to the high point of $1.85 in 1946. The decline over the next four years was considerable, reaching a low point of $1.14 in 1950. Further increases were registered until 1954. The next two years showed declines, and in 1957 the rates jumped back, but only to the 1939 level.

These trend data are discussed by the New Jersey Division of Workmen's Compensation in its 1956 Annual Report. It is claimed that they bear out the development, noted earlier in the report, that "workmen's compensation cost has presented a relatively diminishing factor of production costs in the State." The division goes on to state: "The reduction in cost is clear. In 1946 the average cost per $100.00 of payroll was $1.85. In 1956 the average cost was $1.32 per $100.00 of payroll. The rise from 1950 to 1953 is attributable to the increase in statutory payment rate from $25.00 to $30.00 a week. From 1954 through 1956 the cost again declined. The $1.32 figure for 1956 represents a 28.6 per cent decrease in the average cost of workmen's compensation insurance per $100.00 of payroll despite the statutory increase in weekly payment rates." [34]

Given the time period chosen, there can be no disputing the conclusion that the average rate per $100 of payroll has declined. The question can be raised, however, as to whether it is completely accurate to make the claim implicit in the heading of this section of the division's report which reads, "Cost of Insurance Coverage Reduced."

The average rate has not declined (or remained the same, depending upon choice of base year) because of any decline in earned premiums, but rather because of the increase in payrolls. During policy year 1939, payrolls amounted to $1,126,834,300. They have increased each policy year since then, and in 1955 amounted to $5,527,942,800. [35]

Payrolls increase for two reasons. One is the increase in the number of man-hours worked, the most accurate index of accident exposure, and the second is the increase in wage rates. If an index of average wage rates [36] (column 4 of Table XXII) is used to deflate the payroll figures, the adjusted average insurance rate for 1957 amounts to $4.22, rather than $1.53. But such an adjusted rate is also deficient as a single measure of compensation costs to the employer. Losses are influenced to some extent by increases in wage rates, and, in turn, loss ratios affect insurance rates and hence earned premiums. It should be pointed out, however, that the fact that the average cost per $100 of payroll has declined, does not mean that the average cost of insurance per employer has declined; nor does it indicate that the average cost of insurance per employee, or per man-hour worked has declined.

4) Changes in the general level of rates. At any one time, the general rate level may change because of the combined effects of a change in the compensation statutes, a change in expense loadings or a

[34] New Jersey Division of Workmen's Compensation, *Annual Report*, 1956, p. 22.

[35] These are the total payrolls of all "payroll rated" business. The bureau derives these data from the carriers' unit statistical reports. The 1955 figure is based upon the first reporting, but there is usually little change in payroll totals from one reporting to the next.

[36] These are the average wage rates of employees who filed for compensation claims. Because of reporting lags, the average wage rate for 1957 was not available but was estimated by correlation with national wage statistics. The manufacturing component of the bureau's wage data has a coefficient of correlation of 0.984 with the manufacturing production workers series of the United States Department of Labor, Bureau of Labor Statistics.

change in "experience." The effect of each of these types of changes, and their total effect from 1939 to 1958, are shown in Table XXIII.

Significant increases in the rate level, because of amendments liberalizing the statute, were made in 1946, 1951 and 1957. The cumulative effect of these "law" changes was to increase the rate level by 63 per cent. As far as the expense loadings are concerned, their effect is to induce small yearly changes in the rate level, up or down, principally because of changes in tax loadings. The cumulative effect of the expense loading changes was to increase the rate level about 2 per cent from 1939 to 1958. Whereas both these factors pushed the rate level up, the experience factor moved it down, until the July, 1958, experience level was only 64 per cent of the 1939 level. The combined effect of the three types of changes was to increase the 1958 level about 7 per cent over the 1939 one. The "law" and "expense loading" changes are largely self-explanatory, but it is the changes in the "experience" category which warrant discussion.

As explained above, in determining the change in the general rate level, the permissible loss ratio is contrasted with the modified overall loss ratio for the last calendar year. If the modified loss ratio is less than the permissible one, then the rate level will be decreased by reason of "experience." Put in another way, if the theoretical number of dollars available to pay losses was greater than necessary to pay the losses, shown on the modified basis, then rates would be decreased.

But this does not necessarily mean that accident experience is improving, or that the employer's dollar cost of insurance will decline. What it does mean is that modified losses were less than they should have been according to the established permissible loss ratio. No adjustments are made in these calculations for past or future wage rate changes. If wage rates increase as man-hours of employment remain constant, payrolls, and hence earned premiums, will be increased. This factor alone can account for an improvement in experience.[37]

Insurance rate-making is based upon the assumption that payrolls are the best available measure of exposure, although, in fact, they may reflect changes in wage rates as much as they reflect changes in man-hours of exposure to accident hazards. They are maintained as a

---

[37] An example confined to a single hypothetical firm may clarify matters. Assume that the firm employs 100 workers, each being paid $2 per hour and each working 2,000 hours in a single calendar year. The firm's total payroll is therefore $40,000 a year. If its insurance classification calls for a rate of $1 per $100 of payroll, its total yearly premium would be $4,000, ignoring the expense constants and rating modifications. Assume that during the year several accidents occurred, so that incurred losses amounted to fifty weeks of temporary disability. If each employee qualified for the maximum weekly rate, total incurred losses would amount to $2,000, or a loss ratio of 50 per cent of earned premiums.

Assume that in the next year the firm paid the same insurance rates and employed the same number of employees for the same number of hours, and that the same accident experience was repeated. The only change is that now wage rates have increased by 15 cents per hour. The firm would now pay $4,300 in premiums, and its incurred loss ratio would now be decreased to 46.15 per cent. In short, according to the insurance criterion, its experience has improved because its loss ratios have been reduced. Of course, all that has happened is that wage rates, and hence payrolls, have increased.

Table XXIII. New Jersey Workmen's Compensation Insurance —
General Rate Level Changes, 1939-1958

| | Change in Rate Level Due to: | | | | | | | |
| | Experience | | Expense Loadings | | Law | | Total | |
Effective Date	Actual Change	Accumulated	Actual Change	Accumulated	Actual Change	Accumulated	Actual Change	Accumulated
Jan. 1, 1939								
July 1, 1939	1.025	1.025	n.c.	1.000	n.c.	1.000	1.025	1.025
Jan. 1940	1.000	1.025	n.c.	1.000	n.c.	1.000	1.007	1.032
July 1940	1.024	1.050	n.c.	1.000	n.c	1.000	1.024	1.057
Jan. 1941	—	1.050	—	1.000	—	1.000	—	1.057
July 1941	1.051	1.104	n.c.	1.000	n.c.	1.000	1.051	1.111
Jan. 1942	—	1.104	—	1.000	—	1.000	—	1.111
July 1942	1.060	1.170	n.c.	1.000	n.c.	1.000	1.060	1.178
Jan. 1943	—	1.170	—	1.000	—	1.000	—	1.178
July 1943	.964	1.128	.992	.992	n.c.	1.000	.956	1.126
Jan. 1944	.957	1.079	1.017	1.009	n.c.	1.000	.973	1.096
July 1944	.992	1.070	n.c.	1.009	n.c.	1.000	.992	1.087
Jan. 1945	.947	1.013	.983	.992	n.c.	1.000	.931	1.012
July 1945	.990	1.003	n.c.	.992	1.010	1.010	1.000	1.012
Jan. 1946	.969	.972	n.c.	.992	1.237	1.249	1.199	1.213
July 1946	—	.972	—	.992	— -	1.249	—	1.213
Jan. 1947	.945	.919	n.c.	.992	n.c.	1.249	.945	1.146
July 1947	.945	.868	n.c.	.992	n.c.	1.249	.945	1.083
Jan. 1948	.923	.801	n.c.	.992	n.c.	1.249	.923	1.000
July 1948	.901	.722	n.c.	.992	1.010	1.261	.910	.910
Jan. 1949	.927	.669	n.c.	.992	n.c.	1.261	.927	.844
July 1949	.875	.585	n.c.	.992	n.c.	1.261	.875	.739
Jan. 1950	.972	.569	n.c.	.992	1.012	1.276	.984	.727
July 1950	1.000	.569	n.c.	.992	n.c.	1.276	1.000	.727
Jan 1951	.962	.547	n.c.	.992	1.114	1.421	1.072	.779
July 1951	1.066	.583	n.c.	.992	n.c.	1.421	1.066	.830
Jan 1952	1.060	.618	n.c.	.992	1.002	1.424	1.062	.881
July 1952	1.009	.624	1.044[a]	1.036	n.c.	1.424	1.053	.928
Jan. 1953	1.067	.666	.983[b]	1.018	n.c.	1.424	1.049	.973
July 1953	1.025	.683	n.c.	1.018	1.005	1.431	1.030	1.002
Jan. 1954	—	.683	—	1.018	—	1.431	-—	1.002
July 1954	.992	.678	1.009[c]	1.027	n.c.	1.431	1.001	1.003
Jan. 1955	.982	.666	n.c.	1.027	n.c.	1.431	.982	.985
July 1955	.997	.664	.991[d]	1.018	n.c.	1.431	.988	.973
Jan. 1956	.958	.636	n.c.	1.018	n.c.	1.431	.958	.932
July 1956	.957	.609	.992[e]	1.010	n.c.	1.431	.949	.884
Aug. 1956	—	.609	n.c.	1.010	1.006[f]	1.440	1.006	.889
Jan. 1957	1.045	.636	n.c.	1.010	1.132	1.630	1.183	1.052
July 1957	.979	.623	1.003[g]	1.013	n.c.	1.630	.982	1.033
July 1958	1.031	.642	1.008[c]	1.021	n.c.	1.630	1.039	1.073

Source: New Jersey Compensation Rating and Inspection Bureau. n.c. = no change.
[a]Reflects inclusion of 1 per cent in tax loading for security funds and the addition of a profit loading of 1.5 per cent.
[b]Reflects removal of 1 per cent in tax loading for security funds.
[c]Reflects inclusion of 0.5 per cent in tax loading for security funds.
[d]Reflects exclusion of 0.5 per cent in tax loading for security funds.
[e]Reflects exclusion of 0.45 per cent in tax loading for second injury fund.
[f]Reflects amendment to the United States Longshoremen's and Harbor Workers' Compensation Act, effective July 26, 1956.
[g]Reflects inclusion of 0.45 per cent in tax loading for second injury fund and general revision of other expense elements.

measure of exposure because there is no other measure that can be had so conveniently, and without the necessity of having employers make separate calculations of man-hours worked. All employers keep payroll records, and these can be audited with much less difficulty than could possible alternative statistical measures of exposure.

At one time, payrolls were a much better measure of exposure than they are now, because as payrolls increased due to higher wage rates, compensation benefits, keyed to a percentage of the employees' wages, also increased. But the maximum weekly benefit levels written into the law have destroyed much of the relationship between compensation benefits and an employee's wage. Any worker receiving wages of $67.51 a week or more qualifies for the maximum weekly benefit. This is a wage $10 under the average wage of workers involved in accidents in 1957. When a worker who earns less than the average can qualify for the maximum benefit, then any further increases in wage rates may increase future losses, but not to the extent that they increase premium volume. It must also be remembered that all wages paid the worker enter into the payroll base. There are no limitations because of size of weekly wage, or even amounts paid for vacations or holidays.[38]

The discussion has been largely in terms of wage rates increasing and thus inflating payrolls. Its possible to conceive that if wages decline in times of depression, quite the opposite effect on payrolls and earned premiums may take place. Insurance rate-makers are constantly in the position of making changes in rates based upon past experience but for effect in the future. This is a game of pursuit in which the rules state that in any one year you can only make changes to catch up with the results of that year. It may take several years to catch up, and then if the object of pursuit changes direction, you may be ahead of the quarry rather than behind it.

The changes in the rate level due to experience (Table XXIII) illustrate this curve of pursuit. Increases in the rate level due to experience were made four times from July, 1939, to July, 1942. Then, during the war years, as the number of accidents was increasing, the experience rate level was actually decreasing. Downward adjustments

---

[38] According to the Compensation Rating and Inspection Bureau's, *New Jersey Manual of Rules, Classifications and Rates*, the premium is based on all remuneration paid employees, including commissions, bonuses, wages for holidays, vacations, sickness periods, and payments under piecework, incentive plans and profit sharing arrangements. Contributions made by the employer to group insurance or pension plans are excluded. Penalty payments for overtime may also be excluded if the employer keeps separate records of these penalty payments. Payroll limitation is provided only in the case of executive officers, defined as those officers of a corporation commonly known as President, Vice-President, Secretary and Treasurer. Their salaries are limited to $150 per week (pp. R12, R12a and R24a).

Other states may calculate premiums based on salaries or wages limited to $100 a week, or more recently $300 a week, per employee. The one advantage of the system used in New Jersey is that payroll auditing is simplified because total payrolls are included in the premium base. The premiums paid by New Jersey employers are not necessarily higher than those in other states because New Jersey employers must include all wages and salaries in the computations. The payrolls are only the multiplicand, and the premiums paid depend upon the rate multiplied by the payrolls.

were made in almost every six-month period from 1943 to 1951, but they never really caught up until July, 1951, when it was found that they had gone too far, and it was necessary to increase the rate level because of the experience factor. Two increases were made in each of the following two years, and then, beginning in July, 1954, the experience rate level began to move down. This downward movement was checked in January 1957, but it again moved down in July of that year. In July, 1958, the experience rate level moved up once again.

The conclusion must be that given the way rates are set, over-all changes in the rate level reflect accurately the cost of changes in benefit levels and expense loadings, and they also measure the degree to which the loss ratios of the past year measure up to the expected loss ratios. Changes in the general rate level, however, even when confined to the experience category, do not give a very accurate picture of what is happening to trends in compensation cases, or even compensation costs. This can best be had by examining the records of the number and cost of the various types of compensation cases, and studying these against the backgrounds of employment and wage changes. This has already been done in Chapter 2.

This does not mean that general rate level changes have no significance. To the employer, they are the important multiplier in his cost of compensation insurance. However, one cannot ignore the fact that payrolls are the important multiplicand, or the fact that changes in rate levels must always lag behind actual experience. To the insurance companies, the general rate level is one important factor in determining its principal source of income — earned premiums — and in fixing the amounts of profits or losses due to underwriting experience.

Trends in Insurance Company Profits

Insurance companies have available two potential profit sources from compensation business. One is the profits they earn from investments of the funds entrusted to them, and the other is the profits they earn from their underwriting experience. Data on investment profits can be derived only from financial statements, and it is impossible to segregate the investment profits on New Jersey business from the total investment profits for any one company. Information on aggregate underwriting profits from New Jersey business is available, however.

The current profit loading is 2.5 per cent, but this expected profit margin can actually be realized only if the incurred loss ratio for any given period turns out to be exactly equal to the permissible loss ratio. If the incurred loss ratio were less, the insurance carriers would show underwriting profits in excess of those contemplated by the profit loadings. Of course, if the incurred loss ratio were greater than the permissible one, the companies would suffer underwriting losses. There is nothing in the rate-making procedures that would recapture the profits or make up for the losses in that one year.

Table XXI shows the incurred losses and the loss ratios for all companies, for each policy year since 1939. During these years, the permissible loss ratio hovered around 58 per cent, with changes up or down because of differences in the yearly expense loadings. As a rough approximation, it can be said that each year the actual incurred loss ratio shows a figure of less than 58 per cent, excess underwriting profits were made; each year it was more, losses were incurred.

A more accurate picture can be had by referring to Table XXIV, which is an exhibit of underwriting results derived from schedule W, with all its limitations and advantages. In spite of the fact that this schedule shows actual losses, and not modified losses, it keys fairly well with changes in the general rate level, as shown in Table XXIII. From 1939 to 1942, the general rate level was increasing. The insurance companies showed aggregate losses up to 1942, when an excess profit of 2.13 per cent of earned premiums was earned. From 1942 until 1951, the general rate level due to experience was declining, but not fast enough to eliminate the excess profit, until 1950, when the

Table XXIV. New Jersey Workmen's Compensation Insurance —
Exhibit of Underwriting Results,
Summary of Calendar Year Experience, 1933-1957

Calendar Year (1)	Premiums Earned (2)	Permissible Loss Ratio (3)	Available for Losses (4)	Losses Incurred (5)	Actual Loss Ratio (5)+(2) (6)	Profit or Loss Amt. (4)-(5) (7)	Per cent (7)+(2) (8)
1933	$9,572,038	.5925%	$5,671,433	$5,763,824	60.22%	$-92,391	-0.97%
1934	11,732,965	.5925	6,951,782	6,281,222	53.53	670,560	5.72
1935	13,295,583	.59125	7,861,013	6,518,868	49.03	1,342,145	10.09
1936	14,824,509	.5825	8,635,276	8,254,515	55.68	380,761	2.57
1937	17,546,190	.5825	10,220,656	9,667,536	55.10	553,120	3.15
1938	16,288,651	.5832	9,499,541	9,546,786	58.61	-47,245	-.29
1939	16,088,072	.5873	9,448,525	9,727,592	60.46	-279,067	-1.73
1940	19,008,331	.5880	11,176,899	12,275,410	64.58	-1,098,511	-5.78
1941	24,241,964	.5880	14,254,275	16,033,412	66.14	-1,779,137	-7.34
1942	30,383,118	.5880	17,865,273	17,218,862	56.67	646,411	2.13
1943	37,295,047	.5886	21,951,865	20,204,371	54.17	1,747,494	4.69
1944	38,581,713	.5874	22,662,898	20,881,089	54.12	1,781,809	4.62
1945	36,432,870	.5880	21,422,528	17,443,911	47.88	3,978,617	10.92
1946	41,505,980	.5930	24,613,046	22,292,589	53.71	2,320,457	5.59
1947	53,250,953	.5930	31,577,815	23,431,408	44.00	8,146,407	15.30
1948	53,919,395	.5930	31,974,201	22,336,938	41.43	9,637,263	17.87
1949	47,174,040	.5930	27,974,206	23,427,892	49.66	4,546,314	9.64
1950	39,827,781	.5930	23,617,874	24,985,664	62.73	-1,367,790	-3.43
1951	48,128,799	.5930	28,540,378	33,993,438	70.63	-5,453,060	-11.33
1952	56,688,038	.5899	33,440,274	38,486,362	67.89	-5,046,088	-8.90
1953	67,711,520	.5761	39,008,607	41,310,166	61.01	-2,301,559	-3.40
1954	71,781,985	.5774	41,446,918	40,498,026	56.42	948,892	1.32
1955	76,313,791	.5743	43,827,010	39,685,016	52.00	4,141,994	5.43
1956	76,410,094	.5786	44,210,880	42,442,449	55.55	1,768,431	2.31
1957	86,495,504	.5817	50,314,435	52,464,684	60.66	-2,150,249	-2.49
Total	$1,004,498,931	.5855%	$588,167,608	$565,172,030	56.26%	$22,995,578	2.29%

Source: New Jersey Compensation Rating and Inspection Bureau.

record shows losses of 3.43 per cent. In July, 1951, the experience rate level turned around and began to increase, but the lag in this increase, plus the jump in losses due to the Korean War, combined to produce an underwriting loss of 11.33 per cent. Underwriting losses continued at a diminished rate in 1952 and 1953 as the experience rate level increased, and then they turned into excess profits in 1954. By this time, the experience rate level, in rapid pursuit, began to turn down. The underwriting loss of 1957 is the reflection, on a real basis, of the fact that modified loss ratios were greater than permissible, thus accounting for the increase in rates in July, 1958.

Even though the running inventory records of schedule W tend to iron out the peaks and valleys, it is easy to see that some years have been extraordinarily profitable for the insurance carriers, whereas in other years the carriers have experienced substantial underwriting losses. In 1947 and 1948, for example, when the rate reductions had not yet had a chance to catch up, and when the payrolls were still increasing as the worst of the war years' accident experience was being left behind, the insurance companies showed profits 15.30 per cent and 17.87 per cent greater than that allowed by the profit loadings. On the other hand, as already stated, 1951 showed a record underwriting loss of 11.33 per cent.

On an over-all basis, for the years 1933 to 1957 the records indicate that the compensation insurance business has been profitable for the carriers. On the average, the excess profit over and above that allowed in the loadings was 2.29 per cent of earned premiums. It must be borne in mind that any individual company may have done much worse or much better. Also, these data say nothing about possible investment profits or losses the companies may have been able to earn or incur by investing funds received from premiums or other sources.

Interstate Comparisons of Rates

Participants in the compensation program are often less interested in the trends in rates and costs over time than they are in how one state's rates compare with another. Since workmen's compensation, more than any of the other social insurance programs, is rooted in an individual state, the opportunities for variation in rates among the states are gross and may become a factor when location decisions are discussed.[39]

---

[39] There is little actual evidence to indicate that employers change locations because of compensation rates alone. When employer groups gather to complain about the high costs of doing business within the state, however, workmen's compensation costs are sure to figure prominently on the agenda — as was the case during a series of meetings held throughout the state in 1958, when tax changes were being contemplated.

In a study of location factors in the New York metropolitan area (covering six New Jersey counties) John Griffin asked a limited sample of firms to rank certain factors according to whether they considered them favorable or unfavorable location factors. In each county, workmen's compensation costs were ranked among the unfavorable factors, illustrating, at least, that these costs are not among the factors which can be counted upon to attract em-

In general, rates will vary among states because of differences in benefit levels and in the interpretation of the law, both by the courts and the administrators. At any particular time, the rates for a given classification will vary, not only because of the differences in the general rate level but also because of the accident experience of employers in the same classification. Even if interstate comparisons are confined to one classification that is described in fairly uniform fashion in the jurisdictions, this still is no guarantee that the employers are similarly situated. Although the descriptions may be the same, the logging and lumbering industry, for example, is simply not the same in New Jersey as it is in Texas. In New Jersey its manual rate is $7.90, whereas in Texas it is $15.30. Obviously to compare rates in one classification among the states would be meaningless as an over-all comparison. At the other extreme, comparisons of the average manual rate would give too much effect to the distribution of industry within each state.

We have chosen to compare manual rates in some forty-odd classifications in several states as of November, 1958.[40] The total payrolls for the classifications account for 47.6 per cent of the total payrolls of New Jersey's insured employers in policy year 1955. When each classification's rate is weighted by its payroll, the average manual rate in New Jersey is $1.220.

An average rate for each of the other states was calculated by weighing each state's classification rates by the New Jersey payroll

---

ployers to the northern New Jersey counties. (John I. Griffin, *Industrial Location in the New York Area* [N. Y.: New York Area Research Council, The City College Press, 1956].)

[40]The method used and the classifications and states chosen for the comparison follow closely those used by Roger A. Johnson in his study "Workmen's Compensation Costs," in *Proceedings of the Casualty Actuarial Society*, XL (1953), pp. 10-17. The major difference is that we have weighted each state's classification rates by the New Jersey payroll distribution, whereas Johnson weighted by New York's payroll distribution. Also we have eliminated Pennsylvania, because, as Johnson recognized, the classification system in that state is different from that in the others, which base their system on that of the National Council on Compensation Insurance.

The following of Johnson's classifications have been eliminated because of differences in descriptions among the various states: Newspaper Publishing #4304; Street or Road Construction, Paving, etc. #5506; Hospitals, Professional Employees #8833; and Hospitals, all other Employees #9040. Also, it was necessary in several instances to combine classifications which embraced employers in a single classification in New Jersey. Other minor adjustments were made, but it is believed that none of these changes materially affects the final results.

Johnson's study was first made as of July, 1948, and then as of February 15, 1950, July 1, 1951, and July 1, 1952. New York was high each time, with New Jersey in the 2d, 7th, 4th and 3d place, respectively.

Our study shows manual rates in effect as of November, 1958. Although these were the manual rates actually in effect, they do reflect different experience periods in the various states. In ten of the fifteen states the rates had been revised sometime in 1958; in three states, Massachusetts, Texas and Michigan, the last rate revision was in December, 1957; in Maryland, on October 1, 1957; and in New York, on July 1, 1957.

In some of the states, the rates reflect the inclusion of some administration costs. In New Jersey, for example, the rates include the 0.25 per cent Workmen's Compensation Tax used to support, in part, the Compensation Rating and Inspection Bureau. According to Johnson, the inclusion of these administrative costs has very little effect on the comparisons.

distribution. The resulting averages, and their ratio to New Jersey's average, are shown in column 1 of Table XXV. Essentially these comparisons show what New Jersey employers would have paid, had the other state's rates been in effect in New Jersey.

Table XXV. Inter-State Manual Rate Comparisons

| State | Av. Manual Rate, November, 1958 | | Hewitt's Indexes, May, 1958 |
	(dollars) (1)	(ratio to New Jersey) (2)	(3)
New Jersey	$1.220	1.000	125
Texas	1.303	1.068	125
New York	1.265	1.037	147
Massachusetts	1.212	0.993	135
Connecticut	1.043	0.855	115
California	0.916	0.751	105
Missouri	0.914	0.749	95
Maryland	0.893	0.732	99
Illinois	0.679	0.557	76
Wisconsin	0.667	0.547	72
Michigan	0.590	0.484	63
Indiana	0.541	0.443	—
Iowa	0.525	0.430	—
Virginia	0.483	0.396	—
Alabama	0.460	0.377	—
Pennsylvania	---	---	—

Texas emerges with the highest average rate of $1.303. New York is next with $1.265, and New Jersey is third with $1.220. Massachusetts' rate of $1.212 is closely comparable to New Jersey's, and the other states fall rapidly behind. Connecticut's average rate is 85 per cent of that in New Jersey and California's is 75 per cent, while the rates in Michigan, Wisconsin and Illinois range from 48 per cent to 56 per cent of the average rate in New Jersey.

Using some of the same states, with the addition of Pennsylvania, and using roughly the same classifications, Hewitt has made an inter-state comparison by calculating indexes of manual rates in effect in May, 1958. [41] For each classification, an index of the median manual rates for each of the states was calculated. The final figures used (shown in column 3 of Table XXV) were the medians of the index numbers in each state. This method, which eliminates weighting by pay-rolls, is essentially an index number based upon a median of the medians.

<hr>

[41] The results of this study by Charles C. Hewitt, Jr., a consulting actuary, were presented in a series of fourteen meetings throughout the State of New Jersey sponsored by the New Jersey Manufacturers Association in 1958. Hewitt used twelve of the sixteen states used by Johnson but made minor revisions and eliminated the following classifications: Clothing Manufacturing #2501; Logging and Lumbering #2702; All Foundry classifications #3081, 2, 5; Chauffeurs and their Helpers #7380; Salesmen, Collectors or Messengers #8742; and Clerical Office Employees #8801.

Hewitt shows New York as the highest paying state, with an index number 18 per cent greater than New Jersey's. Massachusetts is the second highest, with New Jersey and Texas both occupying the third rank. (These comparisons were made before the July, 1958, rate revision in New Jersey.) There is little point in arguing which method is best; each shows slightly different things. It is likely that the most appropriate comparison would be one that measured the rates over the period of a business cycle, but such a comparison would be of only historical importance.[42]

Interest in New Jersey has always centered on how its rates compare with those of the neighboring State of New York. Johnson's 1952 comparison of rates showed New York's rates to be more than 80 per cent higher than New Jersey's, and Hewitt's comparisons show an 18 per cent differential, whereas our comparisons show New York's rates to be less than 4 per cent higher. The indications seem to be that New York rates are coming closer to New Jersey's rates.

There is some evidence to bear this out. Table XXVI shows the number of cases, their total incurred cost and their average cost for

Table XXVI. Average Cost Comparison of Workmen's Compensation Cases in New Jersey and New York — All Losses, 1946-1955

Policy Year	No.	Total Incurred Cost	Av. Cost	No.	Total Incurred Cost	Av. Cost	Ratio: N. Y. Av. / N. J. Av.
1946	178,062	$22,218,745	$124	507,630	$91,569,651	$180	1.452
1947	181,519	23,636,524	130	519,570	106,257,686	205	1.577
1948	191,379	24,084,856	126	500,822	115,763,323	231	1.833
1949	199,505	24,490,310	123	495,887	119,170,692	240	1.951
1950	240,200	31,486,650	131	551,898	132,349,739	240	1.832
1951	238,830	36,634,006	153	551,529	132,194,136	240	1.569
1952	238,196	36,091,971	152	541,894	128,093,621	236	1.553
1953	226,038	37,363,729	165	513,636	125,019,677	243	1.473
1954	214,147	38,378,887	179	494,233	123,730,861	250	1.397
1955	216,622	40,714,311	188	496,709	128,168,213	258	1.372

Source: New Jersey Compensation Rating and Inspection Bureau. It should be noted that these data do not pertain to closed compensated cases, and hence they are not comparable with data discussed in chapter 2. These data include all indemnity and medical losses, including medical costs in cases in which no indemnity payments were made. The information is derived from insurance carriers' reports.

[42] R. P. Goddard discusses Johnson's method in *Proceedings of the Casualty Actuarial Society*, XLI (1954), pp. 176 ff. Goddard believes that valid results can be obtained by using unweighted averages of the rates in each state. For a comprehensive comparative analysis of costs which delves into differences in types of losses, with particular reference to New York's experience, see Joseph S. Keiper, "The Imbalance Between Costs and Benefits," in *Studies in Workmen's Compensation* (N. Y.: Commerce and Industry Association of New York, 1954), pp. 1-45.

policy years 1946 to 1955 for both states. The 1952 rate comparison would be influenced by the experience of policy year 1950, and in that year the ratio of New York's average cost to New Jersey's was 1.832. Since then, the average cost has increased in both states, but in New Jersey at a more rapid rate than in New York, and hence the average cost ratio has declined. New York's average cost and average insurance rate are still greater than New Jersey's, but the differences are narrowing.

Under both comparisons shown, New Jersey emerges as a relatively high-cost state. Its rates are less than New York's, comparable to those in Massachusetts and a good deal above those in the industrial states of California, Wisconsin, Connecticut, Illinois and Michigan. One possible reason for the differences is the variation in benefit levels. Interstate comparisons of benefit levels are as difficult to make as insurance rate comparisons, but New Jersey is by no means the most liberal of states when it comes to benefits. When interstate comparisons of the maximum weekly benefit for temporary disability as a percentage of the average weekly wage in each state are made, New Jersey ranks below Wisconsin, California, Connecticut, Pennsylvania, Texas and Massachusetts.[43] Differences in benefit levels do not appear to be wholly responsible for New Jersey's insurance cost ranking. The differences could possibly be accounted for by the fact that New Jersey pays such a high proportion of permanent partial awards. At the very least, it can be said that the different ways the various states distribute the compensation dollar among the different types of losses affect manual rates.[44]

Employer groups are vitally interested in interstate cost comparisons and use them to point to features of the law, or its administration, that they find displeasing. Labor groups are apt to retort by saying that costs could be reduced drastically if private insurance were eliminated from the compensation program, and an exclusive state fund substituted in its place.

State Funds Versus Private Insurance

Of the fifty-four compensation jurisdictions, eight finance compensation benefits through an exclusive state fund, although in two of these

---

[43] Alfred M. Skolnik, "Trends in Workmen's Compensation: Coverage, Benefits and Costs," *Social Security Bulletin*, XXV (August, 1958). Other benefit comparisons have been made in chapter 3. Johnson lists the benefit index of the National Council on Compensation Insurance for July, 1952, for the states used in his rate comparisons. This shows New Jersey's benefit index as being closely comparable to that of Michigan, Maryland and Missouri, and below that of Wisconsin, Illinois, Massachusetts and New York.

[44] Some comparative information on these differences between New Jersey and some of the other states has been presented in chapter 4. The data presented below compare New York and New Jersey experience, not on all losses, as in Table XXVI, but only in major and minor permanent partials, on one hand, and "temporary disability only" cases, on the other. Throughout the years shown, New Jersey exhibits a higher proportion of permanent partial cases than does New York, and devotes a greater proportion of its compensation dollar to these types of cases. The average cost of permanent partials and "temporary only" cases

states, employers are allowed to self-insure. Eleven jurisdictions have competitive state funds. Employers in these jurisdictions have the option of insuring with the state fund or with one or the other of the private insurance carriers that operate in these states; or, if qualified, they may self-insure. Benefits under the Federal Employees' Compensation Act are financed by appropriations from Congress, but in all the remaining jurisdictions the situation is comparable to that prevailing in New Jersey. An employer is obligated to place his business with a private insurance carrier or carry his own risk.[45]

All exclusive state funds, and most competitive ones, were established rather early in the history of the compensation program, usually at the same time that the state's act was adopted. No new exclusive fund has been established since 1920, and among the competitive funds, only Arizona's (1925) and Oklahoma's (1933) were started after that date. This is not to say that the controversy over methods of financing workmen's compensation is a dead issue. Both in the state and nationally, labor organizations have advocated exclusive state funds, and insurance groups have been just as adamant in their defense of the private carrier.

In part, the argument over state versus private insurance is based on rather broad philosophical and political considerations. The proponents of a state fund argue that workmen's compensation is essentially

---

combined is greater in New York than in New Jersey. But the ratio of New York's cost to New Jersey's is closer than when all incurred losses are considered. Permanent total and death cases are not considered in the comparisons, but these are only a minor fraction of the total in both states. More important is the exclusion of medical costs in noncompensable cases. These data would indicate that New Jersey's medical costs in noncompensable cases are substantially less than in New York and would partially account for differences in costs and hence rates.

Comparison of New Jersey and New York: Permanent Partial and Temporary Cases

Policy Year	Major and Minor Permanent Partial Cases				"Temporary Only" Cases				Average Cost Major, Minor and Temporary		Ratio — New York: New Jersey
	Percent of Total				Percent of Total						
	No.		Cost		No.		Cost				
	N.J.	N.Y.	N.J.	N.Y.	N.J.	N.Y.	N.J.	N.Y.	.N.J.	N.Y.	
1946	10.4	5.6	74.1	53.6	9.5	14.3	11.8	26.9	540	728	1.348
1947	10.5	6.0	71.8	52.8	8.7	13.6	10.9	26.0	562	821	1.461
1948	10.4	6.5	72.9	53.2	7.5	13.2	10.1	26.6	585	934	1.597
1949	10.0	6.7	72.1	53.6	7.0	12.9	10.0	27.0	595	989	1.652
1950	10.2	6.5	73.8	51.9	7.0	13.6	10.4	28.6	642	961	1.497
1951	11.3	6.7	74.7	50.3	7.2	13.7	9.8	29.4	701	940	1.340
1952	11.4	6.8	75.0	51.5	6.8	13.7	9.8	29.6	702	934	1.330
1953	12.3	6.6	75.6	49.4	6.9	13.9	9.6	31.4	732	956	1.306
1954	12.7	6.8	74.1	46.6	7.2	14.1	9.7	34.4	754	973	1.290
1955	13.1	7.9	73.9	44.7	7.6	14.7	11.2	38.2	770	947	1.230

Source: New Jersey Compensation Rating and Inspection Bureau.

[45]Nevada, North Dakota, Ohio, Oregon, Puerto Rico, Washington, West Virginia and Wyoming have exclusive state funds; but West Virginia and Wyoming allow self-insurance. Arizona, California, Colorado, Idaho, Maryland, Michigan, Montana, New York, Oklahoma, Pennsylvania and Utah have competitive state funds. The privilege of self-insurance is allowed in all jurisdictions in which private carriers operate, with the exception of Texas.

a social insurance program, that its costs are in the nature of a tax, and that there is no justification for allowing private companies to collect this tax and to make a profit in the bargain.[46] The insurance requirement is made compulsory in order to carry out a social purpose; and, it is contended, there is no place in this scheme of things for private enterprise to function.

On the other hand, advocates of private insurance raise the issue of "socialism" and claim that this is a field in which the encroachment of government monopoly must be resisted. The mere fact that the government requires employers to insure does not, in their view, mean that government ought to provide this insurance, any more than the state's safety requirements mean that the state should sell protective devices. The rights of free enterprise are said to include the right of the insurance carriers to compete for this business and the right of employers to choose among competing carriers.[47]

The controversy sometimes runs in less philosophical and more tactical terms. The insurance carriers, quite naturally, are seeking to maintain and extend their right to do business. Some employers undoubtedly feel that their position in compensation litigation is better protected if an insurance carrier, dependent upon them for continued business, is representing their interests. On the other hand, the AFL-CIO is convinced that benefit rates could be higher if the insurance carriers' cut of the costs were eliminated. Also, it is claimed that the insurance companies spearhead the fight against improved legislation with what, from labor's point of view, are the dollars the employers have set aside for the benefit of injured workers.[48]

Quite apart from either the narrower interests of the participants or the broader social issue of government versus private enterprise, the controversy extends to claims that one system, or the other, excels when it comes to such items as comparative cost, extensiveness of services provided, efficiency of operation, and so on.

Before making comparisons, it is well to recognize that not all state funds are alike. As has been mentioned, eight are exclusive funds, whereas the other eleven are competitive, but differences extend beyond this. Some operate as arms of the state, others as distinct self-supporting entities. Some charge the same rates as private carriers and offer their policyholders rights to participate in dividends;

---

[46]Cited as an argument for a state fund in Herman and Anne Somers, *Workmen's Compensation: Prevention, Insurance and Rehabilitation of Occupational Disability* (N. Y.: John Wiley and Sons, 1954), p. 123.

[47]A short analysis of the arguments pro and con can be found in Michelbacher, ed., pp. 62-63. For an earlier analysis which is sympathetic to the idea of a state fund, see Harry Weiss, "Employers' Liability and Workmen's Compensation," in John R. Commons, *History of Labor in the United States* (N. Y.: The Macmillan Co., 1935), pp. 581-587. A concise statement of the arguments for private insurance arrangements can be found in the publication of the Association of Casualty and Surety Companies, *Better Workmen's Compensation Protection*, January 1, 1958.

[48]AFL-CIO Department of Research, *Labor's Economic Review*, III (August-September, 1958).

others offer advance discounts, and still others combine both features. All of the funds share the common characteristic of operating as non-profit enterprises selling, for the most part, only workmen's compensation insurance within the boundaries of a single state.[49]

The exclusive state funds naturally write all of the compensation insurance in their respective states, with the exception of insurance for the self-insurers in states which permit this. The competitive funds, however, must meet the competition of the private carrier. When measured by the proportion of net cash and medical benefits paid in the nation as a whole, the various state funds and the federal system for government employees accounted for slightly more than 25 per cent of the total benefits paid during the years 1954 to 1956. Private insurance carriers of all types paid a little more than 61 per cent of all benefits, and the balance was accounted for by self-insurance payments.[50]

The proportion of compensation business within a particular state that falls to the competitive state funds varies a good deal. In Arizona, for example, the state fund wrote 98 per cent of the compensation business in 1954. In only three other states did the state funds succeed in writing 50 per cent or more of the premiums. These were Colorado (55 per cent), Utah (53 per cent) and Montana (50 per cent). In the industrially important states of California and New York, about one-quarter of the business is in the hands of the state funds. Although this does not constitute a major portion of the premiums, it does make the New York State Insurance Fund the largest single carrier of compensation insurance within that state. In the remaining states, the competitive funds write approximately 10 per cent or less of the business.[51]

---

[49] The exclusive state funds are usually administered by the same board or commission which carries out the general provisions of the compensation statutes. Competitive funds may follow this pattern or be administered by a separate board or commission. The California fund, for example, is administered by a board consisting of the director of the Department of Industrial Relations and four members appointed by the Governor. The New York State Fund is administered by a board of eight commissioners appointed by the Governor from among the employers who are policyholders in the fund. The state's Industrial Commissioner serves on the board as an ex officio member. The board appoints an executive director to operate the fund under its general control. In contrast, Montana's fund is administered by the state's Industrial Accident Commission.

In some of the funds, California's, for example, the rates charged are the same manual rates as charged by private carriers. These funds are usually participating carriers returning a portion of the collected premiums in the form of dividends. On the other hand, in Arizona, the fund charges rates that are about 90 per cent of those approved for private carriers. In Colorado, the fund charges rates approximately 30 per cent under manual rates for most classifications and pays dividends which, in 1956-1957, ranged from 12 per cent to 28 per cent according to classification. New York's fund offers advance discounts which amount to 25 per cent of manual rates for standard risks. The New York fund is also participating, according to classification of employers in safety groups. No so-called general group policyholders' dividend has been declared since the early 1930's.

Most of the funds do not pay state taxes on premium volume and profits, but there are exceptions. California's fund pays the same premium tax as required of private carriers. (*Best's Insurance Reports — Fire and Casualty* [N. Y.: Alfred M. Best Co., 1958], pp. 653 ff.)

[50] Skolnik, p. 8.

[51] Michelbacher, ed., p. 62.

To bring the controversy down to its more pragmatic side, the question of comparative costs, losses, and so on, may be discussed. Unfortunately, we are in the position of trying to compare apples and oranges, and it is not possible to find any one single measure that will illuminate the cost differences between the private carriers and the state funds.

Table XXVII shows particular loss and expense ratios for stock and mutual companies from 1948 to 1956. This is the country-wide experience of companies that operate in New York State, and comprises about 80 per cent of the compensation business underwritten in the nation as a whole. Incurred losses and incurred expenses are shown as percentages of earned premiums. The incurred loss ratios are about the same for stocks and mutuals, and show approximately the same trends for the two types of companies since 1948. The average for the entire period 1948-1956 shows the loss ratios for both stocks and mutuals to be under 60 per cent. [52]

Table XXVII. Country-wide Experience of Stock and Mutual Companies Operating in the State of New York, 1948-1956

Year	Stocks			Mutuals		
	Ratio to Earned Premiums		Net Gain or Profit	Ratio to Earned Premiums		Net Gain or Profit
	Incurred Losses	Incurred Expenses		Incurred Losses	Incurred Expenses	
1948	52.6	36.8	10.6	52.6	22.9	24.5
1949	52.4	37.3	10.3	57.7	23.6	18.7
1950	61.4	39.0	-0.4	62.1	24.3	13.6
1951	67.0	37.2	-4.2	62.4	24.3	13.3
1952	64.3	35.2	0.5	62.2	23.4	14.4
1953	59.7	34.8	5.5	59.9	23.5	16.6
1954	55.4	34.7	9.9	55.6	23.8	20.6
1955	58.7	34.5	6.8	56.8	24.6	18.6
1956	59.6	34.9	5.5	58.1	25.1	16.8
Av. 1948-1956	*59.1*	*35.8*	*5.1*	*58.6*	*24.0*	*17.4*

Source: Abstracted from insurance expense exhibits filed with the New York Insurance Department. The basic data may also be found in *Journal of Commerce*, July 30, 1958, p. 5, and Skolnik, Table 9. All figures disregard dividends to policyholders.

Table XXVII also shows the incurred expense ratios and the net gain or profit ratios. As might be expected, in light of greater acquisition expenses, and the tendency for stocks to underwrite the smaller risks, this class of carriers has higher expense ratios and hence lower net gain ratios. During the period as a whole the net gain ratio for the stock companies averaged 5.1 per cent, whereas the corresponding

---

[52] The earned premium base used in these computations disregards the dividends issued by mutuals and participating stock carriers. If these were taken into account, the mutual's earned premiums would be less and their loss ratios would consequently be higher.

figure for the mutuals was 17.4 per cent. On the basis of underwriting experience, it is obvious that the compensation business has been more profitable for the mutuals than for the stock companies.

Unfortunately, comparable ratios are not available for the state funds. Table XXVIII shows the ratio of direct losses to direct writings for the private carriers in the nation as a whole and for eighteen state funds, for the period 1950 to 1956. The base used here is not earned premiums but written premiums, and the losses shown are those actually paid in current and past cases.[53] Actual losses or benefits paid do not include reserves for future payments on present or past cases. At a time when wages and compensation rates are increasing, the ratio of incurred losses to earned premiums tends to be greater than the ratio of direct losses to written premiums.

Table XXVIII. Ratios of Direct Losses Paid to Direct Writings for Private Carriers and Ratios of Benefits Paid to Premiums Written for 18 State Funds, 1950-1956

Year	Private Carriers Ratio of Direct Losses Paid to Direct Writings	18 State Funds[a] Ratio of Benefits to Written Premiums
1950	52.8	73.6
1951	52.6	68.8
1952	51.3	69.2
1953	48.8	68.1
1954	50.6	68.9
1955	52.2	68.8
1956	53.6	73.0
Av. 1950-1956	51.7	70.0

Source: Private carrier data from *Spectator: Insurance by States of Fire, Marine, Casualty, Surety and Miscellaneous Lines*, annual issues. State fund data abstracted from Skolnik, Table 10. All figures disregard dividends to policyholders.
[a] For eight state funds, fiscal-year data have been converted to calendar-year data.

In each of the years shown, the loss ratios are higher for the state funds than for the private carriers. For the period 1950 1956 the average loss ratio for the private companies was 51.7 per cent, whereas the loss ratio for the eighteen state funds combined amounted to 70.0 per cent. These loss ratios are not strictly comparable for several reasons. The written premium base, for both the private carriers and the state funds, disregards dividends to policyholders, but some of the state funds provide substantial advance discounts to policyholders. If the state fund premiums were shown at the manual rates instead of at the discounted rates, the loss ratios would tend to be lower. Also,

---

[53] Written premiums are essentially the initial or gross premiums received by the carriers for all policies written during the calendar year. Earned premiums are written premiums after deducting for adjusted premiums, reinsurance premiums paid and, most important, the reserves to cover the unexpired policies for which premiums have been paid.

some of the state funds' premiums need not include either charges for certain services the private carriers perform or, in some cases, allowances for taxes and reserves. Finally, the state funds are required to accept all risks, and undoubtedly these funds write a high proportion of extra-hazardous risks, which help boost their loss ratios.[54]

Table XXIX shows the ratios of expenses to written premiums for stocks, mutuals and the eighteen state funds combined. Again, these are not strictly comparable, since, as noted above, the private carriers have to pay taxes and meet certain charges, including those of the various services offered, whereas some of the state funds are largely exempt from these costs. With these cautions in mind, it can be noted, as was seen in comparing incurred expenses with earned premiums, the mutuals have lower expense ratios than the stocks; but the state funds operate with substantially lower expense ratios than the mutual companies. One reason for this is that the state funds, especially the exclusive funds, spend little or nothing in the way of acquisition expenses. They also have the considerable advantage of being able to concentrate their business in one line of insurance within the boundaries of a single state.

Table XXIX. Average Expense Ratios of Stocks, Mutuals and State Funds

Year	Ratio of Expenses to Premiums Written[a]		
	Stocks	Mutuals	18 State Funds[b]
1951	26.5	16.2	9.1
1952	25.8	15.6	8.9
1953	24.9	15.3	8.8
1954	25.7	16.4	9.1
1955	25.9	17.2	8.7
1956	25.8	17.0	9.1

Source: Data on stocks and mutuals from *Best's Fire and Casualty Aggregates and Averages* (N. Y.: Alfred M. Best Co.), annual issues. State fund data abstracted from Skolnik, Table 10.
[a]For stocks and mutuals, expenses include commissions and brokers' fees and all other underwriting expenses. For state funds, administrative expenses financed through appropriations from general revenues are included. Loss adjustment expenses for certain competitive funds are excluded. The written premiums disregard dividends to policyholders.
[b]For eight states, fiscal-year data have been converted to calendar-year data.

In the area of services offered by the different classes of insurance carriers, it is difficult to secure comparative data on which to base sound judgments. The private carriers point out that a compensation program does not operate itself; risks must be classified, rates determined, claims investigated and adjusted, payrolls audited, and prevention and rehabilitation programs established and maintained.[55]

---

[54] With the exception of Michigan, each of the competitive or exclusive funds is required, either by law or administrative ruling, to take any risk offered for insurance. Michigan, like New Jersey, has an assigned risk plan.

[55] Association of Casualty and Surety Companies, *Better Workmen's Compensation Protection*, p. 18.

Some of the exclusive funds provide few of these services; on the other hand, the New York State Insurance Fund claims to offer a complete line of services to its clients. In some of the states that have exclusive funds, Ohio for example, private service agencies are utilized by employers who feel that the state fund agents do not adequately represent their interest in adjusting claims. [56] To the extent that such services are employed, they constitute an addition to the employer's compensation costs, even though this cost is not part of the insurance premium.

From the point of view of the employer, the least expensive insurance may not be the best buy. Confronted in some states with the choice of insuring with a competitive fund, a mutual company, or a nonparticipating stock company, a small employer may choose the stock company. Although his net premiums will be higher, he has the advantage of dealing with a broker with whom he may be personally acquainted. The broker may give him all possible breaks when it comes to the classification of risks offered, and find for him the lowest-paying classification. Also, in the event of an accident, the broker may take care of all the paper work and settle the claim without litigation, even though it may be a bit questionable. The mutual carrier may offer some of these advantages, whereas the competitive fund is probably least able to bend any of its regulations for the employer's benefit.

The large employer may be less interested in these possible concessions, and is more likely to purchase his insurance only after careful consideration of cost advantages. Also, he may be less willing to compromise claims, especially if his firm is large enough to be experience rated. He may be attracted to a participating company which gives evidence of offering good claims adjustment services and vigorous defense of contested cases.

All employers would be interested in safety work performed by the carriers and some funds. The loading factor in the rate-making process provides about 2.5 per cent of the premium for inspection and accident prevention work, but private carriers probably average less than 2 per cent of premiums for this purpose. [57] There is great variation among these carriers in the effectiveness of their safety program. Some of the large stock and mutual companies have acquired a reputation for this work, and they make their sales appeal on this basis. The smaller carrier, with but a few risks in a geographic area, can afford to do little along these lines. It is probable that the safety work of the exclusive funds cannot compare with that of the largest private carriers.

From the point of view of the private carriers, the establishment of a *competitive* state fund in New Jersey would not be wholly bad. If such a fund were compelled to underwrite all risks, it would remove the burden of assigned risks from the private companies. Employers would be attracted to the fund if it offered substantial advance discounts

---

[56] Somers and Somers, *Workmen's Compensation*, p. 128.
[57] Somers and Somers, *Workmen's Compensation*, p. 129.

of manual rates, and especially if it combined these lower rates with a strong safety program, effective claims service, and an administration free of political entanglements.

Pressures for the establishment of a competitive fund within the state would probably be greater than they are, if it were not for the assigned risk plan, and also the New Jersey Manufacturers Casualty Insurance Company. Reference has already been made to the fact that this participating stock company writes more workmen's compensation insurance in New Jersey than does any other carrier. It was incorporated in 1913, sponsored by a number of large manufacturing concerns closely affiliated with the affairs of the New Jersey Manufacturers Association. The trustees of the association hold title to the shares in the stock company, but these are held for the benefit of the policy-holders under a deed of trust. Business is solicited only from members of the Manufacturers Association and their employees. In conjunction with a sister company, it offers a rather complete line of casualty insurance to its clients.[58]

Although the company is licensed to do business in ten states, all but a miniscule portion of its business is written in New Jersey. During 1956, its ratio of direct losses to direct writings amounted to 51 per cent, within 1 per cent of the same ratio for all carriers within the state. In part, this correspondence is influenced by the fact that the Manufacturers Company writes about one-quarter of all the compensation business in the state. Although its loss ratio is favorable, the more remarkable fact is its extraordinarily low expense ratio.

The company's underwriting expenses incurred have been 6 per cent or less of its written premiums in each year since 1953. In 1957, they were 5.7 per cent. Its combined losses and expenses for the years 1953 to 1957 were only 67.3 per cent of premium volume. This is an indication of what can be done when a company with relatively low acquisition expenses operates in a geographically compact state and charges rates set high enough so that the average stock company can write compensation business.

In a sense, the company operates as type of employers' cooperative. Although it has earned lucrative underwriting profits, no dividends have been paid to its stockholders since 1926. Attractive dividends have been paid, however, to its policyholders according to their individual premium volume. During the years 1955 to 1957, normal dividends amounted to 25 per cent; from 1952 to 1954, they were 30 per cent, and during some years, 1941 and 1946, for example, total dividends paid, both normal and extra, amounted to a return to policyholders of 40 per cent of the premiums paid.

In some respects, the surface analogies between a competitive fund like that of New York State and the New Jersey Manufacturers Casualty

---

[58] Information about the New Jersey Manufacturers Casualty Insurance Company is from *Best's Insurance Reports — Fire and Casualty*, 1958, p. 739; *Best's Fire and Casualty Aggregates and Averages*, 1957, p. 34; and New Jersey Compensation Rating and Inspection Bureau, various *Annual Reports*.

Insurance Company are striking. Both do about the same percentage of compensation business within their respective states, and both have returned the same percentage of premiums to policyholders in recent years. Each is controlled by a board, composed in the main of employers who are also policyholders. Of course, there are basic differences. The New York fund must accept all risks; the New Jersey company is obligated only to underwrite the questionable risks which come to it under the assigned risk program. One is a private company; the other is an instrumentality of the state. The New Jersey company shares its underwriting gains in the form of dividends, whereas the New York fund can offer discounts on manual rates, without reference to the size of the risk.

From the point of view of organized labor, the New Jersey Manufacturers Casualty Insurance Company is merely another insurance carrier which opposes claims, in much the same manner as any other private insurance organization. Furthermore, it is closely allied with an organization which, from labor's point of view, opposes needed improvements in the compensation law. Nothing in the setup of the company meets labor's demands for increased state participation in the financing of workmen's compensation. For some employers, however, the company serves some of the same functions as the New York fund. Of course, neither this company nor New York's competitive fund writes a major share of the available compensation business. Other carriers, whether because of participating features, services rendered, ability to cover nation-wide operations, or other reasons, are able to attract their share of the potential customers.

Conclusions

Insurance companies play the central role in financing the compensation program and naturally are the targets of criticism. The insurance carrier is the "visible" party in the compensation proceedings, offering settlements at the informal levels, and opposing employees' claims at the formal level. Employee representatives tend to blame the companies for inadequate settlements and delays in adjudicating claims, whereas employers, who eventually pay the costs, complain that no matter what they do to reduce accidents, premiums seem to go up.

In none of the other social insurance programs does private insurance play so prominent a role. The basic reasons for this are rooted in the origins of the program. Private carriers sold employers' liability insurance even before the passage of the compensation acts, and it was natural for them to continue coverage as the laws were amended to substitute the compensation principle. New Jersey's 1911 statute did not make this insurance coverage compulsory; it merely set forth the employers' obligation to meet the statutory payments as they came due. When the law was amended in 1917, it required employers to make provision for the security of their obligations, but it continued the existing private insurance arrangements. Even then, the compulsory requirements were not extended to employers of farm labor and domestic servants, although the law covered these categories of employees.

Such exemptions may have made sense in the 1920's, but they are not warranted today. It is probably no great service to any employer to exempt him from the compulsory insurance requirements. A single accident can cost over $50,000 in compensation costs, a sum that would wipe out the assets of many a farmer or householder. Neither does there seem to be any good reason to remove governmental bodies from the compulsory requirements, although this ommission is probably less serious.

Although most employers must insure, they are left free to cover their obligations by placing their insurance with a wide variety of companies. The employer can place his business with a broker connected with a nonparticipating stock company, with a mutual association or with a participating stock company. If large enough, he can qualify for premium discounts or one of two classes of retrospective rating. Although all carriers charge the same initial manual rates, competition for the available business is based upon differences in services offered and the possibility of dividends being returned to policyholders.

The fact that free enterprise is allowed to function in this sector does not remove the question of rates from the realm of social concern. An instrumentality of the state, the Compensation Rating and Inspection Bureau sets these rates in the first place. Their interest is in seeing that the rates are neither excessive nor discriminatory but, at the same time, adequate to meet incurred losses. But the bureau works within a framework prescribed by tradition and national practice. Rates are set so that expected indemnity and medical losses will amount to about 58 per cent of the premiums.

It is the 40-odd per cent of the rates allocated for expenses that causes consternation in labor circles. The lion's share of this is accounted for by the 17.5 per cent acquisition cost item. As Hobbs points out, this item, like all the expense items with the exception of taxes, is a mere estimate based upon judgment. The loadings are fairly uniform from state to state and not based upon a survey of expenses within any one state. Granted that it would be technically difficult to segregate the New Jersey expenses of companies which do business on a national basis, still, if this were done, average expenses would probably be smaller in New Jersey than in many other less industrialized states in which business is thinly distributed. The experience of the one insurance company that confines its operations to the state would seem to bear this out.

Quite apart from geographic considerations, another important reason for the high proportion of premiums allocated for expenses, especially for acquisition costs, is that loadings are set on the basis of the average expense items of the stock companies. The various rating plans reduce the amount of these expense items for the large risks, but if the acquisition loadings were reduced drastically for all risks, some stock companies which operate through brokers would probably be eliminated from the field. To prevent this, rates are set so that the stock company which is of average, or less than average, efficiency can find it profitable to operate within the state. As in any other rate regulating procedure which allows the marginal operator to exist, the more efficient units, under the set rates, may be cutting the melon.

This is the price paid for having a large number of various types of companies competing for business. Advocates of exclusive state funds maintain that it is too high a price. Defendants of the present system point out that any employer has the option of insuring with a participating company, thereby cutting his net costs. If he chooses to remain with his broker, it is maintained that he ought to be allowed this privilege. Unfortunately, however, critics of the high cost of compensation programs measure these costs by premiums, and they fail to distinguish between amounts that must be available for losses and expenses, which would have to be met by any financing method, and those required to satisfy the penchant of employers who wish to do business in a certain way.

Expense loadings currently allow 2.5 per cent of premiums for underwriting profits. But this amount is realized only if aggregate losses turn out exactly as expected by the rate-makers. Examination of the trend data indicates that these expectations are rarely realized; losses as a percentage of premiums usually amount to more or less than the percentages expected. In part, this flows from the difficulty of predicting the future on the basis of past experience. In part, it is accounted for by the fact that payrolls are not the best measure of exposure as wage rates rise. Measured in aggregate terms, the compensation business has been a profitable one in recent years. Inflation is proverbially kind to compensation insurers.[59]

The generally favorable loss experiences of private companies lends ammunition to those who advocate a state fund. Although these profits may be due largely to factors such as rising payrolls, labor groups also complain of the interest that insurance carriers have in compromising an employee's compensation claim for something less than it is worth, or in the words of petitioners' representatives, of "beating a claim." There is no doubt but that a responsible insurance adjuster must be interested in minimizing indemnity and medical claims. Rates are set on the basis of some past experience. An adjuster, working on a current claim, is dealing with an employer who has already paid premiums on the basis of past experience; it is in his company's interest to minimize losses. It is true that any losses that will be paid will eventually be reflected in the classification and total experience, so that the matter of timing, which looms large in the immediate picture, will eventually be less important.

More significantly, any insurance company has an interest in

---

[59] Kulp, p. 152.

minimizing losses so that the risk will come out with better than average experience. With due allowances for modifications under rating plans, the employers' rate will be determined by the experience of all employers in general, and the employers in the same classification, in particular. Any company that can skim the cream by insuring the risks with favorable loss experience will receive rates based on general experience but pay losses based on the more fortunately situated companies — on the whole, a delightful position.

It is not necessarily bad that insurance companies have an economic interest in minimizing claims. The matter of formally adjusting a compensation claim has taken on all the attributes of adversary proceedings, and for this type of proceedings, both sides need strong representation. The opposite type of charge has also been made, that insurance companies fail to contest claims diligently and have a tendency to wash out claims for their nuisance value. Insurance adjusters in private conversation will admit this, but they maintain that in the long run this saves the carrier money.

Insurance companies have the option of refusing to insure risks which they believe will have unfavorable loss experience. An employer refused by insurance carriers can always receive protection provided he is willing to abide by the regulations. The fact that an assigned risk plan exists, plus the fact that employers have the option of insuring in participating companies, particularly the New Jersey Manufacturers Casualty Insurance Company, eliminates most of the pressures for a competitive fund within the state. This leaves the major choice between continuing the present system or substituting an exclusive state fund.

In light of the differences that exist among state funds, the difficulties of making equitable comparisons and the paucity of data on comparative services, it is hazardous to draw conclusions about the relative over-all merits of the exclusive state funds and the private carriers. With due allowance for all necessary cautions that must be observed, it is likely that if New Jersey established an exclusive fund, it would operate with higher loss ratios and lower expense ratios than the private carriers. On balance, the rates charged would probably be less than the present net rates of most private companies. This would be because of the lower over-all expenses of a single carrier operating within a small state, without having to meet any but the most nominal of acquisition costs.

There is always the possibility that such a fund would suffer from administrative weaknesses. Its personnel might be chosen with first regard to political considerations, or the fund might be unable to recruit a first-class staff because of low civil service salaries. Such factors would influence the quality of services offered.

Perhaps, in the final analysis, the fundamental choice between an exclusive fund and private insurance rests on broad philosophical and political considerations. Groups advocating an exclusive fund would probably be willing to tolerate possible administrative weaknesses to gain what they feel is government's rightful place in the financing of this social insurance program. On the other hand, advocates of private financing may be willing to tolerate higher costs to gain the principle of reserving this field for private enterprise.

Those who are unconvinced that any fundamental principles are at stake in this controversy are hard put to make a choice. Decisions are easy only when the well-managed exclusive fund offering a wide range of services is compared with the kind of private carrier which requires a high portion of its premiums for administrative expenses and which is unable to provide effective safety or rehabilitation programs. This choice is equally easy when the politically ridden fund, which requires employers to meet separately the expense of necessary services, is compared with the safety-conscious participating company which offers substantial premium dividends and an extensive range of services. If an exclusive state fund were established in New Jersey, it would be impossible to predict its method of operations, whereas we do know something about the operations of the present system. We ought not to lose sight of the fact that whatever the advantages of a private system, we probably pay a price for the privilege of allowing private carriers to compete in the underwriting of the risks involved in this compulsory social insurance program.

APPENDIX

NEW JERSEY'S RATE-MAKING PROCEDURES

One way to explain the procedures involved in the complicated process of rate-making is to examine the New Jersey Compensation Rating and Inspection Bureau's work at the time of the July 1, 1958, rate revisions. The bureau's first task is to adjust the rate relativity among the separate classifications by determining the pure premiums, that portion of the rates available for losses, for each classification. After this, the general rate level is examined to determine whether it should be increased, lowered or allowed to remain the same. Once this is done, the standard expense loadings are adjusted, and the pure premiums are multiplied by a factor that will translate them into manual rates.

Determining the Pure Premiums

In the usual case, when an accident occurs, the insurance company has no exact way to calculate the amounts it will eventually pay on the claim. It must estimate its incurred losses and, as time passes, make adjustments in these estimates. Consequently, the older the claim, the more accurate the estimate of incurred losses; but, of course, the more aged the experience data, the less likely it is to reflect current conditions. There is no ideal solution to this problem; the bureau takes the most recent information, as reported by the carriers, and adjusts it to reflect more recent conditions.

Insurance companies report to the bureau under the unit statistical plan. The experience of each policy year — the exposure or payroll, the earned premiums and estimated incurred losses — is reported five times. The first reporting is made, as of a date 18 months after the effective date of the policy, and subsequent reportings are made as of 30, 42, 54 and 66 months after the effective date.[1] Hence, as of July, 1958, the bureau had available data from the fifth or final reporting for policy year 1951; the fourth reporting for 1952; the third for 1953; the second for 1954; and the first for 1955. The nature of the reporting process does not allow consideration of more recent experience from policy years 1956 or 1957. The complete first reporting of 1956 experience was not yet due as of July, 1958, and policy year 1957 had not yet expired. Yet, the risks had been paying premiums based upon rates established in July, 1957. Once these so-called present pure premiums, or the loss portion of the rates, have been converted or adjusted, they can be used, together with the average of the five-year experience in each classification, to establish the underlying pure premiums for each classification for the July, 1958, rate revision.

The actual, "as reported" experience, which reflects conditions in each of the past policy years, cannot be used without making several adjustments. The payrolls or exposure can be used as reported, but the losses must be segregated according to type of injury, limited and brought up to the most recent benefit levels as explained below:

1) Subdivision of losses.

Since losses in a single classification vary according to type of injury they are divided into three subclasses. These are: (a) serious losses, which include deaths, permanent totals, and major permanent partial disabilities,[2] (b) nonserious, which include temporary disabilities and minor permanent partials, and (c) medical, which includes all medical costs incurred.

2) Adjustments for law changes.

The reported losses must be adjusted to show what they would have been if the benefit levels which prevailed as of July, 1958, had been in effect during each of the policy years.

3) Loss limitations.

For purposes of adjusting rate relativity, frequency of accidents is thought to be more important than some aspects of severity;

---

[1]New Jersey Compensation Rating and Inspection Bureau, *New Jersey Statistical Plan*, edition of January 1, 1956, p. 9.

[2]A major permanent partial disability is one involving the loss of sight of an eye or the loss of a hand, foot or leg or arm; also every permanent injury involving impairment to the extent of 50 per cent or more of a hand, foot, arm or leg or involving impairment to the extent of 80 per cent or more of an eye; also every permanent injury, whether enumerated in the above categories or not, which is compensated on the basis of 25 per cent or more of permanent total disability. Minor permanent partial disabilities include all cases of permanent partial disabilities which do not fall within the enumerated categories. These definitions are from *New Jersey Statistical Plan*, p. 16.

consequently, the reported losses in individual cases must be limited. Regardless of the reported incurred loss, no permanent total case is included at more than $18,000 (450 times the $40 weekly maximum rate), and medical losses are limited to $3,300 (one-quarter of the average death and permanent total indemnity). Any losses removed by these limitations are later provided for in the multiplier. In effect, this spreads the excess cost of a relatively few fortuitous cases over the entire rate structure.

Adjustments are also made in catastrophe cases, defined as accidents which involve more than two claims. Any catastrophe is limited to $26,400 (twice the average death and permanent total value used in experience rating) in indemnity costs, and in medical costs to $6,600, or twice the usual medical limitation. To make the premiums comparable to losses as limited, the specific and general catastrophe loading elements in the premiums are also eliminated.[3]

4) Inclusion of loss adjustment expenses.

At one time, the claims or loss adjustment expenses were included in the general expense loadings. In 1955, the National Council on Compensation Insurance transferred these expenses to the loss portion of the premium, and this procedure was adopted by New Jersey at the time of the July 1, 1957, rate revision. Consequently, reported losses are increased by 14 per cent to cover these claims expenses. In effect, this transfers the loss adjustment expense from a relativity to premium to a relativity to losses, to which it is more nearly related. This is in accordance with practice in automobile and other liability insurance rate-making.[4] This transfer must be taken into account later in the multiplier calculations.

Table XXX summarizes the reported and converted experience for the five policy years for all classifications. Part A of the table shows the payrolls, premiums (excluding constants), the subdivided losses and the loss ratios as actually reported. Part B of this table shows the same payrolls, but the premiums are those based upon the latest manual rates (July, 1957) excluding catastrophe loadings; and the losses have been adjusted, as described above. This is the converted experience; it shows what the experience would have been if "present" premiums and benefit levels had been in effect in each of these years, if losses were limited and, finally, if loss adjustment expenses had been included.

Actually, in working with these data, the bureau divides the classifications into three groups; (1) manufacturing, (2) construction and erection, and (3) all other classifications. The totals for the five policy years in each of these groups form the basis for calculating factors (shown in Table XXXI) that will convert the present (July, 1957)

---

[3] The general catastrophe loading applicable to most classifications is $0.02 per $100 of payroll. In some classifications, such as office employees and teachers, it is $0.01, whereas other hazardous classifications carry specific catastrophe loadings. The catastrophe loading in the hauling of explosives, for example, is approximately one-half the total rate.

[4] C. A. Kulp, *Casualty Insurance*, 3d ed. (New York: The Ronald Press Co., 1956), p. 475.

Table XXX. Actual and Converted Pure Premiums at Time of July 1, 1958, New Jersey Rate Revision — All Classifications

Policy Year	Payroll (in hundreds)	Premium Excl. Constants	Exhibit of Losses									Loss Ratios			
			Serious		Nonserious		Medical	Total				Ser.	Non-ser.	Med.	Total
			No.	Amt.	No.	Amt.	Amt.	No.	Amt.						
A – Pure Cost of Workmen's Compensation and Employers' Liability Insurance															
1951	$4,305,277.0	$49,597,370	759	$6,055,152	42,959	$21,483,885	$8,412,522	43,718	$35,951,559			12.21%	43.32%	16.96%	72.49%
1952	4,657,672.2	59,808,155	764	6,181,645	42,382	21,036,219	8,315,140	43,146	35,533,004			10.34	35.17	13.90	59.41
1953	4,977,237.3	68,950,363	744	6,229,292	42,207	21,608,587	8,735,798	42,951	36,573,677			9.03	31.34	12.67	53.04
1954	5,108,411.1	70,181,756	805	7,002,584	41,392	21,327,708	9,307,619	42,197	37,637,911			9.98	30.39	13.26	53.63
1955	5,515,210.2	74,120,590	839	6,765,801	43,694	22,917,451	10,247,451	44,533	39,930,329			9.13	30.92	13.82	53.87
Total	$24,563,807.8	$322,658,234	3,911	$32,234,474	212,634	$108,373,476	$45,018,530	216,545	$185,626,480			9.99%	33.59%	13.95%	57.53%
B – Converted Experience on July 1, 1958, Final Conversion Level															
1951	$4,305,277.0	$66,158,229	759	$8,034,618	42,959	$28,767,728	$9,100,626	43,718	$45,902,972			12.14%	43.48%	13.76%	69.38%
1952	4,657,672.2	70,306,371	764	7,848,622	42,382	28,134,945	9,124,451	43,146	45,108,018			11.16	40.02	12.98	64.16
1953	4,977,237.3	74,892,990	744	8,111,122	42,207	28,897,024	9,500,913	42,951	46,509,059			10.83	38.58	12.69	62.10
1954	5,108,411.1	76,385,114	805	9,027,667	41,392	28,542,124	9,979,313	42,197	47,549,104			11.82	37.37	13.06	62.25
1955	5,515,210.2	82,209,230	839	8,870,091	43,694	30,700,630	11,120,607	44,533	50,691,328			10.79	37.34	13.53	61.66
Total	$24,563,807.8	$369,951,934	3,911	$41,892,120	212,634	$145,042,451	$48,825,910	216,545	$235,760,481			11.32%	39.21%	13.20%	63.73%

Source: New Jersey Compensation Rating and Inspection Bureau, "July 1, 1958, Rate Revision," Exhibit IV.

underlying pure premiums to the level adopted for the July, 1958, rate revision. As will be seen, in selecting the pure premiums for each individual classification, the present rate will be compared with the five-year average; but in order to make this comparison, the present rate must be made comparable to the converted experience. The present pure premiums for serious losses in the manufacturing group, for example, would produce losses approximately 3 per cent too high. Hence, the present pure premiums in this subclass of losses in this industry group must be multiplied by .966 to arrive at the converted losses for the five-year period. On the other hand, the present pure premiums for serious losses in the construction and erection group would produce losses that were too low. In this category, the present pure premiums would have to be multiplied by the factor 1.063. Similar factors are presented in Table XXXI for the different subclasses of losses in all three industry groups.

Table XXXI. Factors Which Will Convert July, 1957, Underlying Pure Premiums to the Level Adopted for the July 1, 1958, New Jersey Revision

Industry Group	Types of Losses		
	Serious	Nonserious	Medical
Manufacturing	.966	.966	.975
Construction and Erection	1.063	.927	.986
All Other	1.042	.974	.977

Source: New Jersey Compensation Rating and Inspection Bureau, "July 1, 1958, Rate Revision," p. 4.

At this point in the process of determining the pure premiums, it is necessary to examine each of the classifications separately. Table XXXII presents the data for one of the classifications, "wire insulating and or covering, code number 4470." As in Table XXX, which was a summary for all classifications, the reported losses and payrolls are presented in Part A, whereas Part B shows the same payrolls with the losses placed on the conversion level.

The bottom line of Part B (line 1) shows that total payrolls for the five policy years for this classification amounted to $80,140,500. Fourteen "serious" cases were reported, and the incurred losses, as limited and modified, plus the loss adjustment expenses, were estimated as $114,262. Thus the indicated pure premium for "serious" losses was .14 ($114,262 + $80,150,5 [payroll in hundreds] = .14). Although this could be thought of as $0.14 per $100 of payroll, actually, at this point, these are pure premiums and not dollars. In similar fashion, it can be seen that the indicated pure premium for the "nonserious" losses is .68 and for medical losses, .24. Adding together the pure premiums for each subdivision of losses gives the pure premium of 1.06 for the so-called "five-year indications."

Table XXXII. Actual and Converted Pure Premiums in the "Wire Insulating or Covering" Classification, New Jersey, 1951-1955

Exhibit of Losses

A – Pure Cost of Workmen's Compensation and Employers' Liability Insurance

Actual Losses and Pure Premiums

Policy Year	Payroll (in hundreds)	Serious No.	Serious Amt.	Nonserious No.	Nonserious Amt.	Medical Amt.	Total No.	Total Amt.	PP Serious	PP Nonser.	PP Medical	PP Total
	Actual											
1951	$14,379.8	4	$17,339	193	$81,556	$36,528	197	$135,423	.12	.57	.25	.94
1952	17,550.6	3	22,343	181	84,115	37,272	184	143,730	.13	.48	.21	.82
1953	16,334.7	2	13,869	183	79,991	28,083	185	121,943	.08	.49	.17	.74
1954	15,245.1	2	11,618	179	77,224	33,792	181	122,634	.08	.51	.22	.81
1955	16,630.3	3	18,971	198	86,689	33,417	201	139,077	.11	.52	.20	.83
Total	$80,140.5	14	$84,140	934	$409,575	$169,092	948	$662,807	.10	.51	.21	.82

B – Converted Experience on July 1, 1958, Final Conversion Level

Losses (as Limited) and Pure Premiums on Present Law Level

Policy Year	Payroll (in hundreds)	Serious No.	Serious Amt.	Nonserious No.	Nonserious Amt.	Medical Amt.	Total No.	Total Amt.	PP Serious	PP Nonser.	PP Medical	PP Total
	Adjusted											
1951	$14,379.8	4	$23,613	193	$108,964	$41,641	197	$174,218	.16	.76	.29	1.21
1952	17,550.6	3	30,319	181	112,006	42,491	184	184,816	.17	.64	.24	1.05
1953	16,334.7	2	18,820	183	106,500	32,015	185	157,335	.12	.65	.20	.97
1954	15,245.1	2	15,766	179	103,912	38,523	181	158,201	.10	.68	.25	1.03
1955	16,630.3	3	25,744	198	117,415	38,096	201	181,255	.15	.71	.23	1.09
1-Total	$80,140.5	14	$114,262	934	$548,797	$192,766	948	$855,825	.14	.68	.24	1.06
2-Present Rate									.14	.65	.24	1.03
3-Formula – 30%					100%	100%			.14	.68	.24	1.06
4-Adopted									.14	.68	.24	1.06

Source: New Jersey Compensation Rating and Inspection Bureau, "July 1, 1958, Rate Revision," p. 145.

On line 2, at the bottom of this same Table XXXII, is shown the "present" rate for this classification. Actually, this is the pure premium, applicable to this classification as of July, 1957, modified by the appropriate factors mentioned above. To determine the pure premium that will underly the new rates, the bureau has the task of averaging, in some fashion, the present rate and the five-year average. This averaging is done by weighting with credibility factors. The greater the losses expected in the classification within any subdivision of losses, the higher the credibility factor that will be assigned to the five-year indications. The complement of the weight assigned to the five-year indications is assigned to the present rate. If the expected losses are sufficient, the five-year indications would be given 100 per cent credibility, which means that the present rate would not be given any weight in computating the average.[5]

Line 3 of Table XXXII shows the results of computing the average by means of the credibility formulas. The pure premium attributable to the serious losses is .14, to nonserious, .68 and the medical component, .24, accounting for the total pure premium for this classification of 1.06.

This also was the actual pure premium adopted to underly the July, 1958, rates. Although underwriting judgment may enter the decision, in most instances the "formula pure premiums" are the ones recommended by the staff of the bureau and approved by the governing committee and the Commissioner of Banking and Insurance.

Once the pure premiums have been adopted for each of the classifications, the rate-maker has a measure of the relative hazard of the various classifications. Only the problem of rate relativity has been taken care of; the task of determining the manual rate still lies ahead. To translate pure premiums into money rates it is first necessary to determine if the general rate level should be changed, and then the expense and other loadings must be added.

General Rate Level Changes

The principal guide to the bureau in the matter of general rate level changes is the information filed by each insurance company on so-called schedule W at the end of every calendar year. The information from these schedules is consolidated, and the result is a policy-year analysis of total experience, which is segregated according to calendar

---

[5] The criteria for giving 100 per cent credibility to the "indications" are based on the following: For the serious category there would have to be, on an expected loss basis, the equivalent of 50 average losses; for the nonserious, 300 average losses; and the medical category would have to show losses equal to 80 per cent of the nonserious figure. The formula appearing on line 3 of Table XXXII shows the figures, 30 per cent, 100 per cent, 100 per cent. This shows that the indications have been assigned a credibility of 30 per cent in the serious category because there were less than 50 average losses, and thus the present premium is assigned the complement of 30 per cent or 70 per cent as its weight. In the nonserious and medical categories, the criteria for 100 per cent credibility to the indications are met, thus ignoring, in effect, the present pure premiums for these types of losses.

years. As published by the bureau each year, the schedule W exhibit shows total premiums and losses during each of the last six calendar years for all policies which became effective in each of the last twenty-two years.[6] Unlike the data used in adjusting rate relativity, these are not based upon accident reports, but rather upon the individual company's accounting records. Necessarily, these data are not as refined as the information filed in the various policy-year reportings, but they do have the advantage of allowing the bureau to look at more recent over-all experience.

Schedule W information for the calendar year ending December 31, 1957, the most recent year available at the time of the July, 1958, rate revision, shows the losses actually paid to the end of the year on all policies which became effective in calendar years 1935 to 1957. Also shown are the companies' estimates of the losses still outstanding at the end of the year on policies which became effective in each of the twenty-two years. Adding together the paid losses and the outstanding losses gives the total losses incurred to the end of the year.

In order to segregate the 1957 experience, it is necessary to look at the previous year's data. In round figures, at the end of 1956, losses of $434.5 million had been paid on all policies which became effective from calendar years 1935 to 1956. Naturally, the bulk of this was paid on policies of the earlier years. The estimate of outstanding losses was $61.9 million, most of it accounted for by policies which became effective in more recent years. Adding together these figures gives $496.4 million as the total incurred losses to the end of 1956.

During calendar year 1957, the companies continued to pay losses on past years' policies, which naturally reduced their outstanding losses on these policies. Also, with the passage of another year, estimates of outstanding losses were revised either up or down. In addition, some losses were incurred for compensable accidents under the policies written during calendar 1957. Of course, many of the policies with a 1957 date were of too recent origin to have generated much experience, because some of them were written toward the end of the year and would not expire until some time in calendar 1958. All told, the losses paid to the year 1957 on all policies which had become effective in the last twenty-two years amounted to $477.4 million, whereas the outstanding losses were $71.4 million. This accounts for $548.9 million in incurred losses at the end of calendar year 1957.

It now becomes a simple matter to abstract the experience of calendar year 1957 from this running inventory of accounting records. Deducting incurred losses as of December, 1956 ($496.4 million), from incurred losses as of a year later ($548.9 million) gives $52.5 million as the incurred loss experience for calendar year 1957. In similar fashion, the written and earned premium records can be used to calculate the earned premium experience for calendar year 1957. Dividing incurred losses by earned premiums gives the loss ratio.

---

[6] The full schedule W exhibit is reproduced on the inside cover of the New Jersey Compensation Rating and Inspection Bureau's *Forty-First Annual Report*, 1958.

It must be emphasized that although this is presented as the experience for calendar year 1957, it does not represent the insurance carriers' experience with losses and premiums on policies written during 1957. Such information is available only by policy year, and, in reliable form, only after the experience has had a chance to mature. Schedule W data show the experience during a calendar year with policies written in a little more than a two-decade period. They are based upon continuing accounting records, however, and they do provide some check on the reporting of outstanding losses. If these are estimated too generously in one year, loss ratios would be inflated; but as outstanding losses become paid losses in subsequent years, the reporting should compensate for this with a corresponding deflation of the loss ratios.

Part 1 of Table XXXIII summarizes actual and modified schedule W data for all companies for calendar years 1952 to 1957. Two modifications are made. Earned premiums are multiplied by factors to bring them up to what they would have been had the rates actually charged as of July 1, 1957, been in effect in each of the years. Also, incurred losses were adjusted to show losses as they would have been incurred, had the present benefit levels been in effect. No adjustments were made for changes in the wage levels or changes in medical costs.

Based upon this modified experience for the six years combined, the losses, on the present law level, were 59.66 per cent of the premiums at the July 1, 1957, collectible level.[7] The same modified loss ratio for calendar year 1957 was 59.87 per cent. From 1953 to 1954 the loss ratios were decreasing; from 1955 to 1957 they were increasing. Because of this up and down movement, the average loss ratio for the six years is closely comparable to the 1957 loss ratio. If the average of the last two years, 1956 and 1957, is taken, the loss ratio becomes 58.57 per cent.

One of these loss ratios must be used to compare with the *permissible loss ratio* to determine any possible change in the general level of rates. In most cases, and the 1958 rate revision provided no exception, it is the modified loss ratio of the last calendar year that is taken as being significant for this comparison. If loss ratios had been moving downward, this use of the last calendar year's experience would have meant a more rapid downward adjustment in rates. Actually, loss ratios were moving up for calendar years 1955 to 1957, so this meant a more rapid increase than if the 1956-1957 average had been used, or even slightly greater, in this instance, than if the average of the whole six years had been chosen.

The permissible loss ratio, based upon the July, 1957, collectible rate level was 58.08 per cent. This was the percentage of premiums set aside for expected incurred losses. The balance of the premiums

---

[7] The principal difference between the collectible level of rates and the manual level of premiums is the adjustment for the offbalance of the experience rating plan. Risks that are experience rated may pay more or less than the manual rates, but on balance, they pay less, thus reducing the collectible level below the actual manual level.

Table XXXIII. Indicated Change in Collectible Rate Level in New Jersey Based upon Schedule W Data, 1952-1957

Calendar Year (1)	Actual Experience			Modified Experience		
	Earned Premium (2)	Incurred Losses (3)	Loss Ratio (4)	Premium at July 1, 1957, Collectible Level[a] (5)	Losses on Present Law Level (6)	Loss Ratio (7)
1952	$56,312,593	$38,420,583	68.23%	$68,926,614	$43,914,726	63.71%
1953	67,942,527	41,327,099	60.83	75,280,320	47,071,566	62.53
1954	71,819,382	40,498,026	56.39	76,128,545	46,086,754	60.54
1955	76,324,625	39,588,474	51.87	81,667,349	44,932,918	55.02
1956	76,410,094	42,442,449	55.55	84,127,513	48,172,180	57.26
1957	86,495,504	52,464,684	60.66	86,927,982	52,044,967	59.87
Total, 1952-1957	$435,304,725	$254,741,315	58.52%	$473,058,323	$282,223,111	59.66%
Total, 1956-1957	$162,905,598	$94,907,133	58.26%	$171,055,495	$100,217,147	58.59%
Total, 1956 + 2 x 1957	$249,401,102	$147,371,817	59.09%	$257,983,477	$152,262,114	59.02%

Indicated Change in Collectible Level

Basis	Loss Ratio	Change
1957	59.87%	1.031 or 3.1% Increase
1956 – 1957	58.59	1.009 or 0.9% Increase
1956 + 2 x 1957	59.02	1.016 or 1.6% Increase

Permissible Loss Ratio = 58.08%

Source: New Jersey Compensation Rating and Inspection Bureau, "July 1, 1958, Rate Revision." p. 6. No adjustments have been made for increasing wage levels or medical costs.
[a] Including Loss and Expense Constant Premium.

was allocated for the standard expense items. These include the acquisition costs, taxes, claims expenses, inspection expenses, home office costs, the costs of making payroll audits and lastly the profit item. It is these standard expense items that are set first, and they, in turn, determine the permissible loss ratio.

According to the converted experience of 1957, the loss ratio was 59.87 per cent. The fact that this loss ratio was greater than the permissible loss ratio was a signal to the bureau that the general level of rates should be increased. Dividing the 1957 loss ratio by the permissible one indicates that a 3.1 per cent increase in rates would bring in revenues sufficient for the level of incurred losses contemplated by the permissible loss ratio. Of course, these rates are being tested against a past level of payrolls and will be applied to a future level, but nothing in the rate-making procedure allows for the fact that the wage level may be changing either up or down.

The permissible loss ratio is based upon the expense items, which, with the exception of tax items, remain fairly constant from year to year. As of July, 1958, it became necessary to allow for a collection in the security fund — the funds set up to provide for payments to compensation claimants in the event an insurance company is unable to meet its obligations. In terms of the standard expense loadings, this meant an additional 0.50 per cent in the tax item. This required an additional increase of 0.8 per cent in the rate level. The combined effect of the 3.1 per cent increase, based on the converted experience of calendar year 1957, and the 0.8 per cent increase because of the security fund contributions, resulted in a total change in the collectible rate level adopted for July, 1958, effect, to 3.9 per cent.

Setting the Manual Rates

Since the pure premiums or loss components have already been determined for each individual classification, the task now is to multiply these pure premiums by an appropriate factor that will allow for the expense loadings. Based upon manual rates, and including the increased tax items, the total expense loadings amount to 42.33 per cent, and the permissible loss ratio becomes 57.67 per cent.

These standard loadings include an item amounting to 8.20 per cent for the claims expenses. It will be recalled, however, that the loss adjustment or claims expense has already been included in the pure premiums in each classification, and it cannot be counted twice. If claims expenses are taken out of the expense loadings and included with the loss ratio, the combined loss and loss adjustment ratio comes to 65.87 per cent, and the expense loadings are reduced to 34.13 per cent.

If the expense component as reduced (34.13 per cent) were the only factor to be considered, the multiplier would be 1.518 ($1 \div 1 - 0.3413$, or $1 \div 0.6587 = 1.518$). But account must be taken of the offset for the expense constant, the offbalance of the experience rating plan, the spreading of the losses eliminated when limitations were placed upon the permanent total and medical losses, and the fact that the general rate level must be increased. When each of these factors is given its due weight, the multiplier is increased from 1.518 to 1.666.[8]

To show how this multiplier is used to determine the manual rate it is necessary to turn to Table XXXII, the exhibit showing the experience of the single classification. The adopted pure premium, it will be recalled, was 1.06; but to arrive at the manual rate, this pure premium must be multiplied by 1.666, and the catastrophe loadings must be added as shown below:

1.06	pure premium
+1.666	multiplier
$1.766	
+ .02	catastrophe loading
$1.786	
$1.80	manual rate, rounded off according to interval system used

Thus a manufacturer who fell under this classification would have to pay for his workmen's compensation insurance a manual rate of $1.80 per $100 of payroll, unless his rate was adjusted because of premium discounts or the experience within his own plant. In addition, he would pay $10 as an expense constant. His *minimum* premium would be $19 per year, computed on the basis of five times his rate plus the $10 expense constant.

---

[8] The premiums at the July 1, 1957, collectible level, when applied to the payroll distribution of policy year 1955, were $83,240,466. Increased by 3.9 per cent, the total collectible premium at the new rates becomes $86,486,844. To arrive at the manual level, the premiums must be increased by adjusting for the offbalance of the experience rating plan and by deducting the expense constant and the per capita-rated premiums. The result is the payroll-rated premium at July 1, 1958, manual rates. A portion of this is derived from the general catastrophe loadings. Once this is deducted, the payroll-rated premium at the July 1, 1958, rates amounts to $88,025,340. Expected losses at the July 1, 1958-adopted pure premiums are $52,833,707. Dividing the premium by the losses gives the so-called pure premium multiplier of 1.666 for payroll-rated classifications. (New Jersey Compensation Rating and Inspection Bureau, "July 1, 1958, Rate Revision," Exhibit VII.)

Chapter 8

REHABILITATION AND MEDICAL CARE

Concepts of Rehabilitation

One compensation expert has called the word "rehabilitation a euphemism, a semantic abnormality or abortion."[1] Disagreement exists both about the objectives of rehabilitation and about the nature and extent of the services that should be covered by this term. This lack of precise definition enables most everyone to advocate rehabilitation and to speak glowingly of the fact that rehabilitation of the injured worker should be the prime concern of the compensation system.

In a general sense, rehabilitation can be thought of as the process of assisting persons to reduce the limitations that result from disability, but this raises a number of questions. Assist them in what way, by what methods? And just what constitutes a disability? Is the train announcer with one arm disabled if he can carry on in his normal occupation? Lack of hearing may be a disaster to a musician but an asset to a boilermaker. To phrase the question pointedly, must the disability constitute an employment handicap? Should the objective of rehabilitation be to restore the person to the labor market, or should it be simply to reduce a person's limitation, or his need for medical care, even though he may never return to employment? This depends, in good part, on whether the rehabilitation is being undertaken under the government-sponsored vocational rehabilitation programs or under some other program.

Each of the states has a rehabilitation agency which operates with state and federal funds. Under the law, the agencies may not accept a client for services unless he has a definite employment handicap and unless there is some reasonable expectation that he can eventually enter, or be returned to, gainful employment. This limitation is understandable in light of the rationale for government expenditures in this field: that handicapped people, dependent upon the community for support, should be made self-supporting. But private groups and compensation administrators are under no obligation to accept such a restrictive goal. A United Nations report on the handicapped states: "The rehabilitation program cannot, however, be expected to result in employment in every case. Some persons are so seriously disabled that the goal must be an ability to meet the physical demands of daily life without institutional care or permanent attendance."[2] A Massachusetts

---

[1] Henry H. Kessler, "The Theory and Practice of Rehabilitation," in *Medical Aspects of Rehabilitation* (New York: Commerce and Industry Association, 1953), p. 78.

[2] United Nations, Department of Social Affairs, *Services for the Handicapped* (United Nations, 1954), p. 1.

report construes rehabilitation broadly to include the provision of a wide range of services "necessary to enable the handicapped person to overcome his handicap sufficiently to take his place, in whole or in part, in the normal social and vocational life of his age group."[3] Another widely used definition interprets rehabilitation to mean "the restoration of a handicapped person to the fullest physical, mental, social, vocational and economic usefulness of which he is capable."[4] As long as the objectives modifying the word "usefulness" are interpreted in the disjunctive sense, rehabilitation services would be provided even if there were no possibility of the worker returning to his job.

This difference in goals accounts for the fact that the rehabilitation enthusiasts can say, with evangelical fervor, that the phrase "not feasible for rehabilitation" should be wiped from the books. At the same time, the rehabilitation counselor employed by the state agency is continually writing these words in the case records because the client is too old or too disabled or, for some other reason, is not expected ever to work again. To restore him to an "independent living status" may be a worthwhile social objective, but one which, in itself, has not yet been deemed sufficient to justify the expenditure of government funds.

Disagreement exists about the nature and extent of services that should be encompassed by the term "rehabilitation." For historical reasons, most state rehabilitation agencies have been oriented toward educating and training the disabled, with the result that physical restoration services are comparatively neglected. On the other hand, compensation agencies have been primarily concerned with seeing to it that the worker is provided with medical treatment and physical restoration. This has resulted in a bifurcation of responsibility in compensation cases: The employer or insurance carrier is responsible for physical restoration, and the rehabilitation agency is responsible for the guidance, training and placement activities, if the worker meets eligibility requirements.

The rehabilitation committee of the International Association of Industrial Accident Boards and Commissions states that a rehabilitation program should not be limited to vocational training, pointing out that it may be better to fit a worker for his old job through physical restoration that to retrain him for a new vocation.[5] But segmentation of the rehabilitation program brings other problems. Under modern concepts of the range of services required and the methods of supplying them, there just is no neat dividing line between vocational adjustment and physical restoration.[6]

---

[3] The Commonwealth of Massachusetts, *Rehabilitation and Employment of Handicapped Persons*, Legislative Research Council Report (House No. 2790, February, 1956), p. 18.

[4] Lisbeth Bamberger, "Rehabilitation Under Workmen's Compensation in California," *Industrial Medicine and Surgery*, XXV (February, 1956), 62. (Institute of Industrial Relations, University of California, Los Angeles, Reprint No. 58.)

[5] In *Workmen's Compensation Problems*, IAIABC *Proceedings*, 1950 (United States Department of Labor, Bureau of Labor Standards, Bulletin 142), p. 170.

[6] The temptation is to classify rehabilitation activities into two neat categories, vocational rehabilitation, on one hand, and physical restoration, on the other. In addition to the

Rehabilitation, if it is to take advantage of all the findings of a host of disciplines, requires a medical, vocational, psychological and social evaluation of the client. Only after such a total evaluation can an individual rehabilitation plan for the client be rationally developed. Services offered under such a plan may include all types of medical and surgical services, physical therapy, occupational therapy, perhaps in a prevocational rehabilitation unit where work tolerances can be tested, or a regimen of muscular re-education and training in daily living activities. The person may also require the services of a social worker to aid him and his family in adjusting to his new condition; or psychiatric counseling may be indicated. If a prosthetic device has been prescribed, training in its use is necessary lest it end up in the closet once the person has left the hospital or rehabilitation center. Vocational counseling may be necessary, perhaps from the time he became injured, and a whole host of auxiliary services, ranging from recreational therapy to diet and drug therapy, may be indicated on a continuing basis.

Just where in this wide range of services does physical restoration end, and guidance, training and placement begin? It is almost impossible to say. Yet, this division of activities is required in many of the compensation programs in which the physical restoration and provision of the accompanying medical services lie within the responsibility of the employer and insurance carrier, and the vocational adjustment activities with the state rehabilitation agencies.

Within the area of employer or carrier responsibility for medical services, the compensation laws may be quite restrictive in spelling out just exactly what is required in the way of rehabilitation services. In states which limit medical and surgical care, little can be expected; but even in states in which such care is unlimited, a comprehensive, integrated rehabilitation program may be difficult to achieve.[7]

Regardless of the carrier's statutory responsibilities, some insurance companies have recognized the dimensions of the rehabilitation problem and the need for positive action. The Association of Casualty and Surety Companies has issued a statement acknowledging that where routine medical care is not sufficient to attain maximum physical

---

overriding problem, discussed below, that rehabilitation is best conceived of as an integrated whole, there is a semantic difficulty. Under federal law, "vocational rehabilitation" is used as a generic term to embrace all rehabilitation activity which has a vocational objective, *including physical restoration.* Thus, there is no one neat term left for the nonphysical restoration activities. One is forced to describe these multiple activities, or to use some rather awkward phrase, such as vocational adjustment activities or vocational training, to denote the wide range of activities that do not come under the term physical restoration. Confusion is compounded when writers use the term "vocational rehabilitation" sometimes in the generic sense and sometimes to mean only guidance, training, placement and such related activities.

[7]As of 1957, the laws of forty jurisdictions provided for full medical aid either by statute or by allowing the administrative agency to extend such services indefinitely. In the remaining fourteen jurisdictions, period-of-time or cost limitations, or both, limit such services. See *State Workmen's Compensation Laws* (United States Department of Labor, Bureau of Labor Standards, Bulletin 161, revised August, 1957), pp. 24-26.

recovery and ability to work, the carrier should provide "the specialized therapy of physical medicine, using the developments and modalities of modern medical science, combined with occupational therapy, training in activities of daily living, mental conditioning, vocational counseling and other services required to return the injured man to self-sufficiency."[8] It is also acknowledged that often complete physical restoration can be accomplished only in a specialized rehabilitation center.

According to the association's statement, the insurance industry accepts the premise that physical rehabilitation is part and parcel of medical care under workmen's compensation. The association recommends that each carrier establish a voluntary program with close liaison with the vocational rehabilitation agencies. It believes that with careful planning and utilization of existing facilities, it should be possible to provide complete and satisfactory rehabilitation under the present compensation acts.

Individual insurance companies have done extensive work in the field. Liberty Mutual, for example, is famous for its program. It employs rehabilitation nurses who act in a social work capacity visiting the injured worker and his family, counseling them, and explaining the indicated physical and medical regimen. The company operates its own rehabilitation centers, and its representatives have written extensively about the success it has had in rehabilitating what would seem to be hopeless cases. The company justifies this activity not only on social and humanitarian grounds but also on economic grounds. It is claimed that successful rehabilitation of a severely disabled case, particularly paraplegics, has resulted in a net savings, mainly in reduced medical costs as patients become self-sufficient and no longer require permanent nursing or custodial attendants paid for by the carrier.[9]

---

[8] Association of Casualty and Surety Companies, *A Rehabilitation Program* (statement approved by the Executive Committee, June 26, 1956), p. 1.

[9] The rehabilitation activity is described in various publications of the company. See, for example, *The Rehabilitation Centers*; *A New Way to Reduce the Costs of Workmen's Compensation Services*; *Six Ways to Better Medical Service* (all undated). Various case examples of rehabilitation activity are described in their claims department publication *Medical Service*. See, for example, Nos. 20-56, 21-56, 27-56 and 30-57.

The success in rehabilitating compensation cases is described in W. Scott Allan, "Target for Today in Workmen's Compensation," *Journal of Rehabilitation* (May-June, 1955); W. Scott Allan, "The Liberty Mutual Rehabilitation Program," *Archives of Physical Medicine and Rehabilitation*, XXXVII (July, 1956), 405-407; and Stanwood L. Hanson, "The Cost of Medical Care in Paraplegia and How It May Be Modified by Rehabilitation Services," in Donald Munro, ed., *The Treatment of Injuries to the Nervous System* (Philadelphia: W. B. Saunders Co., 1952), chapter 8.

In a survey of eighty-six cases of paraplegia treated at the company's rehabilitation center in Boston, the company reported that when treatment was completed only four remained in the hospital, thirty-seven either had returned to work or were in business for themselves, and the rest were at home or in convalescent homes without full-time medical care. Although it cost $895,415 to complete the rehabilitation process in these cases, it is estimated that the saving in indemnity and medical costs amounted to $2,719,203. (See, W. Scott Allan, "Rehabilitation, Challenge and Responsibility," *American Economic Security* (September-October, 1956), 7.)

Such dramatic economies are possible only in the cases of severely disabled persons who would be classified as permanent and total cases; but even in cases of permanent par-

Thus, although concepts of rehabilitation differ, there is some general agreement about desirable practices and about what should be done. But still there is the disturbing matter of the separation of the physical and vocational adjustment aspects of rehabilitation, with all its problems of liaison between two agencies. Also, there is a gap between what the law requires of the employer or carrier and what some carriers have been doing voluntarily. As will be seen, this poses problems in individual cases. All apparently agree that an integrated teamwork approach affords the best chance of rehabilitating the severely disabled person; but whether such an approach is possible, given the statutory language, the segmentation of responsibility, and the lack of full agreement about just how far any one party is obligated to go, is another matter.

New Jersey has faced up to these problems in the last few years. A good deal of creative thinking and experimentation is taking place, much of it directed to bridging the administrative gaps between the Rehabilitation Commission and the Division of Workmen's Compensation. Before looking at this activity, it is instructive to take a backward look. What is now being advocated by rehabilitation authorities in the way of cooperation between the rehabilitation and workmen's compensation agencies was accomplished in New Jersey in 1919. At one time, New Jersey had what some considered to be a model program in the field; today, she is faced with the same problems as other states without such experience.

The Rise and Fall of Integrated Procedures — 1919-1945

As early as 1916, the IAIABC annual meetings were being advised that rehabilitation of injured persons and the readaptation of dependents in fatal cases should be the first concern of workmen's compensation, followed by financial relief during the period of readjustment and then accident prevention, in that order.[10] Prior to 1920, twelve states had passed rehabilitation laws, and the influence of workmen's compensation is attested to by the fact that in nine of these states, benefits were restricted to the industrially disabled. In three states, New Jersey, New York and Illinois, the laws were broader in coverage.[11]

The development of rehabilitation might have continued along the lines of individual state legislation closely allied with workmen's compensation, but other factors brought the federal government into the

---

tial disabilities, rehabilitation may be economically wise for the insurance carrier. In a survey of thirty cases labeled by the company as "typical routine industrial injuries" the estimated savings were over $32,000 in compensation costs and over $1,500 in medical costs after the workers were treated at the Boston Rehabilitation Center. (Liberty Mutual Insurance Co., "A Survey of 30 Typical, Routine Industrial Injury Cases Handled at the Boston Rehabilitation Center.")

[10]Francis D. Donoghue, "Restoring the Injured Employee to Work," in IAIABC *Proceedings*, 1916 (United States Department of Labor, Bureau of Labor Statistics, Bulletin 210, 1917), p. 212.

[11]Henry H. Kessler, *Low Back Pain in Industry* (New York: Commerce and Industry Association of New York, 1955), p. 23.

field with programs oriented toward vocational rehabilitation for persons disabled from any cause. Two separate acts in 1917 were important. One was an amendment to the War Risk Insurance Act which established a program of compensating veterans or their families for war-connected death or disability.[12] This also provided hospital care and physical restoration services to veterans. Also, in that same year, Congress passed the Smith-Hughes Act, known as the Vocational Education Act, which created the Federal Board for Vocational Education.[13] This act, which originally had nothing to do with rehabilitation, provided federal funds, to be matched by states, for vocational education at the grade and high school level.

A year later, Congress passed legislation designed to retrain veterans.[14] The prime objective was to make handicapped veterans self-supporting insofar as possible. This act was originally administered by the Federal Board for Vocational Education which was directed to furnish the eligible veteran with an appropriate course of vocational rehabilitation.

The act, passed during the first world war, covered only veterans; but soon after the end of the conflict, pressures from various groups, including workmen's compensation administrators, brought about the passage of legislation generally applicable to the civilian disabled. This was the Fess-Keyson Act, which followed the pattern previously established for veterans.[15] Federal funds were provided, on a matching basis, to states which accepted the act's provisions. The various state boards of vocational education were empowered to cooperate with the Federal Board for Vocational Education in providing vocational rehabilitation.

The act was hailed as a significant accomplishment since it applied the principles which had been successful in the case of veterans to the civilian population. But the veterans who received vocational training had already received physical restoration services in the veterans hospitals.[16] No provision was made in the Fess-Keyson Act for physical habilitation, except that if necessary, artificial appliances could be provided. Administered in most states by the vocational education departments, the orientation was inevitably toward training around a disability, rather than toward eliminating or minimizing it by medical and surgical procedures.

The act provided for rehabilitating all disabled who showed promise of being able to enter the labor market; but if workmen's compensation agencies existed in the individual states, the rehabilitation administrators were directed to establish a plan of cooperation with these agencies. Thus patterns were established early. Physical restoration was

---

[12] 40 Stat. 398 (1917).
[13] 39 Stat. 929 (1917).
[14] 40 Stat. 617 (1918).
[15] 41 Stat. 735 (1920).
[16] For pertinent comment on the consequences of this omission of physical restoration services, see Henry H. Kessler, *Rehabilitation of the Physically Handicapped* (New York: Columbia University Press, 1953), p. 227.

presumably to remain a responsibility of workmen's compensation; training aspects of the program could be handled by the state rehabilitation agency, provided the injured worker was judged capable of eventually re-entering the labor market. Not until 1943 did the federal government make available matching funds for physical restoration services. New Jersey, however, had a functioning rehabilitation commission before the federal government entered the field of rehabilitating civilians. From the beginning, New Jersey's program was unique in that the stress was placed upon physical restoration rather than vocational training.

The American Red Cross had established an Institute for Crippled and Disabled Men in New York in 1917. Under the direction of Robert McMurtrie, the institute, utilizing European experience, was pioneering in rehabilitation work, using a variety of methods to assure self-support for the crippled.[17] McMurtrie was called upon to draft New Jersey's act, and it followed closely a model bill advocated by the Red Cross institute. The act covered all persons disabled from any cause who were, or might be expected to become totally or partially incapacitated for remunerative employment.[18] The term rehabilitation was construed to include physical restoration as well as vocational training and placement.

The Rehabilitation Commission, established under the Act, was composed of the Commissioner of Labor, the Commissioner of Education, the Commissioner of Charities and Correction and three other members representing management, labor and the medical profession. It had an independent status but was closely allied with the Department of Labor, whose Commissioner was instrumental in establishing the first clinic in which surgical restoration work was to be performed. This was Lewis Bryant, whose achievements in the compensation field have already been noted. Bryant worked closely with McMurtrie and Dr. Fred H. Albee, the medical representative on the commission who was elected its first chairman. Albee had the benefit of experience as Chief of Orthopedic Services at the United States Army Base Hospital No. 3 at Colonia, New Jersey, an Army unit which had been used as an amputee center. These men were cognizant of the effective rehabilitation work that had been accomplished at the veterans' hospitals and at the Red Cross Institute and were impressed with the need for the establishment of clinics in which surgical restoration work could be carried on. At the same time, Bryant was anxious to apply these techniques to the rehabilitation of industrially injured workers; workmen's compensation problems had always been among his chief interests. The 1919

---

[17] Kessler, *Rehabilitation of the Physically Handicapped*, p. 225. Information about the early history of New Jersey's Rehabilitation Commission is derived in part from Henry A. Brodkin, M.D., "State Rehabilitation Clinics; A Stage in the Development of Rehabilitation Service in New Jersey" (typewritten, 1957). Dr. Brodkin, Chief Medical Director of the Division of Workmen's Compensation and Medical Administrative Consultant to the Rehabilitation Commission, has been most helpful in supplying information on the current and past relationships between rehabilitation and workmen's compensation.
[18] N.J. Laws 1919, 74.

law authorized the Rehabilitation Commission to arrange with the Commissioner of Labor to receive reports of all compensable permanent disability cases and to proffer rehabilitation services to such industrially injured persons. But the statutory language does not begin to portray the actual cooperation which existed between the Commission and the then Bureau of Workmen's Compensation. Since the two agencies were guided by the same forceful personality, liaison was intimate, direct and continuous.

In 1919, the first State Diagnostic Industrial Surgical Clinic was opened in Newark, in the same building that housed the workmen's compensation hearing rooms and the employment service. The clinic, fully equipped for orthopedic and physical therapy, was under the direction of a medical adviser, half of whose salary was paid by the Department of Labor because he also advised on compensation matters. (Dr. Henry H. Kessler was assistant director of the clinic and later served as director until he was called into service in 1941.) The relationship between rehabilitation and compensation was so close that it was difficult to separate the two. According to Bryant, if a worker came into the compensation center to review the financial adequacy of a settlement, he would be examined not only to determine the correctness of the cash indemnity payment but also to determine whether an improvement in his condition could be accomplished by means of reconstruction surgery. As Bryant stated: "It is our ... purpose to have at these gatherings a representative of the training section of the rehabilitation work so that the problem of the return to industry of each injured worker may be studied by the expert and followed up either by vocational training or intelligent placement of the worker in the industry in which he is physically, mentally, and by past experience best capable of filling." [19]

By 1922, four additional clinics were established in conjunction with compensation hearing rooms in Jersey City, Camden, Trenton, and Paterson. Subsequently, an additional clinic was opened in Atlantic City. These were under the division of clinics, one of the two divisions of the commission. The other was the division of vocational rehabilitation, which had offices in the same building as the clinics. [20]

To build up the confidence of injured workers during the period between completion of medical treatment and the time of their return to remunerative employment an occupational therapy unit, known as the curative workshop, was established in 1927. This was operated in conjunction with the Newark clinic, and its program was patterned after the occupational therapy program of the Colonia Army hospital which had been administered by Albee. Patients were furnished the necessary shop tools to construct practical wooden articles, some of which

---

[19]Lewis T. Bryant, "Industrial Rehabilitation in New Jersey," in IAIABC *Proceedings*, 1920 (United States Department of Labor, Bureau of Labor Statistics, Bulletin 281, 1921), pp. 138-139.

[20]New Jersey Department of Labor and Industry, *Summary of Activities*, July 1, 1953 — June 30, 1954 (Fiftieth Anniversary Report), p. xxxxvii.

were used by the Department of Labor and the Rehabilitation Commission. Facilities were also available for training in printing, photography and certain other trades. The work was under the direction of the Newark district medical director, together with an advisory staff consisting of a psychiatrist, a psychologist, the field agent directing the patients' rehabilitation program and a vocational examiner of the commission. [21]

Although this rehabilitation program was open to persons with employment handicaps from causes other than industrial accidents, the bulk of the work of the commission was concentrated on compensation cases. During fiscal 1924, for example, 75 per cent of the rehabilitants who received treatment at the clinics were persons disabled by reason of a compensable industrial accident; 59 per cent of the rehabilitants who received services from the vocational division were also compensation cases. [22] These were higher percentages than for the nation as a whole, although in these early days compensation cases formed a large part of the work of the rehabilitation agencies in other states. It is estimated that approximately 44 per cent of the persons rehabilitated by all state agencies between 1921 and 1924 were injured in industrial accidents. [23]

Although New Jersey's program embraced both physical restoration and vocational training, primary emphasis was placed upon medical and surgical procedures. The policy of the commission was not to train around the disability, but to attempt to eliminate or modify it. [24]

Operating with scarce funds, the commission was forced to consider the problem of payment for the medical bills in compensation cases. According to Bryant, the insurance carrier was asked to defray the costs of secondary or orthopedic operations and the required aftercare, with the understanding that the expenses would be substantially returned because of the lower costs due to the reduced permanent disability of the worker. If the aggregate costs of the operation and aftercare were greater than the carriers' compensation savings, then the difference was to be reimbursed from rehabilitation funds. Writing in 1920, the Commissioner could report that in none of the cases treated up until that time had the expenses involved been greater than the savings in permanent disability costs. [25] Since in those days the law limited medical liability in the usual case to $50, this meant that the savings had to come in the form of reduced cash indemnity payments.

[21] New Jersey Rehabilitation Commission, *Annual Report*, 1941, p. 52.

[22] New Jersey Rehabilitation Commission, *Annual Report*, 1924, pp. 56-59.

[23] "Report of Committee on Rehabilitation," in IAIABC *Proceedings*, 1931 (United States Department of Labor, Bureau of Labor Statistics, Bulletin 564), pp. 20-22.

[24] This was in sharp contrast to other state programs which were administered by the state departments of vocational education. Bryant felt that the first aim of the program was to get the man as surgically fit as possible, and then to train and place him. (*The Newark News*, April 10, 1922.) Dr. Albee was also of the opinion that physical restoration should occupy first priority. See his "New Jersey Rehabilitation Service," in IAIABC *Proceedings*, 1923 (United States Department of Labor, Bureau of Labor Statistics, Bulletin 359), pp. 127-129.

[25] Bryant, p. 139.

This was making rehabilitation the number one goal of the compensation program in no uncertain terms.

In many respects, New Jersey had achieved in the 1920's a model system of effective rehabilitation of compensation cases. Today, the state is grappling with the problem of how to coordinate the work of the Rehabilitation Commission and the Division of Workmen's Compensation. In 1950, Dr. Kessler, speaking before a national conference on workmen's compensation and rehabilitation and after hearing reports of the latest developments in these fields, could say:

> ... All of these services, all these demonstrations which are taking place today, and all these movies you have seen embody principles and practices which were well outlined over 30 years ago. They were not only outlined, but they were put into practice in five State-established clinics in the State of New Jersey. The great doctor, Fred H. Albee, was one of the pioneers who stimulated the establishment and development of this type of activity — the relationship between industrial accident commissions and their responsibility for following through to the ultimate conclusions, seeing the man put back on the job.
>
> I say I am the greatest failure because today those clinics have been abandoned, despite all of our interest, despite our pioneering, despite our stimulation. We find that we are very much behind in the march of progress in this field.[26]

The question naturally arises: What happened?

Explanations vary. Some persons who are attached to the theory of the importance of individuals in maintaining a social system would place some weight on the departure of Kessler from active management of the clinics. Kessler himself has an interesting explanation which deals with over-all basic forces. He blames, not ineptness, political skulduggery, economy waves or anything of that sort, but the deepseated prejudice of the man-in-the-street toward the handicapped person who is different. Also, he singles out a second psychological disease, akin to the Oedipus complex, which has affected industrial accident commissions who "still like to go back to that maternal breast and suckle at the old idea of employers liability, with the responsibility ending right there."[27] The image is a striking one. The reasoning, if relevant, pertains to all jurisdictions, but there were special reasons in New Jersey which accounted for the drifting apart of the two agencies. The direct liaison was accomplished largely through the clinics, and these were abandoned in 1945 for several reasons.

At the time of their establishment, the clinics were equipped with the most modern modalities of physical medicine then in existence to

---

[26] *Proceedings on National Conference on Workmen's Compensation and Rehabilitation,* March, 1950 (United States Department of Labor, Bureau of Labor Standards, Bulletin 122), p. 85.
[27] *Ibid.,* p. 85.

treat muscle, bone, joint and nerve injuries. They also had the necessary trained personnel to operate them. Surgery was performed in the clinics, X-rays taken, casts applied and deformities corrected. Heat, baking and ultra-violet lamps were used; massage, whirlpool baths and corrective exercises were prescribed.[28] This was at a time when such facilities were rare in hospitals or doctors' offices. By the late twenties, however hospitals and doctors began to buy and use diathermy lamps and heat lamps and certain other equipment of the kind that had been installed in the rehabilitation clinics. Insurance companies now had alternative places to refer clients. Although it may be argued that the "teamwork" approach to rehabilitation, implicit in the clinic's approach, could not be duplicated in a private physician's office, on the surface, the treatment appeared similar.

The consequent decline in the number of patients meant loss of the nominal fees the clinics charged, and this, combined with other financial difficulties, made it difficult for the clinics to keep abreast of the latest in equipment. The federal rehabilitation law, which New Jersey accepted in 1920, did not provide matching funds for physical restoration services, as has already been noted. Nonetheless, the state managed to apply some such funds to the operations of the clinics up until 1928, but then this practice had to be discontinued.[29]

Some financial aid was forthcoming from the compensation program. But these funds were available only sporadically and not in sufficient amounts.[30] State funds were increasingly difficult to come

---

[28]Brodkin, p. 4.

[29]National Institute of Public Administration, *Survey of the Organization and Administration of the State Government of New Jersey* (Trenton: 1930), p. 160.

[30]In 1923, when the second injury or One Per Cent Fund was established, it was specifically provided that balances in the fund at the end of the year could be transferred to the Rehabilitation Commission. Although the fund showed a surplus each year, no withdrawals were made until 1929, largely because of the uncertainties involved in predicting future demands on the fund. But after the first withdrawal in 1929, transfers from the fund became progressively larger. In fiscal years 1933, 1934 and 1935, there were no appropriations from the free treasury fund to the Rehabilitation Commission. The entire expenditures of the commission were financed from clinic fees, federal matching funds for vocational training, and transfers from the One Per Cent Fund.
The One Per Cent Fund law was amended in 1936 (N. J. Laws 1936, ch. 55), and further transfers of funds were prohibited. The Commissioner of Labor had testified before the Advisory Budget Commission that more than $688,000 had been transferred from the fund to the commission, and that this was being used for the rehabilitation of all types of cases, not just those whose disability originated in a compensable accident. (Statement appended to Assembly Bill No. 169, introduced February 10, 1936.) In 1938, the law was again amended to allow withdrawals of up to $15,000 yearly from the fund to be used for the purposes of rehabilitating persons disabled in industry. (N. J. Laws 1938, ch. 198.) There is no record of such funds ever having been transferred, and in 1940 this provision was removed from the law. (N. J. Laws 1940, ch. 133.)
A law, passed in 1924 (N. J. Laws 1924, ch. 128) provided that all fines collected from employers who failed to carry workmen's compensation insurance were to be turned over to the Rehabilitation Commission. According to available records, the fines transferred have never amounted to over $550 a year. (The Governors' budgets show transfers of these fines from 1938 to 1943. The high figure was the $550 in 1941, the low, in 1939, when $27 was transferred.) Although this provision was still in the law as of 1958, since the end of World War II, the Rehabilitation Commission has no records of receiving any funds from this source.

by during the depression. A series of surveys during the 1930's recommended that some of the clinics be abandoned as an economy measure, that the physical restoration aspects of the commission's work be transferred to the Department of Institutions and Agencies and the vocational rehabilitation work put under the Department of Labor,[31] or that the entire operation be integrated with the compensation bureau.[32] None of these surveys resulted in an immediate change in the status of the clinics or the commission. The clinics limped along, with the doctors doing some examining work in informal compensation hearings, some physical restoration work with rehabilitation clients, and evidently offering some services to patients who had no connection with either a compensation or a rehabilitation case.

For purposes of maintaining an integrated program, it was desirable that the same doctor who examined in the informal hearing also be the one to recommend certain rehabilitation procedures. Some of these same doctors, in addition, appeared for one party or another as witnesses in the formal hearing. This led to the controversies that have already been detailed, and probably did nothing to enhance the prestige of rehabilitation. With the passage of time, compensation cases tended increasingly to be decided in formal hearings, and disputes over the exact amount of cash indemnities predominated. With the changed atmosphere, it just was not so easy to work out agreements with insurance carriers to finance surgical operations with the promise that the cash award would be reduced as the disability lessened. The tendency was to litigate first, establish the number of weeks of compensation due, and then perhaps worry about rehabilitation.

In 1943, Congress passed the Barden-La Follete Act, which finally amended the federal rehabilitation law to allow matching funds for physical rehabilitation services.[33] Each state, in order to be eligible for funds, was required to work out a plan for federal-state cooperation. Although New Jersey's law was not revised, corrective surgery, therapeutic treatment and necessary hospitalization could now be financed with the aid of federal funds. Such physical restoration services were to be furnished, without cost, provided the client was able to pass a "needs" test.

Presumably, federal funds could now be used, on a matching basis, to support the work of the clinics; but the funds could also be used to purchase services from other sources. Governor Walter E. Edge appointed a committee to make recommendations on what should be done with the clinics. The committee reported in September, 1945. It noted that the cost of the clinics was not being met by the fees collected; that about one-third of the patients treated in the clinics were rehabilitation cases, another third were purely compensation cases, whereas the rest

---

[31]National Institute of Public Administration, *Survey of the Organization and Administration of the State Government of New Jersey*, p. 160.

[32]New Jersey Legislature, *Report of The Joint Commission on Study of the Workmen's Compensation Act and Practices* (Trenton: April 12, 1935), p. 22.

[33]57 Stat. 374 (1943). This was an amendment to the Fess-Keyson Act.

were evidently cases which had no connection with either rehabilitation or compensation. The committee felt that it would be more convenient and economical if rehabilitation clients were allowed to purchase services in their home communities, and not have to travel to the clinics for treatment.

The spectre of socialized medicine was raised. It was pointed out that insurance companies refer clients for medical treatment and are charged only a nominal fee. According to the committee, "This does not appear to be a function of the Rehabilitation Commission and if such an activity is continued or expanded, it is very probable that medical associations throughout the State will be knocking at the doors with protests, alleging that the State is rendering services in competition with their profession."[34]   The committee also noted the absence of legal authority for treatment of individuals who were neither compensation nor rehabilitation clients. Investigation of the clinics' equipment led to the conclusion that much of it was outmoded and useless, also, the committee found evidences of inefficiency among the clinic staff.

The report sounded the death knell for the clinics, and they were abolished. Personnel were transferred to the compensation division, and the physical facilities were to be used by workmen's compensation for examining rooms. Three years after the clinics were abandoned, the Curative Workshop was also discontinued.

The findings of the committee must be accepted at face value. Times had changed, the equipment had been allowed to deteriorate, inefficiencies in administration had undoubtedly crept in, especially during the war years. There was, however, little recognition that the clinics did present one method of solving the thorny problem of coordinating the work of compensation and rehabilitation. Granted their defects, once the clinics were abolished, a vacuum remained, and more than a decade later attempts were still being made to fill it.

The Hiatus in Relationships

The abandonment of the clinics did not mean that liaison between the two agencies ceased to exist, but cooperation became more involved and difficult than when the two agencies operated under the same roof. Also, in the years subsequent to the passage of the Barden-LaFollete Act, the work of the Rehabilitation Commission began to change. In many ways the changes were desirable from the community's viewpoint, although they contributed to pulling the agencies further apart.

In 1942, in the nation as a whole, the state rehabilitation agencies reported that 21,757 persons were returned to employment as rehabilitated.[35]   The next year the figure doubled, as more funds became

---

[34]"Report and Recommendations to Governor Walter E. Edge on the Administration and Activities of the New Jersey Rehabilitation Commission" (Trenton: September 5, 1945), p. 3.

[35]The United States case statistics are from Federal Security Agency, Office of Vocational Rehabilitation, *Annual Caseload Statistics of State Rehabilitation Agencies*, 1951, p. 1; United States Department of Health, Education and Welfare, Office of Vocational Rehabilita-

available and as the wartime labor shortage made its effects felt. In 1953, more than 61,000 individuals were rehabilitated,[36] and in 1957, the figure, for the first time, passed the 70,000 mark. During fiscal year 1958, 74,320 persons were rehabilitated. But of the number rehabilitated in 1953, only 6 per cent were persons who were injured in a compensable accident. The agencies had found other clients, and the industrially disabled were only a small portion of the total.

In New Jersey, no such dramatic rise in the number of rehabilitants took place. The war years saw a rise in numbers, but after the war, the figures fell drastically. In each of the years 1952 through 1957, the number of rehabilitants fell below the 1,000 mark, but in 1958, the number rose to 1,190. Although the percentage of these persons whose disability could be traced to a compensable employment accident was greater in New Jersey than in the nation as a whole, still these persons were by no means a significant portion of the commission's clients. In 1949 and 1950, when in the nation as a whole a little more than 6 per cent of rehabilitants were persons injured in employment accidents, in New Jersey the comparable figure was approximately 16 per cent. In 1953, when the nation's percentage remained at the 6 per cent figure, in New Jersey the industrially injured were 9 per cent of the rehabilitants. In the ensuing years, however, this figure declined to the 6 per cent mark and below.[37]

If, for recent years, all the states are ranked according to the number of persons rehabilitated per 100,000 population, New Jersey ranks close to the bottom.[38] But it would not be fair to leave it at that. Rehabilitation statistics are tricky, and this is one area where reliance on numbers alone may be misleading. Any person who has received services from the commission, and who returns to employment and manages to stay there for six months, can be classified as rehabilitated. If the statistical record were the sole objective, each counselor could be compelled, or urged, to make his record in terms of numbers, without regard to the kinds of cases accepted. It is undoubtedly easier to rehabilitate a person who simply has need of guidance or some simple prosthesis than it is to restore to, or place originally in, gainful employment a person with epilepsy, a severe cardiac condition or a

tion, *Facts and Figures on Vocational Rehabilitation*, 1953, p. 10; Office of Vocational Rehabilitation, press release, September 30, 1958; and New Jersey Rehabilitation Commission, *Rehabilitation Trends*, September, 1958.

[36]The New Jersey case statistics are from the *Annual Reports* of the New Jersey Rehabilitation Commission, and New Jersey Rehabilitation Commission, *Rehabilitation Trends*, February, 1959.

[37]It should be noted that these percentages include all the rehabilitants whose disability originated in a compensable employment accident, no matter who referred them to the Rehabilitation Commission. A smaller number were referred by the compensation division; the others were referred by insurance carriers, private physicians, social work agencies or other persons or agencies.

[38]In 1957, New Jersey ranked fiftieth among fifty-two states and territories in the number of persons rehabilitated per 100,0u0 of population. The previous year, she had ranked at the very bottom. (See New Jersey Rehabilitation Commission, "Monthly Report of Operations," January, 1958.)

psychosis. The record indicates that the New Jersey commission is attempting to broaden its services to include these persons, even though it is recognized that their rehabilitation will be a slow process.

The new emphasis on the more difficult cases came largely after the federal law was again amended in 1954.[39] These amendments expanded services available to the disabled and provided federal grants-in-aid for special projects, expansion of facilities and other activities. Physical restoration services were redefined to include those "necessary to correct or substantially modify within a reasonable period of time a physical or mental condition which is stable or slowly progressive . . . ." Heretofore, most states would not accept clients unless their condition was static; the new amendments allowed more leeway. Still, a patient had to have a disability that was stable or fairly progressive and one for which the prognosis was good. Fears of being accused of providing a general health program are still present, and the agencies do not accept clients if simple, definitive medical or surgical care would eliminate a transitory condition, or if it is expected that the illness is a terminal one.

Shortly after these amendments, the New Jersey commission underwent some fundamental changes.[40] A full-time director was appointed, and he set about the task of revitalizing the agency. New counselors were hired. During 1954 and 1955 the agency used eighteen counselor man years. This figure jumped to twenty-four in 1956 and thirty in 1957. Given this expansion and the turnover in counselors, the commission could report in 1958 that nearly 90 per cent of the staff were newly hired since 1955.[41]

There can be no doubt about the revival of activity and the commission's new direction since the mid-1950's. Some of this increased

---

[39] 68 Stat. 652 (1954).

[40] New Jersey's law was also fundamentally revised to bring it into conformity with the new federal statute (N. J. Laws 1955, ch. 64). Vocational rehabilitation services were defined broadly to include the whole range of possible services. For the first time, the law was specific as to which of these types of services would be provided at the commission's expense, regardless of the client's economic position, and which would be available without charge only if the client could pass a "needs" test. Diagnostic and related services as well as all guidance, training and placement activities were to be in the first category, whereas all other services, including physical restoration, would be supplied gratis only to those who required financial assistance.

The most significant changes in the New Jersey law were, of course, the broadening of the definitions of disability in conformity with the changes which had been made in the federal amendments.

[41] Some indication of the future is apparent from the fact that the number of referrals to the agency was less than 2,000 in 1954 and 1955 but nearly 4,000 in 1957, and more than 8,000 in fiscal year 1958. Rehabilitation of these clients may not be so swift as in the past since clients have more difficult problems. Cases requiring only counseling and selective placement have declined in number, whereas cases requiring physical restoration, with or without training, have doubled since the most recent amendments. The future activity of the agency is, of course, dependent upon adequate financial support from the state. In fiscal year 1957, New Jersey's per capita expenditure for rehabilitation was $0.20, about one-third that of Delaware and $0.08 less than the national average. Its ranking among the jurisdictions was forty-fifth in 1957 but rose to fortieth in 1958. (New Jersey Rehabilitation Commission: "Monthly Report of Operations," March, 1958; Annual Report, 1958; and Rehabilitation Trends, February, 1959.)

activity is beginning to be reflected in the case statistics. In addition to the 1,190 physically and mentally handicapped persons rehabilitated in 1958, another 469 disabled persons had completed rehabilitation services to the point where they were seeking jobs. But the burst of new enthusiasm did not immediately take into account workmen's compensation problems. In the ordinary case, the client makes an application for services of the commission after being referred from some source.[42] The counselor's first task is to determine whether the client is eligible for the commission's services. This involves having the client undergo a physical examination by a general practitioner and perhaps by specialists. This examination may be done by a physician of the client's own choice and is not ordinarily a responsibility of a staff doctor. From the results of this examination and an interview with the client, the counselor must decide whether the individual is disabled, whether this disability constitutes an employment handicap and whether it would be practical for the commission to furnish services. In evaluating clients, the counselor has the benefit of advice from medical and psychiatric consultants. If it is determined that the client is eligible, the counselor, on the basis of a full case analysis, which may involve all case data, personal, medical, psychological, social, vocational and education, works up a plan of service. This may encompass specific training, an educational course, or even setting up the client in an independent business. If physical restoration and certain other services are indicated, the counselor must evaluate the economic and financial position of the client to determine if these services will be made available without cost to the client. The counselor has the responsibility of following through on the case, giving appropriate counsel and guidance, and eventually cooperating with the employment service in placing him in a job if the program is successful.

But this is the procedure in an ordinary noncompensation case. The compensation cases present particular difficulties. In the period between the abandonment of the clinics and the start of a new program in 1956, the ordinary compensation referral was of the type known as the "bench referral." After the case was adjudicated, the deputy director could refer the man to the commission. But the standards for referral were not too meaningful, and whether or not a worker was referred depended, in good part, upon the rehabilitation consciousness of the individual deputy. Compensation cases which did not reach the adjudication stage never even received the benefit of a possibility of a bench referral. At any rate, the best time for referral had usually long since past by the time the case came to the deputy for decision.

During this same period, the commission personnel came to regard the compensation client as just another routine case. The referral had to be investigated and a medical examination arranged for, just as for

---

[42]Clients may be referred by educational institutions, health and welfare agencies, employers, private physicians or one of several governmental agencies. Once a client is referred or brought to the attention of the commission, he must still make an application for services.

any other client. If the counselor had a waiting list, the compensation case waited its turn on the list. Rehabilitation horizons had expanded, and no special priority was given to compensation matters. At the same time, the compensation case could cause special difficulties to plague the life of the counselor. The referral might not have come about because of the employee's wishes, and he could be quite suspicious of the whole process, fearing some reduction in his award. Also, the matter of financial responsibility was more complicated; physical restoration services could now become the responsibility of an insurance carrier, and he had to be consulted before any plan was established. Or differences of opinion could arise between the counselor and the rehabilitation physician, on one hand, and the insurance carrier and its medical advisors, on the other. In short, the whole atmosphere had changed in a relatively few short years. Instead of being almost the principal concern of the commission, the client injured in a compensable employment accident became an incidental part of the commission's work, and a part likely to bring special problems.

The commission, however, had the statutory responsibility for investigations in connection with permanent and total disability cases. Continuation of payments to these persons beyond the initial 450 weeks was subject to their having submitted to "such physical or educational rehabilitation as may have been ordered by the rehabilitation commission." [43] At the end of this period, if the employee was earning wages, his weekly payments would be reduced by the percentage that his weekly current wages were of his wages at the time of the accident, subject to a minimum payment of $5 per week. Thus if he was earning only 50 per cent of his former wages, this was the percentage amount by which his compensation payments would be reduced. (This is the only passage in the New Jersey law which specifically mentions a wage-loss theory of calculating compensation benefits.) Employees, some time before the expiration of the 450-week period, were referred to the commission to determine whether rehabilitation was feasible. But even in these situations, the person had to meet the eligibility requirements. If because of, say, advanced age, the commission determined that the client would not be able to re-enter the labor market, the case would be marked "not feasible," and so certified to the compensation division. The client might be in dire need of certain rehabilitation services, the fitting and train ng of an artificial appliance, for example, but, if he was not eligible, under the rules of the commission, this would not and could not be provided. Whatever the original meaning of the compensation statute, the phrase, "shall submit to such physical or educational rehabilitation as may have been ordered by the rehabilitation commission," has been interpreted to mean that clients are not required or allowed to submit to any rehabilitation unless they are first declared eligible under whatever the current eligibility rules of the commission may be.

---

[43] N.J. Stat. Ann. (West, 1958), 34:15-12b.

Outside of this area, in which the statute enforced some coordination, liaison between the two agencies was casual. At the same time, the compensation division was doing nothing, itself, in the way of offering rehabilitation services. The responsibility of the employer or carrier to afford medical services to cure and relieve the effects of the injury was clear, as was the obligation to provide prosthetic devices where indicated. If these matters became part of the issue in dispute, they would be handled in the normal course of things. At a time when supervision of cash indemnity payments in voluntary agreement cases was lax, the supervision of medical and related services at this level was practically nonexistent. Individual insurance carriers may have been doing an exemplary job of offering rehabilitation services, but they were doing this voluntarily, and without a great deal of supervision or reporting.

Rebuilding Administrative Bridges

Just as the military experiences during the first world war provided a stimulus to civilian rehabilitation activities, the medical advances during the second world war served to reawaken interest in the field.[44]

The IAIABC, always interested in rehabilitation, surveyed the field and called attention to the areas in which reform was needed.[45] Individual states experimented with ways and means to bring the latest findings about the potentialities of rehabilitation to the industrially disabled.[46] Florida, for example, established a rehabilitation department within its Industrial Commission in 1955. Personnel in this department coordinated the physical restoration responsibilities of the insurance carriers with the vocational adjustment services provided by the state's Division of Vocational Rehabilitation. The Industrial Commission also employed rehabilitation nurses to investigate and follow up individual cases.[47]

---

[44]As an example of the progress made with the rehabilitation of severely disabled persons, Dr. Howard Rusk reports that of the 400 paraplegics in World War I, 90 per cent had died or were dying after the first year from kidney infections or bed sores. In 1953, of the 2,500 paraplegics of World War II, 1,736 were living in their own homes and driving their own cars. Of these, 80 per cent were either working or in school. (Howard A. Rusk, "Application of Rehabilitation to Workmen's Compensation Cases," in *Medical Aspects of Workmen's Compensation* [New York: Commerce and Industry Association of New York, 1953], p. 62.)

[45]See for example, "Report of Rehabilitation Committee," in *Workmen's Compensation Problems*, IAIABC *Proceedings*, 1950 (United States Department of Labor, Bureau of Labor Standards, Bulletin 142), pp. 166-179. Mention should also be made of the interest created by the national conference on workmen's compensation and rehabilitation held in March, 1950, sponsored jointly by the Federal Security Agency and the United States Department of Labor. See *Proceedings of National Conference on Workmen's Compensation and Rehabilitation* (United States Department of Labor, Bureau of Labor Standards, Bulletin 122, 1950).

[46]"Report of Rehabilitation Committee," in *Workmen's Compensation Problems*, IAIABC *Proceedings*, 1955 (United States Department of Labor, Bureau of Labor Standards, Bulletin 186), pp. 127-128.

[47]"The Rehabilitation Program of the Florida Industrial Commission," in *Workmen's Compensation Problems*, IAIABC *Proceedings*, 1957 (United States Department of Labor, Bureau of Labor Standards, Bulletin 195), pp. 147-51.

By 1956, the time was ripe for some such attempt at coordination between the Rehabilitation Commission and the Division of Workmen's Compensation in New Jersey. The need was obvious, and the two agencies were under new directors who recognized the necessity for some action. In October, 1956, a new program was initiated. A workmen's compensation — rehabilitation coordinator was designated to facilitate liaison between the two agencies.[48]

Under this program, reports of accidents submitted to the compensation division were to be screened to discover injured workers who could benefit from vocational rehabilitation. Possible cases were to be referred to the commission to be handled as normal cases if the clients were deemed eligible for services. If, for one reason or other, the injured worker was not eligible, the coordinator was to try to have the insurance carrier or employer provide the necessary medical treatment and functional restoration services. If the client was accepted by the commission, the vocational training, guidance, and so on, would be provided free; but the commission would seek to have the insurance carrier pay for any necessary medical and surgical treatment. If the carrier denied liability, the case would be handled by the coordinator, who would attempt to have the question of liability decided, in one fashion or another.

The screening procedures started in October, 1956, and ran into immediate difficulties. First reports of accidents were screened by personnel within the Division of Workmen's Compensation who were instructed to select the "serious" disabilities for referral to the coordinator. These reports, sent to the division soon after the accident, were sometimes filled out by laymen who may have only second-hand knowledge of the accident. Under the best of circumstances, it was difficult to make an intelligent selection from some of these raw reports. The screening unit was instructed to select amputations and such other serious injuries as head injuries, heart cases, and so on. In this experimental phase, the criteria were necessarily vague and indefinite.

Other forms were also screened by this unit. Follow-up reports, which were submitted if the worker sustained a permanent injury or if he had not returned to work before the end of the one-week waiting period, were scrutinized. Cases involving amputation of more than two fingers, back injuries, eye injuries, head injuries, or other cases which appeared to be serious, were called to the attention of the coordinator. In addition, an attempt was made to screen the direct settlements. The instructions to the examiners were to refer serious cases, as with the other forms, and, in addition, all cases in which the settlement was made for 25 per cent or more of permanent total disability, and also

---

[48] "A Project For The Extension and Improvement of Services to Injured Workmen" (undated memorandum in files of New Jersey Division of Workmen's Compensation), p. 2. Information about the joint program is derived, in part, from extensive interviews with Norman Sprague, who filled the position of coordinator from 1956 to 1958.

all cases in which medical and hospital costs seemed high in proportion to the indemnity award. Although the primary purpose of this scrutiny was to discover possible need for rehabilitation, the almost inevitable by-product was to examine the adequacy of the medical services rendered, even if no rehabilitation was indicated.

The cases selected were examined by the coordinator; and if they passed his scrutiny, they were referred immediately to the commission. At the same time, medical reports were requested from the insurance carrier. After a time lag, on the average six weeks, the reports were received and examined.[49] If the medical report showed the injury to be a minor one, the case was closed and the commission so notified. If it appeared that the carrier was already providing physical restoration services, the coordinator simply kept in touch with the parties to follow the progress of the case.

Cases referred to the commission were handled according to their normal procedure, at least up to a point.[50] Letters were sent to the injured worker, who had to make an application and submit to medical examination and to a determination of eligibility for services. If he was found ineligible, the full report of the counselor was sent to the coordinator, together with any recommendations for physical restoration treatment if such was indicated. The case was then handled as a purely workmen's compensation matter. Nothing in the program contemplated any changes in the criteria for acceptance as set forth in the state-federal regulations governing vocational rehabilitation.

If the worker was accepted as a rehabilitation client, and, for example, certain physical restoration services were indicated, the counselor wrote to the insurance carrier asking whether it would provide the services. If the carrier refused, the records in the case were transferred to the coordinator, who then attempted to negotiate the matter. Only if these negotiations proved fruitless, was the case set down for a hearing. The whole program was organized on a purely administrative basis without specific statutory recognition, and the coordinator had no legal authority to compel the carrier to provide, or the worker to accept, any services. However, if prolonged negotiations or litigations were necessary before liability could be determined, the commission went ahead and provided the services subject to the needs test outlined in the law. If the carrier was subsequently found responsible, presumably it then paid the bills and reimburse the commission.

---

[49] This was the approximate mean time lag, from the date reports were requested until they were received, for a sample of 146 closed cases in the files of the coordinator. This average is influenced, however, by long delays in a few cases. The median time lag was approximately five weeks, whereas the modal lag was two and one-half weeks.

In situations where the medical reports were difficult to interpret, the coordinator, who was not a physician, had the benefit of advice of the medical director, with whom he met on the average of one-half day a week. In certain exceptional cases, the injured worker was examined by the director or a member of the medical staff.

[50] This procedure is described in New Jersey Rehabilitation Commission, "Procedure for Servicing Pre-adjudication Workmen's Compensation Referrals," Casework Memorandum No. 9, revised May 1, 1958.

On the other hand, if the carrier was providing the physical restoration services or accepted responsibility for services recommended,
the coordinator was notified and the other vocational rehabilitation aspects of the program proceeded, either subsequent to, or concurrently
with, the physical restoration services.

From October 10, 1956, to December 31, 1957, approximately
235,000 first reports of accidents were screened. Of these, 272 cases
were referred to the commission, and over 400 medical reports were
requested. As of this latter date, 197 of these cases had been closed
by the coordinator; but of these, only 4 persons were accepted for
services by the commission and only 2 of these were rehabilitated.[51]
In both of these cases, the services of the commission were limited to
the usual diagnostic examinations and guidance and counseling, for both
men found jobs on their own. Rehabilitation programs were started in
the other two cases but then discontinued. In one case, the man returned to work, and in the other, the counselor found that the man's
lawyer was bewildered as to how and why the commission was working
on the case before it was adjudicated. His "bewilderment" may have
contributed to the client's refusal to continue with the rehabilitation
program.

Of more significance perhaps than the low number of rehabilitants
was the fact that no services were required in nearly half the cases.
Either the employees had already returned to work or they had died as
a result of their injuries. In almost all death cases, medical reports
had been requested; and in 22 such cases, referral had already been
made to the commission before it was determined that the injured
worker had succumbed. In most of the cases, death followed shortly
after the accident; but this fact was not known in over half of the cases
until six weeks or more had elapsed after the case was brought to the
attention of the coordinator. If the screening had been done on the basis of reports that came in later than the first reports of accidents,
the needless investigation of most of the death cases would have been
avoided.

The relatively large number of cases which required no services
indicated the weakness of using the screening of the first reports of
accidents as a selection device. These had the great advantage of allowing the coordinator to discover cases early, but it also led to much
wasted effort. According to the commission, in some cases "...the
person on the scene of the accident tended to exaggerate its severity
when filing the first report."[52]

In October, 1957, the procedure of referring cases only on the basis of the screened first reports was discontinued. Instead the coordinator selected the cases from the first reports and then wrote for

_____
[51]Data compiled from monthly reports of the coordinator. Medical reports were requested for at least 409 cases during this period. An exact count is not possible because
this information was not consistently reported prior to January 1, 1957.

[52]New Jersey Rehabilitation Commission, "Monthly Report of Operations," December,
1957.

medical information. Only after evaluation of these medical reports was the case referred to the commission. Although this may not seem much of a change, it meant that more than two months would elapse, in the normal case, between the date of accident and the date the rehabilitation counselor received the case.[53] This change meant sacrificing the principle of early referral for the sake of improving the quality of referrals to the commission. From the commission's point of view, the quality factor is important, since each referral involves the expenditure of time and money. Operating with limited funds and scarce counselor time, the commission may well allot these to referrals by physicians, over 50 per cent of which are accepted for services, or referrals by the tuberculosis groups, nearly all of which are accepted for services.

During calendar year 1958, 182,788 first reports of accidents were screened; 538 cases were selected, 284 medical reports were received and 121 cases were referred to the commission. Also during the year, 313 cases were closed by the coordinator, some of which had been opened during the previous year. Of these cases, only 10 were rehabilitated by the commission; the others were cases in which either no services were required, or the workers were found to be not interested in services, or the workers could not be located, or (in 9 cases) the records were closed because the worker had died.

During fiscal year 1958, the commission reported that it had received 163 pre-adjudication referrals from the division. Also during the year, 23 of the division's referrals were accepted for services, 92 cases were closed after investigation but before the person was accepted for services, 3 cases were closed after being accepted but before being rehabilitated, and 2 cases were closed after being rehabilitated. On the whole, this is not an impressive record, but it is one which was improved over the first year of the program's operations. As the new employer-reporting forms, which call for more detailed medical information come into widespread use, the record should improve further.

The coordinator also has the responsibility of channeling the bench referrals to the commission. During fiscal 1958, 283 of these bench referrals were received. Also, during the year, 85 cases were accepted for services, and 35 cases were rehabilitated. Some of these, of course were cases which had been referred in the previous year.[54]

---

[53] The mean time lag from date of accident to date of receipt of the first report of the accident to the division was three weeks and three days for 196 cases in which both dates could be ascertained. There were several long delays, accounted for, in part, by the fact that self-insured employers are not required to file reports until it has been determined that the injured worker has a disability which extends beyond the waiting period or will be classified as a permanent disability. The median time lag was one week, five days, and the mode fell within the first week. In addition to this time lag, there is the delay of approximately six weeks until the medical reports are received, and an additional, perhaps two weeks for the referral to filter down to the counselor once it has been referred by the coordinator.

[54] Information on 1958 cases from an analysis of cases in the files of the coordinator, and New Jersey Rehabilitation Commission, *Annual Report*, 1958.

The coordinator has not confined his activities to referring cases derived from the screening process to the commission. In actual practice, he became involved with other types of cases. Persons may be referred by physicians or social agencies, and these cases are handled by the coordinator.[55] Also, in investigating the medical reports and in contacting injured workmen, the coordinator finds cases in which rehabilitation was not indicated, but the injured worker has some complaint about the adequacy of the medical services being provided, or even the indemnity settlement. Once these matters are uncovered they cannot be dropped and must be referred to the appropriate division or agency or handled by the coordinator himself. From the point of view of the worker, an inquiry from the coordinator about rehabilitation matters is an inquiry from an official of the compensation division which gives him an opportunity to discuss his general dissatisfactions. In most cases, this may have been the first, or perhaps the only direct personal communication from the division, and it is not surprising to find that the coordinator became involved in all sorts of collateral matters which were only remotely connected with rehabilitation.

In a somewhat informal fashion, the coordinator has been involved in attempts to have employers retain handicapped workers or rehire injured persons and in promoting the general idea of the worthwhileness of employing the handicapped, and in numerous other such activities. These are difficult to quantify, the results often being ephemeral, but it is likely that this sort of activity has proved worthwhile and in accord with the desired objectives of a compensation program.

In addition to these informal tasks, the coordinator has the responsibility of coordinating the work of the commission and the division in relation to commutations. The commission investigates certain applications for commutation in which the injured worker desires to start his own business, and this work flows through the coordinator.

Medical Care and Legal Responsibility

In practice, the New Jersey law requires the employer or carrier to furnish unlimited medical care until it is determined that the petitioner is physically restored. If the carrier stops paying the bills and the disabled worker still feels the need for medical treatment, he can file a petition to determine the carrier's further liability. The case would be heard provided that the petition is timely, that is, if it is filed within the time period fixed by the statute of limitation.[56] The

---

[55]There were a total of 230 closed cases in the coordinator's file as of December 31, 1957: 197 of these were called to the coordinator's attention through first report of accident screening; 14 after screening of other employers' or insurance carriers' compensation reports; 2 from unsolicited medical reports; 4 after direct contact by the injured worker; 2 from other jurisdictions; 2 from miscellaneous sources within the division; and the remaining 9 were cases referred to the coordinator after the injured worker was already a client of the Rehabilitation Commission.

[56]The statute tolls two years after the last payment of compensation, construed to mean receipt of medical care as well as cash indemnities.

procedures are somewhat cumbersome; and from the point of view of the worker's attorney, the results may not be worth the effort. The informal negotiations carried on by the coordinator have served as a substitute for a formal reopening of the case in some instances. But questions arise as to the liability of the carrier for certain types of medical and rehabilitation services.

In New Jersey, the carrier is obligated to furnish necessary artificial limbs and other appliances, including artificial teeth or a glass eye.[57] The law has not been clear as to the responsibility for the repair and replacement of such appliances, although two 1957 court decisions would seem to go a long way toward clarifying matters.[58]

The compensation law requires the employer to furnish medical treatment and hospital service "as shall be necessary to cure and relieve the workmen of the effects of the injury and to restore the functions of the injured member or organ where such restoration is possible...."[59] In one case, the issue was whether the insurance carrier could be required to provide the injured employee with certain nursing care and palliative treatment which designed, not to cure, but to relieve the effects of suffering. The employee had been adjudged permanently and totally disabled, and expert medical opinion indicated that her prognosis as a useful citizen was hopeless, that the pathology was irreversible. The court, noting that the statute was to be construed liberally and in light of its benevolent purposes, held that the words "cure and relieve" must be interpreted in the disjunctive rather than the conjunctive sense. The employer was made liable for treatment which was designed merely to relieve rather than cure the patient.[60]

Under the statute, the obligation of the employer to furnish the initial artificial appliance is clear, whereas under the doctrine in this case, it may be construed that he is responsible for repair and replacement, even though such services are designed merely to relieve the effects of an injury and not to work a fundamental cure. At least such an interpretation is applied in permanent and total cases, and words to this effect are written into the deputies' awards. In a case decided in favor of totally disabled person who petitioned for additional medical services and a replacement of his prothetic device, the division ordered the carrier to provide him with "... proper medical and dental care to effectuate the purposes hereinbefore expressed, in its attempts to relieve or to effect a cure of the petitioner's injury now and in the future, and further to keep in good repair and to maintain in satisfactory condition the dentures here provided to the petitioner, as well

---

[57]N.J. Stat. Ann., 34:15-15. The liability of employers for furnishing artificial appliances has been quite clear in the New Jersey law throughout its history except for an adverse court decision in 1927 (*Peczar* v. *Ryan Leather Co.*, 5 N.J. Misc. 117, Sup. Ct. 1927). The effects of this decision were nullified by a statutory amendment the following year (N.J. Laws 1928, 149).

[58]*Howard* v. *Harwood's Restaurant Co.*, 25 N.J. 72, and *Fierro* v. *Public Service Coordinated Transport*, 44 N.J. Super. 73.

[59] N.J. Stat. Ann., 34:15-15.

[60]*Howard* v. *Harwood's Restaurant Co.*, 25 N.J. 72.

as the prothesis and brace provided for, and to provide a replacement thereof, if and when such further replacement becomes necessary."[61]

This was done in the case of a permanently and totally disabled person whose compensation benefits may continue for the rest of his life. However, the obligation of the carrier to provide continuing care is not so clear in the case of a permanently and partially disabled person if the statute of limitations has already tolled. The coordinator has succeeded in persuading carriers to furnish these repairs and replacements, but this has been done on a voluntary basis. His successes in this regard have been one of the bright spots in the whole program, but the issue has not been formally adjudicated.

Similar issues arise as to the scope of services that can be included under the carriers' obligation to furnish functional restoration. For example, cosmetic gloves for amputees are designed primarily to conceal the fact that fingers are missing. It has been argued that such a glove fulfills a functional as well as a cosmetic purpose, on the grounds that its use will increase function by permitting proximation. Also, its use has been defended on the grounds that it can help relieve amputees of neurotic tendencies. Carriers have been cooperative in providing these gloves when cases have been called to their attention, but, again, these have been provided voluntarily without a legal test of the carrier's specific obligations.

Such voluntary cooperation is commendable, but it must be recognized that only a fraction of cases come to the attention of the coordinator and that the standards in this area remain unclear. Even if the issue of replacement of and repair of prostheses and cosmetic gloves is resolved, undoubtedly medical advances will create new problems of responsibility.

The whole business of a carrier voluntarily providing certain services after negotiation with the coordinator, outside of its possible legal obligations, goes to the heart of the unsupervised nature of the medical provisions. As matters stand, the coordinator can see relatively few cases, and the division has no real way of knowing whether other disabled workers may be uninformed of their rights and fail to demand certain types of services to which they may be legally entitled or which the carrier may voluntarily furnish. This argues for more adequate supervision of the medical care provisions.

The legal liability of the employer for basic physical restoration is clear, but is it possible to go further and require the employer or carrier to pay for any and all vocational rehabilitation services? The answer is evidently in the negative. In one case, a woman lost two fingers of one hand and the disability was fixed at a formal hearing. The deputy director stated in his opinion: "I further find that the petitioner's condition properly warrants rehabilitation in order to assist her in adjusting herself to existing conditions and that such rehabilitation may

---

[61] *Kern* v. *National Movers, Inc.*, New Jersey Division of Workmen's Compensation, CP A-83086 (May 18, 1957).

be supplied in the form of counsel, advice and any directions offered by the New Jersey Rehabilitation Commission with the further provisions that any expenses in connection with same be chargeable to the respondent." [62]

On appeal by the carrier, the court reversed this portion of the deputy's award. The judge could find no authority in the law for requiring the employer to furnish rehabilitation to the extent envisaged in the decision. It was also pointed out that rehabilitation was never an issue between the parties. A literal reading of the court's decision would lead one to believe that the employer had no responsibility under the law for furnishing rehabilitation of any sort. The court, however, was using the term rehabilitation in the sense of guidance, training and placement functions, and this decision would not seem to remove the authority of the division to order functional restoration services. As a matter of fact, in this case the carrier, subsequent to the court's decision, agreed to pay for the costs of removing the malformed nail which had grown over the stump of one finger. In general, this decision reaffirms what has been obvious all along. The statute, as written and enforced, does require a separation of at least the financial responsibility for the two broadly distinguishable phases of rehabilitation-physical restoration, on one hand, and all the guidance, training, placement and related services, on the other. Although such separation of financial liability does not preclude the creation of an integrated program, it certainly makes it more difficult to achieve. The very success of the coordinator's inquiries in particular cases emphasizes the necessity for more rigorous standards or more adequate supervision of the medical care provisions of the law, not only in possible rehabilitation cases but in all cases in which treatment has been rendered.

Litigation and Disability Rating

In many respects, the coordinator has been working in an oasis surrounded by a desert of litigation. The primary function of the compensation system has been to determine a cash indemnity award, and it is not always easy to fit the clinical approach necessary for rehabilitation into this framework. This criticism of compensation has been amply discussed by writers who have noted the fundamental incompatibility of a system of litigation with the objective of rehabilitation. [63] At the same time, we must recognize the possible virtues of New Jersey's system of rating disabilities insofar as rehabilitation is concerned. As has been pointed out, New Jersey litigates a high proportion of its cases, and the atmosphere of the formal hearing can hardly be classified as clinical; yet its theory of disability rating has its advantages for

---

[62] Cited by the court when case was heard on appeal. *Adeline B. Stafford* v. *U. S. Envelope Co., Seaboard Division* (45 N.J. Super. 333).

[63] For example, Herman M. Somers and Anne R. Somers, *Workmen's Compensation: Prevention, Insurance and Rehabilitation of Occupational Disability* (New York: John Wiley and Sons, 1954), chapter 7. Kessler, *Rehabilitation of the Physically Handicapped*, esp. 49-53.

rehabilitation purposes, especially as opposed to a form of the wage-loss theory.[64]

When a worker's cash indemnity settlement is determined by his actual or potential loss in earnings, he may be reluctant to undergo a rehabilitation regimen for fear that his award will be reduced. In a sense, this may be illogical, but the worker has what appears to him to be an assured weekly income. Although it is less than his usual wage, he may be afraid to gamble on his award being eliminated or reduced if he undergoes rehabilitation. This form of "pensionitis" is less likely to occur under New Jersey's system in which the award is based essentially on the worker's physical condition at the time of adjudication, and specifically not on his employment status. However, in New Jersey, an award may be reopened for a redetermination of disability at any time by either party providing the statute of limitations has not tolled. In several cases handled by the coordinator, the fear of reopening may have influenced the petitioner in his decision to accept or reject rehabilitation services.

In one such case, the Rehabilitation Commission furnished the man with physical restoration after the carrier refused liability. The man was subsequently declared successfully rehabilitated, and ways and means were sought to have the carrier pay the medical bills. In order to do this, over the carrier's objections, it is necessary to reopen the case and allow the matter to be adjudicated. Since the carrier denied liability, it had no interest in reopening the case. The injured worker refused to file a petition for a reopening since he ran the risk of having his award reduced because of the improvement in his physical condition. In such a case, neither of the parties wants to proceed, and the only alternative is for the division to proceed on its own motion. Although it is apparently willing to do this in individual cases, this places the division in an unusual role in that it is seeking something neither party desires. If it does not proceed, the Rehabilitation Commission is left footing the bill, and the division will probably be more reluctant to proceed in other cases.

In this case the man was already rehabilitated, but other workers may have rejected services for fear of the possibilities of a reopening. Such situations can occur only after a case has been adjudicated. There is no way of knowing how many persons are reluctant to undertake rehabilitation, before their compensation case is actually heard. Their fear may well be that if successfully rehabilitated, their physical condition will have improved, and the compensation award will be less than it otherwise would have been. The feeling may be that it is better to adjudicate first and rehabilitate later, taking chances on a possible reopening and thus getting the best of the two possible worlds. The difficulty, of course, is that chances of rehabilitation success are greatest

---

[64]The effects of the various theories of disability rating upon rehabilitation are discussed in Morton Lane, *The Effect of the New York Workmen's Compensation Law Upon the Employment of the Handicapped* (N. Y.: The Institute of Physical Medicine and Rehabilitation, New York University-Bellevue Medical Center, Rehabilitation Monograph XI, 1956).

when the process is started early, and not after the months of litigation and shock of having one's disability maximized and emphasized by counsel and medical witnesses in the compensation court. The advantages for rehabilitation of New Jersey's rating theory are greatest in the post-adjudication cases; in the pre-adjudication stages, the psychological obstacles are comparable to those under the wage-loss theory.

It has been suggested that workers who refuse rehabilitation services be penalized in some fashion, and this has been done in several jurisdictions.[65] The problem is that proper motivation is such an essential ingredient in successful rehabilitation that it is difficult to carry through a rehabilitation plan without the whole-hearted cooperation of the worker. A functioning program whose results could be continuously demonstrated to the potential rehabilitant would constitute a positive approach to this problem. The obvious fact that productive income and a self-sufficient life are infinitely preferable to a cash indemnity award needs to be constantly emphasized. Also, the worker needs to be reassured that in certain cases of schedule injury, the law will protect his award, regardless of his earning power. In other cases, in which disability has actually been reduced by rehabilitation, the willingness of the division to reopen cases on its own motion, will go far to prove to the worker that he might just as well have started his program early, even before adjudication, since the final results will eventually be the same.

Maintenance During Rehabilitation

But, in the final analysis, it is the carrot rather than the stick which promises success. A worker may not have sufficient capital resources to meet the daily needs of his family during the rehabilitation period, and he may decide to return to work prematurely. In New Jersey, no special maintenance allowance is paid to industrially disabled workers while they are undergoing rehabilitation. Their payments are limited to the normal temporary disability benefits, the general adequacy of which has already been discussed. In one case handled by the coordinator, the Rehabilitation Commission found that an employee should undergo surgery before he could safely return to his former occupation of house painter. The carrier agreed to pay for necessary medical costs and, in addition, to pay temporary disability

---

[65]The Federal Employees' Compensation Act provides that if a worker fails to undergo rehabilitation that would have increased his earnings, his award can be reduced. Florida has a similar provision which authorizes its commission to suspend or reduce benefits if the worker refuses rehabilitation services without reasonable cause. In New Jersey, payments to a permanently and totally disabled person beyond the initial 450-week period are contingent upon his acceptance of whatever rehabilitation program is prescribed by the commission. This would of course apply only to this category of disability, and not to workers with permanent and partial disabilities. (United States Department of Labor, Bureau of Labor Standards, *State Workmen's Compensation Laws*, Table 14.)

benefits. But the worker felt that he would not be able to support his family on such a stipend and, instead, returned to work.

If a worker is accepted for services by the Rehabilitation Commission and can pass the needs tests, he may qualify for a maintenance allowance of from $10 to $20 a week. But this is the case only if the worker is declared eligible and feasible for vocational rehabilitation. If the worker has need only of certain physical restoration services for which he is eligible under the compensation program, he cannot qualify for this allowance. It seems clear that the commission's maintenance allowance cannot substitute for an allowance administered and financed by the workmen's compensation agency. Eighteen states have provisions for such allowances in their compensation law.[66] Whether or not they fulfill the bill in regard to adequacy, they point in the right direction. Any positive encouragement to the rehabilitation process would seem to be worth careful consideration.

Commutations

One of the poorer features of forms of the wage-loss theory is that cases tend to remain open for extended periods of time. One result is a tendency on the part of both parties to close them out with lump-sum settlements. These aggregate sums may be useful for rehabilitation objectives if used for the purpose of setting the worker up in some worthwhile business enterprise. On the other hand, if loosely supervised, the worker may use the money for some purpose unconnected with rehabilitation; and then he may find himself left with no weekly income and, in some cases, no further rights to medical care.[67]

Such pressures for closing out cases with lump-sum settlements are largely absent under the theory of disability rating employed in New Jersey. A case comes to a proximate end when disability is determined. This fact, plus strict supervision of the commutations granted, accounts for the absence of this problem in New Jersey. Only 30 of 203 petitions for commutations were granted in the state in 1956.[68] The commission and division have cooperated in this regard, and an occasional settlement that will be helpful to the rehabilitation plans of the petitioner has been approved. At the same time, the policy of the division has remained sufficiently restrictive to prevent abuses prevalent in some other jurisdictions.

Toward an Effective Rehabilitation Program — Summary and Conclusions

In several respects New Jersey is more fortunately situated than other jurisdictions when it comes to the possibilities of establishing a

---

[66]United States Department of Labor, Bureau of Labor Standards, *State Workmen's Compensation Laws*, Table 14.

[67]Lane, pp. 26-27.

[68]New Jersey Department of Labor and Industry, *Annual Report*, 1956-1957, p. 56.

potentially effective rehabilitation program. The two agencies directly concerned with the problem have had a tradition of cooperation, and today the Commissioner of Labor and Industry is chairman of both the Rehabilitation Commission and the Division of Workmen's Compensation. The division's method of rating permanent disabilities probably contains fewer obstacles to rehabilitation than the alternative methods which use some form of the wage-loss theory. Lump-sum settlements which may tend to close cases prematurely constitute no real problem; there are no great pressures for commutations, and these have been strictly supervised. In addition, it is worth noting that under New Jersey's law, workers must use the physician chosen by the employer and insurance carrier and that relatively few carriers do the bulk of the insurance underwriting in the state. At least the possibilities that the division can exercise effective supervision over rehabilitation and medical care are greater under such conditions than they would be if the worker had free choice of a physician and the insurance business were less concentrated.[69]

Against these advantages must be set the obstacles to an effective program. The two agencies, at least since 1945, have tended to go their separate ways, in spite of their once close relationship. The primary purpose of the compensation system has been the fixing of cash indemnities in an increasingly litigious atmosphere. Until recently, there has been relatively little supervision of direct settlements, of any kind, and of the medical treatment offered by employers. It also can safely be said that the compensation law does not stress the rehabilitation responsibilities of the employer.

The limited experience of the coordinator illustrates the difficulties of administering a program in which responsibilities are divided between the Rehabilitation Commission and the Division of Workmen's Compensation. In contrast with the situation in 1919, the commission has expanded its horizons beyond the industrially disabled. Counselors are no longer familiar with the details of the compensation law; nor are they impressed with any special obligations toward the client who may be a compensation case. Faced with an enlarged clientele, and operating with limited funds, the commission has treated the compensation client on an equal footing with all other potential clients. If a worker referred to the commission by the coordinator does not respond to written inquiries to file an application for rehabilitation services, other clients are waiting to be served; and these cases are not likely to involve complicated questions of fixing liability for certain services. Industrial accident victims may be in great need of reconstruction surgery, psychological counseling or other services, and yet the eligibility rules of the state-federal rehabilitation program may prevent the commission from accepting such a client if the chances for re-employment are not reasonably good.

---

[69]On the other hand, it has been argued that if the worker had free choice of his physician, he would recover more quickly, since he would have the aid of a physician in whom he had confidence.

These difficulties are likely to persist so long as responsibility for rehabilitation remains divided. Some division is inevitable as long as the rehabilitation law restricts services to those with employment handicaps and the compensation law does not place responsibility for the complete regimen of rehabilitation upon the employer. Yet, the worker suddenly disabled by an industrial accident faces an over-all adjustment problem. Rehabilitation must be fitted to his needs, whether they be medical, social, psychological, or concerned with placement in a new job for which training may be required. A program has better chances of success when it is conceived of as an integrated whole focused on an individual's unique problems.

In the final analysis, the responsibility for the rehabilitation of industrially injured workers belongs to the compensation program. The work done by the coordinator, if not impressive in its over-all results, shows the way to improving the division's rehabilitation services. A one-man unit cannot possibly do the job. An adequately staffed program within the division, charged with coordinating the social, psychological unit would need administrators, physicians and trained social workers, call them rehabilitation nurses or what you will, who would have the responsibility of seeing the injured worker and exercising some supervision over the rehabilitation regimen. These staff workers could be under the supervision of a coordinator who would have the responsibility of seeing to it that matters of liability for treatment were handled in accordance with proper procedures.

Such an expansion of personnel would require additional funds, and this involves questions of financing. But regardless of how this is handled, it would seem that this service is a responsibility of a workmen's compensation program and a legitimate cost to be assessed in some manner against employers or the community. Such outlays would represent a sound investment. both in economic and humanitarian terms.

The establishment of such a unit would not automatically solve all problems. The problem of early identification of potential rehabilitation cases would remain. Screening of employer reports, though eminently desirable, is not the whole answer. In the bulk of its cases, the division deals with a relatively few insurance carriers, and they choose the attending physicians. One of the important functions of such a rehabilitation unit would be to educate these carriers and employers about desirable procedures for referral of cases. Although New Jersey is fortunate in having within its borders excellent comprehensive rehabilitation centers, an expanded program would surely require multiplication of such facilities. The coordinator could maintain close liaison with these centers and assure employers that cases referred to units would receive competent evaluation in accordance with established criteria of the compensation division.

The problem of employee motivation is also one for which there are no ready-made solutions. Although it would require an amendment to the law, the possibilities of establishing a special maintenance allowance for workers while undergoing rehabilitation would solve part of the problem.

The success of the rehabilitation program will depend upon its enthusiastic acceptance by workers, employers and by all of the interest groups. It will also depend upon the general administrative reforms discussed above. As matters stand now, relatively few of the thousands of cases handled each year by the division can benefit by rehabilitation. The whole system is geared to fixing cash indemnities by a method which emphasizes disability and not residual capacities; and it is difficult to make an exception for the cases which need rehabilitation services. It is difficult to substitute the clinical for the forensic approach for only a small portion of the total number of cases. It is asking a lot to have petitioners' attorneys, bent on maximizing disabilities in adversary proceedings, switch tactics in those cases in which the best interests of the employee call for a quick, comprehensive rehabilitation program. This is especially so if it eventually reduces the cash award the employee would have received if he had refused rehabilitation services or if these services are not readily available. Yet the advantages of an effective rehabilitation program to the worker, the employer and the community are transparent and obvious. Advances in medicine, social work and psychology are continually being made, and it would be a criminal waste not to utilize them in cases of industrially disabled workers.

If such a program is to come about, it will have to be at the urging and insistence and under the essential direction of the Division of Workmen's Compensation, with the Rehabilitation Commission playing an auxiliary role in training and placement functions. The need has been demonstrated, the paths have been explored. The time is overdue for placing an expanded program into operation, even under the present statutes.

Chapter 9

SECOND INJURIES AND THE EMPLOYMENT
OF THE HANDICAPPED

If a worker with a pre-existing disease or impairment suffers a compensable injury, the combination of the prior condition and the second injury may result in a disability greater than that which would have resulted from the subsequent injury alone. The classical example is the one-armed worker who, as a result of a compensable accident, loses the other arm. In New Jersey, the second injury alone would require a permanent partial award of 300 weeks, but the loss of two major members automatically renders the worker permanently and totally disabled — a condition which would entitle him to a life-time pension if he were not rehabilitatable. Under New Jersey's second injury fund legislation, the employer would pay only 300 weeks of compensation, and the balance of the liability would be shifted to the fund made up of contributions from all employers.[1]

A second injury fund law is designed to encourage the employment of handicapped workers. The workmen's compensation laws, themselves, added to the already formidable employment obstacles faced by the handicapped. Jurisdictions which assessed the employer for the full liability resulting from the compounded disability were faced with threats on the part of employers to dismiss all handicapped workers. On the other hand, those states which allowed employees to sign waivers to their rights to benefits for an injury caused, or contributed to, by a previous disability found that the practice could get out of hand, with employees signing away rights to which they were entitled under the statute. Other states ignored the fact that the combined injuries could result in a greater disability than that produced by the second injury alone, and they made the employer liable only for the disability resulting from the subsequent injury by itself. This left the worker with inadequate compensation, or at least with less than that prescribed by the statute for his final combined disability.[2]

---

[1]Acknowledgment is made of the work of Joseph N. Seward, a graduate assistant in the Department of Economics at Rutgers, The State University, during the academic year 1956-57, in this field of second injury programs. Seward examined the case materials of the Division of Workmen's Compensation and incorporated his findings in a Master's Essay, "New Jersey's One Per Cent Fund" (Rutgers University, 1957).

[2]According to one employer, speaking before an annual meeting of the International Association of Industrial Accident Boards and Commissions in 1930, one court decision in Oklahoma which held the employer responsible for the combined results of successive disabilities resulted in the displacement of between 7,000 and 8,000 crippled workers in that state in less than thirty days. See the discussion of I. K. Huber, in IAIABC *Proceedings*, 1930 (United States Department of Labor, Bureau of Labor Statistics, Bulletin 536, 1931), p. 272.

The way out of this dilemma was shown by New York, when it passed the first second injury fund law in 1916. During the following two decades, only eleven other states passed such legislation, New Jersey among them.[3] It required the specter of a world war, with the possibility of thousands of handicapped veterans returning to the labor market, to galvanize most of the states to action. Before the war was over, thirty-four states had such laws; later thirteen additional states joined the fold, leaving only five states, Georgia, Louisiana, Nevada, New Mexico and Virginia, without such legislation as of 1958.

Coverage

The normal difficulties of comparing compensation laws are multiplied in the second injury field because two separate disabilities, the relations between them, and their combined result, must all be considered. Matters may be simplified if it is recognized that the extent of coverage is determined by provisions relating to the following three items: (1) The cause and type of the pre-existing disability, and the type of the second injury, (2) the relations between the pre-existing condition and the second injury, and (3) the extent of the first, second and combined disabilities.

Insofar as the first item of coverage is concerned, New Jersey's law and those of fourteen other jurisdictions cover any previous permanent disability, regardless of type or cause. This is in contrast with the remaining thirty-three second injury jurisdictions, whose laws either confine coverage of the pre-existing disability to scheduled injuries or contain some other limitation.[4] New Jersey's law provides for payments: "...to persons totally disabled, as the result of experiencing a permanent disability under conditions entitling such persons to compensation therefor, when such persons had previously been permanently and partially disabled from *some other cause....* "[5] The law contains no limitation as to the type of pre-existing disability; it could be an amputation, loss of use of a limb, a disabling disease or any type of injury which resulted in permanent partial disability. The phrase *some other cause* indicates the lack of restriction as to origin; the previous disability could be congenital or due to a military episode, an automobile accident or any other cause.

In spite of the shortcomings of a waiver system, as of 1957 six states specifically permitted waivers, although in two of these states the administrative agencies reported that the permission required by law was never given. Eighteen other states permitted waivers for an aggravation of a special condition — usually silicosis. See *Second Injury Funds* (United States Department of Labor, Bureau of Labor Standards, Bulletin 190), 1957, Table p. 30. In 1920, fourteen of the forty-two states which had compensation statutes made the employer liable only for the disability resulting from the second injury itself. See *Comparison of State Workmen's Compensation Laws* (United States Department of Labor, Bureau of Labor Statistics, Bulletin 275), 1920, pp. 71 ff.

[3]N.J. Laws 1923, ch 81, p. 163.
[4]*Second Injury Funds*, p. 11.
[5]N.J. Stat. Ann. (West, 1958), 34:15-95. Italics added.

It required a 1936 amendment to the act to establish this unrestricted coverage on a firm basis.[6] The title of the original 1923 act said that payments were to be made when a worker was permanently and totally disabled as a result of "two separate accidents," although the principal provisions of the act were substantially as quoted above. The Commissioners of Labor, obviously guided by the substantive provisions rather than the title, placed many persons on the fund, even though their prior disability was not the result of an accident. In 1934, Commissioner Blunt turned down a petition of one Tony Addotta on the grounds that his prior disability (arthritis) had not resulted from an accident. The Supreme Court, concurring on the grounds that the title revealed legislative intent, stated further that the act must be interpreted as applying only in cases where both accidents were compensable.[7]

As a result of this decision, many persons whose previous disability was not the result of a compensable accident were removed from the second injury fund rolls, until the legislature in 1936 resolved the confusion by changing the title of the act to conform to the text. Subsequent court decisions indicated that the amendments were to be retroactive, and beneficiaries of the fund who had been taken off as a result of the Addotta decision were reinstated and given lump-sum checks to cover the period for which they had been deprived of their benefits.[8] The net effect of the amendment was to restore the practice which had existed prior to the Addotta case, with the result that New Jersey's law can be said to contain the broadest possible coverage provisions, insofar as the cause and type of the pre-existing disability are concerned.

All jurisdictions limit the *cause* of the second disability to those disabling injuries which are found to be compensable, and over one-half of the jurisdictions limit the *type* of this injury to loss, or loss of use of, a hand, arm, foot, leg or eye. New Jersey's law contain no such restrictions — the sole requirement for coverage is that the second injury occur under circumstances which would entitle the worker to compensation. However, the combined injuries, as will be discussed below, must result in permanent and total disability.

The second coverage item pertains to the relationship between the two injuries, a matter dealt with in New Jersey in the 1940 amendments. No person is eligible to receive benefits from the fund:

1. If the disability resulting from the last injury is permanently and totally disabling in itself.

2. If permanent and total disability results from aggravation, activation, or acceleration by the last compensable injury of a pre-existing noncompensable disease or condition.

---

[6]N.J. Laws 1936, ch. 55, p. 146.

[7]*Addotta* v. *Blunt*, 114 N.J.L. 85.

[8]*Wittel* v. *Toohey*, 117 N.J.L. 572 (1937); *Richardson* v. *Essex National Trunk and Bag Co.*, 119 N.J.L. 47 (1937). Addotta was still on the fund as of 1957, receiving payments of $36.93 semimonthly.

3. If the disease or condition existing prior to the last compensable accident is not aggravated or accelerated, but is in itself progressive, and by reason of such progression subsequent to the last compensable accident, renders him totally disabled.

4. If a person who is rendered permanently and partially disabled by the last compensable injury subsequently becomes permanently and totally disabled by reason of progressive physical deterioration or pre-existing condition or disease.[9]

Given the fact that the New Jersey fund is designed to cover only cases where the combined disabilities result in permanent total disability, the provisions of paragraphs (1), (3) and (4) follow logically enough. Each of them is designed to prevent payments from the fund if the permanent and total disability flows from either of the separate disabilities, but not from their combined effects. Paragraph (2), however, blocks payments from the fund when the second injury aggravates the pre-existing disease or condition, and the employer remains fully liable for any compensation award which may be made. These amendments did not introduce this concept, for it was part of the interpretation of the act even before 1940. In one case which preceded the amendments by six months, the "lighting up" or activation principle was used to deny a petition to the fund. The court stated: "This is another of the numerous applications for benefits under the so-called one per cent fund. The difficulty in this class of cases is apparently due to a misunderstanding of the legislative intent as exhibited in the present and preceding acts. This intent is (1) to insure the employee full compensation where a compensable disability succeeds but has no causative connection with the results of a prior disability, the combination of the two leaving the employee permanently and totally disabled. Its purpose is (2) to relieve the employer of the undue burden of a prior disability, with which, or its result, the disability arising in his employ has no causative connection, but which burden the previous broad provisions of the Workmen's Compensation Act were found to impose upon him."[10] In decisions subsequent to the 1940 amendments, the courts have held that under paragraph (2), the payments cannot be made from the fund if the second injury aggravates or accelerates the pre-existing condition. Only if the subsequent injury is unrelated to the first can the employer be relieved of a portion of the liability.[11]

---

[9]N.J. Laws 1940, ch. 133, pp. 288-291.
[10]*Application of Glennon*, 18 N.J. Misc. 196 (1940).
[11]*Vacaro* v. *Walter Kidde and Co.*, 134 N.J.L. 491 (1946). In this case an employee who had congenital astigmatism to the extent of an estimated 36 per cent loss of vision was blinded in an industrial accident. The entire permanent total disability award was charged to the employer on grounds of aggravation. In *Balash* v. *Harper*, 3 N.J. 437, the One Per Cent Fund petition was denied by the Commissioner on the grounds that the subsequent injury, a coronary occlusion, aggravated and accelerated the pre-existing generalized arteriosclerotic condition and an inoperative inguinal hernia. The Supreme Court affirmed the County Court's reversal of the Commissioner's decision on the grounds that the subsequent injury was unrelated to the previous condition. The decision was based upon medical opinion indicating that the strain on the hernia affected everything that the man attempted to do, and that the added strain and undue burden imposed on the other factors, namely the arterio-

This is by no means a black or white situation. As Larson points out, "Nothing is better established in compensation law than the rule that when industrial injury precipitates disability from a latent prior condition, such as heart disease, cancer, back weakness and the like, the entire disability is compensable, and, except in three states having special statutes on aggravation of disease, no attempt is made to weigh the relative contribution of the accident and the pre-existing condition to the final disability." [12]   However, if the disability is known to the employer (the obvious case is an amputation), and if the second injury aggravates it, this could be considered in a different category. The question obviously turns on what is meant by employer knowledge, and the relationship this has to employment obstacles.

These considerations lead directly to the third item of coverage, the extent of the first, second and combined injuries. In New Jersey, aside from the fact that the combined injury must not result from an aggravation of a pre-existing condition by the second injury, the prior condition must be capable of being fixed in extent. In the words of the New Jersey Supreme Court: "This previous permanent and partial disability must be as certain and as capable of ascertainment as a previously incurred permanent partial disability through the loss of one hand, one arm, one foot, one leg or one eye." [13]   In another case, the Appellate Division of the Superior Court objected to an application to the fund on a number of grounds, including the fact that the previous disability was not measurable. The court stated: "With respect to the finding that petitioner had a pre-existing 'condition which was disabling to a certain extent' it is noted that the certain extent is not stated in terms of a percentage of total disability. Nor does there appear in the record any basis for a measurement of such pre-existing disability." [14]
The courts quite naturally insist that the pre-existing disability be definitely fixed in extent, because this is vitally necessary for deciding the apportionment of liability between the fund and the employer. But other considerations are involved if the broader social purposes of the law are kept in mind.

The IAIABC committee on second injury funds advocated broad coverage but recognized that the extent of the previous and subsequent disabilities could properly be restricted to that degree of disablement

---

sclerosis, and the aftereffects of the coronary occlusion, were more than the man could cope with. The court also found that these conditions added to the risks of the operation on the hernia. In *Davenport* v. *Alvord Hotel*, 21 N.J. Super. 493 (1951), a seventy-one-year-old woman who had pre-existing disabilities of hypertension, a squint in one eye and a congenital curvature of the spine fell from heat exhaustion and suffered shock, a concussion and a back injury. The court denied benefits from the One Per Cent Fund on the grounds that the compensable injury aggravated the pre-existing conditions. See also *Gorman* v. *Miner-Edgar Chemical Corp.*, 16 N.J. Misc. 170.

[12] Arthur Larson, *The Law of Workmen's Compensation* (Albany: Matthew Bender and Co., 1952), II, 56.

[13] *Gorman* v. *Miner-Edgar Chemical Corp.*, 16 N.J. Misc. 170.

[14] *Kalson* v. *Star Electric Co.*, 15 N.J. Super. 565.

which would prejudice the worker's employment chances.[15] This is easier to accept in principle than it is to translate into practice. Various jurisdictions have attempted to meet the problem in different ways. Some states, notably Wisconsin, require that both the first and second injuries meet minimum threshold qualifying requirements. In Wisconsin, the prior disability must be one which, if it had occurred in industrial employment, would merit a compensation award of 250 weeks. The subsequent compensable disability must also be entitled to 250 weeks of compensation.[16]

On the other hand, Ohio does not specify the extent of the disability, but provides that any employer may give notice to the commission, prior to an injury, that it is employing a handicapped person.[17] If the employer gives such notice, then, presumably, the handicap is noticeable and of sufficient gravity to constitute an employment handicap. One difficulty with Ohio's method is that employers may be reluctant to go through the red tape necessary to advise the commission and, instead, may refuse to hire handicapped workers. Or, employers may require rigid pre-employment physicals to weed out employees with latent disabilities that would not ordinarily constitute an employment handicap. Unlike Wisconsin, Ohio does not restrict the extent of the second disability, but covers any injury which is either aggravated by, or could not have occurred except for, the pre-existing condition.

New York approaches this problem in yet another way in that it limits coverage of prior disabilities to those that are likely to be "a hindrance or obstacle" to employment. The compounded disability must be "materially and substantially greater" than that which would have resulted from the second injury alone.[18] Although an employer need not file notice of the fact that he is employing a handicapped worker, the New York administrators require that an employer have knowledge of the handicap, and in the case of a prior latent condition, he must have acted upon this knowledge in some manner. The rationale here again is that if the employer did not know of the handicap, it could not have constituted an employment obstacle. Since the act has neither the "notice" requirement of the Ohio law nor the mechanical "rating" provisions of the Wisconsin law, the administrators are left with a great deal of flexibility in interpreting its provisions.

---

[15] "Report of Subcommittee on Second Injury Funds," in *Workmen's Compensation Problems*, IAIABC *Proceedings*, 1955 (United States Department of Labor, Bureau of Labor Standards, Bulletin 186), p. 71.

[16] In case of both the previous and subsequent disability, this 250-week figure is reduced by $2\frac{1}{2}$ per cent for each year of the worker's age above fifty, with no reduction greater than 50 per cent. Wisc. Stat., Sect. 102.59, excerpts of which appear in *Second Injury Funds*, p. 42.

[17] The Ohio statutes provide, however, that: "Any employer who fails to so notify the commission but makes application for a determination hereunder shall be entitled to a determination if the commission finds that the failure to give notice of the employment of such a handicapped worker has not made it impossible for the commission to make the determination...." (Page's Ohio Rev. Code Ann., Sect. 4123:343, quoted in *Second Injury Funds*, p. 41.)

[18] N. Y. Consol. Laws, ch. 67, Sect. 15 (8) (d).

New Jersey's law has no limitation on the extent of the first injury or condition, except that it must be capable of being measured; neither is there any restriction on the extent of the second injury. It must be compensable and unrelated to the first. When it comes to the combined effects of the injuries, however, New Jersey, unlike New York, does not require simply that the disability resulting from the combined injuries be greater than that caused by the subsequent injury alone. Payments can be made from the second injury fund only if the worker is permanently and totally disabled as a result of the successive unrelated disabilities. If the combined result is classified only as permanent partial disability, the employer is wholly liable, regardless of the contribution of the pre-existing condition to the final result. Likewise, if death results from a combination of a pre-existing condition and a subsequent injury, the law would not countenance payments from the fund.

The rationale for this limitation is not clear. However, only six of the states whose second injury funds cover previous disabilities without restriction as to type or cause, allow recoveries from the fund where the final disability is classified as less than permanent total; and only five states, in all, allow recoveries from the fund in certain types of death cases.[19] Thus, although New Jersey is not alone in these restrictions, it should be noted that such jurisdictions as New York, California and Wisconsin are more liberal in allowing the fund to share liability if the disability is both less serious and more serious than a permanent total disability.

Apportioning the Liability

The IAIABC has been unable to lay down any definite guide lines about exactly how liability should be apportioned between the employer and the fund, but its committee has counseled: "The provisions should not be so restrictive as to prevent the employment of the physically handicapped nor so liberal as to make the maintenance of the fund a burden on employers and insurers."[20] But more than the financing of a fund is involved here; if the provisions are too liberal, however that may be defined, the fundamental basis of the compensation laws — making individual employers liable for their own accidents — may be shaken.

Various methods are used by the states to apportion liability. The most common method is the one followed in New Jersey in which the fund pays the difference between the amount payable for the subsequent injury, taken alone, and the total award. The necessity of measuring

---

[19] California, Florida, Missouri, New York, Utah and Wisconsin allow second injury fund payments if the final disability is less than permanent total disability. Florida, Massachusetts, New York, Ohio and Rhode Island allow payments in death cases.

[20] "Report of Subcommittee on Second Injury Funds," in *Workmen's Compensation Problems*, IAIABC *Proceedings*, 1955, p. 72.

precisely the extent of the pre-existing disability is obvious under this method of apportioning liability.

Such measurement is also necessary under a second method used by Wisconsin. If the combination of the first and second injury results in permanent total disability, Wisconsin follows the same method as is used in New Jersey. However, if the successive disabilities result in permanent partial disability, the employer is liable for the greater of the two disabilities and the fund for the lesser.

Because of the difficulties inherent in attempting to measure precisely the extent of the pre-existing disability, months or years after it occurred, some states have devised methods which eliminate this measurement. In New York and Florida, once the employer can show the existence of a known pre-employment handicap, which together with the subsequent disability resulted in a combined disability materially and substantially greater than would have resulted from the second injury alone, he is relieved of liability for all payments beyond the first 104 weeks. After this period, payments are made from the fund. If the combined disability requires payments of less than 104 weeks' duration, the employer would be liable for the entire amount. The great advantage here is an administrative one, because no controversy need develop as to the precise extent of the pre-existing condition. In Massachusetts, the employer may be reimbursed from the fund for 50 per cent of the liability, except where total disability is the result of an aggravation of a pre-existing condition by a schedule injury. In such a case, the employer is responsible for the full benefits for the last injury, according to the schedule, and the fund shares, on a 50-50 basis, the balance of the award.

Other states reduce the fund's liability by the amounts of any payments made to the employee on account of the pre-existing disability, or for the compensable value of the previously lost member. If the latter deduction is made, the employee may gain very little additional from the fund. Although New Jersey does not make these deductions, only cash indemnity payments can be made from the fund. Under the existing law, the fund does not pay for medical or hospitalization costs, although these may constitute a significant portion of the total costs in an ordinary permanent and total disability case.

Financing the Fund

In general, three different methods are used to finance these funds in the various jurisdictions, although the details may vary considerably.

1) The most common method is to require employers to pay a stated amount into the fund in no-dependency death cases, compensation cases in which the fatally injured worker leaves no dependents.[21] Such

---

[21] The various methods of financing the fund are described in "Report of Subcommittee on Second Injury Funds," in *Workmen's Compensation Problems*, IAIABC *Proceedings*, 1955,

payments, of course, can bear no relation to the requirements of the fund. They are based on the notion that such cases involve "windfalls" to the employer; however, such cases are anticipated when insurance rates are set. The only warrant for such a method appears to be that tradition recommends it; it was the method used by New York in its original 1916 law, although that state has since abandoned it.

2) New Jersey and seven other states, Connecticut, Delaware, Florida, Indiana, Kentucky, Missouri and New York, finance the program by assessments levied against insurance carriers and self-insurers. In New Jersey, each insurance carrier and self-insurer is assessed 1 per cent of the compensation payments (excluding the cost of medical benefits) made during the calendar year preceding the date of collection. Hence, the second injury fund in New Jersey is known as the One Per Cent Fund. Some other states assess on the basis of a percentage of insurance premiums written. New York's method seems best calculated to assure a close correspondence between its fund's income and its expenditures. Total disbursements from the fund are calculated, and each insurance carrier is assessed a proportion of these disbursements equal to the proportion which the total compensation payments of the carrier bore to the total compensation payments made by all carriers during the year. Thus, if one carrier paid out 10 per cent of all compensation during the year, it would be assessed 10 per cent of the amount needed to replenish the fund.

3) As coverage of the funds becomes broader, and includes pre-existing conditions which are not industrial in origin, the argument is made that the costs ought to be borne by society as a whole, rather than employers as a group. Two states, California and Pennsylvania, finance their funds entirely by legislative appropriation. Under this system, the costs are borne by the general taxpayer rather than the employers or insurance carriers. [22]

According to the methods used in most states, the liability falls on all employers as a group, to be absorbed or passed on according to market situations. But there is certainly nothing that the last employer can do to eliminate the pre-existing disabilities, and if these disabilities are not even industrially connected, there is nothing that employers as a group can do, or could have done. Hence the burden of the fund can be considered as a public liability for which governments can make sufficient cost provisions. One disturbing thing about this, aside from the fact that some pre-existing disabilities may have been industrially connected, is that if the reasoning gains currency, it may

---

pp. 72-73, and also *Second Injury Funds*, chapter VI. According to this latter publication, "Fifteen jurisdictions finance their funds entirely by this method. Five others, however, use this method in conjunction with employer payments in certain permanent partial disability cases, and another three combine no-dependency death payments with annual assessments against insurance carriers" (p. 23).

[22] Massachusetts, which has a separate second injury fund for veterans, provides for direct payment from the state's general funds if the special fund becomes exhausted. Jurisdictions with exclusive state insurance systems pay benefits from the general state insurance fund or from special funds, without charging the employer's experience rating.

also be applied in the case of an aggravation or activation of a latent prior disability in which the second injury fund payments may not even be involved. Probing almost any aspect of second injuries leads one directly to the cases where only one disability is involved. As our compensation laws broaden in coverage to include not only the schedule injuries but also the occupational diseases and other ills to which everyone is susceptible, the difficulties of separating out the employment-connected disability from the general disability becomes more difficult. The rationale for using public funds to finance second injury cases may some day be applied to the ordinary disability, with a consequent change in the whole compensation structure.

But such considerations involve speculations about the future. At the present time New Jersey does not use public funds to finance any part of its fund. The assessment is made against each carrier and self-insurer according to the amount of cash compensation benefits paid and, of course, is reflected in insurance rates. The original 1923 law did not provide for any maximum limit on the size of the fund, but in 1938, as compensation benefits began to increase, the legislature imposed a maximum limit of $200,000. During the second world war it was anticipated that handicapped veterans would be returning to industry in large numbers, and to protect their job chances, the maximum limit was increased drastically to $1,500,000.[23] As the law now stands, collections cease whenever the amount in the fund, including accumulated interest, exceeds this sum, with collections to resume whenever payments from the fund's balance cause the balance to fall below the $1,500,000 figure. Collections have been made each year from 1945 to 1958, with the exception of 1956, when the fund's balance exceeded the statutory maximum.

As can be seen from Table XXXIV, covering the years 1953 to 1957, the annual income of the fund has been sufficient to cover the yearly payments to the permanently and totally disabled (with the exception of 1956, when no assessments were made). Given this recent experience, the balances in the fund are more than adequate. As a matter of fact, as of July 1, 1956, the balance in New Jersey's fund was higher than that of any of the other jurisdictions for which second injury fund information was available to the United States Department of Labor.[24] New Jersey's balance was $1,595,042, whereas the only state with a balance at all comparable was Washington, with $1,225,828. The next highest ranking state was New York, whose balance was $818,094. It should be noted that Washington has an exclusive state insurance system, benefits being paid directly from the special fund without charging an employer's experience rating, whereas New York's method of financing does not require a large surplus fund.

Because New Jersey's fund is sizable in relation to its expenditures, and because this is the only fund in New Jersey that is paid for

[23]This bill removing the $200,000 limit was passed after Governor Edge urged the new limit as a means of protecting the veterans returning to industry. (*The Newark News,* January 30, 1945.)

[24]*Second Injury Funds,* Table p. 22.

Table XXXIV. Income and Expenditures of New Jersey's
One Per Cent Fund, 1953-1957

Year Ending Dec. 31	Income				Expenditures				Balance in Fund at End of Year
	from Insurance Co.	from Self-Insurers	Interest and Other	Total	Payt. to Totally Disabled Persons	Auth. Admin. Expenses	Other Payt.[a]	Total Expenditures	
1952									$1,316,010.28
1953	$245,103.32	$93,782.94	$14,587.42	$299,473.68	$82,994.31	$12,500.00	$100,000	$195,494.31	1,419,989.65
1954	263,917.39	43,248.00	16,034.77	323,200.16	116,649.50	7,917.50	164,232.08	288,799.08	1,454,390.73
1955	269,104.78	45,977.90	22,924.61	338,007.29	121,838.77	10,943.17	-----	132,781.94	1,659,616.08
1956	31.63	-----	16,974.26	17,005.39	208,668.18	11,662.50	100,000	320,330.68	1,356,291.29
1957	287,665.84	43,210.75	28,399.90	359,276.49	279,138.41	11,870.10	-----	291,008.51	1,424,599.27

Source: New Jersey Compensation Rating and Inspection Bureau, *Annual Reports*.
[a] Includes veterans' payments and transfers to the general state fund to be applied to costs of administration of the Division of Workmen's Compensation. Such transfers cannot exceed $50,000 for any one fiscal year, but one appropriation is made for two fiscal years.

by employers as a group, the temptation is ever present to use the monies for purposes other than payments to the totally disabled. One such logical use is to pay for the costs of administering the fund. The statute authorizes a sum not to exceed $12,500 per year for the purposes of administration, including costs of appeals and proceedings for review of decisions on applications for benefits from the fund. In 1952, the law was amended to allow the legislature to appropriate from the fund an amount not to exceed $50,000 for any one fiscal year for purposes of meeting general administrative expenses of the division as a whole. The appropriation may be made only when the balance in the fund exceeds $1,250,000 and may consist of no more than $50,000 of such excess.[25]

Another use made of the fund is to supplement compensation benefits to veterans of World War II and of the Korean War who use their G.I. benefits under the Servicemen's Readjustment Act of 1944 or similar acts for purposes of on-the-job training. Payments are made from the fund to make up the difference between the compensation benefit to which their low weekly wage entitles them and the maximum weekly benefit.[26] Quantitatively, these amounts have not been very significant. In most cases, these veterans have suffered relatively minor disabilities, and the One Per Cent Fund payment has been made in one lump sum. Up to mid-1957, only fifty-two veterans, in all, had received benefits from the fund since the passage of the legislation in 1951. Few would quarrel with the idea of supplementing these benefits, but why impose this liability on the One Per Cent Fund? The rationale is not obvious, except that in the absence of any appropriations from general funds, the One Per Cent Fund is an eligible source, if for no reason than it has generous cash balances.

Proposals have been made, from time to time, to tap the fund for other purposes. The inadequacy of benefit payments to permanently and totally disabled persons and to survivors in death cases, whose benefits are calculated according to a past weekly maximum, has prompted demands that these payments be increased to current benefit levels. The method of financing such increases has always been a stumbling block, and the One Per Cent Fund has been suggested as an eligible source. Aside from the desirability or lack of desirability of making these adjustments, the question of whether One Per Cent Fund balances should be used for these purposes must be decided in light of whether these funds are to be considered as dedicated to second injury purposes, or whether no such dedication is implied. As a matter of good financial housekeeping, it would seem preferable to assess the needs and finance each kind separately, but there probably is no more difficult political problem than to find a new revenue source. At least, financing benefit increases to long-term compensation receivers, or even paying administrative costs from the fund, involves no violence to

---

[25]N.J. Laws 1952, ch. 80, p. 411.
[26]N.J. Stat. Ann., 34:15-12.1-12.6.

the principle that such payments are a liability of all employers and should be shared among them.

Administrative Procedures

Before any claimant can receive benefits from New Jersey's One Per Cent Fund, a hearing must be held and a determination made. No individual employer or insurance carrier is involved in the hearing. The fund is represented by someone from the Attorney General's office who acts for the Commissioner of Labor and Industry, and the injured worker, whose petition to the fund must be filed within two years after the last compensation payment has been made, is usually represented by a lawyer. One Per Cent Fund cases may not occupy a high priority on a petitioner's attorney schedule since the fees allowed are relatively low ($150 to $200 per case) and are chargeable directly to the petitioner and not against the fund. If the petition to the fund is not successful, the attorney receives no fee from any source.

Procedural innovations introduced in 1957 were designed to shorten the traditional time lag between the date of the petition and the final award. Once a petition is received, arrangements are made for a medical examination of the claimant. All medical reports and the deputy director's findings from previous cases are made available to the division's examining physician. An advisory hearing before a deputy director is supposed to take place within four weeks of this examination.

After the hearing at which medical evidence and testimony are heard, the deputy director files an advisory report with the Commissioner. The supervisor of the One Per Cent Fund also makes a personal investigation of the petitioner to determine his age, marital status, number of dependents, physical condition, employment status, earnings and other sources of income. The Commissioner then weighs the advisory report and the supervisor's report to arrive at a decision. It is seldom that the supervisor and the deputy disagree, but when this happens, the Commissioner may order a further hearing.

The order placing the man on the fund can come only from the Commissioner. The deputy director adjudicating the compensation claim that arose by reason of the second disability cannot make any binding apportionment of liability between the last employer and the fund. At one time, the courts held that the Commissioner was bound by decisions of the deputies in regard to apportionment, at the time of the hearing on the workmen's compensation claim; but amendments to the One Per Cent Fund law in 1938 prescribed the present procedure.[27] Nonetheless, in their workmen's compensation decisions, deputy directors sometimes adjudge the worker to be permanently and totally

---

[27] *Walker* v. *Albright*, 119 N.J.L. 285, *Voessler* v. *Palm Fetcheler and Co.*, 120 N.J.L. 553, *affirmed* 122 N.J.L. 434. The 1938 amendments can be found in, N.J. Laws 1938, ch. 198, p. 475.

disabled, but at the same time, the employer is made liable only for the disability attributable to the subsequent accident. Such determinations obviously facilitate the acceptance of future petitions to the fund, but the Commissioner is no longer bound by such determinations.

For the 163 persons on the fund as of April, 1957, the average number of months elapsing between the dates of their petitions and the dates of the awards placing them on the fund was 11.37 (Table XXXV). When the same time periods are calculated for beneficiaries with effective dates in 1956, the time lags have been cut in half. This illustrates the efforts that have been made to shorten these time lags. Something more than administrative niceties is involved here because a period of time may elapse during which the worker receives no compensation benefits, either from his last employer or from the fund. This is shown by the size of the lump-sum awards granted when the petitioner is placed upon the fund. These are calculated by multiplying

Table XXXV. Time Expiring Between Date of Petition to New Jersey
One Per Cent Fund and Date of Award

A – All One Per Cent Fund Beneficiaries, as of April, 1957

Mos. Expiring	No. of Beneficiaries	Per cent of Total
0- 3	15	9.2
4- 6	38	23.3
7- 9	31	19.0
10-12	22	13.5
13-15	12	7.4
16-18	11	6.7
19-21	10	6.1
22-24	7	4.3
Over 24	13	8.0
Unknown	4	2.5
	163	100.0

Av. no. of mos. – 11.37

B – One Per Cent Fund Beneficiaries Placed on the Fund in 1956

Mos. Expiring	No. of Beneficiaries	Per cent of Total
0-1	1	3.5
1-1.9	0	0
2-2.9	1	3.5
3-3.9	1	3.5
4-4.9	8	27.6
5-5.9	6	20.6
6-6.9	5	17.2
7-7.9	3	10.3
8-8.9	4	13.8
	29	100.0

Av. no. of mos. – 5.2

Source: Files of New Jersey Division of Workmen's Compensation

the worker's benefit rate by the number of weeks between the date of petition or the date of the last payment of compensation (whichever is later) and the date of the award. Table XXXVI shows that the largest lump-sum award necessary during 1956 was not in excess of $1,250, whereas awards in excess of that amount were common in earlier years, when compensation rates in some cases were lower.

The one 1957 case with a lump-sum award in excess of $1,500 illustrates the difficulties in trying to speed the disposition of these cases under the present law and procedures. Rather than press the petition to the fund, the attorney for the injured worker chose to file a petition for increased disability attributable to the second injury. Only

Table XXXVI. Lump-Sum Awards Paid to Persons Receiving Benefits from the New Jersey One Per Cent Fund as of April, 1957

Year Placed on Fund	No. of Lump-Sum Awards								Total No. of Beneficiaries
	$0	$1-250	$250-500	$501-750	$751-1,000	$1,001-1,250	$1,251-1,500	Over $1,500	
1926	1	0	0	0	0	0	0	0	1
1929	0	0	0	0	0	0	0	1	1
1930	0	0	0	0	0	0	0	0	0
1931	1	0	0	0	0	0	0	0	1
1932	0	0	0	0	0	0	0	0	0
1933	0	0	0	0	0	0	0	3	3
1934	1	0	0	0	1	0	0	1	3
1935	0	0	0	0	0	0	0	1	1
1936	0	4	1	0	1	0	0	0	6
1937	0	1	1	0	0	0	0	1	3
1938	0	0	0	0	0	0	1	0	1
1939	0	0	2	0	0	0	0	0	2
1940	0	0	0	0	0	2	0	0	2
1941	0	0	0	0	1	0	0	1	2
1942	0	0	0	0	0	0	0	0	0
1943	0	0	0	0	1	0	1	0	2
1944	1	1	1	0	0	1	0	0	4
1945	0	0	2	0	0	1	0	1	4
1946	0	1	0	1	1	0	0	2	5
1947	0	1	0	0	1	0	1	1	4
1948	0	0	0	1	2	0	2	1	6
1949	0	1	0	2	1	0	2	0	6
1950	0	1	1	0	0	1	0	4	7
1951	2	1	3	1	1	1	0	1	10
1952	0	0	0	0	0	1	0	2	3
1953	0	0	0	2	0	3	3	2	10
1954	0	0	2	2	4	6	2	5	21
1955	0	1	2	5	6	5	1	5	26
1956	1	0	7	12	7	2	0	0	29
1957	0	0	0	0	0	0	0	1	1
Total No. of Beneficiaries	7	12	22	26	27	23	13	33	163

Source: Files of New Jersey Division of Workmen's Compensation.

when this was unsuccessful was the petition to the fund pursued. In the two-year interim between the date of last payment from the employer and time the petitioner was put on the fund, he was without any compensation income and found it necessary to apply for public assistance.[28] The time lag in this case cannot fairly be charged to administrative lacity, since petitions to the fund are not acted upon until after all claims pending against the employer are decided.

Trends in One Per Cent Fund Activity

The outstanding thing about recent One Per Cent Fund activity is the increase in the number of persons placed on the fund. On December 10, 1938, only forty-two persons were receiving benefits from the fund. In contrast, in the relatively short period, July, 1956, to April, 1957, forty-six persons were newly placed on the fund. Eight beneficiaries died during that period; hence there was a net increase of thirty-eight persons in a period less than a year.

Table XXXVII shows the number of persons on the fund's payroll for various dates since 1952; although the increase is apparent, it does not give the full picture because of the turnover, due largely to deaths. On January 15, 1959, 234 persons were receiving benefits from the fund. Certainly neither the accident rate nor the statutory changes can account for this increase in fund activity. It must be accounted for by an increased willingness on the part of the administrators to allow payments from the fund. But there is no objective evidence, other than the record of the increase in the number of persons placed on the fund, to prove or disprove this.

Table XXXVII. New Jersey One Per Cent Fund Payroll, 1952-1959

Date	No. of Persons	Total Amt. of Payroll	Av. Semimonthly Amt. per Person
Feb. 15, 1952	81	$---	$---
Jan. 7, 1954	90	3,211.43	35.68
Mar. 25, 1954	91	3,472.12	38.15
July 6, 1954	89	3,393.09	38.12
Oct. 7, 1954	96	3,748.77	39.05
Apr. 1, 1955	108	4,360.96	40.38
June 16, 1955	113	4,348.09	38.47
Dec. 22, 1955	114	4,587.07	40.23
Mar. 28, 1956	110	4,815.17	40.80
June 30, 1957	180	8,665.30	48.14
June 30, 1958	208	10,307.92	49.56
Jan. 15, 1959	234	12,205.54	52.16

Source: Files of New Jersey Division of Workmen's Compensation.

---

[28]This man received payments from the county welfare board and ran into some difficulty in reimbursing the county agency when he finally received his lump-sum award. The matter was settled only after the supervisor of the One Per Cent Fund intervened. (Seward, p. 55.)

The age distribution of the 163 fund beneficiaries is shown in Table XXXVIII. The average age in 1957 was 62.4 years; 15.3 per cent of the beneficiaries were 75 years of age and over. The average age of the group at the time they were placed on the fund was 55.1 years, with 29.5 per cent having been 65 and over. At the time of the disabling accident, the average age for the group was 49.8 years, with 28.2 per cent having been age 60 or over.

Table XXXVIII. Age Distribution of New Jersey One Per Cent Fund Beneficiaries, 1957

Ages	At Time of Accident		At Time Placed on Fund		In 1957	
	No. of Beneficiaries	% of Total Cases	No. of Beneficiaries	% of Total Cases	No. of Beneficiaries	% of Total Cases
Under 40	34	21.0%	25	15.3%	9	5.5%
40-49	28	17.2	28	17.2	16	9.8
50-54	22	13.4	15	9.2	12	7.3
55-59	24	14.7	19	11.6	18	11.1
60-64	27	16.5	23	14.1	27	16.5
65-69	13	8.0	28	17.2	27	16.5
70-74	5	3.0	16	9.8	24	14.7
75 and over	1	.7	4	2.5	25	15.3
Unknown	9	5.5	5	3.1	5	3.3
Total	163	100.0%	163	100.0%	163	100.0%
Av. Age	49.8 yrs.		55.1 yrs.		62.4 yrs.	

Source: Files of New Jersey Division of Workmen's Compensation.

The nature of the pre-existing disability does not lend itself to statistical evaluation since the pre-existing disability is usually multiple in nature, but it is clear that arteriosclerosis, arthritis and other ailments common to persons of advanced years are the most prevalent types of pre-existing disabilities. Pre-existing eye disabilities are also very common, but in many cases the eye disability is combined with some degenerative disease, and it is impossible to separate out the crucial disability for statistical purposes. [29]

One thing remains certain. Under New Jersey's broad coverage of pre-existing disabilities, the path is open to accept many persons who could not recover from the fund if the restrictions on the pre-existing disability were confined to scheduled disabilities, as in some other states. To think of restricting the type of pre-existing disability would be a regressive step if the object is to remove obstacles to the employment of the handicapped. On the other hand, the fund was never meant to be a means of providing old-age assistance or a way to remove liability from employers if it properly belongs with them.

In the nature of the case, it is difficult to separate out the seriousness of the previous disability after a subsequent injury has been superimposed. A deputy hearing the compensation case may be sorely

---

[29] Seward, p. 59.

tempted to settle the matter by noting that the man is permanently and totally disabled, and then assessing the employer for only some portion of the disability. The financial difference between a permanent partial award, of any amount, and the potential liability involved in a permanent total assessment can be considerable; and pressure may be exerted by an employer and his insurance carrier to shift liability to the fund. Once the fund has been "set up," humane considerations make it difficult for the commissioner and the deputy director conducting the advisory hearing to deny the injured worker's petition.

Procedures in a state like New York have the twin advantages of eliminating time lags and providing a solid method of defending the fund. The injured workmen is always awarded compensation for the full disability, and it is then up to the employer to petition the fund for all benefits paid or payable after the first 104 weeks. It is the employer or his insurance carrier, rather than the worker, who must make the application, because it is the employer who seeks to transfer liability. The New York law also provides that the chairman of the workmen's compensation board appoint a representative to defend the fund; but if an employer or insurance company group's attorney has been appointed to act for his clients, the chairman may designate him as a representative of the fund to defend its interests.[30]

This brings the two contenders together: on one side, the individual employer who seeks to transfer liability to the fund and, on the other, the representative of the companies and carriers who finance the fund. Under New Jersey's procedure, both of these parties are absent from any One Per Cent Fund hearing. On one side there is the injured workman and on the other, a representative of the state, in spite of the fact that no public funds are used to finance the fund. If a representative of the financially interested carriers defended the fund, questionable claims would be rigorously contested. At the same time, if New York's method of apportioning liability were adopted, this would guarantee that if the claim was not successful, the injured workmen would not suffer; the amount and duration of compensation have already been determined in his case, and benefit checks are presumably being received without delay.

Toward a More Adequate Second Injury Fund Law

All second injury cases involve the assessment of the nature and extent of disabilities and, in part, are similar to any other case. Whatever defects may be present in the method of deciding ordinary compensation cases will be reflected in the second injury fund proceedings; and if reforms are made in, say, definitions of disability in the ordinary case, these reforms should help ease some of the problems here. But aside from these general reforms, the comparison of practices in the

---

[30] N.Y. *Consol. Laws*, ch. 67, Sect. 15 (8) (i).

various second injury jurisdictions suggests ways in which New Jersey's law could be improved.

Much underbrush could be cleared away if the second injury fund provisions contained a frank statement of objectives.[31] The historical development of these provisions argues that their essential purpose is to remove hindrances to the employment of the handicapped that were introduced by the compensation laws. Second injury funds, alone, will never automatically open the gates to disabled persons, but their purpose is to remove at least one set of obstacles. A simple declaration of legislative intent spelling out this purpose would aid the courts in their interpretation of the law.

In keeping with this fundamental objective, New Jersey's law contains no restrictions either on the type or cause of the pre-existing condition or on the type of the second injury. Certainly it would be a backward step to impose any such restrictions.

But when it comes to the relationship between the first and second disabilities, New Jersey prevents recovery from the fund if the second aggravates the first. Such a restriction may have merit if the first disability consisted of a prior latent condition unknown to the employer at the time of hiring. If it was not known, it could not constitute an employment obstacle. If, however, the condition was apparent, the employer, apprehensive of the potential compensation liability in the event of another injury, might be reluctant to hire the man. The effects of such a provision on the employment of diabetics or others with diseases that could be activated or aggravated by an injury of the kind that would result only in a minor disability in a healthier person, are obvious. If the fundamental intent is to further the employment of the handicapped, such a provision denying the fund's liability in the aggravation, acceleration or activation cases does not appear warranted. Of course, if the second injury itself results in permanent and total disability, or if this condition is the result of the pre-existing disability itself, then there is no reason why payments should be made from the fund. The fund cannot be used to provide indemnity payments in lieu of a general health insurance scheme.

If the aggravation clauses are stricken from the act, some provisions must be made to assure that the fund is not flooded with applications by reason of employers' claims that the fund should pay a share of the award because the employee had some pre-existing condition. As discussed above, each of the methods used to prevent this has its own advantages and disadvantages. Ohio's method of having employers notify the compensation authorities that they are employing a disabled person would seem best designed to assure that the handicap was known prior to the second injury. But employers may be reluctant to bother

---

[31] As part of its declaration of policy and legislative intent, the New York State law says: "That any plan which will reasonably, equitably and practically operate to break down hindrances and remove obstacles to the employment of partially disabled persons honorably discharged from our armed forces, or any other physically handicapped persons, is of vital importance to the State and its people and is of concern to this legislature;..." (N.Y. Consol. Laws, ch. 67, Sect. 15 [8] [a].)

with this notification, and, instead, they may take the easier path of refusing to hire the handicapped person.

Wisconsin's threshold requirements for both the pre-existing and the subsequent disability have the advantage of preventing minor cases from receiving payments from the fund. Presumably, disabilities that do not exceed the minimum requirements are not considered grave employment obstacles. The disadvantages here relate to the somewhat mechanical approach involved in arbitrarily classifying disabilities which merit more than 250 weeks as employment handicaps. Also, such a system seems better suited to a jurisdiction which has succeeded in promulgating widely its standards of disability determination.

New York's provisions are more general, because coverage is limited to those disabilities likely to be a hindrance to employment, and this requirement is coupled with a "knowledge of the employer" requirement. The theory behind this is most logical, but lacking either the notice requirement or the threshold requirement, the law leaves a great deal of discretion in the hands of the administrators. Whether one supports this solution, in preference to the others, will depend on the degree of confidence one has in the administration of the New Jersey law.

It is possible, of course, to propose an eclectic solution which would borrow provisions from all these methods of dealing with the problem. This would take the form of a law which allowed, but did not require, employer notices, which had a threshold-qualifying requirement and which contained the New York provision limiting coverages to those disabilities constituting some hindrance to employment. Of course, such a solution would embrace not only all the advantages of the methods, but the combined disadvantages as well.

The New Jersey law requires that the combined disabilities result in permanent and total disability. With the expanded coverage of the compensation laws, this limitation is difficult to justify. The combined disabilities may also result in a permanent partial condition calling for greater indemnity payments than if there were no pre-existing condition. Or, at the other end of the scale, the compounded disabilities may result in a death that would not have occurred except for the pre-existing condition. If the object is to aid the employment of the handicapped, it is necessary to broaden the New Jersey law to encompass both the disabilities that are less serious and those that are more serious than permanent total disabilities. If this is done, the problem arises as to the definition of those disabilities that should be covered. Here again, the solutions lie in adopting some minimum threshold qualifications or in specifying, in general terms, that the combined injuries should result in a disability which is materially greater than that caused by the second injury alone.

The question of the method of apportioning liability is intimately connected with administrative procedures. In New Jersey, although no notice or knowledge requirement is present, the pre-existing disability must be fixed in extent. This, at times, is a difficult task once the second injury has occurred, and yet it is a vitally necessary one, because the employer is liable only for the results of the second injury standing alone. Also, the employee may secure an award for the disability due to the subsequent injury, but then have to wait six months or a year before he can discover whether he is entitled to payments from the fund. In the interim, he may be without income from any source. Although New York's solution may appear arbitrary, it does have the great advantage of eliminating time lags and a large element of controversy. Once it is established that the employer had knowledge of the pre-existing condition that was a hindrance to employment, and once it is shown that the combined injuries resulted in disabilities materially greater than would have occurred in the absence of the pre-existing condition, the whole award runs initially against the individual employer. Payments for compensation begin and continue without interruption. If, however, the liability extends beyond the 104-week period, the employer can petition the fund, as outlined above. These provisions bring the real contenders together. The fund can be defended by a representative of the insurance or employer interests, of the very persons who contribute to the fund. The introduction of such a provision would go far toward preventing unjustified "raids" on the fund.

The present limitation on the uses of the monies in the One Per Cent Fund to payments of cash indemnities is another of the provisions with some historical rationale but little justification in light of current conditions. When medical and hospitalization payments were limited, it made little difference who paid them; but when they can amount to thousands of dollars, the apportionment of these costs should stand on the same basis as the indemnity payments. Whatever the reasons for the liability, indemnity payments or medical costs, the rules for sharing ought to be the same.

In spite of the recent increase in numbers of persons on the fund, the financial reserves appear to be more than adequate. Although some thought may be given to supplementing the fund with public appropriations to take care of cases in which the pre-existing disability was not industrially connected, the important thing is that the monies be available to meet the demands on the fund, including the necessary costs of administering and defending the fund. Whether the fund should be tapped for purposes extraneous to the problem of second injuries is largely an accounting matter. It would seem preferable, from a financial housekeeping point of view, to confine outlays from the fund to second injury purposes, but practical political exigencies may dictate otherwise. At any rate, there seems to be little point in allowing idle cash balances to accumulate. To go to the other extreme of putting the fund on a "pay-as-you-go" basis may be equally inadvisable. It would be possible, starting with present reserves, to place the fund on a fully-funded or partially-funded basis. The future potential liabilities of the fund could be calculated on an actuarial basis, and the contributions assessed according to need of the fund each year. These contributions could be divided among the carriers and self-insurers proportionately, according to the compensation paid or premiums written. Some such scheme would accomplish the desired goal of bringing contributions more nearly in line with the needs of the fund.

An incidental consideration may be mentioned, although it is more important from the equity point of view than the financial one. Employers not required to insure are not required to contribute anything to the fund, and yet their employees are entitled to reimbursement under appropriate conditions. If contributions are to be assessed on the basis of compensation paid, it would be administratively feasible to require these employees to contribute to the fund. Such assessments could be made at the same time the compensation awards or direct settlements are made.

A good second injury fund law, combined with sound administration and wide publicity, should help to scotch the fears of employers that their compensation liability will be increased if they employ handicapped workers, regardless of these workers' known pre-existing conditions or subsequent disability if an accidental injury should occur. An ideal second injury fund should not allow administrators to settle difficult cases of, say, older workers by shifting liability from the employer, on whose shoulders it belongs, to all employers as a group. If such a change in the method of financing compensation is to be made, it ought to be made openly, frankly, and not under the guise of second injury legislation.

Chapter 10

HEART CASES AND RADIATION HAZARDS —
TWO UNRESOLVED PROBLEMS

In workmen's compensation, as in any other social insurance program, the passage of time brings problems which test the viability of the program. Threats to its existence can come from changes in the medical, industrial or economic world, or from developments and trends in the program itself. Some of these challenges have already been discussed. Inflation threatens the stability of the benefit structure; the system tends to be unable to keep up with medical advances in rehabilitation, and so on. The list could be extended further, but two problem areas have been singled out for special discussion. One stems from trends and interpretations in the compensation field, although it is certainly not unrelated to changes in medical thinking. This is the whole problem of the degenerative diseases and their treatment under workmen's compensation. Another arises by reason of discoveries in the scientific field and the application of this new knowledge to industry. This is the area of radiation hazards, which poses the problem of whether the system can adapt itself to encompass, if not a new problem, at least one with which compensation has never had to deal to the extent that it may have to, in view of the proposed applications of atomic energy to industry. Examination of these two problem areas will give some perspective with which to judge the future of workmen's compensation.

Degenerative Diseases — The Heart Cases

In the main the problems of degenerative diseases have come to the fore only since the compensation laws have been broadened to include all occupational diseases. We have chosen to illustrate the problems with the example of the heart disease cases, but the developments have broader applicability.

In the case of heart disease, as well as any other disease or disability, the employee must show that his injury was the result of an accident which arose out of and in the course of employment before he is eligible for workmen's compensation benefits. Stated as simply as possible, the phrase "in the course of employment" means during employment, while the worker is under the effective direction of his employer. Problems are encountered in interpreting this phrase, especially in the so-called "coming and going" cases, when the employee is on his way to work, or is returning from work, or is on some errand for his employer and makes some detour, and so on. Decisions in individual cases are of fundamental importance to the litigants, but essentially they pose borderline legal questions which are best left to the law textbooks. We cannot, however, ignore some aspects of the interpretation of this phrase, because it is intimately connected with its companion phrase, "arising out of employment."

Suppose an employee falls and severely injures his head on the factory floor during an epileptic seizure. Granted that this occurred in the course of employment, would it be compensable, would it be an accident which arose out of employment? One could argue in the negative, on the grounds that the man was subject to seizures, that the accident would have occurred if he had not been at work, and that nothing in the work environment caused the injury. Suppose, however, he fell and hit his head against some moving machinery and was injured in this fashion. Could it then be argued that the same disability would have resulted if he had not been at work? One could argue that if it had not been for the moving machinery, his injury would not have been the same, and that even if it would have been, the machinery contributed, in some measure, to the final result. In New Jersey, the worker who hit his head on the floor would probably not collect compensation, whereas the worker whose head met the machinery probably would.[1]

This may seem like a distinction without a difference, a strange flight from reality on the part of the legal profession, fond as it is of making abstruse distinctions. But this may be too harsh a judgment. Two things must be recognized as basic to the theory of compensation law. One is that the employer takes the man as he finds him, with all of his weaknesses and predispositions to accidents and diseases; the other, that in the State of New Jersey there is no apportionment of liability in the ordinary case. Either the employer is liable or he is not. If the work situation contributes to the cause of the injury, in any degree, then the employer becomes wholly liable for the compensation benefits. Given these basic postulates, the fact the man was subject to the seizures, or the fact that he might have been injured in much the same manner and with the same results if he had been at home, would not defeat the compensation claim. It can be argued that the work situation, the moving machinery, did *contribute* to the final result. Some part of the rationale for this thinking will be discussed below.

Courts have dealt in a variety of ways with difficult borderline cases in which there has been some doubt about whether an accident arose out of employment.[2] At one time, courts insisted that in order to collect compensation benefits, the worker must encounter some risk peculiar to his employment, and not a risk to which the general public was exposed. This was abandoned in favor of the "increased risk"

---

[1]*Henderson* v. *Celanese Corp.*, 16 N.J. 208 (1954), and *Reynolds* v. *Passaic Valley Sewerage Commissioners*, 130 N.J.L. 437 (Sup. Ct. 1943), *affirmed* 131 N.J.L. 327 (E. and A. 1944). The distinction between these cases is discussed by Robert E. Rodes, Jr., in "Workmen's Compensation," *Rutgers Law Review*, XI (1956-1957), 142-144.

[2]Arthur Larson, "The Legal Aspects of Causation in Workmen's Compensation," *Rutgers Law Review*, VIII (1953-1954), 423-434. For a fuller discussion, see Arthur Larson, *Workmen's Compensation Law* (Albany: Matthew Bender and Co., 1952), I, chapter 3.

test, under which it was necessary for the claimant to show the existence of a quantitatively greater risk than would be encountered by the public, even though the risk was not peculiar to his employment. The increased risk test gave way to an "actual risk" doctrine, under which the employee merely had to demonstrate that the risk he encountered was actually a risk associated with his employment, even though others who were not working also ran the same type of risk.

New Jersey courts have moved further and have adopted what has been variously termed a "positional risk," a "but for" or a "neutral risk" doctrine; this theory combines, in effect, the arising and the course factors. If an employee's job duties bring him to the place where he is injured at the time of the accident, compensation will be granted, provided the risk is a neutral one, and not one personal to the worker.

Thus, in the Gargiulo case, a clerk was in the back of the shop burning trash when he was blinded by an arrow shot by a boy playing in the neighborhood.[3] The compensation award was upheld on the grounds that the clerk's work duties placed him in the position of danger. But for the fact that he was engaged in the work of the employer, he would not have been hit at the time he was. The decision would have been different if it had been shown that the person who shot the arrow was motivated by personal animus against the clerk. If the archer had sworn revenge for some real or fancied wrong, the fact that the clerk was attacked while at work would not make the disability compensable. The risk must be a neutral one.

This is further illustrated in the Howard case, in which an employee was savagely attacked by a fellow employee.[4] There was some doubt as to the motive for the attack. One side claimed that the attacker was thwarted in a robbery attempt, whereas the other alleged he was the victim of an insane delusion. The court refused to make the choice, holding that the employee was entitled to compensation in either case. In so doing, the court specifically adopted the "positional risk," or "but for" doctrine. The court cited the Gargiulo case and an earlier case which involved a compensation claim growing out of a fight between two truck drivers that took place as an aftermath of a traffic accident. In the latter case the court had stated: "...without the collision of the trucks there would not have been an inquiry for the license number, and but for the inquiry there would not have been an exchange of words, and without the exchange of words there would not have been an assault.[5]

The employer in the Howard case contended that the adoption of the "but for" test (reminiscent of the saying "but for the nail the shoe was lost," and so on) would, inevitably, make the employer the guarantor of every evil that might befall a workman within the physical time and space of his employment. The court thought otherwise, pointing out that a standard of reasonable probability is implied. It must be shown

---

[3] *Gargiulo* v. *Gargiulo*, 13 N.J. 8 (1953).
[4] *Howard* v. *Harwood's Restaurant Co.*, 25 N.J. 72 (1957).
[5] *Sanders* v. *Jarka Corporation*, 1 N.J. 36 (1948).

that it is more probably true than not that the injury would have occurred at the time and place of employment than at another time or place; also, it is necessary to show that the risk was a neutral one. In the Howard case, the court recognized that the employer had no control over the irrational impulses of a workman and that it was not a risk directly related to employment, but maintained that it was at least a neutral risk.

The justification for this type of reasoning is summarized neatly by Larson: "...if it is said that the harm has nothing to do with the employment it is equally true that it has less to do with the claimant personally; it has more to do with the employment than with the personal life of the claimant, since the employment contributed the one slender causal fact: if it had not been for the duties or conditions of employment, the injury would not have happened."[6]

Granted the impeccability of the legal logic involved, these cases do broaden the scope of the phrase "arising out of and in the course of employment," and hence the range of injuries for which the employer is responsible. But there is still the word "accident" to be considered. In the Gargiulo and Howard cases there can be little doubt that an accident occurred, but other cases cause trouble. Generally speaking, the word "accident" can refer to the cause or to the result. For example, if a worker is struck on his forehead by a flying bolt, which inflicts a deep gash, the accident may be considered as the specific incident which caused the gash; or the accident may be considered as the result, or the injury itself. It may seem that it makes little difference, except perhaps to the safety statisticians, how this is decided; but the distinction can be important.[7] Consider the case of a man who lifts 100-pound sacks of flour day in and day out. One morning, while engaged in this lifting, he strains his back and becomes disabled to the extent that he cannot continue working. Has an identifiable accident occurred within the meaning of the compensation law?

In 1913, a New Jersey court, borrowing words from an English decision of a decade earlier, defined an accident as "an unlooked for

[6] Larson, "The Legal Aspects of Causation in Workmen's Compensation," p. 427.

[7] The safety statisticians have struggled with the problem, and some now recognize the usefulness of making a distinction. It is possible to define the incident as the "accident" and to compile data on causes of "accidents" defined in this fashion. Thus, in the above example, the accident may have been caused by someone not fastening a nut on the bolt. Determination of such causes can lead to clues for changes in existing safety practices. The result of the accident, the gash on the forehead, would be defined as the "injury," and it is obviously useful to know and classify the causes of the injury separately, and apart, from the causes of the accident. In this case, the injury was caused by a flying object, the part of the body injured was the forehead, and so on. The statistician clearly satisfies his purposes by separating the identifiable incident from the result and calling one the accident and the other the injury. As will be seen, the compensation tribunals have other and more complex problems. This distinction between accident and injury is advocated by Frank S. McElroy of the Industrial Hazards Division, Bureau of Labor Statistics, United States Department of Labor. See "A Modification of Z16.2" (an undated mimeographed release of the Bureau of Labor Statistics). Z16.2 refers to The American Standard Method of Compiling Industrial Accident Causes, Z16.2 (N. Y.: American Standards Association, 1941).

mishap or untoward event which is not expected or designed."[8] The man lifting flour was doing nothing on the day of his injury that he had not been doing on other days. Nothing untoward or unexpected can be discovered in the tasks he was performing. But if the word accident refers to the *result*, rather than to the *cause*, then it is not difficult to pick out the untoward, undesigned and unexpected result. He did not expect the strained back: This was an unlooked for mishap.

The same problems can be illustrated in the case of an employee who drops dead from a heart attack while at work performing routine tasks. No one can deny the unexpected quality of this act. But if the term accident is applied to the result, and it is not necessary to show an accidental cause, then does the employer become responsible for death benefits regardless of the cause of the coronary occlusion? Not quite, since the employer's responsibility would depend on whether the accident, the resultant heart attack, actually arose out of employment. Note, however, that it may be extraordinarily difficult to demonstrate such causal connection, especially if it is not necessary to show that any special exertion or unusual activity precipitated the attack. More of this later.

There is another ingredient in the accident definition of most jurisdictions which, at first glance, would seem to dispose of the problem. The accident must be "traceable, within reasonable limits, to a definite time, place and occasion or cause."[9] Here again, however, the same difficulties apply. Is the reference to the cause or to the result, to the incidents surrounding the event or to the resulting injury? Actually, both interpretations may be placed upon both of these requirements of unexpectedness, and of a definite time and place.[10] To compound confusion, some courts have admitted that the injury may be the unexpected event, but that in order for it to be accidental, it must be the result of unusual conditions or unusual exertion, and not merely produced by the usual work performed in the usual fashion.[11]

New Jersey, for a time, was committed to the unusual exertion theory and then dropped it for everything but heart cases. Thus, in New Jersey, if an employee after mere routine exertion suffers a back injury or ruptures a intervertebral disc, he could collect compensation. If climatic conditions on the job cause heat exhaustion, sunstroke, or frozen fingers, an employee's claim may prevail. He may be called upon to show that the risk of his employment was greater than that experienced by the general public, but not that there was anything unusual about the conditions at the time of the injury. Routine job exposure which causes pneumonia follows the same rule.[12] But until 1958,

[8] *Bryant, Adm'x* v. *Fissel*, 84 N.J.L. 72 (Sup. Ct. 1913).

[9] *Liondale Bleach Dye and Paint Works* v. *Riker*, 85 N.J.L. 426 (1914).

[10] Larson, *Workmen's Compensation Law*, p. 514.

[11] Stefan Riesenfeld and Richard Maxwell, *Modern Social Legislation* (Brooklyn, The Foundation Press, 1950), p. 200.

[12] A back injury was involved in *Mills* v. *Monti Christi Corporation*, 10 N.J.S. 162 (1950), *petition for certification denied*, 6 N.J. 315 (1951); heat exhaustion in *Douglas* v. *Riggs Disler Co.*, 120 N.J.L. 583 (1938); sunstroke in *Higham* v. *Preakness Hills Country Club*, 10 N.J.

employees suffering from myocardial infarcts or coronary occlusions, as distinguished from ruptures and hemorrhages, had to show that some unusual strain or exertion caused the injury. In these cases, the court was applying the term "accident" to the cause, and not merely to the result.

These are cases in which the employee may have had a medical history of heart trouble, and the thrombosis could possibly have occurred at any time or any place. If it happened while at work, the New Jersey courts were constrained to look for some unusual exertion, some incident that could be identified as the accident, before they were willing to grant compensation. The search for the unusual exertion could lead to some strange results, but at least the doctrine served to prevent compensation payments in many cases in which employment conditions did not contribute to the final result.[13]

In the Lohndorf case, decided in 1946, the court held that there was a presumption that any death from heart disease is the result of natural causes and that "to render an injury compensable, there must be an accident or happening beyond the mere employment itself, which brings about the result or contributes thereto, and without which the injury or death would not have resulted ... to hold otherwise is to constitute an employer an insurer of the health and life of his employees."[14]

In the 1949 Seiken case, the employee worked as a "snapper" or a straw boss. As part of his duties, he assisted other employees in loading and unloading materials and in keeping the yard clean of scrap. In the course of his work he suffered a heart attack after he and a co-worker lifted a piece of scrap weighing between 200 and 250 pounds, a task the court found to be a usual one in his particular job. Compensation was denied on the grounds that no evidence of unusual strain or exertion was produced to rebut the presumption that a heart ailment was due to natural causes.[15]

Shortly after the Seiken decision, it became apparent that the unusual strain or exertion doctrine would be confined specifically to heart cases. This was clearly stated in the Neylon case, in which the employee suffered a sacroiliac sprain following usual exertion. The injury was orthopedic, and hence presumptively traumatic, and no proof of unusual strain or exertion was required.[16] The line was drawn in rather fine fashion. Compensation would be granted in the so-called "breakage" cases, the rupturing of an intervertebral disc or even a cerebral hemorrhage, following usual exertion.[17] The fact that something broke or let go in some part of the body was likened to the usual

Misc. 889 (1930); frozen fingers in *Matthews* v. *Woodbridge Township*, 14 N.J. Misc. 143 (1936); and pneumonia in *Richter* v. *E. J. Dupont*, 118 N.J.L. 404 (1937).

[13] Larson, "Legal Aspects in Workmen's Compensation," pp. 430-431.

[14] *Lohndorf* v. *Peper Bros. Paint Co.*, 134 N.J.L. 156 (Sup. Ct. 1946), *affirmed* 135 N.J.L. 352 (E. and A. 1947).

[15] *Seiken* v. *Todd Dry Dock, Inc.*, 2 N.J. 469 (1949).

[16] *Neylon* v. *Ford Motor Co.*, 10 N.J. 325 (1952).

[17] Larson, *Workmen's Compensation Law*, I, 519-525.

traumatic injury, and it was not necessary to rebut the presumption that this was due to natural causes.

From a legal point of view this distinction was unsatisfactory. For one thing, it meant that the term "accident" was to be applied to the result in most cases, but to the cause in the generalized heart cases. It also meant that the courts were hard put to distinguish between the usual and the unusual — a task of inordinate difficulty in borderline cases.

The necessity for making the distinction was eliminated by the 1958 decision in the Ciuba case. Frank Ciuba worked as a millwright, setting up machinery weighing as much as 500 pounds; on occasion he handled pieces weighing as much as 1,500 pounds. After installing an oven-drive unit, which required him to lift machinery weighing between 200 and 300 pounds, he suffered a myocardial infarction, followed by immediate disablement and death ten days later.

Ciuba had consulted a doctor fifteen years before, and his complaint had been diagnosed as angina pectoris, but there had been no symptomatic recurrence of the condition. The deputy director and the lower court denied his widow compensation on the grounds that there was no proof of unusual strain, nor was there any showing that the coronary incident was related to any occupational disease or hazard.

The Supreme Court reversed the decision. It stated that the accident requirement was to apply to the result, and not the cause, in heart cases, as well as in other types of injuries or diseases. An accident occurs: "...where a heart ravaged by disease succumbs to strain or exertion arising from doing the master's work, even though it be but a normal incident of services in no sense extraordinary, and such as a sound heart could withstand."[18] This was a recognition of the doctrine that the employer takes the man as he finds him and that a compensable injury occurs if employment conditions aggravate or accelerate the progress of a pre-existing disease or physical infirmity. As the court saw it, the basic question was not whether an accident caused the injury, but rather whether the accident, that is, the accidental injury, the myocaridal infarct, came from the disease alone, or whether the employment contributed to it. This leaves the essential issue as one of medical causation, rather than one of a determination of whether an accident, in the sense of an accidental cause, did or did not happen.

While the decision in the Seiken case was specifically overruled, the court affirmed the holding that it is to be presumed that injury or death from heart disease is the result of natural physiological causes; and the onus was placed upon the claimant to prove, by a preponderance of the probabilities, that the employment was a contributing cause of the injury or death. Note that employment conditions need not be the sole cause, but merely a contributory cause. The difficulty of showing this in cases of coronary occlusion, myocarditis or dilatation of the heart was admitted; nonetheless, the issue becomes one of sustaining

---

[18] *Agnes Ciuba* v. *Irvington Varnish and Insulator Co.*, 27 N.J. 127 (1958).

this burden of proof, and not one of showing the existence of an unusual strain. In large part, this is a factual issue for the deputy directors to determine; the courts' principal function is to lay down the guide lines to show the necessary quanta of proof and to determine if the tests have been met.

When it comes to deciding whether the disability arose out of employment, the standard is one of "reasonable probability," and not one of certainty. In the Ciuba case, the court found irresistible the inference that the physical exertion of doing the work aggravated the disease and brought on the fatal collapse. It conceded that the occlusion and the exertion could have been coincidental but also that the exertion could have precipitated the occlusion, and it was felt that the latter was the more probable hypothesis.

Given the trend of New Jersey decisions, the Ciuba decision was almost inevitable. There was simply no sound legal reason to treat heart cases differently from the other cases. If we compensate the man with a weak back for a sacroiliac sprain after routine exertion, or the epileptic who has a seizure and falls against the machinery, then there is no sound legal reason why the man with the impaired heart should be denied compensation simply because the evidence does not show unusual exertion or strain, as these terms may be defined. But two very practical problems emerge as a result of these decisions. One relates to the difficult and essentially medical problem of deciding whether the employment caused the injury, and the second relates to the possible employment effects of the decisions.

Although the onus is placed upon the claimant, he need only show that employment contributed in some slender manner, and not necessarily that it was the principal cause of the injury. Even this does not have to be sustained with certainty, but merely with reasonable probability, as the standard of persuasion. Given the present state of medical knowledge, however, the relationship between normal, routine exertion on the job and coronary occlusions is something on which the medical experts violently disagree.

This is nowhere better illustrated than in an IAIABC panel discussion on the effect of exertion on the production of coronary occlusion. One distinguished doctor on the panel had this to say: "The one thing that I cannot emphasize too strongly ... is that attacks of coronary insufficiency or angina pectoris, or myocardial infarction with or without thrombosis, occur with sufficient frequency among employees engaged in work involving strenuous physical strain and emotional stress, as to invalidate those opinions which hold that these events are purely coincidental."[19]   On the other hand, his medical colleague on the panel, after reviewing studies of three pathologic groups, stated: "Therefore, if we accept these conclusions, as I believe we must, then we must also

---

[19]Moses Barron, a panel member discussing the topic "The Effect of Exercise, Exertion and Excitement on the Production of Coronary Occlusion," in *Workmen's Compensation Problems*, IAIABC *Proceedings*, 1957 (United States Department of Labor, Bureau of Labor Standards, Bulletin 195), p. 86.

agree that attacks of coronary occlusion arise from progressive arteriosclerotic disease within the arterial wall, and that exercise, exertion, or excitement are not precipitating events, but merely coincidental occurrences." [20]

The medical consultant to a Moreland Act Commission in New York sampled expert medical opinion on this question of the relation of work to heart disease.[21] A majority of the 398 physicians responding were of the opinion that work does not produce heart disease, and that coronary occlusion occurring during moderately heavy work without unusual exertion is not causally related to employment.

But these were not unanimous opinions. This is further shown in the responses to a hypothetical question relating to the case of a sixty-year-old man who was employed for twenty years at a job which required the lifting of 100-pound weights. During the course of this customary work, it is supposed that he develops a coronary occlusion with a myocardial infarction. The specific question asked was whether the doctor would consider the attack to be causally related to the lifting of the weight.

A total of 185, or 46.6 per cent, of the doctors gave some sort of an affirmative answer: either that there was some causal relationship or a possible relationship, or that the work precipitated the attack, or that a myocardial infarction could have occurred without an occlusion; 197, or 49.5 per cent, of the physicians believed that there was no causal relationship between his employment and the attack. Sixteen of the physicians felt that the question could not be answered.

Such questionnaires have limited value because each case may be different from the next. Also, medical truths cannot be reached by democratic voting procedures. The findings are presented merely to indicate the lack of agreement among the medical experts.[22] Although one might conclude that reliable determination of the causes of an

---

[20] *Ibid.*, p. 94 (Charles N. Honsel).

[21] Joseph M. Callahan, *Costs, Operations, and Procedures under the Workmen's Compensation Law of the State of New York* (N. Y.: January 28, 1957). The medical consultant to the commission was Dr. Hermann Ehrlich. A summary of his findings is presented by Callahan on p. 13. Details of the study are set forth in Appendix A of the report.

[22] In a California study, a panel of physicians reviewed the abstracts of 398 cardiac cases decided by the California Industrial Accident Commission in which compensation had been awarded on the theory that there was a causal connection between the employee's disability and his employment. Five physicians reviewed each of the cases for a total of 1,990 reviews. In 786 reviews (39.5 per cent), the doctors agreed with the judgment of the commission that there was some employment connection; and in 796 reviews (40.0 per cent), they did not; 408 reviews resulted in an undecided answer. Of 240 reviews made by board-certified cardiologists, 94 of these were in agreement with the judgment of the commission; 107, or nearly 20 per cent, of the specialists were undecided. In only 47 of 319 cases did the five reviewers agree among themselves. As a matter of fact, there was not complete agreement by physicians even with themselves when, to test the results, the same case was given to the same person for a second review. Rodney M. Beard presented the results of the study with accompanying tables as part of a panel discussion on "Industrial Compensation Aspects of Heart Disease," in *Employment and Heart Disease* (proceedings of the first Western Conference presented by the California Heart Association and its affiliates in cooperation with the Institute of Industrial Relations, University of California, Berkeley, 1955), pp. 42-58.

attack is not possible, the fact remains that this issue must be settled by the hearing officer, in one fashion or the other. It becomes a factual medical issue, the resolution of which is sometimes predicated upon the answer of an expert medical witness to a hypothetical question asked during the compensation hearing. Because there is a substantial body of medical opinion which holds that normal exertion can produce an occlusion, a spate of cases in which compensation is granted for various types of heart failures must inevitably follow the Ciuba decision. The findings, in accordance with the preponderance of probabilities, will be that employment conditions contributed to the occlusion and that the employer should be liable. The accident requirement is no longer available to prevent compensation for injuries or death not caused in any substantial degree by work.

Does this make the employer the insurer of the health and life of his employees, as the court predicted in the Lohndorf case? Is workmen's compensation well on its way to becoming a general health insurance program? Are the flood gates now open so that every internal failure becomes an accident, just because it happens? Larson believes not. He cites the examples of states that have no statutory requirement that an accident be demonstrated before compensation can be awarded and claims that "...an examination of California, Iowa and Massachusetts cases will show that getting an exertion or exposure award is no 'pushover' there, the only difference is that the battle is fought on the fundamental causation issue."[23]

But California and Massachusetts are two states in which the second problem comes to the fore, the problem of the employment of cardiacs. A California attorney calls that state's treatment of heart cases in compensation "one of the biggest barriers to the employment of those afflicted with heart disease." He goes on to say that in California "...any employer that indulges in a free and uninhibited cardiac employment policy would be either: first, ignorant of the law, or secondly, so altruistic and public-spirited that he was willing to subordinate the interests of his company and its stockholders and pay the economic penalty for such a policy."[24]

It goes without saying that it is to the interest of everyone, employee, employers, and the community, to see to it that no worker is placed in a job that may constitute a hazard to his health and safety. But, if properly placed, cardiacs can and do work successfully. Of course, sooner or later, the worker is going to die and perhaps as a result of a cardiac failure. The Ciuba decision has certainly increased the probabilities that if this should happen while the man is employed, the employer will become liable for a substantial compensation award. This may mean that a burden has been placed upon the employer which does not properly belong to him; but, more important, the employer

[23] Larson, *Workmen's Compensation Lcv*, I, 564.
[24] Remarks of Howard J. Scott during panel discussion on the subject of "Industrial Compensation Aspects of Heart Disease," in *Employment and Heart Disease*, p. 74.

may now become leery about hiring others with weakened heart conditions.

The employment effects of this decision have not been missed in New Jersey. The Rehabilitation Commission cites the statistics on death from heart diseases, pointing out that they are the number one killer; that in the nation, 635,000 man-years are lost each year in industry due to heart disease disabilities; and that about 30 per cent of the persons who die from cardiovascular-renal diseases are of working age. The fear is expressed that the broadened coverage of heart cases under workmen's compensation will mean a further increase in insurance costs, in employers screening out physically impaired workers, and in their refusal to hire job seekers who are victims of heart disease. [25]

On the one hand, we have medical science making rapid strides toward rehabilitation of cardiacs, with work as part of the prescribed regimen; and on the other, we have logical, supposedly liberal and humanitarian trends in workmen's compensation which may prevent the employment of those so afflicted. [26] A bushel of suggestions has been advanced to solve this problem, but none of them is guaranteed to work, nor would any of them be easy to put into effect.

One suggestion is to reinstate the requirement of an accident, by legislative, judicial or administrative action. [27] The purpose would be to spell out the degree of unexpectedness required, the definitiveness of the occurrence, and the extent to which these criteria would apply to the cause or the result. This, of course, would mean that we are right back to trying to distinguish between usual and unusual exertion, with all the attendant problems.

An opposite type of suggestion advanced is to be content with the elimination of the accident requirement as it applies to the cause, and to concentrate on improving methods of determining whether employment contributed to the disability. It has been suggested that a committee composed of medical men be asked to devise standards for determining causal relationships between employment and the cardiac and degenerative diseases. [28] Utah has gone even further. In that state, a medical panel has drawn up a set of principles and criteria for compensation of heart cases, and members of the panel advise the compensation commission in individual cases. [29] The idea of an expert medical panel has been discussed in connection with the problem of permanent

---

[25] New Jersey Rehabilitation Commission, "Monthly Report of Operations," May, 1958.

[26] Morton Lane, *The Effect of the New York Workmen's Compensation Law Upon the Employment of the Handicapped* (N. Y.: The Institute of Physical Medicine and Rehabilitation, New York University-Bellevue Medical Center, Rehabilitation Monograph XI, 1956), p. 43.

[27] Callahan, pp. 14-15.

[28] Lane, pp. 47-48.

[29] L. E. Viko, "Medico-Legal Problems of the Heart in Relationship to Injury," *Utah Bar Bulletin*, XXIII (March, 1953), 47-58. Also, remarks of Richard J. Clark, panelist discussing, "Medical Aspects in Determining Responsibility in Heart Cases," in *Workmen's Compensation Problems*, IAIABC *Proceedings*, 1956 (United States Department of Labor, Bureau of Labor Standards, Bulletin 192), p. 122.

partial disabilities, and much the same advantages and disadvantages would obtain in the heart cases. It is worth noting that nothing in New Jersey's procedures bars the use of impartial medical advice if the deputy feels that it would be helpful in resolving an issue in a case.

Another suggestion is to reintroduce a system of waivers into compensation. Employees over a certain age would be allowed to waive their rights to compensation for the aggravation of a degenerative disease.[30] This may amount to solving the problem by ignoring it, and it would be a return to practices which have been abandoned in some jurisdictions only after years of struggle. The one telling argument in favor of this proposition is that employees may be better off without compensation protection for jobs they can get than with theoretical compensation protection for jobs which may be denied them.

It has been advocated that the second injury or One Per Cent Fund provisions be used to fill the breach. As has already been discussed, the present New Jersey One Per Cent Fund provisions specifically exclude cases in which the second injury aggravates a pre-existing condition; but even if this provision were removed, there seems to be little hope from this method of dealing with the problem.

In the case of a person with an orthopedic handicap, there is no good reason to assume that he will be any more susceptible to a second injury than an unimpaired person. But the passage of time alone aggravates a degenerative disease. A person with a cardiac condition is more likely to suffer from a coronary episode than a person without such a history.[31] Even if the cardiac condition were classified as a pre-existing disability for which the employer was not liable, the incidence of subsequent disabilities is likely to be greater. This alone may make employers hesitant about hiring such people.

Another point is relevant. Unless radical changes are made in financing the fund, assessments against it become a liability of industry as a whole. Even if a single employer could be indifferent to these charges and hence not hesitate to employ persons with these handicaps, the same would not necessarily be true of all employers or insurance carriers considered as a group. It can be expected that they would make their views known about the appropriate hiring policy employers should follow. As mentioned above, certain changes in New Jersey's One Per Cent Fund law seem desirable for their own sake, but it would be a sham and delusion to hold out these amendments as a final solution to the employment problems of persons with degenerative diseases.

More radical solutions proceed on the theory that many claims involve both physical strain or emotional disturbance and pre-existing pathology, and that it is simply impossible to separate these factors in any meaningful fashion. One suggestion is to reduce the compensation award in such cases by a legislatively determined percentage and to have the difference paid as a benefit under some other social

---

[30]Lane, p. 49.
[31]Lane, pp. 48-49.

insurance program. In New York, it has been advocated that the difference be paid under the Disability Benefits Law and that this statute be revised to include medical care and dependents' benefits. [32]

It is possible to go further and advocate that the degenerative disease be taken out of compensation entirely and that benefits be paid under some other social insurance scheme. Under such a proposal, it would not become necessary to determine whether employment contributed to the condition. The fact that the condition existed would be sufficient to enable the employee to collect benefits. If such a scheme were adopted for the degenerative diseases, there might be compelling reasons to argue that it should be extended to other types of cases. This would mean the abandonment of the traditional workmen's compensation arrangements in favor of some integrated scheme of social insurance, a prospect that will be considered in the final chapter.

Radiation Hazards

Radiation hazards are not an entirely new phenomena either to the general public or to workers in industry. Ever since the universe began, certain amounts of radiation have been present, and the famous incident of the radium dial painters caused a flurry of concern over this problem more than a generation ago. But the dawn of the atomic age in 1939 changed the dimensions of the problem.

Radiation can come from various sources. Radon and thoron gases are always present in the air; the soil and drinking water contain a certain amount of radioactive materials; marketed products may contain radium; and cosmic rays from outer space may add to the radiation to which an individual is exposed. Medical and dental X-rays are another possible source, and there is some fall-out from the testing of atomic weapons. [33] But from the standpoint of workmen's compensation, the significant problem arises from the industrial uses of atomic energy.

The Atomic Energy Commission, in May, 1957, had less than 7,000 employees, and most of these were professional and clerical employees who were not exposed to radiation hazards and who did not come within the scope of the various state compensation laws. At this time, however, a total of approximately 112,000 nongovernmental employees were engaged in contract work for the commission. [34] Almost all of them ran

---

[32]Callahan, p. 14.

[33] J. F. Edge, Jr., "Evaluation and Control of Radiation Hazards," in *Workmen's Compensation Problems*, IAIABC *Proceedings*, 1955 (United States Department of Labor, Bureau of Labor Standards, Bulletin 186), p. 180. "Report of the Department of Labor Atomic Energy Study Group on Labor Implications of Atomic Energy" (United States Department of Labor, July 30, 1956), p. 52. See also excerpts from the "Report of the United Nations Scientific Committee on the Effects of Atomic Radiation," *The New York Times*, August 11, 1958, p. 6.

[34]Clay Shackelford, "Report of Atomic Energy Committee," in *Workmen's Compensation Problems*, IAIABC *Proceedings*, 1957, pp. 68-80. According to this report and the exhibits presented with it, the Atomic Energy Commission as of May, 1957, had granted 191 licenses for the use of radioactive isotopes in New Jersey, two licenses for the use of special nuclear materials, such as uranium 235, uranium 233 or plutonium, and 41 active source material

the risk of potential exposure to radiation, and, with inconsequential exceptions, all were covered by state compensation laws.

The program of peaceful application of atomic energy started after the second world war, but it received its significant impetus with the passage of the 1954 Atomic Energy Act, and it can fairly be said that the program is in its infancy. The responsibility for damage to persons and property is placed upon contractors who are licensees of the Atomic Energy Commission. The federal government is freed of all liability arising from these industrial uses of atomic energy. Licencees are required to carry insurance policies covering their liability under the applicable state compensation acts, with endorsements providing for unlimited medical coverage.

In general, there are two different types of radiation hazards.[35] One stems from external beam radiation and the other from radioactive particles or dustlike materials which may be ingested or inhaled and deposited in the body. When fission occurs in a reactor, alpha and beta particles and gamma and neutron rays are released. As an external source of radiation, alpha emitters may be insignificant. While they produce intense ionization, they can be stopped by a few sheets of paper or the human skin. Beta particles have less ionizing, but greater penetrating, power than the alpha particles. Although they can be stopped by a few millimeters of body tissue, they can penetrate the skin and cause lesions and internal injuries.

Gamma rays are physically similar to X-rays, but of different origin in the atom. They have great penetrating power and travel long distances before losing their energy by ionizing the air through which they pass. Neutron rays have no charge and produce ionization only indirectly through the production of charged nuclei. They move with the speed of light, travel great distances and have great penetrating power. They constitute primarily a radiation rather than an inhalation problem.

Radioisotopes taken inside the body present greater hazards than those encountered externally because the radioactive sources may be in contact with delicate body tissue, perhaps that of a critical organ. They irradiate continuously until eliminated, and their measurement and detection pose difficult problems. Exposure to radiation of any type may cause severe injury, shorten life or even result in genetic damage. In addition to radiation effects, some radioisotopes, such as strontium-90, pose other problems because of their extreme toxicity.

The acknowledged potential dangers from radiation hazards give rise to certain problems for workmen's compensation. It is an open question whether these problems are essentially different from problems posed by occupational diseases or even traumatic injuries. But they differ in degree, and the great amount of attention devoted to this

---

licenses in the state. As of this date, a total of 24 reactors and critical facilities were being operated by employers, other than the commission, in the nation as a whole. Licenses had been granted for 16 others, including one in the State of New Jersey.

[35] A concise description of various types of radiation hazards can be found in "Report of the Department of Labor Atomic Energy Study Group," pp. 52-55; and in Ege, pp. 180-185.

"new" hazard has served to focus attention on some critical unsolved issues in the fields of compensation and industrial health and safety.[36]

One source of these problems is that effects of exposure to radiation may not become apparent until twenty-five or thirty or more years after the date of exposure. Bone tumors were seen among the radium dial painters of the 1920's as little as two years after exposure; but in the case of one woman, a bone tumor, allegedly caused by this exposure, appeared in 1955, thirty-six years after her work experience. Admittedly, this is a lengthy period of latency, but it must be noted that diseases such as berryliosis, lung cancer from exposure to chrome, and so on, also may not manifest themselves until years after initial exposure. Another difficulty is that a worker cannot tell when he is being exposed to radiation. A moderate dose may go undetected and yet have serious consequences in the future, especially since continued low dose exposures can have a cumulative effect.[37]

In some jurisdictions, the limited coverage of occupational diseases makes it almost impossible to deal with radiation hazards under the workmen's compensation laws. Two states (Mississippi and Wyoming) do not include any occupational diseases within their compensation statutes.[38] Nineteen jurisdictions limit coverage to specific occupational diseases listed in their schedules. Thirteen of these include certain diseases due to radiation exposure, but there is no assurance that any and all possible effects would be covered in these jurisdictions. The remaining six of these jurisdictions, and of course the two which provide no occupational disease coverage, have solved the existing problems by the simple expedient of ignoring them. Thirty-three jurisdictions, including New Jersey, provide coverage for all occupational diseases, and the trend appears to be in the direction of providing blanket coverage.[39]

In jurisdictions whose compensation laws purport to cover the effects of radiation hazards, the facts that exposure may go by undetected, that latent periods may be lengthy and that the precise effects of the

---

[36] See for example Earl F. Cheit, "Radiation Hazards: A New Challenge to Workmen's Compensation," *Insurance Law Journal* (December, 1957), 743-751. The State of New Jersey has been alive to these problems. The Governor has appointed an Advisory Committee on Radiation Protection, and the Department of Labor and Industry has an actively functioning Committee on Atomic Energy and Radiation Safety.

[37] Robert J. Hasterlik, "Long Term Results of Radiation Exposure," in *Workmen's Compensation Problems*, IAIABC *Proceedings*, 1955, pp. 190-192. Also see Ashley St. Clair, "What Protection Do Present Day Workmen's Compensation Laws Afford Workers and Their Families Against Wage Loss for Disability or Death from Occupational Diseases?" (An address prepared for presentation at the Annual Convention of the IAIABC, September 9, 1958, pp. 5-6.)

[38] Montana might be included as another state which covers no occupational diseases under its workmen's compensation law. However, a separate act in that state allows payments from public funds to persons totally disabled from silicosis.

[39] Information about coverage of occupational diseases in the various states is from *State Workmen's Compensation Laws* (United States Department of Labor, Bureau of Labor Standards, Bulletin 161, rev. August, 1957), pp. 18-20. See also St. Clair, Exhibits A, B and C. In New Jersey, blanket coverage of all occupational diseases has existed only since 1950.

hazards are not well established, give rise to basic difficulties. One of these has to do with the time limitations on filing of claims.

In any sort of compensation claim, the worker must give notice to his employer within a definite period of time. In New Jersey, the notice to the employer that the worker has contracted an occupational disease must be given within five months after the employee ceased to be exposed to the disease, or "within ninety days after the employee knew or ought to have known the nature of his disability and its relation to his employment, whichever period is later in duration,... "[40] Although this ninety-day period is short in comparison with that in some other states, it does allow calculation of the time from the date of *awareness of the disability*, and not just from the date of exposure. In eighteen states, the time for notifying the employer runs from date of last exposure, and this would preclude claims with long latent periods even if the causal relationship could be established.[41]

Notice to the employer is only part of the problem. In case of a disputed claim, timely notice must also be filed with the compensation tribunal. As with notice to the employer, the time can run either from the date of last exposure (or last day worked for the employer) or, as in the majority of jurisdictions, from date of disability, or the date the worker should have been aware of the disease or disability.

New Jersey's statute is a bit complicated. It bars claims for compensation unless a petition is filed within two years of date of exposure, or within one year after the worker knew, or should have known, about the disability, whichever is later. In case a direct settlement had been made on account of the occupational disease and the employer had been paying compensation, the claim must be filed within one year after the employer fails to make payment according to the agreement, or within two years after the date of the last payment.

If the statutes said only this, they could be classified as being able to meet the problem of radiation hazards, at least to the extent any statute of limitations is able to deal with this problem. But the law goes on to say that a compensable occupational disease claim is barred unless the petition is filed "within five years after the date on which the employee ceased to be exposed in the course of employment with the employer to such occupational disease."[42] The only exception provided is in the case of the death of an employee who had been receiving compensation on account of a disease. In such a situation, a petition by dependents would be timely if filed within two years after the date of last payment even if this was after the five-year period.

Given the fact that the latency period might run much beyond the five years specified, the law apparently would bar claims if the disability was discovered after this period of time, even if it could clearly be shown that the disability arose out of and in the course of a particular employment experience.

---

[40] N.J. Stat. Ann., 34:15-33 (West, 1958).
[41] Cheit, p. 746.
[42] N.J. Stat. Ann., 34:15-34.

A statute of limitations has its place in compensation law. Its purpose is to prevent abuses, to protect employers and to allow insurance carriers to set rates in a meaningful fashion; but given the five-year provision, radiation hazards would not be treated on a par with other occupational diseases which have shorter periods of latency. Although it may seem ludicrous to fix liability on an employer decades after the worker has left his employ, the fact remains that a worker may not suffer the consequences until years after the initial exposure to a radiation hazard.

One solution to the problem would be to delete from the statute the section which bars claims unless filed within five years after date of last exposure. This would still leave the other provisions which would allow a claim to be heard if it was filed within one year after the disability became apparent. If it is not feasible to eliminate the five-year period for all occupational diseases, then consideration could be given to making it inapplicable in the case of claims for radiation disease.

Other aspects of the compensation laws which cause concern are the medical care provisions. In New Jersey, the worker is entitled to unlimited medical and hospital care. The law contains monetary limitations, but these are almost automatically extended; and there is no real danger that the victim of radiation will be denied adequate medical care because of these statutory provisions. There is, however, the related matter of the choice of physician. Except under special circumstances, the worker must use the physician chosen by his employer or the insurance carrier.[43] The IAIABC 1957 Committee on Atomic Energy, recognizing that some physicians may not have the specialized knowledge necessary to cope with radiation hazards, has recommended that the compensation agency and the appropriate state medical body be authorized to designate attending physicians and hospital and rehabilitation facilities in cases of radiation injury and disease.[44]

This may be a step in the right direction, but it presupposes that the state agencies are a good deal more active in supervising medical care than many may actually do. These problems relating to the extent to which the agency ought to supervise medical care and rehabilitation are present in cases other than radiation cases. If some improvements were devised in the general method of supervising medical care, the benefits would undoubtedly spill over to the radiation cases. Of course, if the compensation agency were authorized to designate the attending physician, it would have a powerful weapon to enforce compliance with any recommendations it would make along these lines. To become effective such authorization would require not only a law amendment but also an expansion of personnel to undertake the necessary supervisory tasks. Very similar problems have already been discussed in connection with rehabilitation.

---

[43] N.J. Stat. Ann., 34:15-15.
[44] Clay Shackelford, "Report of Atomic Energy Committee," in *Workmen's Compensation Problems* IAIABC *Proceedings*, 1957, p. 73.

Radiation hazards magnify the ever-present problem of how to fix liability for compensation upon an individual employer. How can causality be established with the necessary degree of proof to substantiate a compensation claim against a particular employer? The difficulties are multiplied if the worker was exposed some years before and has worked for several employers since. Can it be established that the accident arose out of and in the course of employment with a particular employer? If the worker develops leukemia or a malignant tumor, or if he suffers genetic damage, not because of a single primary exposure, but because of cumulative exposure while working at various jobs, which employer shall be assessed?

These, of course, are some of the very problems which lie beneath the surface in other types of cases not connected with radiation hazards. The worker who has a coronary attack while working at a particular job may have suffered some undetected heart damage years before, while working in a different industry. Even the worker disabled by a traumatic injury may have acquired a predisposition to this type of accident sometime in the past, or a previous injury can compound and aggravate the effects of a subsequent accidental injury. Broadening legal concepts of causation brought these problems to compensation administrators years before atomic energy became important. Radiation hazards pose some long-standing problems in dramatic form.

Insofar as the problem of establishing the connection between employment and disability is concerned, it has been proposed that this be solved by changing the nature and quanta of proof required to establish this relationship. As things stand now, the burden of proof rests with the claimant. It has been recommended that this be shifted to the employer under certain circumstances. The employee would be required to show that his condition was the result, or the probable result, of radiation exposure; to demonstrate the top and bottom limits of the possible period of latency; and to show that radiation to which he could have been exposed existed in connection with his employment during that period. Such evidence would be available only if radiation exposure records were kept for all workers. These records would have to be accurately compiled and carefully preserved over the years by all employers engaged in operations with radiation hazards. This is especially important since nuclear workers may move from job to job and since the effects of exposure can be cumulative.

The recommendation is that once these facts have been demonstrated during litigation, a prima facie case of liability should be established. The responsibility would then be placed upon the employer to rebut the presumption that the injury resulted from the demonstrated exposure.[45] This is an extreme solution, which would fundamentally

---

[45]These are the recommendations of Sol D. Kapelsohn of the Committee on Atomic Energy and Radiation Safety appointed by the Commissioner of the New Jersey Department of Labor and Industry, March 22, 1957. Mr. Kapelsohn, a member of the committee, is an attorney who often represents petitioners in the compensation courts. His typewritten undated report is in the files of the New Jersey Division of Workmen's Compensation.

change existing evidential law, but it is difficult to chart any course that would assure compensation payments to affected workers without disturbing existing practices. As with other problems connected with the determination of cause of disability and its connection with employment, our knowledge is largely in terms of the over-all statistics and probabilities, which may not be applicable to an individual case. The probability of injury depends not only on the quantity and type of radiation absorbed, the length of time of absorption and the relative quantities absorbed by different parts of the body, but also on the individual's relative radiosensitivity. The amounts of radiation injurious to one person may not affect another.[46]

Even if it could be shown that the worker suffered a radiation disease due to some exposure, the problem would be one of fixing liability on a particular employer. This task becomes more difficult if the worker has been employed over the years in several employments, each with possible radiation hazards. Some states provide for a pro-rating of the liability among several employers, a task which requires extensive investigation and prolonged litigation. Because of this, a prominent representative of the insurance industry has recommended that the last of the several successive employers of a claimant be made solely liable for the total amount of compensation awarded.[47] It is claimed that this would save the time of compensation administrators and, in the final analysis, time and expense for employers and their insurance carriers.

Such a scheme could cause some employment difficulties for those workers whose cumulative records show them to be close to their maximum exposure limits, but it does have the virtue of preserving the traditional arrangements of fixing liability on a single employer. An IAIABC committee has taken a different tack in recommending that in cases of exposures in multiple employments, the employee should be eligible for benefits from the second injury fund.[48] In New Jersey, one recommendation has been made that a special radiation injuries fund

---

[46] In this connection, the Atomic Energy Study Group of the United States Department of Labor states: "... evidence for compensation claims based upon statistics of tolerance might frequently be unsatisfactory. For example, 1,500 roentgens of radiation has generally been assumed to be unharmful when delivered to a small area of the skin. In one authenticated case, however, a child developed a skin cancer twenty years after receiving such an amount of roentgen exposure. Moreover, since large numbers of persons are subjected to radiation in medical therapy, the effects of which might be identical, the determination of whether to ascribe a given condition to a medical exposure or job exposure presents additional difficulties." ("Report of the Department of Labor Atomic Energy Study Group," pp. 59-60.)

[47] St. Clair, p. 6. Mr. St. Clair is counsel to the Liberty Mutual Insurance Company. He discusses in his address another related insurance problem. An employer may be found liable for a compensation claim which was due to exposure in his plant over the course of many years. During this time, the employer may have placed his insurance business with various carriers. As Mr. St. Clair points out, the new Standard Provisions Workmen's Compensation and Employer's Liability Policy, put into use in 1954, provides that the insurance carrier on the risk on the last day of the last injurious exposure to conditions causing a disease is liable for all of the compensation due the claimant from that employer.

[48] Shackelford, p. 73.

be established with contributions from all employers (or their insurance carriers) who expect to offer employment in which an occupational radiation hazard is found to exist.[49] Use of such funds would bring us one step closer to placing the burden of industrial accidents and diseases on industry generally rather than on any one employer in particular.

The use of such funds raises other questions. During the period of latency, a nuclear worker may have been employed in several states, and exposure in each of his jobs may have contributed to his final disability. If a special radiation injuries fund were established, it would be logical to make it a nation-wide fund, with the possibility of having the federal government enter the picture in an administrative capacity. This would certainly weaken one of the basic tenets of the existing system.

Also, if radiation exposure can stem from other than employment-connected sources, and if it is difficult to distinguish among sources when it comes to a particular theory, why should liability be restricted to industry? Why not to the community or to society at large? If this were done, it would amount to removing these disabilities from the compensation system as it has traditionally been known. And if exceptions are made for radiation hazards, a list of ailments for other possible exceptions would not be difficult to propose. After all, this is exactly the same sort of problem encountered in discussing the degenerative diseases.

Radiation hazards pose other issues which can only be mentioned.[50] A person suffering genetic damage may not be handicapped in an employment sense. Even if it is deemed equitable to indemnify him, the real disability would become apparent only in his progeny; and nothing in the existing compensation laws would take their plight into account. Also, another type of problem is posed by the worker who has undergone exposure to the maximum permissible limit for a year or some other period of time. He may not be disabled in any physical sense, and yet safety considerations may prevent him from working at his accustomed job until some months have elapsed. This problem could be left for the unemployment insurance system rather than workmen's compensation, but there is also the case of a worker who has received his maximum permissible lifetime limit of exposure and who would forever be barred from working where he might possibly be exposed to radiation. Although such a worker who has not actually suffered any injury might not be eligible for cash indemnities, still he would be a candidate for rehabilitation services and retraining for another job. Even if rehabilitation services offered by workmen's compensation

---

[49] Report of Sol D. Kapelsohn.

[50] One listing of problems and issues is contained in the "Report of the Special Committee on Atomic Energy Law," prepared for the annual meeting of the American Bar Association, 1957. An excerpt from Section V of this report dealing with workmen's compensation has been mimeographed and distributed by the Bureau of Labor Standards of the United States Department of Labor (September, 1957).

were expanded, it is an open question whether a worker in such a situation would be eligible for such services.

Perhaps enough of the various problems have been discussed to make the point that radiation hazards, although not essentially different from other occupational disease hazards, may force us to reconsider the whole role of workmen's compensation. The one fundamental question is whether the system can accommodate itself to this challenge or whether it will have to be replaced by essentially different arrangements.

The IAIABC's 1958 atomic energy committee has expressed confidence that the problems of radiation hazards can be met within the present state system of workmen's compensation arrangements if some changes are made. It has recommended that the United States Atomic Energy Commission retain responsibility for the licensing of the construction, use and operation of nuclear reactors and for the possession and use of radioisotopes. At the same time, it is urged that the Atomic Energy Commission establish minimum standards for safety codes for operations which involve radiation hazards, and also standards for safety supervision and inspection methods and procedures. The committee also outlined minimum uniform workmen's compensation standards. These include provisions for maintaining individual exposure records for workers exposed to radiation in industry, to be kept at a central agency available to the individual worker; provisions for monitoring sources of radiation emissions; unlimited medical care, with authority given to the state agency to supervise such care; and provisions in state laws which would allow the time limitation for instituting a compensation claim, and notifying the employer of such intention, to run from the date the employee knew, or should have known, the injury was sustained. Also, the committee recommended the establishment of radiation injury claim funds in each state, to be made up of contributions from insurance carriers and self-insurers. Such a fund would pay all medical costs and compensation benefits in radiation hazards cases. In the opinion of the committee, placing the liability solely on the last employer would result in such employers refusing to hire workers who had long, or moderately long, experience in radiation industries.

The 1958 IAIABC committee recognized that the recommendations of previous IAIABC committees on this subject had been largely ignored. In order to give some force and effect to the recommended standards for both safety and workmen's compensation, it proposed that Congress permit the Atomic Energy Commission to issue licenses, contingent upon the states' adopting these minimum requirements. If such legislation is not in effect in a particular state before January 1, 1960, it proposed that the Atomic Energy Commission be authorized to refuse to issue new licenses and that it be empowered to recall old ones until such time as the standards are adopted.[51]

---

[51] "Report of Atomic Energy Committee," prepared for presentation at the Annual Convention of the IAIABC, September 9, 1958. Ned J. Parsekian, former director of New Jersey's Division of Workmen's Compensation, was chairman of this committee.

These recommendations are an ingenious attempt to preserve the state system of workmen's compensation and, at the same time, guarantee protection and benefits to possible industrial victims of radiation hazards. The difficulties involved in translating the recommendations into practice are enormous. An individual state radiation injuries fund poses problems in the case of workers who work in several states during their lifetime; supervision of medical care involves the expenditures of scarce or nonexistent funds, and so on. In addition, difficulties would be encountered in persuading Congress to authorize the Atomic Energy Commission to deny licenses in particular jurisdictions which failed to meet the suggested standards. At the same time, it must be recognized that there are no easy solutions to the problems posed by radiation hazards. Exhortation to the individual states to revise their compensation laws has not proved very fruitful. Perhaps basic reforms will come only after some dramatic incidents involving radiation injuries have come to the attention of the public. By that time it will be too late for many workers, and the dissatisfaction may result in some broad, sweeping changes which are not carefully designed to preserve existing workmen's compensation agreements.

Chapter 11

THE FUTURE OF WORKMEN'S COMPENSATION

In the past, general crises in state government or particular crises in the workmen's compensation program have brought forth a rash of criticisms, some of which have been detailed in foregoing chapters. In too many instances, the discussion has not been on the highest plane as one interest group attacked the other. The debates have so often focused on outstandingly outrageous individual instances, and not on a consideration of the program as a whole with its complex interrelationships. Perhaps this is the path we are doomed to follow until the whole program collapses from the weight of its own inadequacies.

On the whole, one must be rather pessimistic about the chances of arousing public opinion to support solutions for existing workmen's compensation problems. Perhaps the national programs of social security, which affect people more directly, have stolen the spotlight. The public may not be aware of all the technical aspects of the federal social security program, but a high proportion of the population expects to collect benefits one day. Congress is well aware that changes in the federal program are of continuing public interest and concern. The state legislatures probably feel no such comparable broad concern about workmen's compensation. The average worker is only mildly interested until he becomes hurt in the shop, an expectation he probably discounts liberally. Even should this happen, today, in contrast to the situation of a generation ago, he may look to his company-union plan for a share of his expected benefits. If dissatisfied with his treatment, his recourse may be to amend the collective bargaining agreement as much as to protest to the state legislature.

In light of these considerations, it is not being unrealistic to ask whether the compensation program can continue. Certainly, by this time, the statement that workmen's compensation faces a crisis has become a truism. But this question is still relevant: Can an essentially privately financed state program, under which individual employers are liable for industrial injuries without consideration of fault, and employees abjure negligence suits in exchange for a surer but more modest remedy, survive in its present form? The question demands a consideration of the alternatives to the present type of program. At the risk of drastic oversimplification, the following alternatives may be sketched:

One possibility would be to maintain the present system but to allow the workers access to a supplemental remedy of civil suits against employers if employer negligence can be shown.[1] If a worker were

---

[1] One prominent advocate of such a proposal is Samuel B. Horovitz, executive editor of

injured, he would prosecute his compensation case and also be allowed to file suit if he claimed that the employer was guilty of negligence. The legislature would have to lay down the ground rules for such suits and decide which, if any, of the traditional common law defenses would be allowed. If the employee were successful in his court action, some or all of the compensation award would be returned; if his suit failed, the compensation award would be allowed to stand.]

Current experience with automobile and personal negligence suits makes one wary of greeting this alternative with enthusiasm. High proportions of the amounts recovered would be swallowed up in court costs and attorneys' fees, and decisions would inevitably be delayed. But at least this form of lottery would result in substantial awards in some cases. The game might be worth the candle to the winner, for in the current situation extensive litigation results in niggardly awards. The contrast between compensation benefits and the munificent settlements detailed by the newspapers in personal negligence suits is striking.

[Industry is not likely to support such a change. In effect, this is what the employer thought he was rid of when the compensation system was adopted. Its reinstatement would mean that industry would have to bear the costs of compensation and, in addition, the costs of defending lawsuits and paying successful claimants the rather high awards.] Of course, if there is any truth in the allegation that compensation costs bring heightened safety consciousness, then the higher costs of the possible judgments ought to redouble employer efforts in this direction.

[If such a solution seems far-fetched, we need only recall that this is the alternative chosen in West Germany and Great Britain. In Great Britain, since 1946, the industrial injury benefits are paid from the National Insurance Fund maintained by employer and employee contributions.] These are flat uniform benefits, unrelated to an employee's wages, but somewhat higher than the benefits paid in the case of ordinary illnesses. Medical treatment is provided by the National Health Service. Compensation controversies are settled in Great Britain by administrative tribunals, with lawyers pretty largely excluded. Medical questions relating to extent of disability are determined by boards composed exclusively of medical practitioners. The right of an employee to file suit in the event of alleged negligence has been restored, with the fellow servant common law defense specifically abolished. No

National Association of Claimants' Compensation Attorneys, Law Journal. A discussion of this alternative is found in Herman and Anne Somers, *Workmen's Compensation: Prevention, Insurance and Rehabilitation of Occupational Disability* (N. Y.: John Wiley and Sons, 1954), pp. 191-193.

[2]Douglas Potter and D. H. Stansfeld, *National Insurance (Industrial Injuries)* (London: Butterworth, 1950). A résumé of the British system can be found in Somers and Somers, *Workmen's Compensation*, Appendix B., pp. 299-308. For a critical analysis of the British system, see Warren H. Pillsbury, "Present Dangers to Workmen's Compensation," in *Workmen's Compensation Problems*, IAIABC *Proceedings*, 1956 (United States Department of Labor, Bureau of Labor Standards, Bulletin 192), pp. 132-136.

monetary limits are placed on potential damages, but half of the compensation paid to an employee is credited against any judgment.

One reason for this change was the desire of labor unions to reform a system which had become unduly litigious and which resulted in rather modest awards. It was thought desirable to integrate compensation with the other social insurances and, at the same time, allow some special treatment for the worker who was exposed to the risks of employment. The solution adopted was to make the administration of compensation simpler, even at the expense of eliminating some of the safeguards traditionally associated with due process and, at the same time, to allow workers to press claims in courts where the litigation might result in substantial judgments. Although it is true that in this country we have no integrated system of social insurance, we do have a proliferation of social insurance programs, and one hears the same complaints about the futility of compensation litigation that prompted the British changes.

Another alternative would be to integrate our system of paying compensation benefits into one or the other of the existing social insurance programs. As one example of how this could be done, the payments for temporary disability under compensation could be merged with the Temporary Disability Insurance program now in existence in New Jersey and three other states. Changes in financing would have to be made, but if the two programs were combined, it would make no difference insofar as payments for *temporary* disability were concerned, whether a person was injured on the job or off the job. Benefits would flow from the same source and presumably be of the same amount in either case.

It is possible to conceive of permanent disability benefits and payments to dependents in the event of fatal accidents being integrated with a revised Old-Age, Survivors, and Disability Insurance program (OASDI). Survivor benefits are already paid under this program, and persons who become permanently and totally disabled can collect benefits beginning at age fifty. The age threshold could be abandoned and the definitions of permanent and total disability liberalized to meet more nearly current criteria of the compensation programs.

This would leave medical benefits and payments for permanent partial benefits, which do not fit neatly into any of the existing social insurance programs. Medical and hospital benefits could possibly be taken care of by an amendment to the Temporary Disability Insurance law or by extension of the present voluntary plans for pre-payment of hospital and medical bills, such as the Blue Cross and Blue Shield plans. Experience has certainly shown the worth of full and unlimited medical care to compensation clients, and it would be a backward step to accept anything less in an integrated program. But to accomplish this under an integrated program, the community would have to be willing to offer full and unlimited medical care to all the sick or injured, regardless of the origin of their disability. It is also possible to visualize an expanded rehabilitation program offering medical and hospital care to all the disabled, regardless of employment prospects or financial need.

No existing governmental program other than workmen's compensation pays benefits in the case of permanent partial disabilities. Private insurance carriers sell policies which pay cash indemnities in cases of specific disabilities and dismemberments, and presumably a program of this type could be underwritten by the government. If extended to the general population, such a program would require some simplified method of determining the nature and extent of disability. To be content with the method presently used in compensation would be to compound confusion.

There is much that is appealing in the idea of integrating workmen's compensation into some general scheme of social insurance. It would eliminate the problem that administrative tribunals have in deciding whether or not a particular disability arose out of and in the course of employment. It would, of course, also diminish whatever incentives to a safety program the special workmen's compensation benefits provide. If one adopts the theory that the worker is exposed to special hazards and that, therefore, he is entitled to greater benefits than the person whose disability originates outside the employment relation, full integration with a parity of benefits contains fatal defects. This leads back to Britain's solution, under which the industrially injured worker is entitled to slightly greater than normal benefits, with the opportunity to file a civil suit.

Another alternative would be to maintain the present system of compensation but to place its administration at the federal level. The objects of such a change would be to equalize medical and cash benefits, presumably at the level of the highest-paying jurisdictions; to make uniform the rather senseless distinctions that now exist among the several states in coverage of employees and disabilities; and to introduce a single over-all system of financing, possibly with private insurance carriers excluded from the field.

A federal system would have the advantage of operating more in the public eye than the present separate state systems. More complete information about what is happening in this field would become available, and there would be greater possibility of increased public interest in the program. The disadvantages of such a step are obvious. States would no longer be free to meet new problems with experimental solutions, although it must be admitted that such innovations have not been overly plentiful in recent years. Also, procedures may become more bureaucratic and less flexible as the program is further removed from its participants.

One's reaction to the idea of federalization is dependent, in good part, upon one's notion of the appropriate roles of the federal and state governments. Labor unions, convinced that the state legislatures are constitutionally and inherently stacked against their interests, have tended to favor increased participation of the federal government, which they visualize as being more responsive to the needs of the workers.

On the other hand, the Secretary of Labor, and other officials of the Eisenhower administration, have made countless speeches urging the revitalization of the state programs, on the theory that responsibility for such programs belongs, not to the federal government, but to the individual states.

There is of course much middle ground. The federal government could participate in some aspects of the program without taking over entirely the role of individual states. Unemployment insurance and the various grant-in-aid programs operate with federal-state participation. Regardless of prevailing social philosophies, however, certain compensation problems may bring some federal participation almost through the back door. Radiation hazards are an example. It is hard to conceive of a national radiation injuries fund without some supervision or administration by the federal government.

These are but some of the alternatives that could be adopted. Of course, it is always possible that the subtle changes that are continuously occurring in the compensation system will transform it without overt action. The increasing coverage of diseases which have dubious employment connections, or the widespread extension of second injury and other special funds, to mention but two aspects of the problem, might transform the program into a general health insurance program without resolving any of the complex problems of responsibility that are involved. On the other hand, continuation of these trends might result in pressures to scrap the system and to start new.

We cannot ignore the fact that the country from which we derived our program has modified it drastically, and what has happened in England can happen here. But if such radical changes come, they will probably have to come on a national basis. Whatever the long-term trends, there is no evidence that such basic reforms are in the immediate offing. In the meantime, the State of New Jersey, like other states, must live and seek at least partial solutions within the present framework.

Reforms in the general administration of New Jersey's program are basic to any set of solutions. There is no good reason why an injured worker should not be able to collect what is due him without resort to long-drawn-out procedures which culminate in a trial, indistinguishable in outward appearances from proceedings in a court of law. Given the way the law has developed in New Jersey, these procedures are understandable; but understanding need not result in tolerance. The interest groups cannot be depended upon to press hard for administrative reforms; the task is one which belongs to the administrators of the program. They must see to it that injured workers receive medical care and equitable indemnity payments with a minimum of technicalities and expense.

Insurance carriers should be required to make payments promptly and in accordance with well-defined standards. The administrator's task is to check these payments and to supervise medical care and rehabilitation. Concentration must be placed upon the direct settlement level — an area which was almost completely neglected until the Division of Workmen's Compensation began some spot checking in 1956. If this level of settlement can be made to work effectively, then the informal and formal stages will not have such clogged calendars. Informal hearings should be reserved for cases in which the division is unable to bring about a settlement, and in which further useful information can be had by calling the parties in for a conference.

If the division strengthened the direct settlement stage, then only genuine controversies should be allowed on the formal level. Attorneys who persist in bringing cases in which formal awards are not substantially different from those offered previously by insurance carriers should have their fees reduced, as is provided by law. Insurance carriers whose cases at the formal level result in awards substantially identical with those suggested by the division at the noncontested level should be penalized by having costs assessed against them. The defects of the formal level cannot be charged wholly against one side. This has been a symbiotic relationship, and reforms require changes in practices of representatives of both the petitioner and the respondent.

At the same time, the deputies should be given wide discretion in fixing fees so that adequate allowances can be allowed professional men in complicated cases. An appeals board within the division would assure some uniformity of decisions among deputies and allow greater administrative control over the hearing officers' fixing of these medical and legal fees as well as control of such other matters as the referral of clients in need of rehabilitation.

These administrative reforms presuppose that the problem of permanent partial disabilities can be solved. From the employer's point of view, this is the outstanding problem in workmen's compensation. Almost any interview with an employer brings forth complaints about individual cases in which it is claimed awards were made with no justification. When employer representatives are asked to explain the reasons for this, the reactions range from bewilderment, to lack of understanding about how any of these awards are made, to accusations that the whole compensation program is one big racket involving doctors, lawyers and compensation hearing officials.

The history of the administration of the program is replete with accusations that ambulance-chasing doctor and lawyer rackets have existed; that runners have been hired to solicit cases; and that shop stewards have been employed by compensation lawyers to discover and maximize any injuries they can find. The accusations have always been more plentiful than the evidence that such activities actually have taken place. If fraudulent practices exist, they should be stamped out; but the basic solutions would seem to lie in administrative reforms that would make most formal hearings unnecessary.

Some of the employers' charges of unjustified awards stem from a lack of understanding of basic workmen's compensation theory. The employer takes the worker as he finds him; and if he suffers an injury which can be said to flow from the employment circumstances, then the employer becomes wholly liable for the resulting disability. The development of such a theory has already been sketched in connection with the heart cases. Although application of this theory may be softened with changes in the second injury legislation, it will remain as a fundamental aspect of workmen's compensation theory unless the entire program is integrated into some general system of social insurance. Until this happens, the problems associated with determining whether a particular disability arose "out of and in the course of employment" will remain, and it is inevitable that the tests will be broadened and liberalized. At least, in this area, the fundamental changes are the product of court decisions made in full public view.

Employer complaints also stem from a lack of understanding of the rating system which measures the extent of permanent partial disability. As has been pointed out, the disability concept is a blend of medical and employment factors. Under New Jersey's system, awards are paid for physical disability as such, and the worker need not show any actual or potential wage loss. In this writer's opinion, the disadvantages of switching over to some form of the wage-loss theory would outweigh the possible gains. There is nothing basically wrong with a rating system, or with compensating the worker for the physical disability as such, as long as the disability is "permanent in quality," as the law requires. But without the limitations inherent in a wage-loss system, awards may be made in the absence of any permenent disability. Nelson, and other observers of the New Jersey law, have pointed to the tendency to compensate for physical disabilities in cases that other states would throw out of court. The differences in the proportion of all cases which end up with some finding of permanent disability are strikingly different in this state, as compared with similar industrial states. The differences among counties within the state in this regard are equally striking. A high proportion of the compensation dollar is spent on these awards, whereas the permanently and totally disabled workers receive less than enough to live on.

Mere mechanical changes in procedures will not solve this problem. Fundamental changes in administrative attitudes are required. It has already been suggested that the standards for the evaluation of permanent partial disabilities be promulgated. If we are compensating for all fractures, no matter how well healed, then let the administrators publicize this fact. If certain disabilities automatically carry an award for neurosis, then let this fact be known. The very act of publication, along with the research and thinking that will have to go into the formulation of these standards, may serve to eliminate situations which cannot stand the light of day.

Of course, complaints will be heard that this cannot be done; that each case is different and that each requires the *expertise* of doctors and lawyers before the estimates of permanent disability can have any meaning. Given the way the system operates, this is perfectly true. But this is not to say that it must continue to be true. Wisconsin and other states have been able to inform their insurance carriers of what is expected of them in direct settlements. There is no reason why New Jersey cannot do the same.

This presupposes the continuation of the present private financing arrangements. The advantages and disadvantages of supplanting these arrangements with an exclusive state fund have already been discussed. If private insurance carriers are to continue their prominent role, it should be with the definite understanding that participation in this field is a privilege and not a right. Compensation insurance is not simply another branch of the casualty insurance field; it is part of a vital social insurance program. Carriers have definite obligations to settle cases directly, to provide basic safety services and to cooperate in rehabilitation matters. The law should provide for detailed reporting on the part of each carrier to the New Jersey Division of Workmen's Compensation so that an individual company's performance can be fairly appraised.

We need more information not only about the actual expenses of insurance carriers in handling business within the state but also about the net cost of insurance coverage to employers after dividends, discounts and rating modifications. Whether because of the futility of resistence or because the carriers merely act as conduits of funds paid by employers, they apparently have been willing to put up with the present system of determining claims. If there is truth in the widespread allegations of "consolation awards," in which monies are paid in the absence of genuine permanent disability, then a portion of the responsibility belongs to the insurance carrier.

Once reforms are made to revitalize the direct settlement level and standards of evaluation of permanent disabilities are devised, then both the loss and expense portions of the insurance rates should be effected. The rate-making procedures will take care of the loss portions automatically, but the expense provisions are set on the basis of national and not state criteria. We need constant examination of this portion of the rates. The compensation business has been a profitable one for insurance carriers, and if private financing arrangements are to continue, profits are necessary. It is not obvious, however, that this social insurance program requires insurance rates under which an inefficient stock carrier which does a small proportion of its business within the state, can operate.

Recommendations have already been made in the case of second injury problems. The One Per Cent Fund was never meant as a substitute for old-age assistance or as a way for the deputies to resolve complex cases. It has a limited but essential purpose: to encourage employers to hire the handicapped by dividing equitably any compensation liability in the event of a second injury. There is no justification for confining the fund to cases wherein the combined injury results only in permanent and total disability, or for excluding all cases wherein the second injury aggravates the pre-existing condition.

New York has pointed the way to solutions in this area. If it is established that the employer had knowledge of the pre-existing employment disability, and if the combined injuries result in a disability materially greater than would have occurred in the absence of the pre-existing disability, then the whole award should run initially against the employer. If liability extends beyond a predetermined period (in New York's case, 104 weeks), then the employer should be able to petition the fund for relief. If it becomes necessary to hold a hearing in the case, the employer and the representatives of the insurance carriers should be brought together as the contending parties. The worker is entitled to compensation payments and medical benefits because of his combined disabilities, and he ought not be involved in whether the employer or the fund is liable.

Even an ideal second injury fund is useless unless it is accompanied by wide publicity. Conversations with employers indicate that many of them do not even know of the existence of the One Per Cent Fund. Without such knowledge, it is obvious that the fund cannot operate so as to encourage employment of the handicapped.

The ironic factor in the rehabilitation picture is that New Jersey once had such an effective program of rehabilitating compensation cases that it attracted nation-wide attention. The story of the decline and eventual death of this cooperative program has already been told. The hiring of the Workmen's Compensation-Rehabilitation Coordinator indicates that, once again, attention is being paid to the vital problems of rehabilitation. Given the way the federal-state rehabilitation program has developed over the years, the Rehabilitation Commission can no longer be asked to carry the main burden of the rehabilitation of compensation cases. This responsibility devolves upon the Workmen's Compensation Division. The law should make clear the responsibility of the insurance carriers for the effective rehabilitation of the injured workers, and the division should hire sufficient personnel to supervise this phase of the operations.

This keys in with other proposed administrative reforms. An effective direct payments program requires a thorough check on employer and insurance carriers' reports, and this should simplify the task of selecting candidates for rehabilitation. A rehabilitation program cannot be grafted onto a program which is concerned only with the adjudication of disputed claims over the amounts of cash indemnities. But it fits in neatly with a program wherein administrators actively supervise cash payments and medical treatment at the non-contested level. This would be the orientation of the administrators if they operated under a direct payment philosophy.

Basic reforms of the program should be accompanied by solutions to the problem of the inadequate level of cash benefits. The most glaring deficiencies exist in the case of survivors and totally disabled persons who are living in the present on benefit levels of the past. Ways of financing increases to bring these past benefits up to a more realistic level have already been discussed. The problem of inadequacy extends to those receiving benefits at the current level. The existence of a maximum weekly benefit operates to prevent most workers from recovering that percentage of wage loss contemplated during most of the act's history. Workers who have foregone their right to bring suits for accidental injuries are entitled to 66 2/3 per cent, or some predetermined percentage of their wage as a compensation payment. If maximum benefits levels must remain in the law, they should not prevent the worker who receives the average wage from recovering the predetermined percentage of his wage loss. The solution is not for the legislature merely to increase the maximum weekly benefit now in the law. We live in a dynamic economy wherein prices and wages are continually changing. The legislature should allow the maximum weekly benefit to change automatically as the average wage level changes in the state.

These are but some of the partial solutions that appear to be necessary if we are to continue to work within the present framework of an essentially privately financed program under which employees receive benefits for work-incurred injuries. This was a pioneering social program which devised a rational method of sharing the costs of industrial work injuries. In spite of the plethora of investigations over the years, the program has remained comparatively neglected, and the community has paid a price for this neglect. We do not say that the present system can continue; perhaps it will eventually be replaced by one of the alternatives sketched above. But if the present program is to be maintained, the time for making reforms is past due.

SELECTED BIBLIOGRAPHY

General

American Federation of Labor — Congress of Industrial Organizations, Department of Research. "Workmen's Compensation," *Labor Economic Review*, III (August and September, 1958).

The federation's analysis of the program, which emphasizes the low benefit levels and deficiencies in rehabilitation and methods of financing. Contains excerpts of resolutions passed at the AFL-CIO's second Constitutional Convention held December, 1957, advocating the enactment of a Federal Workmen's Compensation Act or legislation fixing minimum standards for the states.

American Medical Association. *Medical Relations in Workmen's Compensation*. Chicago: American Medical Association, December, 1955.

A statement adopted by the House of Delegates emphasizing the medical profession's interest in the formulation of policy in the fields of workmen's compensation and rehabilitation.

Association of Casualty and Surety Companies. *Better Workmen's Compensation Protection*. New York: Association of Casualty and Surety Companies, 1958.

A vigorous presentation of the point of view that private insurance carriers have proved superior to monopoly state funds in financing workmen's compensation.

Association of Casualty and Surety Companies. *A Rehabilitation Program*. New York: Association of Casualty and Surety Companies, 1957.

Presents a rehabilitation program prepared by the Advisory Committee of the Claims Bureau, Association of Casualty and Surety Companies, which was approved by the Executive Committee on June 26, 1957, and recommended for the consideration of the association's member companies.

Association of Casualty and Surety Companies. *Statement of Principles on Insurance Claims Management and Practices in the Field of Workmen's Compensation*. New York: Association of Casualty and Surety Companies, 1958.

A revision of a 1943 statement. Lists eight principles which the association urges upon those engaged in claims management. These include the idea that formal claims and appeals should be minimized, that complete rehabilitation of the injured worker should be the goal of the insurer, that claims should be paid promptly, etc.

Black, S. Bruce. "The Anomalies of Workmen's Compensation," *Industrial and Labor Relations Review*, VII (October, 1953), 42-50.

An official of the leading compensation insurance carrier discusses what he feels are disturbing trends in the compensation program. This is an article in the *Review's* 1953 symposium on workmen's compensation.

Black, S. Bruce. *Free Institutions and the Quest for Security: The Development of Workmen's Compensation in the U. S. A.*, address at the "1951 Massachusetts Dinner" of the Newcomen Society of England at Boston, December 27, 1951. Princeton: Princeton University Press, 1951.

Deals with the development of Workmen's Compensation in the United States and with the history of Liberty Mutual Insurance Companies.

Bowers, Edison L. *Is it Safe to Work? A Study of Industrial Accidents.* New York: Houghton Mifflin Company, 1930.

A survey of the development and operations of compensation laws. The book treats a wider range of subjects than is suggested by its title. Specific attention is paid to rehabilitation and to factors involved in a disability rating schedule.

Burns, Eveline M. *The American Social Security System.* New York: Houghton Mifflin Company, 1949.

Although subsequent legislative amendments have outmoded the factual data, this is still a basic work in the field. Chapter 8, "Sickness and Disability Insurance," contains an analysis of workmen's compensation programs.

Burns, Eveline M. *Social Security and Public Policy.* New York: McGraw-Hill Book Company, 1956.

Instead of a program by program approach, this book attempts an analytical approach to the problems. Major questions of public policy in the field of social security are identified and discussed.

Chamber of Commerce of the United States. *Analysis of Workmen's Compensation Laws, 1956.* Washington, D. C.: 1956. Supplement published in January, 1957.

A useful compilation with many tabular presentations showing provisions of the laws in the various jurisdictions.

Cheit, Earl F. "Radiation Hazards: A New Challenge to Workmen's Compensation," *Insurance Law Journal* (December, 1957), 743-51. Available from the Institute of Industrial Relations, University of California, Los Angeles, as Reprint No. 105.

An excellent analysis of the adequacy of present compensation laws to meet the problem of radiation hazards.

Commons, John R., and John B. Andrews. *Principles of Labor Legislation.* 4th rev. ed. New York: Harper and Brothers, 1936.

Although time has taken its toll, this text by a pioneer in the field of labor economics, and the secretary of the American Association for Labor Legislation, was once the leader in its field. Chapter V, Part 1, "Industrial Accident Insurance," deals with workmen's compensation.

Congress of Industrial Organization, Department of Education and Research. *Workmen's Compensation — A Story of Failure*. Pamphlet No. 202. Washington, D. C.: 1952.
An exposition of the CIO's dissatisfaction with the level of benefits and general operations of the compensation programs.

Dawson, Marshall. *The Development of Workmen's Compensation Claims Administration in the United States and Canada*. Washington, D. C.: International Association of Industrial Accident Boards and Commissions, 1951.
A report by Mr. Dawson to the IAIABC, October 4, 1951, contrasting systems of claims administration in Ontario, New York, Wisconsin and other jurisdictions.

Dawson, Marshall. *Problems of Workmen's Compensation Administration in the United States and Canada*. United States Bureau of Labor Statistics, Bulletin 672, 1940.
Although written in 1940, this still contains useful information and penetrating comments. Based on visits to each jurisdiction, this survey covers problems relating to adequacy of benefits, medical care, relations of compensation to rehabilitation and coverage under the various laws, as well as claims administration.

Dodd, Walter F. *Administration of Workmen's Compensation*. New York: Commonwealth Fund, 1936.
One of the few pre-World War II full-dress reviews of the field.

Donoghue, Francis D. "Restoring the Injured Employee to Work." In International Association of Industrial Accident Boards and Commissions *Proceedings, 1916*. United States Bureau of Labor Statistics, Bulletin 210, 1917. Pp. 212-20.
An early statement in which it is maintained that the first basic principle of a compensation law should be the rehabilitation of injured persons.

Downey, E. H. *Workmen's Compensation*. New York: The MacMillan Company, 1924.
An early standard work in the field and still useful in spite of the fact that much of it is now outmoded.

Dublin, Louis I., and Alfred J. Lotka. *The Money Value of a Man*. Rev. ed. New York: The Ronald Press Company, 1946.
As its title states, this is an attempt to compute the money value of a man by estimating present value of gross and net future earnings under various assumptions.

Fox, Harland. "Company Supplements to Workmen's Compensation," National Industrial Conference Board, *Management Record*, XVII (January, 1955), 19-22.

A survey of the practices of various firms in supplementary compensation benefits.

Gagliardo, Domenico. *American Social Insurance*. Rev. ed. New York: Harper and Brothers, 1955.
A widely used textbook whose virtues are also its defects. It is almost encyclopedic in its details, but unfortunately recent law amendments make some of its details inapplicable. Part 4: "Occupational Injuries," pp. 373-430, deals with workmen's compensation and related problems.

Hanson, Stanwood L. "Results of Rehabilitation in the Field of Workmen's Compensation," *Journal of Chronic Diseases*, III (March, 1956), 323-30. Reprint available from Liberty Mutual Insurance Company, Boston, Massachusetts.
One of a number of articles written by the staff of the Liberty Mutual Insurance Company describing that carrier's program and interest in the field of rehabilitation.

Hobbs, Clarence W. *Workmen's Compensation Insurance*. 2d ed. New York: McGraw-Hill Book Company, 1939.
Parts of this book are now outmoded but the student who wishes to understand the compensation insurance field would be well advised to start with this volume.

Hookstadt, Carl. *Comparison of Workmen's Compensation Insurance and Administration*. United States Bureau of Labor Statistics, Bulletin 301, 1922.
One of the earliest studies of administrative experience sponsored by the United States Department of Labor and the IAIABC. The investigation, begun in 1919, covered twenty states and two Canadian provinces.

Hookstadt, Carl. *Comparison of Workmen's Compensation Laws of the United States and Canada up to January, 1, 1920*. United States Bureau of Labor Statistics, Bulletin 272, 1920.
Detailed comparisons of early laws and their administration by a pioneering student of the field.

Horovitz, Samuel B. *Injury and Death under Workmen's Compensation Laws*. (Horovitz on Workmen's Compensation) Boston: Wright and Potter Printing Company, 1944.
An exposition of the law by a prominent workmen's compensation attorney who has been active in the National Association of Claimants' Compensation Attorneys (NACCA).

International Association of Industrial Accident Boards and Commissions. *Proceedings of the Annual Meetings*.
These discussions at the meetings of the professional association of administrators in this field are a basic source of information. From 1916 to 1932, they were published under the title of *Proceedings of the Annual Meetings of the IAIABC* as bulletins of the United States

Department of Labor, Bureau of Labor Statistics, In 1933 and from 1939 to 1948, they were published under the title of *Discussion of Industrial Accidents and Diseases* by the United States Department of Labor, Division of, or Bureau of, Labor Standards. Since 1949 they have continued to be published by the Bureau of Labor Standards and have been entitled *Workmen's Compensation Problems*.

International Association of Industrial Accident Boards and Commissions. *Workmen's Compensation Statistics – Glossary of Terms.* Washington, D. C.: United States Bureau of Labor Standards, 1954.

An attempt to explain the sometimes confusing use of terms in workmen's compensation statistical compilations.

Katz, Harold A., and Estelle M. Wierpel. "Workmen's Compensation 1910-1952: Are Present Benefits Adequate?" *Labor Law Journal,* IV (March, 1953), 164-179.

An indictment of the low level of cash benefits. Illustrations drawn largely from the experience in Illinois.

Kessler, Henry H. *Accidental Injuries: The Medico-Legal Aspects of Workmen's Compensation and Public Liability.* Philadelphia: Lea and Febiger, 1931.

A comprehensive survey covering not only the medical details but the problems involved in rating disabilities of all types.

Kessler, Henry H. *Low Back Pain in Industry.* New York: Commerce and Industry Association of New York, 1955.

Primarily a statistical analysis and clinical summary of case histories, but the book also contains recommendations for dealing with this perplexing problem. This is one of the series of publications issued as part of the association's study of workmen's compensation.

Kessler, Henry H. *Rehabilitation of the Physically Handicapped.* Rev. ed. New York: Columbia University Press, 1953.

Treats the problems involved in rehabilitating of persons with all types of handicaps. Chapter IV deals specifically with the injured worker. Contains many references to Kessler's New Jersey experiences.

Kessler, Henry H. "Whole Man Theory." In *Workmen's Compensation Problems,* International Association of Industrial Accident Boards and Commissions *Proceedings,* 1956. United States Bureau of Labor Standards, Bulletin 192, 1957. Pp. 76-79.

A statement of Kessler's ideas on the problems involved in disability rating.

Kulp, C. A. *Casualty Insurance.* 3d ed. New York: The Ronald Press Company, 1956.

An analytical survey of casualty hazards and policies which cover the whole field of casualty insurance. A prime source of information on compensation insurers, principles of compensation insurance rate-making, rate regulations, etc. Particularly useful since it enables the reader to contrast workmen's compensation insurance with other casualty insurances.

Larson, Arthur. *The Law of Workmen's Compensation.* 2 vols., with Cumulative Supplement for 1957. New York: Matthew Bender and Company, 1957.

Written primarily for the legal profession, this mammoth survey of the law is enhanced by Larson's lack of hesitation in presenting his own point of view.

Larson, Arthur. "The Legal Aspects of Causation in Workmen's Compensation," *Rutgers Law Review,* VIII (1954), 423-434.

There is some discussion of New Jersey cases in this excellent analysis of the legal problems involved in determining causation. This is written in a style which the layman can easily comprehend.

Larson, Arthur. *The Model Workmen's Compensation Act,* address by Under Secretary of Labor Arthur Larson at Sixth Annual Conference of Southern Association of Workmen's Compensation Administrators, Orlando, Florida, October 28, 1954. Available from United States Department of Labor, Bureau of Labor Standards.

An exposition of the "Model Act" at one time was advocated by the federal government as a means of attempting to bring some uniformity to the laws of the several jurisdictions.

MacIntyre, Duncan M. "Workmen's Compensation and Private Benefit Programs," *Industrial and Labor Relations Review,* VII (October, 1953), 63-72.

One of the few attempts to bring together the information on the private supplementation of workmen's compensation benefits. Part of the *Review's* 1953 symposium on workmen's compensation.

Michelbacher, G. F., ed., *Multiple Line Insurance.* New York: McGraw-Hill Book Company, 1957.

Written with the cooperation of a group of specialists, many of whom participated in the writing of older editions, under the title *Casualty Insurance.* No specific section of the book is devoted to workmen's compensation insurance, but the general analysis of underwriting, claims, rate-making, etc., includes discussion of problems of workmen's compensation insurance.

National Rehabilitation Association. *Journal of Rehabilitation.* Published bimonthly, 1025 Vermont Avenue, Washington 5, D. C.

A useful source of current articles on various phases of rehabilitation.

Pollack, Jerome. "A Policy Decision for Workmen's Compensation," *Industrial and Labor Relations Review,* VII (October, 1953), 51-62.

A critical look at some of the problems by the consultant on social insurances to the UAW, AFL-CIO. Pollack calls for more adequate benefit levels and a comprehensive system of medical care and rehabilitation. One of the articles in the *Review's* 1953 symposium.

Potter, Douglas, and D. H. Stansfeld. *National Insurance (Industrial Injuries)*. London: Butterworth, 1950.
A useful source of information on the system adopted in the United Kingdom to supplant older workmen's compensation arrangements.

President's Commission on Veterans' Pensions. *Compensation for Service-Connected Disabilities. A General Analysis of Veterans' and Military Disability Benefits, Mortality Rates, Disability Standards in Federal Programs, Workmen's Compensation, and Rehabilitation.* House Committee Print 281, 84th Congress, 2d session, August 3, 1956.
Especially valuable is Chapter VII, "Disability Rating: Veterans Administration contrasted with Workmen's Compensation Experience." This chapter analyzes the various types of rating systems used by the states in workmen's compensation.

Reede, Arthur H. *Adequacy of Workmen's Compensation.* Cambridge: Harvard University Press, 1947.
Although parts of this are now out of date, this is still a scholarly and exhaustive study of the problems involved in evaluating adequacy.

Riesenfeld, Stefan A., and Richard C. Maxwell. *Modern Social Legislation.* Brooklyn: The Foundation Press, 1950.
This is a legal case book supplemented by expository material, much of it written by the authors. Especially valuable is Division 2, "Insurance Against Industrial Accidents and Diseases," pp. 127-441.

Skolnik, Alfred M. "Trends in Workmen's Compensation: Coverage, Benefits and Costs," *Social Security Bulletin*, XXI (August, 1958), 4 ff.
The latest of a series of articles published in the *Social Security Bulletin* in which nation-wide estimates of benefit payments, coverage and cost are included. The series began in 1942 with an estimate of benefit payments: Michalina M. Libman, "Workmen's Compensation Benefits in the United States, 1939 and 1940" in the January issue of the *Bulletin*. The next article, Dorothy McCamman, "Workmen's Compensation: Coverage, Premiums and Payments," in the July, 1950, issue, estimated coverage along with other data. The article in the March, 1954, issue, Dorothy McCamman and Alfred M. Skolnik, "Workmen's Compensation: Measures of Accomplishment," was expanded to include cost estimates and measures of the scope and adequacy of the program. A series incorporating estimates of benefit payments and other data have been published annually in the *Bulletin*, in recent years in the December issues.

Somers, Herman M. "Myth and Reality in Workmen's Compensation." In *Workmen's Compensation Problems*, International Association of Industrial Accident Boards and Commissions *Proceedings*, 1956. United States Bureau of Labor Standards, Bulletin 192, 1957. Pp. 18-31. Available from the Institute of Industrial Relations, University of California, Los Angeles, as Reprint No. 99.

This address before the IAIABC poses the problem of whether the fundamental compensation "bargain" struck in the early 1900's must be considered as inviolable and fixed for all time.

Somers, Herman M., and Anne R. Somers. "Industrial Safety and Health in the United States," *Industrial and Labor Relations Review*, VI (July, 1953), 475-496.

In this article, which preceded the publication of their book, the Somerses question whether workmen's compensation has proved to be a sufficient stimulant to the adoption of industrial health and safety measures.

Somers, Herman M., and Anne R. Somers. *Workmen's Compensation: Prevention, Insurance and Rehabilitation of Occupational Disability.* New York: John Wiley and Sons, 1954.

The definitive work in the field, responsible for much of the resurgence of interest in these areas.

Somers, Herman M., and Anne R. Somers. "Workmen's Compensation: Unfulfilled Promise," *Industrial and Labor Relations Review*, VII (October, 1953), 32-42.

Part of a symposium on workmen's compensation. Contains in short compass some of the materials and ideas treated in fuller length in the Somerses' volume, *Workmen's Compensation*.

Switzer, Mary E., and Howard Rusk. *Doing Something for the Disabled.* Public Affairs Pamphlet No. 197. New York: Public Affairs Committee, June, 1953.

A popular exposition of the problems involved in rehabilitation.

Thompson, Davis M. *The Company and the Physically Impaired Worker.* Studies in Personnel Policy, No. 163. New York: National Industrial Conference Board, 1957.

An analysis of the experience of various companies with the employment of the physically impaired worker.

Turnbull, John J., Arthur C. Williams, and Earl F. Cheit. *Economic and Social Security.* New York: The Ronald Press Company, 1957.

A modern textbook in the field. Chapters 9 and 10 deal with problems of occupational disability and workmen's compensation, and the beginning and concluding chapters contain general observations pertinent to this social insurance program.

United States Department of Labor, Bureau of Labor Standards. *Proceedings of the National Conference on Workmen's Compensation and Rehabilitation, March 22 and 23, 1950.* Bulletin 122, 1950.

An examination of common problems by administrators and others concerned with both rehabilitation and workmen's compensation.

Second Injury Funds: Standards and Patterns in State Legislation. Bulletin 190, 1957.

An excellent short survey of the laws and program of the various jurisdictions which points up existing problems.

State Workmen's Compensation Laws. Bulletin 161, August, 1957.

Although this bulletin does not contain very much detail on the laws, its tables are the best source of information on the benefits level for all types of disability and other basic provisions of the laws in each jurisdiction. The bureau revises this bulletin periodically.

United States Department of Labor, Bureau of Labor Statistics. *Workmen's Compensation in the United States.* Bulletin 1149, 1954.

Reprint of a series of eight articles which appeared in *Monthly Labor Review* during 1953. These are:

    I. "An Appraisal," Max D. Kossorvis
    II. "Court Proceedings," Warren H. Pillsbury
    III. "Federal Legislation," John Petzko
    IV. "Occupational Diseases," Bruce A. Greene
    V. "Medical Services," Bruce A. Greene
    VI. "Accident Prevention," William L. Connolly
    VII. "Problems of Administration," Paul E. Gurske
    VIII. "Rehabilitation," Jerome Pollack

United States Senate. *A Study of the Report of the Commission of the American Federation of Labor and the National Civic Federation.* Document 419, 63d Congress, 2d session, January 15, 1914.

Incorporates findings of surveys of operations of compensation laws in various states by a joint labor-management commission.

Witte, Edwin E. "The Theory of Workmen's Compensation," *American Labor Legislation Review*, XX (December, 1930), 411-18.

One of the few basic articles which examine the theoretical foundations of the system. In it, Witte propounds the principle of "least social costs" maintaining that workmen's compensation minimizes the losses occasioned by accidents.

New Jersey's Experience

Albee, Fred H. "New Jersey Rehabilitation Service." In International Association of Industrial Accident Boards and Commissions *ceedings, 1923*. United States Bureau of Labor Statistics, Bulletin 359, 1924. Pp. 127-9.

An optimistic report on the operation of the state clinics by the man who played a leading role in the establishment of the Rehabilitation Commission in New Jersey.

American Association for Labor Legislation, Social Insurance Committee. "Three Years under the New Jersey Workmen's Compensation Law," *American Labor Legislation Review*, V (March, 1915), 31-102.

An early survey of the act which influenced basic changes in the administration of the program.

Brodkin, Henry A. "State Rehabilitation Clinics - A Stage in the Development of Rehabilitation Service in New Jersey" (typewritten, c. 1954).

An analysis of the rise and decline of the clinics by a physician who has served on the medical staffs of both the Division of Workmen's Compensation and the Rehabilitation Commission.

Bryant, Lewis T. "Industrial Rehabilitation in New Jersey." In International Association of Industrial Accident Boards and Commissions *Proceedings, 1920.* United States Bureau of Labor Statistics, Bulletin 281, 1921. Pp. 138-40.

An early report on the problem which optimistically looked forward to close coordination of workmen's compensation and rehabilitation.

Chance, R. Robinson. *The Workmen's Compensation Law of New Jersey.* 2d. ed. Newark: Soney and Sage, 1918.

An early annotated and indexed compilation of the law.

Malone, Wex S. "Workmen's Compensation," *Rutgers Law Review,* VIII (1953-54), 97-110.

A survey of the developments in the court's interpretation of the law — a continuation of the periodic surveys previously written by Harland J. Scarborough.

National Institute of Public Administration. *Report on a Survey of the Organization and Administration of the State Government of New Jersey.* Trenton: 1930.

Chapter IX of this survey, by Luther H. Gulick, contains proposals for changes in the administration of workmen's compensation and rehabilitation.

New Jersey. *Message of the Governor of New Jersey Transmitting to the Legislature the Report of the Commission on Employer's Liability Together with the Evidence and Testimony Taken; also a Proposed Act in Relation Thereto.* Trenton: January 16, 1911.

The basic report which led to the adoption of the original law.

New Jersey. "Report and Recommendations to Governor Walter E. Edge on the Administration and Activities of the New Jersey Rehabilitation Commission." Trenton: September 5, 1945 (mim., 1945).

This report influenced the decision to discontinue the state rehabilitation clinics.

New Jersey Commission on Post-War Economic Welfare. *Labor Security in the Post-War Period,* Second Report. Trenton: 1945.

Contains recommendations for improvements in the workmen's compensation law.

New Jersey Compensation Rating and Inspection Bureau. *Annual Reports of the Chairman and Manager.*

Each of these reports contains a complete analysis of the year's experience in the field of compensation insurance within the state.

New Jersey Department of Labor and Industry. *Annual Reports.*
For fiscal years 1949 through 1954, these have been published
under the title *Summary of Activities.* In fiscal years 1955 and 1957
the report was simply entitled *Annual Report.* No reports were published for fiscal years 1953 and 1956. Each of these reports contains
data on workmen's compensation, safety and rehabilitation. The fiftieth
anniversary report for fiscal year 1954 has a historical review of the
activities in each of these fields.

New Jersey Department of Labor and Industry, Division of Workmen's
   Compensation. *Annual Report, 1956.*
A report of the activities of the division. Includes a historical
accident analysis from 1946 to 1956. Prior to this report, the division
published annually an *Industrial Accident Report,* with summaries of
case data and an analysis of compensable accidental injuries as to
type, cause, part of body affected, etc. These were discontinued and
will eventually be replaced by a fuller analysis of all industrial accidents within the state.

New Jersey Employers' Liability Commission. *Annual Reports, 1912,*
   1913, 1914, 1915.
The early reports of the legislative "watch-dog" committee, set up
to observe the operations of the act in its earliest years.

New Jersey Legislature.
   Report of the Commission to Study Laws Affecting Industrial Devel-
   opment. Trenton: June, 1957.
Chapter 2, on "Social Insurance," contains recommendations on
workmen's compensation that are similar to proposals made by various
employer groups.

   Report of the Joint Commission on Study of the Workmen's Compen-
   sation Act and Practices. Trenton: 1935.
A thoroughly critical survey of the act and its operations by a commission headed by Dr. Andrew F. McBride, one-time Commissioner of
the Department of Labor.

   Report of the Joint Legislative Survey Committee of New Jersey.
   Trenton: 1925.
A report of the committee headed by Senator W. H. Bright on the
costs of administration of the state government of New Jersey. Includes recommendations for reorganization of the Department of
Labor, especially for the inclusion of the Rehabilitation Commission
within this department.

New Jersey Manufacturers Association. *New Jersey Workmen's Com-*
   pensation Act. Trenton: 1957.
An exposition of the act prepared for the use of employers.

New Jersey Rehabilitation Commission. *Annual Reports.*
Each year's report contains an analysis of the cases rehabilitated,
types of disabilities involved, sources of referral, etc. In recent years,

the reports also contain an analysis of the problems faced by the commission in discharging its statutory obligations.

New Jersey State CIO Council, Legal Department. *The New Jersey Workmen's Compensation Law: What Every Worker Should Know About It.* Newark: rev. ed., 1957.
A popular booklet prepared for the information of workers; contains questions and answers on the compensation law.

New Jersey Statutes Annotated (West, 1958).
A convenient compilation of the statutes annotated with references to judicial decisions. Yearly supplements bring statutes and cases up to date.

New Jersey Workmen's Compensation Advisory Commission. *Report To the Commissioner of Labor.* Trenton: March 11, 1931.
Report of commission appointed by Colonel Charles R. Blunt, Commissioner of Labor, which recommended changes in hearings and appeals procedures.

New Jersey Workmen's Compensation Aid Bureau. *Report,* 1916.
The initial report of the short-lived agency which was set up to administer the act in 1916. It was supplanted in 1918 by the Workmen's Compensation Bureau.

Newman, Philip Charles. *Labor Legislation in New Jersey.* Washington, D. C.: American Council on Public Affairs, 1943.
This general survey is not primarily concerned with workmen's compensation but does contain information on the background of the act.

O'Neal, Arthur J., Jr. "Problems in the Rehabilitation of New Jersey's Industrially Disabled." M.A. thesis, Rutgers University, September, 1958.
An analysis of the problems involved in the rehabilitation of the industrially injured with particular reference to New Jersey's experience. Contains recommendations for the improvement of the program.

Princeton University School of Public and International Affairs. *Report on a Survey of Administration and Expenditures of the State Government of New Jersey with Recommendations for the Fiscal Year 1933-1934.* December, 1932.
Includes proposals relevant to rehabilitation and workmen's compensation in New Jersey.

Ritchie, Fred. "An Appraisal of Workmen's Compensation Legislation in New Jersey." Ph.D. dissertation, Princeton University, Apr. 1942. Ann Arbor: University Microfilms, 1952.
A good survey of the legislation and some of the court decisions. Does not contain very much on the actual practices or administration of the act.

Rodes, Robert E., Jr. "Workmen's Compensation," *Rutgers Law Review,* XI (1956-57), 140-59.

A continuation, after a four-year gap, of the series of articles reviewing developments in the law. Previous article in the series were by Harland Scarborough and Wex Malone.

Scarborough, Harland J. "Workmen's Compensation," *Rutgers Law Review*, IV (1949-50), 122-38; V (1950-51), 130-45; VI (1951-52), 144-54; VII (1952-53), 123-32.

Periodic reviews of developments in the courts' interpretations of the law by a faculty member of the Rutgers Law School.

Seward, Joseph M. "New Jersey's One Per Cent Fund." M.A. Thesis, Rutgers University, June, 1957.

A survey of New Jersey's experiences, with recommendations for administrative and statutory changes.

Weiner, Max. *Workmen's Compensation in New Jersey.* Newark: The Newark News, 1955.

A reprinting of a series of popular articles from *The Newark News* of November 14-23, 1955, which succeeded in stimulating public interest in various aspects of the program.

Weiner, Max. *Workmen's Compensation in New Jersey: A Postscript.* Newark: The Newark News, 1957.

A reprinting of articles from *The Newark News* of January, 1957, following up Weiner's 1955 examination of the program, pointing out some of the improvements since the last series of articles.

Experience of Other Jurisdictions

Bamberger, Lisbeth. "Rehabilitation under Workmen's Compensation in California," *Industrial Medicine and Surgery*, XXV (February, 1956), 62-72. Available from the Institute of Industrial Relations, University of California, Los Angeles, as Reprint No. 58.

Barton, Sam B. *How Texas Cares for Her Injured Workers.* Denton: North Texas State College, August, 1956.

British Columbia Workmen's Compensation Board. *Report of the Commissioner Relating to the Workmen's Compensation Act and Board.* Vancouver: 1952.

Brown, Ray Andrews. *The Administration of Workmen's Compensation.* University of Wisconsin Studies in the Social Sciences and History, No. 19. Madison: 1933.

Callahan, Joseph M. *Costs, Operations and Procedures under the Workmen's Compensation Law of the State of New York.* Reports to the Honorable Averell Harriman, Governor of the State of New York. First Report, January 28, 1957; Second Report, December 29, 1958.

Canada, Department of Labour. *Workmen's Compensation in Canada — A Comparison of Provincial Laws.* Ottawa: December, 1954.

Commerce and Industry Association of New York. *Medical Aspects of Workmen's Compensation: Two Symposia before the Special Committee on Workmen's Compensation.* New York: Commerce and Industry Association of New York, 1953.

Dawson, Archie O. *Administration of the Workmen's Compensation Law in the State of New York.* First report to Governor Thomas E. Dewey, March 31, 1954.

Hamilton, Charles S., Jr. *Administration of the Workmen's Compensation Law in the State of New York.* Interim Report to Governor Thomas E. Dewey, December 30, 1954.

Holly, J. Fred, and Bevars D. Mabry. *Protective Labor Legislation and Its Administration in Tennessee.* Knoxville: University of Tennessee Press, 1955.

Horlacher, John P. *The Results of Workmen's Compensation in Pennsylvania: A Study of the Pennsylvania System from the Point of View of the Injured Worker.* Pennsylvania Department of Labor and Industry, Advisory Committee on Workmen's Compensation. Philadelphia: 1934.

Keiper, Joseph S. *Forces that Spiral Workmen's Compensation Costs.* New York: Commerce and Industry Association of New York, 1953.

Keiper, Joseph S., M. William Zucker, James J. Regan, and Mahlon Z. Eubank. *Studies in Workmen's Compensation.* New York: Commerce and Industry Association of New York, 1954.

Lane, Morton. *The Effect of the New York Workmen's Compensation Law upon the Employment of the Handicapped.* Rehabilitation Monograph XI. New York: The Institute of Physical Medicine and Rehabilitation, New York University — Bellevue Medical Center, 1956.

MacIntyre, Duncan M. *Workmen's Compensation in New York State.* Ithaca: Cornell University, New York State School of Industrial and Labor Relations, May, 1953.

Massachusetts, Legislative Research Council. *Rehabilitation and Employment of Handicapped Persons.* Feb. 22, 1956, House No. 2790.

Mayer, Marian. *Workmen's Compensation Law in Louisiana: A Case Study.* Baton Rouge: Louisiana State University Press, 1937.

Minnesota Legislature. *Report of the Interim Commission on Workmen's Compensation.* St. Paul: 1953.

Mitchell, John. "Operation of the New York Workmen's Compensation Law," *American Labor Legislation Review,* V (March, 1915), 15-19.

National Industrial Conference Board. *The Workmen's Compensation Problem in New York State.* New York: National Industrial Conference Board, 1927.

Ohio Legislative Service Commission.
Workmen's Compensation and Industrial Relations in Ohio. Columbus: 1957.

Workmen's Compensation in Ohio. Research Report No. 10. Columbus: 1955.

Owen, John P. *What's Wrong With Workmen's Compensation.* Houston Studies in Business and Economics, No. 4. Houston: Bureau of Business and Economic Research, College of Business Administration, University of Houston, 1956.

Roach, Justice W. D. *Report on the Workmen's Compensation Act.* Ontario Workmen's Compensation Board. Toronto: 1950.

Sayer, Henry D. *Workmen's Compensation in New York: Its Development and Operation.* New York: Commerce and Industry Association of New York, 1953.

Singleton, Evelyn E. *Workmen's Compensation in Maryland.* Baltimore: The Johns Hopkins Press, 1935.

Soderstrom, Reuben G. *How Can We Improve the Workmen's Compensation Law and Its Administration?* Champaign: University of Illinois, Institute of Labor and Industrial Relations, 1954.

Weber, Arnold Robert. *Workmen's Compensation in Illinois.* Bulletin 25. Urbana: University of Illinois, Institute of Labor and Industrial Relations, 1955.

INDEX

N